'*Prince of Europe* is a superbly funny, colourful and debauched journey through the palaces and bedrooms, taverns and battle-fields of emperors, charlatans, philosophers and prostitutes with the wittiest and naughtiest charmer in Europe. I wished it had been twice as long'

Simon Sebag Montefiore, *Sunday Times*

'This highly entertaining book ... it has been very thoroughly and professionally researched in twenty-five archives in eleven different countries ... it brings an intelligent and constructively benign eye to bear on a phenomenon which continues to elude most anglophone (and indeed francophone) historians, namely the Holy Roman Empire. What Mansel demonstrates so successfully through his subject is the unique political culture which kept this amorphous, polycentric, confusing but durable structure in being ... this excellent and important book'

Tim Blanning, *Times Literary Supplement*

'To read it is also to read a history of the second half of the long 18th century, ending, with its subject, at the Congress of Vienna ... Mansel presents the fruits of his massive labours with delicate care, and the book is written in readable, anec-dotal, explanatory prose. It is scholarly without being pedantic, and he has had the wisdom to see that the life of the man Basil Guy has elsewhere called "the paradoxical prince" needs no imported rhetorical colouring'

Min Wild, *Independent on Sunday*

'Vibrant and enjoyable ... This book should be required reading for the politicians and civil servants now struggling to agree on the final text of a constitution for the European Union ... Mansel takes us on a dazzling journey through the Europe of the eighteenth and early nineteenth century'

Alfred Latham-Koenig, *The Tablet*

'As well as profiting from the scholarship, I really enjoyed reading Philip Mansel's *Prince of Europe*'

Antonia Fraser, *BBC History magazine*

Philip Mansel is a historian and Fellow of the Royal Historical Society. His previous books include *Louis XVIII, Constantinople: City of the World's Desire, Sultans in Splendour* and *Paris Between Empires: Monarchy and Revolution*. Six of his books have been translated into French, including an earlier version of this biography. He lives in London. His website can be visited at www.philipmansel.com.

By Philip Mansel

Louis XVIII
Pillars of Monarchy
Sultans in Splendour: Monarchs of the Middle East 1869–1945
The Court of France 1789–1830
Constantinople: City of the World's Desire 1453–1924
Paris Between Empires: Monarchy and Revolution 1814–1852
Prince of Europe: The Life of Charles-Joseph de Ligne 1735–1814

Prince of Europe

The Life of Charles-Joseph de Ligne 1735–1814

PHILIP MANSEL

PHOENIX

To Didier Girard

A PHOENIX PAPERBACK

First published in Great Britain in 2003
by Weidenfeld & Nicolson
This paperback edition published in 2005
by Phoenix,
an imprint of Orion Books Ltd,
Orion House, 5 Upper St Martin's Lane,
London WC2H 9EA

A CIP catalogue record for this book
is available from the British Library.

ISBN 0 75381 855 8

Typeset by Butler & Tanner Ltd, Frome and London

Printed and bound in Great Britain by
Clays Ltd, St Ives plc

www.orionbooks.co.uk

J'aime mon état d'étranger partout.
The Prince de Ligne to Mme de Coigny, 1787

Contents

North
Sea

Baltic
Sea

P R U

London 1767 ●

● Brussels
Beloeil

Berlin 1760,
1780, 1804 ●

HOLY
ROMAN
EMPIRE

Dresden ●

Leuthen
1757

Teplitz

Kolin
1757

Versailles ● ● Paris

● Edelstetten 1803

Prague

Vienna ●
Pressburg
1805, 1808

● Ferney 1763

A U S

Late eighteenth-century Europe

Showing the travels of the Prince de Ligne

0   100   200   300   400 km

Gulf of Finland St Petersburg
1780, 1787

• Moscow 1787

RUSSIA

SSIA

POLAND

• Warsaw 1780

• Kiev 1787

Elizabethgorod
1787

• Jassy 1788   Ochakov   *Sea of Azov*
1788

• Pest 1809

TRIA   • Bahceseray 1787

Belgrade   *Black Sea*
1789   OTTOMAN   EMPIRE

Acknowledgements

The author would like to express his gratitude to all those who have helped in the preparation of this book: in particular to the staffs of the British Library, the London Library, the Bibliothèque Nationale and the Haus-, Hof- und Staatsarchiv; and to Olivier Aaron, S. A. S. Prince Carlos d'Arenberg, Professor Derek Beales, Christiane Besse, F. W. P. Broadley, Abbé Bernard de Brye, Arminée Choukassizian, the late Georges Englebert, Professor Basil Guy, Marco Leeflang, S. A. the Prince de Ligne, S. A. Prince Michel de Ligne, S. A. Prince Charles-Antoine de Ligne, Dr Luc Lowagie, Jaromir Macek, J. M. P. McErlean, André Nieuwazsny, the Marquis of Normanby, Dr Robert Oresko, Alexandre Pradère, Serge Proutchenko, Baronne Elie de Rothschild, Francis Russell, Andrée Scufflaire, Simon Sebag Montefiore, Anke and Lienke van Nugteren, Professor Jeroom Vercruysse and Adam Zamoyski. He is particularly grateful to Aouni Abdulrahim, Didier Girard, Sara Menguç and Fouad Nahas for their comments on the manuscript. Special thanks to Bing Taylor for helping the Prince de Ligne to acquire an English identity.

AUTHOR'S NOTE

The Prince of Europe is a revised and expanded version of an earlier manuscript, *The Courtier. Charles-Joseph, Prince de Ligne, 1735–1814*, published in a French translation as *Charles-Joseph de Ligne. Le charmeur de l'Europe (1735–1814)* (Stock, 1992).

Illustrations

12. View of Dresden, 1765, by Bernardo Bellotto *(Staatlichen Kunsthalle, Karlsruhe)*

13. Schönbrunn Palace, a residence of the Empress Maria Theresa, in 1759, by Bernardo Bellotto *(Kunsthistorisches Museum, Vienna)*

14. View of Belgrade, August 1789, by Captain Mancini *(Teplice Castle)*

15. The Emperor Joseph II in a circle of friends. Anon. *(Liechtenstein collection)*

16. Parade of Walloon grenadiers in the presence of Joseph II during his visit to the Austrian Netherlands, 26 June 1781, by Sauveur Legros

17. Prince Potemkin, patron and ally of the Prince de Ligne, by G. B. Lampi (attrib.) *(Suvorov Museum, St Petersburg)*

18. Catherine II in travelling costume, 1787, by Mikhail Shibanov *(State Russian Museum, St Petersburg)*

19. The Prince de Ligne in bed at Beloeil, 22 September 1793, by Sauveur Legros *(Private collection)*

20. Interior of the Hôtel de Ligne on the Moelkerbastei, Vienna, by Sauveur Legros *(Former coll. of Georges Englebert)*

21. A page of the manuscript of *Fragments de l'Histoire de Ma Vie (Reproduced in the Leuridant edition of 1927)*

22. A view of Mont Ligne outside Teplitz. Anon. *(Private collection)*

23. Marshal Berthier requesting the hand of the Archduchess Marie Louise in marriage, 1810, by J. B. Hoechle *(Kunsthistorisches Museum, Vienna)*

24. The Prince de Ligne in 1812, at the age of 77, by Emile Legros *(Fondation Ligne, Beloeil. Photo: J. Cussac)*

25. The Prince de Ligne driving in the Augarten, 1814. Anon. *(Former Clary collection, reproduced in the* Annales Prince de Ligne)

26. The knight in armour who followed the funeral procession of the Prince de Ligne on 15 December 1814. Anon. *(Historisches Museum der Stadt, Wien)*

The House of Habsburg

(Only individuals mentioned in the text are included)

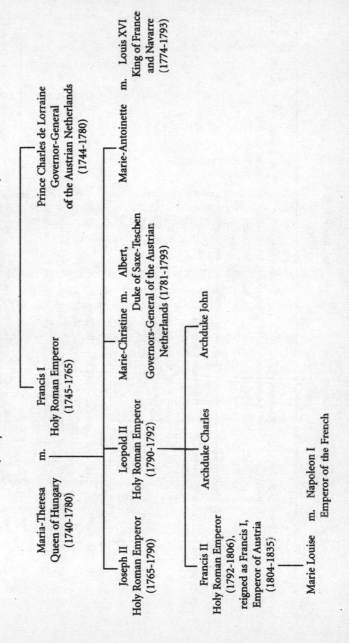

Maria-Theresa
Queen of Hungary
(1740-1780)

m.

Francis I
Holy Roman Emperor
(1745-1765)

Prince Charles de Lorraine
Governor-General
of the Austrian Netherlands
(1744-1780)

Joseph II
Holy Roman Emperor
(1765-1790)

Leopold II
Holy Roman Emperor
(1790-1792)

Marie-Christine   m.   Albert,
Duke of Saxe-Teschen
Governors-General of the Austrian
Netherlands (1781-1793)

Marie-Antoinette   m.   Louis XVI
King of France
and Navarre
(1774-1793)

Francis II
Holy Roman Emperor
(1792-1806),
reigned as Francis I,
Emperor of Austria
(1804-1835)

Archduke Charles

Archduke John

Marie Louise   m.   Napoleon I
Emperor of the French

The Family of the Prince de Ligne

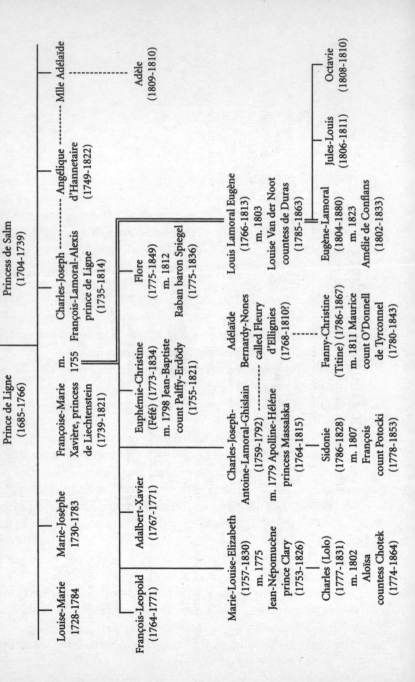

Beloeil

The chateau of Beloeil lies forty miles south-west of Brussels. Set in the middle of flat fertile farm land in the province of Hainaut, it appears to be an embodiment of aristocratic order. Iron gates crowned by a princely coat of arms keep the village at a distance; beech hedges fade into woods and lakes; a moat surrounds the E-shaped stone and brick classical building.

Beloeil has been the seat of the Counts, later Princes, of Ligne (the name of a nearby village) since the eleventh century. Reconstructed in 1900–1906 after a fire, the chateau has high slate roofs, four turrets and a moat. Although extremely large, it looks like many other chateaux in France and Belgium.

Beloeil, however, is distinguished by its European character. Situated between the English Channel, the French border, and the frontiers of the Netherlands and Germany, Beloeil is at a crossroads of Europe. It is European by history as well as geography. For the Ligne family, as the pictures and genealogies on display in Beloeil make clear, the history of Europe was family history. The Lignes were not content to remain landowners in Hainaut. In 1187 Wauthier de Ligne went on the Third Crusade with the Kings of England and France, Richard Coeur de Lion and Philip Augustus; a hundred and thirty years later Michel de Ligne helped Isabella of France dethrone King Edward II of England. Lignes fought in the fields of Flanders, the mountains of Castile and the marches of Prussia.

Their titles reflect their European history. As a result of dynastic inheritance and international treaties, the southern Netherlands (roughly present-day Belgium), including the province of Hainaut in which Beloeil lies, were long ruled by foreign sovereigns: first by the Dukes of Burgundy; then by their heirs the Emperor Charles V and the Habsburg Kings of Spain; after the War of the Spanish Succession, by the Habsburg Holy Roman Emperors. The Ligne family acquired a triple identity. They were not only Princes de Ligne in the southern Netherlands (where Prince was a noble title, below Duke and above Marquis), and peers of Hainaut, Artois and Flanders, but also, by the early seventeenth century, grandees of Spain and princes of the Holy Roman Empire.

The Lignes rose high in their sovereigns' service. Two massive narrative pictures in a downstairs salon, by Van Tilborgh and F. Du Chastel respectively, depict the entry of Prince Claude Lamoral I de Ligne, with a suite of 254, into London in 1660 and his reception in the Banqueting Hall of Whitehall Palace. He had been sent by Philip IV of Spain on an embassy to congratulate their mutual cousin King Charles II on his restoration to the throne. This Prince de Ligne subsequently became one of the leading figures in the Spanish monarchy, first Governor-General of Milan, then Viceroy of Sicily, before dying in Madrid, a grandee of Spain and President of the War Council, in 1679. One of his sons chose a Portuguese heiress and became a grandee of Portugal; another married a French heiress and settled in France.[1]

For the Lignes were Europeans by matrimony as well as by history and geography. Possibly from a conscious strategy, possibly because no neighbours were considered grand enough, more than any other noble family of the region the Princes de Ligne married foreign princesses. They came from sovereign dynasties, with names like Aragon, Lorraine, Luxembourg and Nassau. The portraits on the walls of Beloeil reflect the ramifications of the Lignes' royal connections: by the eighteenth century they were seventh or eighth cousins of the Holy Roman Emperor, the Kings of Spain, France, England, Prussia, and Poland, the Elector of Bavaria and the Prince of Orange – and acknowledged as such.[2]

One room in Beloeil, however, contains not royal portraits or narrative pictures, but personal relics: the visiting cards, shaving bowl and earring of Charles-Joseph de Ligne, the seventh prince. At once the most famous and the most European member of the family, he is the subject of this book. It is a voyage into the Europe of his time, as well as the biography of a prince. For by the end of his life Charles-Joseph de Ligne had travelled so widely, and acquired so many identities, that he could write, as no other European has been able to: 'I have six or seven fatherlands, the Empire, Flanders, France, Spain, Austria, Poland, Russia and nearly Hungary.'[3] He was not only the epitome of Europe: he was also a field marshal in the Austrian army; a brilliant, subversive writer, whose works (thirty-five volumes published in his lifetime, as many since) are a key to the politics and passions of the Enlightenment and the Counter-revolution; and the charmer of the age, seducing everyone he met, from Mme du Barry to Mme de Staël. His funeral, on 15 December 1814 in Vienna, was a European event.

His baptism, however, was a family occasion, taking place in Brussels, in the family *hôtel*, on 23 January 1735 (the date of his birth is unknown).[4] His mother, a princess of Salm, an enclave of the Holy Roman Empire in eastern France, died when he was only five. She added yet another strand to the Lignes' European web. If Catholicism had not been a barrier, she would have had a better claim to the throne of England than her cousin the reigning monarch, George II: the Salms descended from a Catholic son, rather than (like George II) a Protestant daughter, of Charles I's sister the Queen of Bohemia.[5]

Few details about Ligne's early years are available. A mother-less only son, he was brought up by a nurse and a governess, Mlle du Coron. She loved him so much, he later recollected in his memoirs, that she played with him in strange ways, and made him dance and sleep with her naked. He remembered that he was a naughty child who told lies, stole food and drank the altar wine.[6] He infuriated his proud and difficult father, Claude Lamoral II, sixth Prince de Ligne (1685–1766). Equally aggressive on the battlefield and in the drawing room, Claude Lamoral

II devoted much of his time to beautifying Beloeil; it was he who created the sixty-three-acre park surrounding the chateau. Around a long lake are laid out a series of 'rooms' formed by walls of thick beech hedge, and colonnades of beech trees. Each room encloses a pool of water and opens into another room, like an enfilade in an eighteenth-century palace. They have such names as *Le Rieu d'Amour*, *Le Bassin des Dames* and *La Salle du Grand Diable*.* At the end of the lake, opposite the chateau, he installed a superb statue of Neptune, trident in hand, accompanied by sea horses and monsters, the work of a pupil of Pigalle called Henrion. Even today the long vistas of beech and grass, the marriage of water, nature and silence, have few rivals in Europe. Claude Lamoral I was also an efficient manager of the family patrimony: by the eighteenth century the Princes de Ligne owned seventeen *terres à clocher*, or parishes, in Hainaut, with names like Quevaucamps, Silly, Rumpst, as well as ten in the neighbouring provinces of Limburg and Brabant.[7]

Ligne regarded his father with a mixture of admiration and dismay. In his memoirs he wrote, in his elegant, disabused language:

> My father did not like me. I do not know why, for we did not know each other ... The sound of his voice made everyone, the salon, the children and the valets, tremble for an hour at a time ... His cane had the air of a sceptre or a whip ... He treated god as an old general who had a few more quarterings than himself ... The only person of whom he had any good to say was Louis XIV and even then it was for his gardens ... Occasionally he made love, *en grand seigneur*, in order to exercise one more form of domination, without fear of being dominated by it. You had to prove your genealogy to enter his heart.

He lived like a king, but forbade his servants to serve wine to the

---

* Named after Antoine de Ligne, known as *le grand diable de Ligne*, since he kept a seraglio filled with neighbours' wives and daughters and was rude to his sovereign the Emperor Charles V.

local priest at dinner, saying: 'Beer is good enough for such people.'[8]

Ligne had even less in common with his sisters, Marie-Louise-Elisabeth and Marie-Josèphe, who were respectively seven and five years older than he. Neither was beautiful. The Lignes were not rich by the standards of European *grands seigneurs* and their father had no desire to waste money on dowries for ugly daughters. They were despatched to nunneries. Ligne writes in his memoirs of Marie-Louise-Elizabeth: 'I barely saw either her or my other sister, hardly less ugly, provost of the chapter of Essen, who was apparently quite delightful.'[9] They made no appearance in his life except to plead, usually in vain, for the regular payment of their allowances.

For the Maison de Ligne, as for other European dynasties, rank and money were the priorities. Those who did not contribute to the family glory were treated with little consideration. An even harsher warning than his sisters' fate was that of an uncle called Antoine de Ligne. Brave, handsome and an elder son, he had fallen in love with a woman who, although noble (or, in the French phrase of the period, *de condition*), was not equal in rank to the Lignes. Forced to renounce his inheritance, his military career and contact with his own class, he became a novice in the Franciscan order, living in seclusion on the third floor of the small Hôtel de Ligne in Brussels.[10] His nephew never knew of his existence until his death.

Another uncle, Field Marshal Prince Ferdinand de Ligne, took more interest in his nephew, but criticised him for impertinence and excessive interest in his own appearance. He fostered his nephew's taste for war, constantly talking about it and sending him to visit his regiment, Ligne-Dragons. In Ligne's world, birth was not enough. Nobles were expected to 'illustrate' the family name, preferably by exploits on the battlefield. War was the most honoured occupation of European nobles, the basis of their values and of much of their wealth.

This was especially true in the southern Netherlands. Beloeil lies in the 'cockpit of Europe', a region where, Ligne later wrote, 'there has always been war'. Every town or village bears the name of a battle: Rocroi (1643), Ramillies (1706), Malplaquet (1709), Fontenoy (1745), Waterloo (1815), Ypres (1915) are all near Beloeil.[11] Even today the nearby town of Mons, site of two battles in World War I, houses the headquarters of SHAPE, the military branch of NATO. In an upstairs gallery in the chateau of Beloeil, a series of pictures of sieges and battles commemorates the Lignes' prowess on the battlefield.

The first conscious thought the young Ligne could remember was the desire to be a second Prince Eugène – the great Austrian general who had won so many victories over French armies in the War of the Spanish Succession, as a result of which the southern Netherlands had passed from Spanish to Austrian control, and the Lignes had become Austrian subjects.[12] He could not sleep for thinking about other great generals such as *le grand Condé* and Charles XII of Sweden. He knew their battles by heart, and was *fou de gloire*.[13] The first portrait of the young prince shows him, at the age of seven, standing in front of the chateau of Beloeil, dressed for war. In accordance with contemporary fashion, he wears a fantasy hussar uniform and head-dress. From his belt hangs a sword; in his hand he holds a gun almost as big as he is.

Throughout Ligne's life, preparing for, writing about and making war would be one of his principal occupations. Most wars were against France. It was the largest and most bellicose country in Europe, with a population of 25 million, compared to 20 million in the Holy Roman Empire, 6 million in England and 2 million in the southern Netherlands. In the eighteenth century the powers of Europe were so competitive and aggressive that the number of dead in battle, in relation to the whole population, would be higher than in the wars of the nineteenth century. Wars often started over questions of dynastic succession, which Paul Schroeder calls 'the most numerous, bitterly contested and critical issues of high European politics'.[14]

In 1740, when Ligne was five, the War of the Austrian Succession broke out between France and Austria over whether

Maria Theresa, daughter of the Emperor Charles VI, should succeed to the entire Habsburg inheritance, including the southern Netherlands. By the age of ten Ligne had witnessed four sieges by French forces of local towns (Tournai, Mons, Ath, and Brussels itself, where his father and uncle were taken prisoners). On 11 May 1745 he heard the sound of the cannon of Fontenoy, a victory for France over the Habsburgs and their British allies, and one of the four battles – the other three being Leuze (1648), Ath (1654) and Oudenarde (1708) – to take place on the Lignes' extensive estates (one of Ligne's descendants, Prince Charles-Antoine de Ligne, still finds helmets and breastplates from this battle on his land).[15] Thus from an early age Ligne, like much of Europe, regarded France, the constant invader, as arrogant, warlike and cruel. His uncle the Field Marshal, who had fought so frequently against the French, was especially voluble in expressing his hatred of them.[16] Ligne himself would later write that he ended his life, as he had begun it, by hating 'this nation'.[17]

However, if France was feared as a military power, it was revered as a centre of the arts and graces. From London to St Petersburg, French was the language of educated Europe, of foreign writers such as Gibbon and Alfieri, as well as of foreign monarchs such as George II, Catherine the Great and Frederick the Great. With the best schools and writers, Paris was considered the capital of European culture and, particularly, of the new movement of the Enlightenment, using reason to challenge received ideas and traditions, including Christianity itself.[18] The Austrian Netherlands, in contrast, were an intellectual backwater, whose provinces – Brabant, Flanders, Hainaut, Luxembourg – were distinguished by the fervour of their Catholicism and their attachment to their traditional constitutions and privileges. In 1740 the most famous author of the day, Voltaire, the leader of the Enlightenment, had written: 'Brussels is the extinguisher of imagination ... It is the home of ignorance and stupid indifference.'[19]

Therefore the Lignes turned to France for their education. Hating France but admiring French culture, Prince Claude

Lamoral, who himself had studied in Paris, received special permission from Vienna, despite the war, to choose his son's tutors
in 'the French nation'. In all Ligne had eight governors in eleven
years (five priests, three soldiers) – proof of his father's irascibil-
ity. The first, a Jesuit called the Abbé du Verdier, was dismissed
for stealing money from his employers, thefts which he tried to
manipulate his young pupil into covering up for him.[20] His successor, M. Duport du Tertre, lost his job for letting Ligne read
pornographic books such as *Thérèse Philosophe* (1748) and *Le
Prince Apprius* (1728), which preached the religion of sexual
pleasure; the next tutor, a brave but limited French officer called
the Chevalier des Essarts de La Roche-Vallin, complained about
the food and the servants, and left in 1748, suspected of
Jansenism. He was replaced by the Chevalier de Saint Maurice,
sacked in his turn for writing an 'extremely tender letter' to his
pupil. Ligne's education was not going well. Unhappy, starved
of affection, Ligne fell ill, and developed a tic in his eyes.[21]

Finally, in 1751, the Chevalier de La Porte, a product of one
of the best schools of the eighteenth century, the Jesuit-run
Collège Louis-le-Grand in Paris, proved a success: he taught his
pupil Latin, literature and the conventional Catholicism of the
day. La Porte dedicated a poem on the Death of the Redeemer
to him: Ligne ended one of his own earliest writings, a *Discours
sur la profession des armes*, with an apostrophe to Mars and his
tutor. He later wrote that he owed the Chevalier 'all that flower
of humanities, literature and urbanity which is the charm of my
life'. They read Caesar, Horace, Cicero, Corneille and Bossuet
together. Ligne made extracts from and commentaries on both
French and classical authors; he adored French literature, later
writing that no other country had produced such geniuses as
Bossuet, La Fontaine and Molière.[22] He soon conceived the
ambition of being a writer as well as a fighter.

French memoirs, the number and quality of which had no
parallel in other literatures, also had a lasting effect on Ligne.
Through their analyses of power, love, fame and wit they had as
much influence on the European elite as the court of Versailles

itself. Ligne's favourite was the memoirs of the great seven
teenth-century French general, the Maréchal de Turenne, by the
Chevalier de Ramsay. Others were the memoirs of a debauchee,
the Comte de Gramont, and of Mme de Maintenon's niece Mme
de Caylus, full of 'those little things which seem to be nothings',
but gave pleasure a hundred years later. Mathematics, science
and card games, however, he could never learn.[23]

His own ancestry was another of Ligne's subjects of study. La
Porte warned Ligne that everyone must submit to the same yoke
and that he should forget worldly grandeur; the family genea-
logist M. Maloteau taught Ligne that his own family was one of
the oldest, most illustrious and most generous in Europe, a race
of heroes and generals descended from Charlemagne.[24] The simplicity of their coat of arms, one diagonal pink line (i.e. *ligne*) on
a yellow background, was a sign of their antiquity. The glory of
his family, however, occasionally palled on Ligne. He covered
margins in his *Grand Dictionnaire Français et Latin* with carica-
tures, drawings of the family chateaux, lists of their titles and the
maddened remark: 'Jean de Ligne three hundred years ago was a
fool about whom I know nothing.'[25]

The Princes de Ligne were a European dynasty. Yet they
were proud of their Belgian or, to use the term current in the
eighteenth century, Flemish* identity. Brussels and Beloeil
were, at this stage, the centre of Ligne's world. In Ligne's youth
the Austrian Netherlands were ruled by the most popular governor in their history, his cousin Prince Charles of Lorraine,
brother-in-law of the Habsburg Empress Maria Theresa: she had
married his brother Francis, the last hereditary Duke of
Lorraine, before its absorption by the ever-expanding power of
France in 1735.

Charles of Lorraine's government of the Austrian
Netherlands is still remembered as a golden age. He lived in
state, served by a household of hundreds and escorted by a
swarm of hussars, valets and pages, as he moved from the white
Nassau-Lorraine Palace in Brussels to his country houses of

* The word 'Walloon' was then generally applied to the poor.

Mariemont and Tervueren. In the park at Tervueren this cultivated connoisseur built factories teaching the crafts practised in
the Austrian Netherlands: porcelain, textiles, iron smelting, and
he installed physics and chemistry laboratories next to his
bedroom. He was trying to help the economy of the Austrian
Netherlands, which had never recovered since the United
Provinces had closed the Scheldt, the waterway leading to the
great port of Antwerp, a hundred years before: in the mid-
eighteenth century fifty per cent of the population were paupers.
His popularity was increased by the tact with which he reconciled the increasing financial demands of the Habsburg government in Vienna with the inhabitants' passionate defence of the
traditional privileges of their cities and provinces.[26]

Charles of Lorraine frequently visited Beloeil, where Prince
Claude Lamoral entertained on a royal scale; after the end of the
War of the Austrian Succession, in 1749, in his honour there
were hunts, dinners and a masquerade called *Les Amusements des
Héros*, in which the young Ligne appeared, prophetically, as
Pleasure. Charles of Lorraine also epitomised the eighteenth
century's cult of pleasure, which equalled its cult of war. An
amorous widower, he used a special sign language for arranging
rendezvous from his box at the theatre: two fingers meant
'Monday', holding his nose 'I must speak to you', passing his
hand over his forehead 'I cannot come'. On one occasion, when
he was staying at Beloeil with a party of princes, it was said that
he 'fooled around (*polissonait*) all day long, making a terrible
noise'.

During another of the Prince's visits a prophetic portrait of
Ligne was recorded in the diary of his friend and neighbour the
cultivated, slightly solemn Duc de Croÿ. A member of another
great Netherlands family, whose estates were separated from the
Lignes' by the French frontier, Croÿ was saddened by what he
saw. Croÿ agreed with Ligne's view of his father, but saw some
of the qualities and defects that would affect Ligne himself
throughout his life:

That day I witnessed the odious harshness of the Prince de Ligne towards his son and I had a curious educational conversation with M. de Laporte, the governor for whose presence he was very grateful. The Prince de Ligne seemed to hate his children and deserved that they returned the feeling ... he detested the idea of having an heir and wanted to do everything himself and although he was more than seventy years old, he never wanted to stop nor ever believe that anything could succeed him. His son, who felt his difficult position deeply, was bubbling over inside with wit, confidence, the desire for glory, all on the grandest scale and wanted to be a hero to such an extent that he might subsequently either become truly great or, if he followed his presumption or his imagination, turn out very badly; I was the person in whom he had most confidence. He gave me some of his writings to read, above all a parallel between Turenne and Eugène; one cannot conceive the vivacity, the talent and the audacity there was in them and it was startling how well written it was when it was done so casually.[27]

In 1751, at the age of sixteen, Ligne was taken by his father on his first journey outside the Netherlands, to be presented to the Emperor and Empress in Vienna. After a brief, intoxicating visit to Paris, they crossed the Rhine at Strasbourg, and entered the Holy Roman Empire.

This legendary realm had shaped European history for a thousand years since Charlemagne had been crowned Emperor of a restored Roman Empire in St Peter's, Rome, in AD 800: its fate dominated the lives of the people of central Europe and of the Princes de Ligne themselves. The Holy Roman Empire has often been the object of mockery by nationalists and rationalists. Voltaire said that it was neither Holy nor Roman nor an Empire. In reality it followed a different concept of a state from that accepted in France and England. As the Emperor Charles IV had proclaimed in 1356 when establishing the right of seven princes known as Electors to elect each new Emperor: 'The fame of the Holy Roman Empire arises from the variety of customs, ways of life and languages found in the various nations which compose it.' (After the Reformation there was variety of religion as well.)[28]

Rather than a centralised nation state, it was a federation of semi-sovereign states with a shared legal, cultural and economic framework, like the modern European Union. A network of 294 principalities, free cities, and ecclesiastical states, stretching from the Baltic to the Adriatic and from Flanders to Silesia, all owed allegiance to the Habsburg Holy Roman Emperor in Vienna. There were two central law courts, the Reichshofrat in Vienna and the Reichskammergericht in Wetzlar in the Rhineland, whose decisions could decide the constitutions, and on occasion the existence, of the smaller states. The Empire was divided into ten administrative circles and the Diet, or parliament, sitting in Regensburg could still raise taxes and put an army in the field. The citizens of the Empire were proud to be part of a state that they considered the successor of the Roman Empire. As successor of Constantine, the 'thirteenth apostle', and Charlemagne, the Holy Roman Emperor was addressed as 'Sacred Majesty'.

In an age that worshipped titles, the Emperor was the fount of honour in Europe, able to award the grandest and most coveted titles of all, both within and outside the Empire. In 1701 he had made the Elector of Brandenburg King in Prussia. This title so increased the unity and prestige of the Prussian state that Frederick the Great himself, no admirer of empty forms, wrote that the minister who had advised the Emperor to grant it should have been hanged for high treason.[29]

In 1602 the Prince de Ligne of the day had been created a Prince of the Holy Roman Empire, a title of such prestige that it was the ambition of Polish, Hungarian and Russian, as well as German, nobles. It satisfied nobles' craving for equality of status with royalty. By enabling them to become sovereigns, if they also owned a sovereign territory in the Empire and were accepted by one of the circles of the Empire, they could also marry into royal dynasties. The Lignes had that opportunity since, in addition to their extensive estates in the Austrian Netherlands, they

owned the sovereign territory of Fagnolles, a small estate
centred on a ruined medieval castle sixty miles south-east of
Brussels, which owed allegiance not to the government in
Brussels but to the Holy Roman Emperor in Vienna. If it had
survived today, it would be a modern Belgian equivalent of
those other relics of the Holy Roman Empire, the sovereign
principalities of Liechtenstein and Monaco.

Ligne always defended the Holy Roman Empire. Two years
before its extinction, he wrote: 'This body, monstrous in appearance by the singularity of its Constitution, is as good in practice
as it is bad in theory.'[30] He appreciated the splendour and originality of the princes of the Empire, recalling nostalgically at the
end of his life, in his memoirs,

> the fêtes of duke Charles of Wurttemberg, the *galanterie*, the
> French theatre and all the sociable pleasures of the court of the
> last Margrave of Bayreuth. The luxury and etiquette of Bonn
> and Mainz. The solidity and bonhomie of the court of
> Carlsruhe. Mannheim, Munich, Erlangen and Stuttgart, the
> court of the Archduchess, that of Liège (no more need be said),
> which shone under two princes of Bavaria...that of the last
> [sovereign] Prince of Thurn und Taxis which was no less
> magnificent for being ridiculous.[31]

Since, as hereditary postmasters of the Holy Roman Empire, the
Princes of Thurn und Taxis ran the postal system of central
Europe, they were rich and could afford a magnificent court.

Since the sixteenth century, princes and court cities such as
Munich, Dresden and Berlin had replaced great merchant cities
like Augsburg and Nuremberg as centres of German power and
culture. Foreigners might sneer at 'petty German princes', but
many were powerful sovereigns who, once they had fulfilled
their obligations to the Holy Roman Empire, were able to raise
their own armies and play an important part in the great game of
European politics. The Elector of Saxony, by protecting Luther
from persecution by the rest of the Empire, had ensured the survival of Protestantism; his descendants returned to Catholicism

and became Kings of Poland in 1697. The Princes of Orange had helped create a state out of the seven United Provinces of the northern Netherlands. The Electors of Hanover had become Kings of England. The cultural life flourishing in the courts of the Empire, many of which had their own picture galleries, theatres, opera houses, universities, porcelain factories and printing presses, was considered one of the justifications of its existence.

In 1751, however, Ligne's father allowed no time to explore the courts of the Empire. From Ulm they travelled by barge down the Danube and entered Austria. The service of Austria would govern the course of Ligne's life.

Austria

Europeans by history, geography and matrimony, the Princes de Ligne were Austrians by allegiance. When Ligne wrote *nous*, or *chez nous*, he was referring to Austria.[1] Austria in 1751 was not the small, neutral, landlocked state of today. It was a multi-national monarchy of fifteen million people, stretching from Flanders, through Hither Austria on the upper Rhine opposite France, to include modern Austria, Hungary, the Czech Republic, Slovakia, Slovenia, Croatia and the western half of Romania.

Plurality was its essence. Austria was a collection of provinces with their own languages, traditions and parliaments: the Kingdom of Bohemia, the Archduchies of Upper and Lower Austria, the Kingdoms of Hungary and Croatia, the Principality of Transylvania, the County of Tyrol and many others. As the Empress Maria Theresa noted with regret, it was quite different from a united nation like France.[2] All these provinces, except Hungary, were in the Holy Roman Empire. Their ruler was (usually) the Holy Roman Emperor, the titular head of Christendom. Yet Austria was already thought of as separate from the Empire. As the author of a book with the momentous title *Oesterreich über alles, wenn es nur will* ('Austria above everything, if it so desires') wrote, it was 'a natural body ... a small world of its own which can look after itself'.[3] The Holy Roman Empire was referred to as 'the Empire', Austria as 'the monarchy'. Ligne often used the phrase *aller en Empire* when he left Austria for what is now Germany.[4]

We are used to thinking of Austria in terms of the empire of Franz Joseph, lurching from defeat to defeat until the self-inflicted cataclysm of World War I. In Ligne's lifetime, and for long afterwards, it was the backbone of Europe, an ambitious state with an appetite for expansion and a sense of grandeur at least as powerful as that of France — one reason, in addition to family tradition, why Austrian service would suit the Prince de Ligne.

Many factors united the lands of the Austrian monarchy: geography, Catholicism, a common fear of the Turks; but the main force keeping these different peoples together for over three hundred years was dynasticism. They were all hereditary possessions of the Habsburg dynasty or, as it was usually called in the eighteenth century, the House of Austria. The Habsburgs took their name from the castle of Habsburg, in what is now Switzerland, which they had built in 1020. They had ruled Upper and Lower Austria since 1278 and were so confident of themselves and of their superiority over other German dynasties that, since the fourteenth century, they had used the title Archduke and had called themselves the Arch-house. Their political skills, luck in marrying heiresses and almost continuous election as Holy Roman Emperor since 1438 were the causes of their rise. As A. J. P. Taylor has written, they were 'the greatest dynasty of modern history, and the history of central Europe revolves round them, not they round it.'[5]

Austria's dynastic nature, and lack of a national base, later became causes of weakness (although dynastic loyalty could outweigh nationalism even in the twentieth century); but in the eighteenth century, when national sentiment was much weaker, the title of Holy Roman Emperor and the multinational character of the dynasty (Ligne later remembered that Maria Theresa's son Joseph II spoke French, German, Italian, Hungarian, Czech and Latin*) gave it the confidence to expand in any direction it chose. In Ligne's lifetime, it would acquire new German, Polish, Italian and Moldavian provinces. Such acquisitions did not contradict the nature of the monarchy, as they did when France, Prussia or Russia attempted to expand outside their linguistic

* Ligne himself spoke French, and some Italian and German.

frontiers. Allegiance to the Emperor in Vienna was the national identity. In the eighteenth century the different peoples of the monarchy – Germans, Czechs, Croats, Hungarians – vied in the extravagance of their declarations of loyalty, rather than of their nationalist protest.

Allegiance to the Emperor and the House of Austria was also part of the identity of the Princes de Ligne. Almost alone of the great noble families of the Netherlands, they had not joined the revolts of the late sixteenth century, which had led to the independence of the northern Netherlands under the leadership of the Princes of Orange. In 1741, by conquering the rich Austrian province of Silesia, in what is now south-west Poland, Frederick II, King in Prussia, had launched the long struggle between Prussia and Austria for the domination of Germany that, until his death, would be one of the parameters of Ligne's life. Competition between the courts of Europe for the services of nobles and officials was as intense as that between modern corporations 'head-hunting' executives. Frederick II tried to entice Prince Claude Lamoral into his service by demanding allegiance for his estate of Wachtendonck in Westphalia. The Prince refused, with the words: 'The house of the Prince de Ligne is accustomed to make still greater sacrifices to the august House of Austria, considering the inviolable fidelity which his ancestors have shown it for almost three centuries.'[6] The Ligne family motto, *Quo res cumque cadunt, stat semper linea recta* ('When other things fall, Ligne always remains straight'), celebrates this ancient loyalty.

His son too would serve the House of Austria, against Prussia or France, throughout his life. Its sovereigns would be as important to him as members of his own family: indeed, by an exceptional favour, 'in gratitude for the zeal and fidelity of this family', the Emperor Charles VI and his wife the Empress Elizabeth Christine had consented to be his godparents. Ligne's first two Christian names were Habsburg, not Ligne, family names: Charles, after his godfather the Emperor; Joseph, after the previous Emperor, Joseph I.[7]

The rise of Vienna was another sign of the magnetism of the Austrian monarchy. With the retreat of the Ottoman Empire and the advance of Austria into the Balkans, Europe's centre of gravity had shifted east. For the first time there was a great dynastic capital that could rival London and Paris. By the middle of the eighteenth century Vienna was the fifth largest city in Europe, after London, Paris, Constantinople and Naples. Its population, which lived either within the walls in high houses, or in greater comfort in the suburbs beyond, was 175,609 in 1750, rising to 232,637 by 1800 (in 1750 London and Paris were both over 500,000). The prints of Charles Schlitz and the paintings of Bellotto show a city of baroque churches and palaces, with streets crowded with priests and soldiers; the imperial double-headed eagle can be seen above doors, on balustrades and on shop-fronts.

Vienna was becoming a destination on the Grand Tour. The English traveller Nathaniel Wraxall wrote: 'Few European cities offer more resources to a stranger who does not place his felicity in absolute dissipation.' King George III used to say, to fathers with sons setting out on their travels: 'You cannot do better than send your son to Vienna.' His ambassador presented four hundred young gentlemen to the Emperor in twelve years.[8]

It was not the bitter, provincial city of post-1918, fallen from its glory and seeking a role, but a confident, imperial capital, sometimes hailed as the new Rome or the new Jerusalem. It would be the backdrop to Ligne's life. Ligne loved Vienna. He wrote that the smallness of its centre made it surprising and agreeable; and he hoped that it would become the capital of Europe as well as of the Empire.[9] Just as the Habsburgs had been traditional enemies of France since the sixteenth century, so Vienna prided itself on being the rival of Paris, with different values, ambitions and manners. Unlike Paris, which was already a conurbation of 600,000, it combined the splendour of a capital with the familiarity of a village. It was a city where everyone knew everyone else; the trees on the surrounding hills could be smelt in the heart of the city.

Although Vienna later prided itself on being a stronghold of German language and culture, in the eighteenth century French was the second language of the Imperial family, the government and the salons. The easy-going, high-spirited Holy Roman Emperor Francis I, husband of Maria Theresa and brother of Prince Charles of Lorraine, spoke French, like the many inhabitants of Lorraine who followed him to Vienna; many books were published in Vienna in French and there was a French-language theatre from 1752 until 1772.[10] Italian was heard in the streets of Vienna almost as much as French; the great Italian poet Metastasio taught Ligne Italian in Vienna in the early 1750s.

Another difference between Paris and Vienna was that, whereas Paris had commerce, the university and the law courts as reasons for existence, Vienna had no independent traditions or institutions of its own. It was a court city, whose purpose was the service of the Emperor. The second floor of every house in the city was reserved for the employees of the court.[11] The Emperor's principal residence, the Hofburg (meaning 'court castle'), was a city within the city that occupied the western quarter of Vienna. The lack of unity of its plain, almost simple, exterior horrified French visitors accustomed to the grandeur of Versailles and the Louvre. However, its roofs and façades hid a hive of courtyards, wings, apartments for the Emperor's family and courtiers, a treasury, the administrative headquarters of the Holy Roman Empire and, in the baroque library and riding school by the great architect Fischer von Erlach, two of the finest rooms in Europe.

The Habsburgs and the Hofburg were part of Ligne's life from the moment he arrived in Vienna in 1751. His father was scolding him for being in the room in the palace reserved for chamberlains. 'That is just what he is. I wanted to surprise you,' said the Emperor Francis I. Ligne wrote: 'My joy at this title! A courtier at fifteen! ... I did not make one drawing or write one line without putting Charles de Ligne chamberlain.'[12] Ligne was part of the wave of chamberlains (all of whom had to prove eight noble ancestors on their father's side) through whom the Empress hoped to bind the nobility more closely to herself. She created so many that by 1780 there were 1500, more than in any other court.[13]

As a chamberlain, Ligne swore the chamberlain's oath, 'that I will conduct myself in every way as a faithful servant and chamberlain towards my master and mistress'.[14] The honour of serving the Habsburgs was so great that, at court, Ligne was prepared to perform duties reserved, in his own household, for footmen; the Emperor's cousin was transformed into a personal servant. When he was in waiting, Ligne admitted people with audiences to curtsey to the Emperor or Empress (in Vienna respect for the monarch was so great that you did not simply bow or kiss hands, as at St James's). The chamberlains' antechamber, following the guardroom, the pages' room and the audience room, and preceding the Emperor's private study, was the room he knew best in the Hofburg. He later wrote a poem called 'Dans l'Antichambre', with the refrain that Love, like the Emperor, admitted him only to its antechamber, never to its chamber.[15]

Since his rank and looks made him an ornament to the Imperial court, he served at special ceremonies, accompanying the Emperor to mass, holding the *dais* – the canopy that was a sign of sovereignty – above the Emperor at the adoration of the Cross in the court chapel. In 1770, at the Feast of the Order of the Golden Fleece in the great gallery in the Hofburg, Lady Mary Coke (an eccentric Englishwoman known as the 'Virgin Mary', because she had no lovers) wrote: 'The Prince de Ligne the Chamberlain in waiting presented the glass of water to the Emperor upon his knees, pouring a little first into the gilt salver and drinking it.' He had carefully practised the gesture the day before in front of a group of friends.[16]

As a chamberlain, Ligne was a courtier, a species more familiar today serving presidents and prime ministers than hereditary monarchs. By upbringing and instinct a royalist, Ligne had no difficulty in following the advice of a Jesuit friend, the historian Père Griffet, to 'stick to the throne', and always be on the side of those who sign simply with their own names: Marie-Thérèse, Louis, George.[17]

Courts are often thought of as superficial or, worse, as extinguishers of talents: 'Qui va à la cour se dérobe à son art,' wrote Molière. In the eighteenth century, however, courts' love of and need for the arts, as well as their roles as centres of power, sociability and job-creation, meant that they could provide favourable conditions, both material and mental, to stimulate rather than extinguish creativity. The most famous writer of the age, Voltaire, wanted to live at a court. In 1745 he was appointed a *gentilhomme ordinaire du roi* and *historiographe du roi* at Versailles; he also lived at Potsdam in 1750–53, with the title of Chamberlain of Frederick II of Prussia, and was a frequent resident at the courts of Nancy and Mannheim. As both Louis XV and Frederick II learnt, Voltaire was too argumentative and independent to be a natural courtier. However, another Enlightenment writer and friend of Ligne, Marmontel, remembered the five years he spent at Versailles in the 1750s, as secretary to Mme de Pompadour's brother, as among the best of his life.[18] Mozart, having served at the court of Salzburg, was a *kammermusikus* at the court of Vienna from 1787 until his death – although some of his best patrons came from the Viennese middle class, rather than the court and nobility.[19] Ligne too would provide proof that life as a courtier, far from extinguishing creativity and originality, could nurture them.

Far from being cut off from the outside world, because it was considered a duty for monarchs to show themselves and their families to their subjects, courts were more accessible than most parliaments. The Viennese roamed in and out of the Hofburg as if they owned it, to attend mass in the court chapel, to watch plays and operas in the court theatre or, during the carnival season, to dance, alongside the Emperor and his family, in balls in the three ballrooms in the palace. Since the accession of Francis I and Maria Theresa, relations between the Viennese and the Habsburgs were particularly relaxed. The chamberlains' antechamber saw the rags of the poor as well as the embroidered coats of the nobility. In Wraxall's words, 'With a view to obtain information she [the Empress] sets apart particular hours when the lowest and meanest of her subjects are not only admitted to see her but are permitted to speak to her independently and freely.'[20] This tradition of public audiences, which had no parallel in other monarchies, was maintained by her successors until the fall of the monarchy in 1918.

After his visit to Vienna in 1751 Ligne had to return to Brussels and Beloeil. His education continued under M. de La Porte: he pursued his studies and learnt riding, fencing and the other skills considered suitable for young nobles. His father still treated him as a child: he claims that to have spending money he had to sell the game he shot while hunting. In 1755, however, when he was twenty, his father took him to Vienna again and married him, on 6 August, to the fourteen-year-old Princess Francisca-Xaviera of Liechtenstein. At the wedding festivities in one of the many castles of the Liechtensteins, Feldsberg in Moravia (now Valtice in the Czech Republic) his father was so happy that he looked more like the bridegroom than Ligne himself. He and his wife did not know each other and had hardly exchanged a word. The wedding night was made uncomfortable by the holy relics the ladies of the household had put under his pillows; next morning Ligne rose at six and went hunting.[21]

In his memoirs Ligne faced life head on. Avoiding both reticence and obscenity, he is equally frank recording eighteenth-century sex and eighteenth-century courts. As a youth he had practised pleasures that 'depended on no one but himself' – of whose existence he had learnt only through his confessor's probing questions.[22]At the age of sixteen he had received his sexual initiation, from a maid in the Black Bear Inn in Munich, 'in a little corner of the house which it is not right to name'. His wife was plain, shy and five years younger than himself. A few crisp sentences record the fate of the marriage: 'In such a fashion took place what is claimed to be the most important event in life. I found it ridiculous for a few weeks and then a matter of indifference.'[23] On their way to visit her aunt the Princess of Saxe-Weissenfels in Dresden, he committed 'my first infidelity, passing through Prague. In the Hôtel de Waldstein, a maid of a Madame de Nostitz. I had been married for three weeks.'[24]

The new Princesse de Ligne was, at this stage of their marriage, timid: Croÿ compared her to 'an eel under a rock'.[25] She spent most of her time in Brussels and Beloeil bringing up their children Christine and Charles, born in 1757 and 1759 respectively. Since the correspondence between husband and wife has not survived, little is known, at this stage, about their marriage. It is probable that, like Ligne's relationship with his father, it remained cold and distant.

If his marriage did little to advance his happiness, it did much to advance his career. Marriage to a Liechtenstein linked him to Austria as firmly as his status as an Austrian subject and his post as court chamberlain. The grandest family in the Austrian nobility, the Liechtensteins had been great landowners in Austria and Bohemia for as long as the Lignes in Hainaut. Arch-loyal to the Habsburgs, since the fourteenth century they had frequently served as *Oliersthofmeister*. They had further increased their wealth while presiding over the redistribution of Bohemian rebels' lands after the Battle of the White Mountain in 1620. The reigning prince was said to be the richest subject in the monarchy with an income of £60,000 p.a. – as well as one of its finest art collections.[26] The second-largest *arc de triomphe* in Europe, after that of Paris, would be built by a Liechtenstein on one of their Bohemian estates in the early nineteenth century.

Ligne's wife's uncle, Prince Joseph Wenzel, whose names show the combination of German and Czech influences in his background, had helped make the Austrian artillery, on which he was said to have spent 10 million florins of his own money, the admiration of Europe. Ligne revered him for his magnificence, the presents he made to sovereigns, his zeal for the Austrian service, his embassies, his entertainments and his hunts.[27] They often discussed military matters and Liechtenstein gave many of his military manuscripts to Ligne.[28]

Like the Habsburgs and the Hofburg, the Austrian nobility, its attitudes and palaces formed part of the background to Ligne's life for the next sixty years. His mother was a Salm, his grandmother a Dietrichstein; two of his sisters-in-law married a

Palffy and a Kinsky, wealthy Hungarian and Czech nobles respectively, who maintained palaces in Vienna. Ligne had no need to feel a stranger among the crowds of princes waiting in the antechambers of the Hofburg. Throughout his life he would be invited to the balls and dinners they gave in their massive baroque palaces (the largest of which, the Palais Liechtenstein beside the Hofburg, was Ligne's second home in Vienna) and to the hunts, plays and operas they organised on their estates.

Even compared to other European nobilities, the Austrians were ostentatious. Lady Mary Coke wrote from Vienna: 'Tis astonishing the magnificent manner in which everyone here lives: everything is the same, dress, dinners, Houses, furniture etc: the Magnificence in everything greatly exceeds either Paris or London.'[29] The Comte de Guibert, a French military reformer, wrote of the 'extraordinary splendour' he observed in one of Prince Esterhazy's residences, the castle of Eisenstadt south of Vienna. Prince Esterhazy (who had married a Liechtenstein) had an income of seven million florins a year, 200 guards, ownership of an Italian opera, German and French theatre troupes and Haydn to conduct his orchestra: 'The state of our greatest lords is nothing in comparison.'[30]

However much the English traveller Nathaniel Wraxall liked the women and the conversation in Vienna, he found the young nobles 'in general insupportable ... distinguished only by pride, ignorance and illiberality, regarding themselves as superior to every other European nation, because their sovereign is titular head of the German Empire'.[31] This pride, which he was not alone in noticing, was the essence of the Austrian monarchy.* It provides the explanation for many of the wars of Ligne's

---

* Art also reveals Austria's pride. In the magnificent baroque monastery of Saint Florian in Upper Austria, past which Ligne travelled on his way to Vienna, one room is decorated with symbols of the Babylonian, Persian, Greek and Roman Empires and portraits of Maria Theresa, Francis I and their son Joseph; an inscription states that, whilst those empires fell, the Austrian would last for ever. On the ceiling of the Marble Hall, a genius flies past the Emperor Charles VI – Ligne's godfather – dressed as a Roman emperor, bearing a flag with the inscription, from Virgil: 'I have given you Empire without limits [*sine fine*] of time or space.'

lifetime. Indeed Ligne himself shared it. His solution to the problems of Europe was simple. He hoped 'the monarchy' would one day stretch from the North Sea to the Black Sea.[32]

His court office as chamberlain gave Ligne not only a link with Austria but also a courtier's view of human nature. As Lord Chesterfield, a Lord of the Bedchamber to George II, wrote (in his celebrated *Letters to his Son*, which Samuel Johnson, a former protégé, described as teaching 'the morals of a whore, and the manners of a dancing master'): 'Courts are the best key to character: there every passion is busy, every art exerted, every character analysed.'[33] Ligne agreed. He wrote: 'The Court is a good furnace,' and believed that living with sovereigns, in the society of courts and women, was the best way to judge the world.[34] He approved of etiquette, 'because you must win the respect of the grandees so that they can win the respect of the humble and in this way establish a cascade of consideration'.[35] He saw nature and politics in terms of courts, describing farmers who watched the dawn as the sun's first courtiers[36] and making the word 'court' synonymous with government – as indeed it was in an age when a royal tutor could become chief minister (Lord Bute in 1762) and a royal mistress influence French foreign policy (Mme de Pompadour).

Meeting so many different people, seeing sovereigns and ministers at close quarters, he was convinced that personalities and emotions, like the pride of the Duchess of Marlborough or Frederick II's jokes about Mme de Pompadour, had greater influence on issues and events than impersonal forces such as geography, religion or nationalism. Pride, self-interest and vengeance were 'the three great causes of events throughout the centuries'.[37] 'It is private interest, ambition, vengeance, the feelings of logic or resentment of the man or woman in favour which often affect decisions which are attributed to a profound political calculation. It is almost always personal factors which have started wars.'[38]

The war of 1756 proved his point. Its principal cause was Maria Theresa's determination to recover Silesia and perhaps subsequently Alsace and Lorraine, to which she and her husband had hereditary claims. Maria Theresa's personal determination had also helped save Austria after her father's death in 1740, when most of Europe was against her, her German and Czech provinces were wavering, her own ministers had despaired and there were riots in Vienna itself. Pious and conservative by nature, yet prepared to listen to unwelcome advice and enforce radical measures when convinced of their necessity, she governed in person. Her striking blonde looks and impressive bearing added to her impact. Her admiring chamberlain, Count von Khevenhuller, wrote: 'God has given this woman the gift of winning people and bending them to her will by a kindly demeanour.' In 1741 a dramatic appearance in black, bearing the crown of Saint Stephen on her head and her heir Joseph in her arms, had won her the hearts of the Hungarians, who thereafter provided some of her best troops.

Maria Theresa was the first of her dynasty to be thoroughly Austrian. She was more interested in recovering Silesia and uniting her hereditary territories than in the Crown of the Holy Roman Empire. When her beloved husband Francis of Lorraine was crowned Emperor at Frankfurt in 1745, she refused to be crowned Empress Consort.[39]

Ligne revered Maria Theresa, although he found her a little cold. Her court had the glory to resemble no other: 'One adored Maria Theresa: one liked her son Joseph II without telling them. The first obliged one to feel enthusiasm. The second to feel respect. However that did not stop us criticising them. They knew it and did not find it bad.'[40] Ligne admired her love of the army, which she called 'the only branch of state administration for which I harboured a real personal interest'. *Mater castrorum*, she attended maneouvres, called the soldiers 'my children', from 1751 admitted all army officers to court receptions in uniform, whatever their birth (to the horror of some of the great nobility) and in 1752 founded the Wiener Neustadt Military Academy.[41] Whereas it had been difficult for the Habsburgs, even with the help of British subsidies, to keep 100,000 men in the field in the wars of Prince Eugène, under Maria Theresa the Austrian army was approaching 250,000 – roughly the same as France and 50,000 more than Prussia.[42] It was not going to remain unused.

By the diplomatic revolution of 1756, for the first time in their history the two traditional enemies, France and Austria, formed an alliance. The principal motives were personal: Maria Theresa's resolve to recover Silesia, Louis XV's hostility to Frederick the Great (fuelled, in Ligne's opinion, by the latter's unwise jokes about Mme de Pompadour). One of Austria's strengths was its ability, by its dynastic grandeur and strategic importance, to attract the support of foreign statesmen, from Louis XV in the eighteenth century to Talleyrand in the nineteenth. Louis XV promised men and money to help Austria deprive Prussia of all its acquisitions since 1618. In return his cousin the Prince de Conti would receive the Crown of Poland, his son-in-law the Duke of Parma the Austrian Netherlands – recognition of the growing feeling that the land of Ligne's birth should one day form an independent state. Russia also joined the alliance against Prussia. Rather than wait to be devoured, Frederick seized the initiative and invaded the Electorate of Saxony, which occupied a strategic position between Prussia and Austria. The Seven Years' War had begun.

Ligne took to war as eagerly as he had taken to court life. It was not only the profession that he had worshipped since he was a boy, but also an opportunity to escape his father and his wife. Despite his lack of formal military training, he began to serve as a captain in his father's regiment, Ligne Infanterie.[43] The first winter, 1756–7, they were stationed in the Austrian Netherlands, at Mons, the capital of Hainaut, where the Ligne family kept a house. He fell in love with a 'celestial, naive, amiable and sensitive' Englishwoman, 'one of the most beautiful creatures I have seen', who was living there in a convent. He fought a duel over her with a rival admirer, had a rendezvous at a masked ball and spent evenings disguised as a woman, waiting to enter her convent.[44]

Soon he had other concerns. In 1757 he moved with his

regiment to Europe's other cockpit, Saxony, Bohemia and Silesia, which, in recent wars, had seen as many battles as the Low Countries. On the way, passing through Bayreuth, Ligne dined with Frederick's brilliant sister the Margravine of Bayreuth. When she asked a fellow officer what he thought of Frederick's prospects, he replied: 'I believe, Madame, that he is f—.'

She rejoined: 'Monsieur, that would make me sad as he is my brother,' to which he responded: 'In that case, Madame, it is I who am.'[45]

Throughout his life Ligne suffered from, or enjoyed, graphomania, the constant desire to write. He regretted the day he neither read nor wrote.[46] He served Austria with his pen as well as his sword. As he often complained, the French were skilled at celebrating themselves: 'There is not one little success in the French Armies which does not have thirty Historians... our Emperors do not have Historiographers.'* As a result, Turenne and Condé were better known than Austrian generals such as Wallenstein and Prince Eugène of Savoy. Even French defeats were celebrated. Ligne was determined to redress the balance. Thus one interest of Ligne's writings is not only their originality and vivacity, but also their Austrian point of view. The diary he kept during the Seven Years' War was published forty years later, extensively rewritten, as *Mon Journal de la Guerre de Sept ans*.[47]

The army in which he served was even more international than the monarchy. In a memorable phrase of Christopher Duffy, who considers Ligne's writings the best source on the army of Maria Theresa: 'No other army of the time could have produced a column of regiments chattering variously in German, Czech, French, Flemish, Raeto-Romance, Italian, Magyar and Serbo-Croatian, and all passing in review under the eyes of a general who was cursing to himself in Gaelic.'[48] The regiments had names such as Los Rios, Esterhazy, Ligne

---

* In France Racine and Voltaire, among others, served as *Historiographes du roi*, writing official histories of the campaigns of Louis XIV and Louis XV respectively.

Infanterie. Ligne himself sometimes commanded a force of 100 Walloons, 100 Hungarians and 200 Germans: he particularly appreciated the Hungarians, whose loyalty and gallantry had helped save the monarchy in 1740.[49]

In battles that could decide the fate of the monarchy, crying 'Vivat Maria Theresa!', or 'Vive Marie-Thérèse, la bayonette et les Wallons!', he found the battlefield more exciting than the most passionate love affair.[50] With characteristic frivolity, he said that victory was a woman who needed to be abducted. The moment two armies met on the crest of a hill he compared to 'a moment of flux and reflux like that at the pit of the opera'.[51] In the midst of battle he quoted poetry and between battles conducted love affairs so pressing that one coachman was let off his rent for the rest of his life as a reward for driving Ligne to a rendezvous on time. When there was no action and he was bored, he started it up again by firing cannon at a mass of blue – the enemy in Prussian-blue uniforms.[52]

At first Austria resumed the victorious tradition of Prince Eugène. On 18 June 1757 Ligne fought in the Battle of Kolin, east of Prague, where Marshal Daun defeated Frederick the Great and saved Bohemia from Prussian occupation. In a dramatic charge in which Ligne participated, the regiment of Ligne Dragons under Field Marshal Prince Ferdinand de Ligne cut a square of Prussian infantry to pieces in a minute. Thereafter the Prussians collapsed. Despite Frederick's pleas in his half-French German, 'Aber mein herren Generals, wollen sie nicht attackieren?', he failed to rally his exhausted and outnumbered troops and fled the field of battle.

Kolin finally proved that Austria could defeat Prussia. The estatic Empress, showing her belief that her army was the basis of her monarchy, called it 'the day of the birth of the monarchy'. Marshal Daun was 'my best, my true, and reliable friend'. In commemoration she founded the great Austrian military Order of Maria Theresa, to reward acts of outstanding gallantry on the battlefield, which became the ambition of every officer in her armies.[53] The joy Ligne and his friends felt the night after the battle was augmented by their astonishment at having defeated the genius of the age.[54] Unfortunately Prince Charles of Lorraine, in command of the pursuit, proved as cautious on the battlefields of Bohemia as he had been reckless in the corridors of Beloeil. Another general might have annihilated the Prussian army and captured its King.

At the Battle of Leuthen, on 5 December 1757, the Austrians under Prince Charles of Lorraine were defeated by the Prussian Guards. In the middle of defeat, surrounded by dying comrades, Ligne took advantage of a dispute over precedence between two superior officers, assumed command of his regiment, rallied it under fire and led it back to safety. He was promoted lieutenant colonel as a reward.[55] At the Battles of Görlitz and Kittlitz, in 1758, he was again mentioned in despatches and that winter was promoted to the rank of colonel commanding the regiment of Ligne Infanterie. Exasperated by the debts his son was accumulating by borrowing from Jewish moneylenders, as well as by his mere existence, his father commented: 'It was already sufficiently unfortunate for me, Monsieur, to have you as my son, without having you as my colonel.'[56]

Since Prussia had broken the peace by invading Saxony, Austria was assisted by the army of the Holy Roman Empire, raised by the Imperial circles; Ligne, who had no respect for their fighting qualities, called them 'the empiricals'. In addition, at least a fifth of the Austrian army, officers and soldiers, was raised outside the Monarchy, in the Empire. One of Ligne's greatest friends in the army, Prince Louis of Württemberg, came from the most important principality in the south-west of the Empire. While in winter quarters in the Saxon capital Dresden in 1758–9, the two young princes amused themselves by running through the streets at night rattling chains and pretending to be ghosts, changing shop signs around, crying 'Fire!' and spraying water on the people who appeared at the windows.[57]

Ligne was not only a wild young officer at the start of his career but also a writer with a sense of the past, and of personalities: he already saw people he met as historical figures. In 1758 he visited a relic of the past, the Comtesse de Cosel, the most famous mistress of Augustus the Strong, 'the Louis XIV of Germany', Elector of Saxony and King of Poland. She had borne him three children and had reigned in Dresden as an uncrowned queen. Since a quarrel in 1716 (possibly in a fit of jealousy, she had tried to kill him), she had lived as a prisoner in the fortress of Stolpen near Meissen.[58] When he died after a drinking bout in 1733, she had decided to stay in prison since she knew no one outside.

Like many old women, she was captivated by Ligne, telling him stories of her lover, whose passion for porcelain had led him to found the first factory in Europe at Meissen in 1710. Through the splendour of his court and collections, he had made his capital Dresden, in Ligne's opinion, one of the finest in the world. The contrast between Saxony and Prussia was shown by Augustus the Strong's gift to the King of Prussia of one of the best regiments in the Saxon army, in exchange for a roomful of porcelain from a Prussian palace. Mme de Cosel said that, having had the time to study all religions, she had chosen the Jewish and advised Ligne to do the same. When Ligne asked her if her lover had been as 'strong' as he was said to be (one author credited him with 354 illegitimate children), she replied: 'Alas no. I hardly noticed it. He drank a lot; and I often spent the night sobering him up with glasses of water.'[59]

At Maxen near Dresden on 20 and 21 November 1759, Marshal Daun won a further victory over the Prussians under the King's brother Prince Henry, capturing nine generals, 12,000 men and nearly one-tenth of the Prussian officer corps. Austrian artillery proved itself superior in number and firepower to the Prussians'. Ligne, who again distinguished himself, later wrote that he had never been so happy as after Maxen: 'I was beside myself with joy.'[60] Austria reoccupied Silesia and in Vienna Frederick was expected to sue for peace; but the King of Prussia would not give up.

Ligne had his first experience of the court of Versailles when he was sent there with news of the victory. Louis XV asked

whether he was younger than the Prince de Condé, whether
Marshal Daun wore a wig, and gave Ligne a ring and a gold
snuff box (he pawned the first and sold the second to the
Empress). He was then presented to Mme de Pompadour as if
she was a minister – as indeed she was, since she was consulted
by the King on politics. After a lot of 'politico-ministerial and
politico-military rubbish', and a search for Maxen on the map of
Saxony, she asked why the Imperial court did not send its silver to
be melted down as the French had, and why the ladies of Prague
did not pay court more often to the sisters of Mme la Dauphine.

In Paris, Ligne's elegant Austrian uniform and excellent
French helped make him fashionable. 'Drunk with pleasure,
parties, surprises, enchantments ...' Ligne spent the most enjoyable winter of his life, 1759–60, guided by a handsome young
heartbreaker called the Marquis de Lestorière. Ligne went on
the first sledge party in Paris with the beautiful Duchesse de
Mazarin and drove to the opera ball behind the carriage of Lady
Sarah Bunbury, dressed as a sequinned footman.[61]

In 1760 Ligne tore himself from Paris 'with pain and pleasure
at the same time as it was to return to the army'. In October 1760,
for the second time in the war, Austrian forces occupied Berlin.
In the palace of Charlottenburg, sacked by Cossacks and
Hungarian hussars, soldiers walked up to their knees in shattered
porcelain and crystal. However, Ligne helped ensure that the
King's private residence at Sans Souci was saved from pillage,
though he himself took a pen from the great man's desk.[62]

Even Ligne acknowledged the horrors of war. In Berlin, soldiers were so drunk that they sold, took back and resold two or
three times the same things. Ligne himself was beaten by
Russian soldiers for taking Prussian uniforms. The Prussians
outraged civilised opinion by setting fire to Dresden. The
Austrian destruction of Zittau, a Silesian city under Prussian
occupation, in which ten thousand civilians died, was, Ligne
wrote, 'capable of putting one off war for ever'.[63]

The campaigns of 1761 and 1762 passed with little incident. In
1762, however, the miracle of the House of Brandenburg

occurred. Frederick's enemy the Empress Elizabeth of Russia was succeeded by her pro-Prussian nephew Peter III. Since Russia withdrew from the war, Frederick recovered the initiative.[64] Ligne attributed Prussian resilience in part to the *énergie communicative* of the officer corps, which came from the poor country nobility rather than, as with the Austrians, from princes or parvenus. Ligne pointed out that Austrian generals such as Marshal Loudon (a soldier of fortune from the Baltic provinces, who could not speak French) were too cautious and methodical to exploit their advantages: they lacked the killer instinct. Frederick the Great, however, was a genius, always capable of surprising his enemies. At the peace of Hubertusburg in 1763, despite all the Austrian victories, Frederick recovered Silesia.

After the fighting was over, Ligne devoted himself to the pursuit of pleasure in Vienna. Once, he was in a hurry dashing to a rendezvous with a new mistress but found his way blocked by one of the slow-moving religious processions that obstructed the streets of Vienna in the reign of Maria Theresa. Screaming *Fahrt zu zum Teufel*, he dealt out sword blows right and left until the pilgrims fled. He reached his mistress on time but the resulting law suit, which was finally dropped by the chief of police, cannot have endeared him to his pious sovereign.[65] Ligne began to win the reputation of being, in Zinzendorf's words, 'a scatterbrain who has no manners and commits acts of insolence'.[66]

The Empress's maids, who told her the gossip of Vienna, may have added that he shared the favours, with her own husband, of the young and beautiful Princess Auersperg, famous for her luxuriant chestnut hair and brilliant conversation. On one occasion the Emperor, slipping into the Princess's box at the theatre, found her alone with Ligne. He asked the name of the play being performed only to be told by Ligne, who then rushed away half embarrassed and half dying of laughter, that it was *Crispin rival de son maître*.

One of the best accounts of Ligne's Vienna is to be found in the diary of his friend and contemporary Count von Zinzendorf, known as *le petit Zinzin*. Detached and meticulous, the diary rolls on in French, recording the Count's travels in Europe and life in Vienna, without interruption from 1761 to his death in 1813. A typical entry says: 'Dined at Marshal Batthyany's with Princess Esterhazy, the Schönborn, the Los Rios, the Lobkowitz, Madame Batthyany my sister in law, M. de Windischgraetz, the Canale, Nassau, Ligne, Boufflers, Durand. We admired the prince's monkey' – which prince is not specified. Foreigners sometimes claimed that there was no conversation in Vienna, but Zinzendorf wrote that when Ligne was at supper you had to sew up his lips to have a chance to speak.[67]

In addition to the great nobles, Ligne knew many of the foreigners who flocked to Vienna. The grandeur of the House of Austria, and the cosmopolitanism of the monarchy, meant that, in an age when talent was hard to find, the Emperor could draw on the largest talent pool in Europe. Foreigners – the most illustrious of whom being the half-French, half-Piedmontese Prince Eugène of Savoy – felt at ease in Austria.[68] Among the people drawn to serve the Emperor rather than their own sovereign were Zinzendorf himself (a Saxon) and Marshal Lacy, son of an Irish Jacobite serving in the Russian army, under whom Ligne had fought in the Seven Years' War.

A handsome, convivial bachelor, one of the most admired soldiers in the Austrian army, Lacy became President of the Council of War at the age of forty-one. He helped make the Austrian army a professional, modernising force, based on recruitment by canton and absorbing at least fifty per cent of the budget of the monarchy.[69] Showing Ligne more affection than his own father, Lacy, who was ten years older than the Prince, acted as his patron in Vienna until Lacy's death in 1801. Lacy called Ligne *notre fol ami Charlot* ('our mad friend Charlie' – *Charlot* was a term for a clown in French), tried to advance his career and often visited the fashionable resort of Spa in the Ardennes with him.[70] He said that Ligne might become wiser but could not become dearer to Lacy than he already was. He trusted him enough to ask Ligne to find him new toupees and a reliable and literate military secretary.[71]

Ligne revered Lacy as 'my master', 'the best of generals and the bravest of soldiers'.[72] His diary of the Seven Years' War celebrates Lacy as an infallible strategist.[73] A letter from Lacy to Ligne describes the life they led in Vienna in peacetime. It is always the same, he wrote on 13 July 1763: 'We get up when the sun has already burnt the whole city. We yawn, dress carelessly, pay visits, dine, go to the theatre, to the Promenade,* to supper and then return to bed, exhausted from having done nothing all day.'[74]

The glories and pleasures of a career in the Austrian army could have defined the rest of Ligne's life, as they did Lacy's. For Ligne, however, Austria was not enough. He had other worlds to conquer.

---

* The Augarten, a fashionable garden, like the Tuileries or St James's, where society promenaded, in search of company, news, and amorous adventure.

The Republic of Letters

In 1763, Ligne left Austria to visit a country that he would inhabit for the rest of his life – the only republic that ever appealed to him: the republic of letters. In the eighteenth century, helped by the appeal of the French language and the abundance of French publishers in Amsterdam, London and Vienna, a 'republic of letters', of French-speaking writers and readers, flourished across Europe at the same time as the national literatures of England, Spain, Italy and Germany.[1] English authors such as Gibbon and Beckford wrote and published in French. French authors were read widely abroad; Ligne would call the letters of Mme de Sévigné *le bréviaire du Nord*.

One of the capitals of the republic of letters was the chateau of Ferney near Geneva. It was there that Voltaire had settled in 1760, when he had abandoned his attempts to live at the French, Prussian or other courts. Maria Theresa's dismay at Ligne's offhand behaviour towards her, her suspicion that he had been an intermediary in a love affair between Prince Louis of Württemberg and her favourite daughter Marie Christine and her horror at the infrequency of his attendance at mass gave him the incentive to leave Vienna.[2] A story Ligne wrote at this time, *Amabile* (*c*.1763), about a younger brother of Candide, hero of Voltaire's most famous tale, is in part an attack on the harshness, stupidity and boredom of the court of Vienna. At court some officials could not read the dates of gala days in the almanac and had to learn them by heart. Society hardly existed; courtiers yawned in their sovereign's presence; but priests and monks were powerful. The hero then goes to pay a visit to Tarivole, M. de Voltaire.[3]

Ligne had admired Voltaire since his youth, when he had read his works in secret at night, since his father and his tutors considered them too daring. After a brief visit to Venice, Ligne arrived at Ferney in June, equipped with an introduction from his friend the Marquis du Châtelet, French ambassador in Vienna and son of Voltaire's adored deceased mistress Emilie du Châtelet.

Ligne's perception and sophistication can be seen by comparing his account of his visit to that written, a year later, by another young man eager to win a literary reputation, James Boswell. Boswell was self-conscious: he describes, at length, his own effect on the great man; they talked mainly about each other's favourite topics: English literature and the Catholic Church. Ligne was more successful both in making Voltaire talk and in winning his hospitality: he stayed eight days, compared to Boswell's two. Voltaire did not simply see him at meals, like Boswell, but came to sit on Ligne's bed in the morning. Ligne was so happy that he wrote: 'I was always drunk' – high praise from a man who needed constant intoxication. More penetrating than Boswell, he not only admired the writer but laughed at his lack of taste, his desire to act the European statesman, his grey shoes and small black velvet bonnet. In his account of *Mes conversations avec Mr. de Voltaire*, Ligne began: 'What would have been best for me to do, was not to have any. I only spoke to him, to make him speak. I stayed with him for eight days and I wish I could remember the sublime, simple, gay, kindly remarks he made without stopping.' They talked about gondoliers singing songs from Tasso, Voltaire's maids' beautiful white necks, the English constitution, Geneva and the defects of Montesquieu – Voltaire said Montesquieu's book should be called *De l'Esprit sur les lois*, rather than *De l'Esprit des lois*: 'I do not have the honour to understand it.' Frederick the Great was another subject of conversation: Voltaire said that the only gratitude the King had ever felt was for the horse on which he had fled from the field of Mollwitz (an Austrian victory in 1742). Ligne saw Voltaire act the lord of the manor with his peasants, addressing them as if they were Roman ambassadors: 'he ennobled everything'.[4]

After Ligne left, Voltaire and his niece and mistress Mme Denis wrote that the only consolation for not being able to see him was to read his letters. No one inspired so much attachment and so many regrets. Thereafter, about once a year, they wrote to each other, letters that Ligne was able to hand around the salons of Europe. Whereas most writers behaved towards Voltaire as disciples towards the god of a new religion – the radical scepticism of the eighteenth century – Ligne acted as a courtier towards a monarch. He called himself a grandee in Voltaire's kingdom, saying, 'You are the only court where I solicit favours. You have no ministers, I am sure to obtain what I want.'[5] He wrote that he had two portraits of Voltaire by his bed, his works in his head and his philosophy in his heart.[6] In 1778, the year of his death, Voltaire wrote a poem to Ligne comparing him to a swan with a silver neck.[7]

With his historian's instinct and ambition to win a literary reputation, Ligne was as eager to 'acquire' famous writers as Boswell was to acquire Dr Johnson. Having visited Voltaire in 1763, he went to see his most famous rival, Rousseau, seven years later. Rousseau was one of a new breed of writers who were beginning to live from their pens and to dispense with courts and patrons (although he received a pension from George III, which continued to be paid to his widow, in 1766).[8] Rousseau's *La Nouvelle Héloise* with its cult of natural emotions had swept Europe in 1762. Pretending he had come to the wrong address, Ligne went to Rousseau's attic in the Rue Platrière in Paris, 'the home of rats but the sanctuary of Virtue and Genius'. Ligne regarded Rousseau as a sage with a new view of humanity, rather than a political revolutionary, and was trembling when he arrived. At first Rousseau continued making a list of plants. Then Ligne asked him about his work copying sheets of music, until Rousseau started to complain about the human race. Ligne replied: 'Those who complain of them are also men and may be mistaken about other men.' They talked about the difficulty of feeling gratitude towards people you neither like nor respect, and about David Hume, occasionally interrupted by questions from Rousseau's mistress about the soup or the laundry. Ligne wrote that, if Rousseau had wanted to, he could have ennobled a bit of cheese and that his eyes were like two stars. After a moment of silent veneration as he looked straight at the author of *La Nouvelle Héloise*, Ligne took his leave. When Rousseau returned his visit, Ligne felt like Louis XIV receiving the ambassador of Siam: they started to talk of the crimes of the *parlement* and the clergy. Ligne let Rousseau see that he knew *La Nouvelle Héloise* by heart and advised him to live in the country. In Paris, he said, 'the more you hide yourself, the more conspicuous you are'. When Rousseau left, Ligne felt 'the same emptiness that you feel when you wake from a beautiful dream'.[9] That year, in a letter that, no doubt owing to the Prince's love of celebrity, was at once printed in the *Gazette universelle* and the *Gentleman's Magazine*, Ligne offered Rousseau asylum at Fagnolles or Beloeil. However, the great writer preferred to continue to suffer in Paris.[10]

Having received the blessings of the two gods of the Enlightenment (as useful then, for young writers, as those of Sartre and de Beauvoir two hundred years later), Ligne could begin to establish himself as a writer. Every genre appealed to him. A skilled stylist, he could write over two hundred lines of verse ending in the suffix -*ine* in 1759 while taking news of Maxen to Versailles, in *Epitre à M. le Duc de Bragance*.* In all he wrote fourteen volumes of *vers de société*, on such subjects as his desire to be buried beside his soldiers' barracks; a dog who warned him of a husband's return; his own heart ('O théâtre d'inconséquence, séjour plein d'agitation!'); and 'a pretty young woman of Paris who had made me happy and who once told me to write immediately afterwards'.

In the late 1760s and early 1770s, while travelling in carriages between the three poles of his life, Paris, Vienna and Beloeil, he also filled his spare time writing thoughts or epigrams, in

---

* The Duke of Braganza, a cousin of the King of Portugal and of Ligne, one of Ligne's greatest friends, resided in Vienna but later returned to Lisbon, and founded the Portuguese Academy of Sciences.

paragraphs or sentences. They were then copied in three red-covered manuscript volumes, intended for publication, called *Mes livres rouges*, either by his secretary Sauveur Legros, a writer twenty years younger than he, son of an officer of the royal kitchens at Versailles, who had fled to Brussels to escape a love affair, or by his German archivist Nicolas Leygeb.[11]

Epigrams are a form that suited Ligne since, as Roland Mortier writes, they enabled him to give free rein to his taste for paradox, humour and concision. In this domain, although not in many others, Mortier is right to claim: 'The apparent ease of the prince is the fruit of carefully concealed effort, of a conscious search for concision, contrast and ellipsis ... the miracle of the prince is to search for the serious below the casual, gravity beneath detachment as he hid his literary effort beneath an apparent facility.[12]

Amid innumerable reflections on ambition, love and friendship, his 'red books' contain remarks such as: 'It is as disagreeable in Society to change your opinion at once, as to uphold it too forcefully'; or, 'The most honourable man without intelligence does a hundred times more harm than an intelligent rascal.' Self-importance amused him: 'The Captain of Guards of the Abbot of Fulda [a Prince of the Holy Roman Empire] ... speaks of his monk, praises his kindness, his affability, the gentleness of his private life, as M. de Beauvau speaks of his Master [the King of France]. A village registrar is as pleased with himself by the evening after working all day as M. de Lacy.'[13]

Ligne's mind ignored boundaries of time, space and convention. The Prince's frivolity in society and conservative attitudes in public were in part screens to mask the radicalism of his views in private. By the 1760s, despite his Catholic education, Ligne was a scornful atheist, who in his own words:

> de tous les erreurs complice,
> des juifs dédaignait le Roi.
> [guilty of every error,
> despised the King of the Jews].

He 'defied the king of kings' and made 'the most infamous' drawings of the most sacred mysteries.[14] Like many contemporaries, including Voltaire, he felt that the progress of science removed all credibility from Christianity. There was no point in leaving 'the temple of love, of this charming little God who preaches only ease, taste, delicacy, liberty, to run to the altars of another God who is called good and whom they make terrible ... whose service is rude and whose favourites are such bad company'.[15] Possessing one of the few copies of the atheist work *Le Traité des trois imposteurs* (Moses, Jesus, Mohammed), printed in The Hague in 1719, he considered Zoroastrianism the most reasonable religion, as it acknowledged the balance between good and evil in the world.[16] This did not, however, prevent him from rejecting Voltaire's offer to send him atheist books for his library, in order to spread Voltaire's gospel of atheism and anticlericalism in the Austrian Netherlands.[17] Ligne was too much part of court society to want to advertise his private radicalism.

Ligne's view of marriage was equally radical. Attacking early, arranged marriages, he wrote: 'We marry too early to love each other. We do not know what it means. The only pleasure of marriage is to be delivered from your relations ... But what an abuse of the most sacred matters! One has a wife like one has a regiment, a government position: to have.' He lamented the injustice of a wife's property belonging to her husband and believed that there should be two trial marriages before the real one. He said that people who were lazy did not know how lucky they were and advocated an inheritance tax on large fortunes to benefit foundations and hospitals.[18]

Not content with scorning Christianity, he also claimed: 'If people opened their eyes, there would be no more thrones or curule chairs [senates]. All seated on the same bench. The world would not work any worse.' He also attacked his own class: 'One good thing that Philosophy [the Enlightenment] has brought with it, in almost all countries, is a complete contempt for *les grands seigneurs*.' Equality was possible: 'The people is like a horse. It allows itself to be ridden because it does not know its strength ... This is one of those maxims which it is dangerous to think!'[19]

The piquancy of these revolutionary remarks is heightened by the fact that they were written at the moment when Ligne himself had become a *grand seigneur*. Ligne had hardly seen his father since the end of the Seven Years' War. Enraged by his son's debts, the Prince had quarrelled with his son as he quarrelled with everyone, even with Prince Charles of Lorraine, over the price of a house in Mons. Finally the old Prince died on 7 April 1766, from eating a surfeit of strawberries grown in his own greenhouse. Ligne was now his own master.[20]

The estates he inherited from his father in 1766 produced a gross revenue of 109,000 florins a year. Although much of it was absorbed by running expenses and pensions, it was a splendid sum at a time when a general's salary was 10,000 florins a year. Ligne spent it on the pursuit of pleasure rather than, like many of his contemporaries, the 'improvement' of his estates. He left them in the capable hands of M. Vandenbroucke, Intendant-Général des Affaires et Maison de S. A. Monseigneur le Prince de Ligne, whose calm and industry he respected more than his advice to economise.[21] Under Vandenbroucke Ligne was served by a full princely household in Beloeil and Brussels, which included a treasurer, a maître d'hôtel, an adjutant, two secretaries and twenty-four footmen, cooks, postillions and coachmen, in addition to the separate staffs attached to each chateau.[22] Henceforth Ligne had the money to do what he wanted.

The contradiction between acts and words is seen in Ligne's attitude to sex, as well as in his attitude to class. For a man who frequently proclaimed the ease and number of his female conquests, Ligne is exceptionally well informed about people with other inclinations. In one 'red book' he wrote: 'Why call Pederasty – against nature? One always starts that way. One is in love with one's school-fellows until twenty: that taste goes from school to the army and it is not the worst place for it: for those who have it escape those horrible diseases which make two thirds of officers incapable of finishing a campaign. Besides it costs nothing: and whatever people say, it is enjoyable. One is not a B ... for f ... one's man from time to time.' The next paragraph continues: 'One does not keep this taste because there is danger, effort, difficulty and rarity; and because one grows old. It is no longer worth anything when one cannot have returned to one what one has given.' Women, with their delicious curves and satin skin, are far more attractive.

Such remarks probably represent Ligne's desire to shock, or a *jeu de société* characteristic of the age. He read out his defence of pederasty in a Vienna salon and hoped that the daring and originality of his Red Books would increase their impact when published, although in fact they remained unpublished, until discovered by the present author, in 1991, in a turret of the Château d'Antoing.[23] Ligne's defence of the pleasure and practical advantages of daily masturbation, in a poem called 'For the Good of the Empress's Service' (because it stopped her troops catching diseases), did not prove that he practised it.*[24]

On the other hand Ligne's remarks and knowledge probably also reflect, to an unknown degree, his own experience, at least when young. He himself refers to his 'facility'. In his memoirs he admitted – with a disclaimer of reluctance: 'A M. de Rodonan, my comrade in the riding-school, an ensign who mounted my first guard with me and then a prince Menzikoff later taught me more about it than I wanted to know.'[25] Two of his closest friends were the Duke of Braganza, who married only at the end of his life, and Marshal Lacy, who never did.

---

* Among the poem's lines are:

> C'est du plaisir de la branlade,
> Dont je fais aujour'hui parade.
> Ah! lorsque ma main me caresse
> Que je suis dans la douce ivresse ...
> Mon sort est toujours en mes doigts,
> Tous les ménages je menace,
> A personne je ne fais grâce:
> Je fais cinq cocus à la fois.

Ligne's short story 'Les deux amis', written about 1765 and published forty years later, may be the first homosexual love story in modern European literature. Zerbin, the prettiest blonde in the world, is chasing the dark-haired Zimaton. Zimaton is frightened of what people will say. Zerbin replies: 'Custom is a word. [The fear of] what people say is ridiculous. Reputation is a matter of prejudice.' Women are not worth the effort, least of all cold and hideous Englishwomen: 'Why look elsewhere for what we have ourselves?' In the end Zimaton yields when they see Carthusian monks 'talking' together in the same cell in a monastery. Ligne concludes: 'They kiss each other very often, love each other to distraction and are perfectly happy.' The interest of this story lies above all in Ligne's attitude. In an age when sodomy was still punishable by death, none of the writers he knew – neither Voltaire nor Rousseau nor the stars of the Paris salons – dealt so lightly and openly with this forbidden topic. On the other hand, if Ligne had been homosexual, he would not have written about it so much.

Ligne also wrote an obscene short story called 'Supplément à Apprius', probably around 1764, since it refers to a peace recently concluded with Frederick the Great. Ligne is the first writer to compare homosexuals to Freemasons: he claims they both have special means of recognition while shaking hands or embracing. It is a hilarious account, transposed into the language of courts and warfare, of the relations of the Bralides (Lesbians), Chedabars (*bardaches*: passive homosexuals), and Ebugors (*bougres*/buggers). Other characters are Litocris/clitoris, King Lucanus/cul-anus (Frederick the Great, whose private life had few secrets for the Prince de Ligne), Apprius/Priapus, Mina/Main, Gemidoche/dildo (*godemiche*), Dandre/bander, suna/anus, Brularne/Branleur, and an 'abbé si joli qu'il était pour tel employé', in countries representing different sexual tastes: Medoso (Sodome), Gherromo (Gomorrhe) and so on. One characteristic passage recounts the tactics of the *Ebugors* who 'were marvellously skilled at attacking positions from heights, especially if they dominated a valley. They went themselves to search through neighbouring woods, whose existence others would hardly suspect, and they only advanced into these valleys if they were very sure of themselves. They did not neglect hills, seized them when appropriate, knew the advantage of Ravines and that of taking all camps from behind if they present their flanks.' They have many adventures until the sexual inclinations sign a treaty of peace. As a final tribute to inversion, Ligne puts the preface at the end.[26]

The theatre occupied almost as much of Ligne's energy as writing poems, stories and epigrams. For the eighteenth century the theatre combined the magic of television, cinema and the stage: it was the principal form of public entertainment and Ligne thought that it had as much influence as education in making manners and language the same throughout Europe. He loved the intoxication and excitement of the theatre, visiting the director of the Grand Théâtre, M. d'Hannetaire, every day when he was in Brussels, and boasting to Voltaire about the Brussels theatre: 'The pomp of our productions, our respect for the author's intentions, the faithfulness of our costumes should prejudice people in our favour. There is so little of all that in Paris, at this moment.'[27]

Ligne also enjoyed playing in what were known as *troupes de société* (amateur theatricals), defending them with this cry from the heart: 'Anything is better than spending the evening in malicious gossip or knitting without saying anything.'[28] Ligne himself acted in amateur productions in Brussels, at Beloeil, and at Hervelé, seat of his cousin the Duc d'Arenberg.* In 1769, with many d'Arenbergs and Starhembergs, he applauded the Duc de Croÿ's amateur actors at Croÿ's Château de l'Hermitage, and tried to steal them for his own troupe. His enthusiasm was greater than his skill. Zinzendorf wrote that in *L'Ecole d'un bourgeois* at Ghent in January 1770 he was 'stiff and did not even pronounce his words distinctly'.[29]

Writing was so much part of Ligne's life that he wrote books

---

* The Arenbergs, a junior branch of the Lignes, were nevertheless wealthier and in some respects more successful and frequently aroused Ligne's jealousy.

for publication in his lifetime, as well as epigrams, verses and stories to be read out loud in a salon, and letters and memoirs for posterity; Ligne was the first *grand seigneur* to be a professional published author. The Duc de Saint-Simon had also seen himself as a writer, and had ensured the preservation of the manuscripts of his memoirs with a view to publication; but they were written for posterity, like those of many other princes and nobles, and were only published posthumously. Saint-Simon did not, like Ligne, arrange publication of his works in his lifetime. Out of respect for the tradition by which princes did not publish, Ligne did not, at this stage, print his name on the title page; however, by stating 'L. P. D. L.', 'M. le Prince de L****', or 'un officer autrichien', as the author's name, he ensured that his identity was an open secret.

One of Ligne's first books, *Lettres à Eugénie sur les spectacles*, published in Paris anonymously and at his own expense in 1774, was a sparkling account of the eighteenth-century theatre, much copied by subsequent writers. Ligne devoted much care to its publication.[30] Unlike Rousseau, Ligne advocates removing the social and religious stigma still attached to the profession of actor. It was well received in the Paris press, although the *Journal Encyclopédique* cruelly suggested that it had a slightly provincial tone.[31] In it Ligne wrote: 'The world is a Comedy ... We are often more actors than those who appear before us from six to nine p.m. ... we act the lover, we act the husband, the gentleman, and it is often the last role we play worst.'[32]

Ligne wanted to be a great military writer as well as a great general. In addition to his account of the Seven Years' War, in 1770 he wrote a *Mémoire raisonné sur plusieurs ordres de bataille* and, between 1773 and 1783, a learned catalogue of 492 military books in his library, including forty-two military manuscripts he had inherited from Prince Joseph Wenzel Liechtenstein. More than a catalogue, it is an exposé of the books he considered necessary for the intellectual formation of a modern officer. The works discussed range from the Commentaries of Caesar and works by Chinese authors to the *Rêveries* of the Maréchal de Saxe and the *Instruction du roi de Prusse à ses généraux* of Frederick the Great. Many modern treatises on the advantages of lines and columns are analysed. It is a reminder, like Ligne's own life, of the connections between writing and fighting.[33]

Ligne also continued his work as an Austrian historian, intent on giving the Empire and Austria their rightful place in European historiography. In 1773 he published in Liège (under the false place name of Paris) the memoirs of a seventeenth-century general who had served in the Austrian army, the Comte de Bussy-Rabutin, from a manuscript in his uncle's library.[34] Another military work, *Préjugés Militaires par un offici-er autrichien*, dedicated 'to my master' Marshal Lacy, was published in 1781 in two volumes (the second being titled *Fantaisies Militaires*) in Paris (although allegedly, since it had been refused official permission by the French censors, at Kralovelhota, the name of a Bohemian village), again at Ligne's expense. The work on it had begun as early as 1773. In ten years only 249 of 300 printed copies were sold .[35]

However, it remains the best account of life in the army of Maria Theresa. With the help of thirty-seven excellent engravings by the publisher Pierre Philippe Choffard, and diagrams, it describes every aspect of warfare, from baggage to bodyguards, from horses' fodder to officers' manners. There is praise for the 'Pre-eminence of Our Army', which he thought the best, and the best-clothed in Europe;[36] an attack on the effect of marriage on soldiers; and a description of the controversy between the merits of the 'oblique line' or the 'direct line' on the battlefield about which, because military affairs were then fashionable, ordinary civilians would converse for hours. Ligne's philosophy of battle expressed his attitude to life: 'One should despair of nothing, dare everything, push down one's hat. The battle is won.'[37]

The only masterpiece he wrote in this period, however, dealt neither with armies, courts nor the theatre, but with gardens. Like his father, he shared the *jardinomanie* of the eighteenth century – almost as strong as its cult of war. Its fervour was in part due to the desire to escape, in gardens, from the rules of behaviour and pressures of rank – and servants – reigning inside palace and chateau walls. Gardens were thought to be a means to happiness and an escape from formality. From the second quarter of the eighteenth century those gardens known as *jardins anglo-chinois*, since their exoticism, informality and lack of symmetry were inspired by England and China, were more fashionable than the traditional *jardins français* of rigid lines and well-ordered flower beds. *Jardins anglo-chinois* shared a 'common currency' of ruins, temples, pagodas and philosophers' huts. Secluded grottoes were places to make love; temples to Wisdom and hermits' cottages had a message for Freemasons.[38]

In 1767 Ligne travelled to England in search of landscape gardens, and a loan. He stayed there from 20 July to 6 August.[39] For Voltaire, who had lived and published there in 1726–9, England was a model of freedom. In Ligne's eyes, however, it did not live up to its reputation. The clergy was almost as ignorant, proud and corrupt as in Flanders. Politics were dominated by corruption and deceit; without the English Channel, the English constitution would not last a month. Characteristically putting emotions before institutions, he wrote to Voltaire that, although they had the pleasure of abusing their King and cutting off his head when they felt like it, the English were subject to the same passions as other peoples. Frustrated, illogical, they were like hares, 'mad when young and then desperately sad'.[40]

However, he had loved English gardens such as Blenheim, Wilton and Windsor (although he considered Horace Walpole's house at Strawberry Hill outside London a bad dream). In his garden book *Coup d'oeil sur Beloeil et la plus grande partie des jardins de l'Europe*, he later wrote:

What more superb than Windsor? What a forest! what majesty! such were the oaks that uttered oracles in Dodona's forest of old [home of a classical sooth-sayer]. I was tempted to consult those of Windsor in like fashion, for they inspired that awe that used to overcome true believers as they aproached the Deity ... We have a great obligation to the English; even their faults are virtues. I defy anyone to work really well with Nature who has not been in England if only to learn neatness. Go into the finest palace precincts of France or into the residences of the Holy Roman Empire; I think more highly of the suburban pleasure garden of a London cobbler, where the furniture is polished like a snuff box, the turf like a billiard table and the shrubs combed like the hair of a pretty woman.[41]

Coup d'oeil sur Beloeil et sur la plus grande partie des jardins de l'Europe is one of the finest, certainly the most European, literary monuments of eighteenth-century garden culture. An early version was being passed around the salons of Vienna in 1770, and it was the first work to be printed, in 1781, on the private printing press Ligne set up that year in this *hôtel* in Brussels, with his son Charles, who sometimes did the printing work himself. One motive was to avoid a repetition of the difficulties experienced in publishing *Préjugés Militaires* in Paris.*[42]

Writing in his favourite form – fragments separated by straight black lines – Ligne shows enthusiasm and originality. He regarded gardens as one of the secrets of happiness, and self-knowledge: 'Fathers of families, inspire gardenmania in your children! They will only be the better for it ... the love of poetry suits the love of gardening admirably. And these two loves – with a few others – will always take pride of place in my heart ... Love of the countryside increases with age, inspires, fulfils, consoles, and makes life worth living.'[43] Gardening is 'a branch to be seized by someone about to drown in the ocean of the great world'. The secret of life is 'to plant with flowers the little distance that separates, as I have shown in my garden of allegory, the cradle of infancy from the sanctuary of death'.[44]

'Labourers' were not excluded. Addressing fellow-landowners, he wrote: 'Have your agents concern themselves with the health of your workmen, restraining too much zeal in the heat of the

---

* The press probably ceased functioning two years later, in 1783.

day. Compel the labourers to rest in the shade of trees and give them milk and bread.' Women should garden; 'the sex increases daily in strength and is excellent for gardening'. In conclusion: 'A wise government should protect the art of gardens and those who cultivate them.'[45]

At the height of the fashion for English gardens, he wrote that they had become as boring and predictable as formal French gardens, and expressed admiration for the grandeur and straight lines of the latter. Gardeners should be more imaginative. They should disobey the orders of Vitruvius and create their own, building Peruvian huts or Lapp cottages rather than endless parodies of classical temples: 'We must make modern gardens still more modern, by imitating nobody.' 'Ruin yourself to make ruins,' he wrote, and he proposed that the French navy should go to the 'Levant to snatch from the infidel the remains of divine temples to rebuild them on his [the King's] lawns as they used to be (Greece, Persepolis and Palmyra would be astounded at finding themselves together)'.[46]

Ligne, who attacked preconceived ideas and categories all his life, also professed: 'I like gardens to look like forests, and forests like gardens': they should neither be too natural nor too obviously planted.[47] 'I recommend attention in marrying perfumes just as I have in marrying the colours of a flower bed. Why not create a bouquet in a bosquet?'[48]

The final edition of *Coup d'oeil sur Beloeil*, published in 1795, is a guide to the Europe of gardens, as well as a collection of principles and instructions: it described over fifty gardens that Ligne had visited, from Bahceseray in the Crimea, to Tsarskoe Seloe, Potsdam, Laxenburg, Esterhaza. He particularly praised Wörlitz, the park of the Prince of Anhalt Dessau south-west of Berlin; Marshal Lacy's garden at Neuwaldegg in the hills outside Vienna, laid out like an order of battle, with a temple, Chinese pavilion and waterfall; and the garden at Hohenheim outside Stuttgart, where the Duke of Württemburg had reproduced more than sixty Roman ruins, such as the Golden House of Nero, and Diocletian's Baths, separated by trees, hedges and rivers.[49]

His favourite garden, however, was his own, at Beloeil:

Everywhere there are ornamental lakes; one is surrounded by
a marble balustrade, another by slender bars of iron ... I have
left tall arbors of elms as frames with which to enclose secluded
gardens, Italian or magic bowers ... there are wooded rooms, a
charming cloister around a pool, round flower beds, and a little
forest of roses ... On all sides flow the loveliest streams in the
world, pure, limpid, sparkling, each connecting with the
others. All my paths are green and lead into the forest
beyond ... My sheep are my gardeners; they make my lawn or
rather my green velvet carpet.

He admitted, however, that most visitors preferred to admire
the French garden of his father rather than to dream in his own
English garden. 'The glory of Beloeil is due to my father; he
won thereby as much honour as if he had written an epic poem.
Credit for all that is grand, dignified, noble, majestic belongs to
him.'[50]

Paris

Restless and frivolous, Ligne was always in search of new pleasures and challenges. Despite the praise he lavished on Beloeil in his books, he did not let it become a prison. Indeed one of its attractions was that it was so easy to get away. As he wrote: 'What a fortunate situation! ... Within twenty hours I could be in Paris, London, The Hague or Spa.'*[1]

After his father's death, on 7 April 1766, Ligne had a further reason to travel. He was furious that he had received neither the promotion in the Austrian army, nor the governorship, nor the highest order of the Austrian monarchy, the Golden Fleece (founded by a Duke of Burgundy in 1430), which, like many *grands seigneurs*, he considered his by right. Maria Theresa deliberately kept him waiting.[2] His anger with the court of Vienna was heightened by a feeling that it was positively ill-intentioned for him. He sold his father's house at Klosterneuburg outside Vienna at a bad price, and in a letter to the Empress's secretary Neny issued the noble's ultimate threat: to change courts. 'Born in a country where there are no slaves, I can take my small merit and my fortune elsewhere.' Thwarted ambition led Ligne to turn to France. Soon he was 'mad about Paris and disgusted with Vienna'.[3]

In his first years as master of Beloeil, after 1766, Ligne visited Paris for several months every year. Since he did not want, in Vienna, to have the air of being established in Paris, he did not acquire a house of his own, and usually stayed in the Hôtel du

* The road between Paris and the Austrian Netherlands was exceptionally good. It took five to six days by coach to go from Paris to Lyons: René Pomeau, *L'Europe des Lumières. Cosmopolitism et unité européene au XVIIIe siècle*, 1991 edn., p. 13.

Parlement d'Angleterre or the Hôtel de Rome, Rue Jacob, near Saint Germain des Près on the left bank.[4]

For Ligne the tension between France and Austria was also a tension between pleasure and duty. As an officer in the Austrian army, in theory each time he went to France he had to obtain permission from Vienna. This was particularly true after he was appointed colonel of infantry regiment number 30 in the Austrian army, in 1771, and began to spend part of his time with it at Mons, the capital of Hainaut, where he had a town house, and Ghent, capital of Flanders, where he kept an apartment in the Hôtel des Armes d'Angleterre: they are respectively no more than fifteen and fifty-five kilometres from Beloeil. Although the lieutenant colonel was the actual commander, the colonel of a regiment was expected to look after its well-being, choose its officers and, if zealous, train it in person. However, Ligne often used the influence of Marshal Lacy to secure permission to leave Austria. Lacy complained that Ligne did not spend enough time with his regiment and preferred escorting the duchesses of the court and the (Opéra) corridors in Paris to attending army manoeuvres in Hungary or Transylvania.[5]

Since Ligne was an Austrian subject, Paris was a foreign city, but the word 'foreign' had no meaning for him. Born into a European family, confident of his status and identity, exceptionally open-minded, he felt at home throughout Europe (except in England), and acquired new nationalities as easily as new friends. Like other cosmopolitans, he made a philosophy out of his multiple identities. Mazarin had written: 'Al galantuomo ogni paese e patria.' Byron considered himself 'a citizen of the world, content where I am now – but able to find a country elsewhere'.[6] Ligne wrote in his memoirs: 'I was happy to be German in France, almost French in Austria, and Walloon in the army. You lose respect in the country where you always live ... I like my condition of being everywhere a foreigner; French in Austria, Austrian in France, both in Russia, it is the way of enjoying yourself everywhere and so being dependent nowhere.'[7]

His appetite for life and travel was so great that he could lead different lives at the same time in France, Austria and the Austrian Netherlands. The sharpness of vision, the expansion of experience, the freedom from rules and constraints resulting from being *abroad* suited his character. If he had stayed in one place, he would have bored himself and exhausted his friends and relations. To facilitate his travels, Ligne maintained a separate *maison ambulante*, in addition to the princely household in Beloeil and Brussels.[8] He later estimated that he had spent three or four years in a carriage (one of his specially fabricated travelling carriages would later be borrowed by the Emperor Joseph II himself), had travelled to Vienna at least forty times, and from Brussels to Paris over 200 times.[9]

Ligne soon became popular in Paris: he found it easy to obtain the formal introductions that oiled the machinery of social life in Paris, in contrast to smaller cities such as Vienna and Warsaw, where people started talking to each other without them.[10] Moreover, in the eighteenth century it was common for educated travellers like Ligne, Boswell, or Zinzendorf to travel round Europe, from city to city, in the same world of *la bonne société*.[11] In addition to his wealth and rank as a Prince of the Holy Roman Empire, another reason for Ligne's success was his physical charm. Tall, with an open, commanding face and excellent health, he was cheerful and vivacious, with an endless appetite for new people, and adventures. Goethe would call him 'the most cheerful man of the century' even when he was seventy-five.

Ligne's manners were another element in his charm. When Lord and Lady Spencer were visiting Ghent in 1772, Ligne sent musicians dressed in Turkish costume to entertain them. Their daughter Harriet, aged twelve, wrote: 'He is a very pleasant man, and when we were caught in a shower of rain sent for his coach, which is almost all glass, and painted over at bottom with large figures. He would never get in but ran along in the rain by the side of the coach.' Such almost unfailing politeness came from the heart. He liked people, and claimed that he once sold a desert scene by Salvatore Rosa because 'a picture without people is like the end of the world'.[12]

Ligne's variety of interests increased his charm. As his books show, he was a free spirit, with enough energy of mind to be interested in gardens and warfare, politics and pederasty, princes and peasants. He even wrote on painting and hunting, though for fear of gaining the reputation of trying to be a universal man he left these works to be published after his death.[13] He was not afraid to push life to the limits, to try any career or pleasure, to visit every country he could, to say anything that came into his head, to 'attack' sovereigns in conversation. His energy and confidence were such that, as Zinzendorf had written, if Ligne was in a room, you had to sew up his lips to have a chance to speak.[14] He was even prepared – unlike most eighteenth-century wits – to risk ridicule. The man who could write, at the beginning of *Préjugés militaires*, 'I believe everything: I believe in everything: above all in what is forbidden to me,' was clearly unlike other princes.[15]

One French friend, the Comte d'Escars, wrote that 'the flashes of his wit and the originality of his manners' were the key to his popularity in France. The Baronne d'Oberkirch called him 'indeed a magician of words and looks. He played on people's minds as he liked.'[16] A few of his remarks have remained famous. When Count Hoyos approached him yawning, Ligne said, 'My dear count, you forestall me.' A prince of the Holy Roman Empire asked whom Ligne recommended to paint his portrait in Paris. Ligne replied, 'Try Oudry' – the painter of animals. The bankruptcy of Ligne's friend the Prince de Rohan-Guémenée was known, from his exalted rank and colossal debts, as the Most Serene Bankruptcy. Ligne wrote to invite him to Beloeil: 'Since, like your wife, I have acquired a taste for English gardens, I cannot erect a finer ruin in mine than my dear friend Guémenée.' Such remarks flashed around Paris; Ligne won a reputation for being unable to resist an opportunity to make a joke.[17]

Ligne was considered so amusing that, when Frederick the

Great attended Austrian manoeuvres in Moravia in 1770, the Emperor Joseph II insisted that Ligne supped every day at his table. He soothed both monarchs with graceful compliments and, when asked what he would like in life, replied: 'I would like to be a pretty woman until thirty, then a very fortunate and very clever general until sixty ... and a cardinal until eighty.'[18]

Wit, charm and originality had their price. Among stuffier friends such as Zinzendorf, Ligne acquired a reputation for lack of common sense, as well as the nickname *Charlot*.[19] In one of his letters urging Ligne to spend more time with his regiment, Marshal Lacy wrote in 1770 complaining of 'yet another of the old light-headed tricks of our mad friend Charlot, with whom I beg the Prince de Ligne kindly to pick a quarrel, on his own behalf as well as mine, making him understand at the same time that it is only on condition that he rapidly reforms himself that I can obtain for him a good reception both at court and in town and in the champ de Mars and from Mars himself'.[20]

At this stage, however, 'Charlot' dominated the Prince de Ligne. It was an age that deified sexual pleasure. Prints and pictures suggest that it was perfectly natural to find people courting, or making love, both in and out of doors. A travel writer called Risbech describes the Prater outside Vienna as a park 'where nature itself invites men to enjoy a free intercourse'; the thickets were filled with disappearing couples. Indeed Ligne himself once made love there as thirty deer jumped overhead, later writing: 'It was enough to stop the most hardened sinner.' Brussels was a more conventional city. Yet Zinzendorf noted that in its salons 'women's conversations between themselves are very lubricious. They know all the dimensions.' They talked about the small testicles of Prince Charles Liechtenstein, the King of Denmark's visits to brothels or Count Cobenzl's regularly gratified passion for his own daughter.[21]

Paris, which one foreigner called 'the island of lunatics', was even wilder.[22] An exchange between the wit and officer the Chevalier de Boufflers and his mother gives an idea of conversation among Ligne's Paris friends. The Marquise de Boufflers, known as the Lady of Pleasure, was complaining that she could never bring herself to love God. Her son told his mother not to be so certain; if He became Man again, she would love Him like all the others.[23]

For many, physical pleasure was a career. In one of Ligne's short stories 'Histoire trop véritable ou Conte qui n'en est pas un', which begins in a brothel and ends in a bout of venereal disease, the hero says, after 'attacking' many different women, 'The pleasure of the act had passed; but the honour of it remained to me. I had shown my comrades who I was, what I was worth, what I was capable of doing.' Ligne shared his hero's belief in the 'honour' of sexual conquest.[24]

His wife and family were no restraint on his behaviour. The Princesse de Ligne continued to live in Beloeil, where she helped bring up their children. To Christine and Charles were added Louis, born in 1766, Euphémie Christine, in 1773, Flore in 1775. Ligne described his wife with transparent lack of enthusiasm. 'My wife is an excellent woman, full of delicacy, sensitivity and nobility ... She has no drawbacks, for she has a very good heart. She is sometimes a bit contrary and after having taken an attitude which perhaps gives her pleasure for a short moment, she gives her children what they ask her and is even obliging to me.'[25]

Her contemporaries agreed that the Princesse de Ligne lacked both charm and beauty. Zinzendorf wrote: 'She is not an amiable woman although she behaves rather well towards her husband.' On another occasion, he remarked that the Princesse de Ligne 'was less disagreeable than usual'. It is probable that she found ways to console herself for the void in her marriage. In 1770 Zinzendorf recorded that she seemed very cheerful after a lunch tête à tête with a Comte d'Ursel; and she had her own small chateau and 'hermitage' near Brussels.[26] The seriousness of her affairs is not known. A Russian chamberlain and writer called Count Fedor Golovkine, who knew Ligne forty years later, claimed that only Ligne's eldest child Christine was his own; but Golovkine was notoriously malicious.[27]

Ligne's desire to avoid ridicule for his wife's infidelities, however, is clear from the following lines in a letter he wrote to the Austrian Chancellor Prince Kaunitz: 'My wife, my Prince, charges me with presenting you her best wishes. She has great difficulty in consoling herself for the loss of M. de Flemming [a Saxon diplomat, one of her lovers]. I would have advised her M. de Burmania. But he too has died. She will return to Vienna only when she will be able again to make such a good choice as the gentle minister of Saxony.'[28]

The same year, on his way to Paris, according to his travelling companion Zinzendorf, Ligne tried to seduce a maid in an inn at four in the morning. When he arrived, he hunted by day and gambled or made love by night. After two or three hours' sleep, he repaired the devastation of champagne with a hot bath and lemonade.[29] Among the women he 'had', by his own account, were Mme de Maghes, who knew nobody, and Mme de Bussy, 'beautiful without being amiable'; he would leave her at midnight to go to the house of another Mme de Bussy, who could not be 'had' but where conversation was so amusing that people stayed, chatting by the fireside, until six in the morning.[30] Other mistresses probably included the Duchesse d'Ursel (called Flore, in whose honour he created the Ile de Flore and erected the Temple de Flore, in the park at Beloeil), Mmes de Konigsegg, de Rohault, de Schönfeld and others; he later described aspects of their affairs in his *Contes Immoraux*.[31]

Like his friend the Neapolitan ambassador Caracciolo who, when asked by the King whether he made love often in Paris, replied, 'No, Sire, I buy it ready made,' Ligne also frequented the parallel world of brothels. Whereas Vienna had a chastity commission and prostitutes leagued with the police to trap young men *in flagrante delicto*, in Paris sex was, already, a well-regulated industry. In bureaucratic prose, the police recorded the names and preferences of prostitutes and their clients. Procurers (and sometimes parents) guarded a girl's virginity for financial rather than moral reasons, in order to sell it to the highest bidder; some procurers ran a subscription service, guaranteeing clients a certain number of new girls every month.[32]

The leading procurer in Paris was the Comte du Barry, who bought girls like pictures and supplied Ligne with Mlle Dorothée of the Opéra, among others. Despite complaining that the pleasure was as low as the price, Ligne continued to use prostitutes.[33] He had affairs with Mlle Julie of the Comédie Italienne; Mlle Bigottini, whose first communion he arranged to prevent her dying excommunicated; and Mlle Raucourt, a bisexual actress of the Comédie Française, who took refuge with him in 1776 from the scandal of her love affair with the beautiful Mme Souck.[34] He was also a friend of the witty, amorous Sophie Arnould, a famous actress who said that, to encourage attendance at the Opéra, ballets should be long, and skirts short. In her salon Ligne met dazzling young debauchees such as Comtes Alexandre de Tilly, de Ségur and Louis de Narbonne, and the Abbé de Périgord.[35]

His principal companion in the pursuit of pleasure was a rich and powerful prince of the blood his own age, the Duc de Chartres, a member of the House of Orléans, a younger branch of the royal family that held court in the Palais-Royal in Paris, while the King lived at Versailles. Chartres's parents, the Duc and Duchesse d'Orléans, had made love so openly in front of other people that her mother had said that they made marriage itself look indecent. They soon turned elsewhere. When asked the name of Chartres's father, his mother had said: 'When you fall into a bed of thistles, how do you know which one has pricked you?' Despite a subsequent rift, Ligne remembered Chartres as a kind, distinguished man who once risked his own life to save one of his servants. They often gambled together until three or four in the morning in the salons of the Palais Royal, and Chartres visited Ligne at Beloeil in 1773.[36]

Chartres was also Grand Master of the French branch of the Order of Freemasons. For some masons, such as Mozart and Casanova, freemasonry was a new, international world of reason, brotherhood and enlightenment, breaking down the barriers between individuals imposed by the Church and the social hierarchy. The lodges were open to nobles and non-nobles, men and women, Christians and deists.[37] Ligne too was attracted to freemasonry. After he had become a member of the Loge La Vraie et Parfaite Harmonie in Mons in 1770, he also became a member of lodges in Ghent, Versailles and Brussels, and attended lodge meetings in Paris with Chartres and Mme de Genlis. However, he later claimed he found the rituals ridiculous, and remembered that there was nothing more comic than to hear Mme de Genlis, who had been the Duchesse de Chartres's best friend before becoming the Duke's mistress, boast that she had given six strawberries to a sick old woman, in order to receive a certificate of virtue.[38]

Ligne once attended an orgy at Mousseau, belonging to Chartres, one of the *pavillons* outside Paris often built for purposes of seduction rather than accommodation. Friends had been teasing him about lack of 'vigour', so he offered to submit to an examination. Despite all their mockery, Ligne was, by his own account in his memoirs, 'firm, unshakeable' on top of a girl supplied by Chartres. He drank punch from a glass-cooler held by the Marquis de Conflans as he finished 'my abomination, to the great admiration of all the spectators and their redoubled applause' – an act of daring rather than desire, he explained in his memoirs. Ligne enjoyed what was called 'bad company', and believed that girls and gambling kept men alert and made them fight like devils.[39] Nevertheless he also wrote: 'In reality very often one amuses oneself much better in normal society than at those suppers of debauch where there is so often so little expenditure of imagination that it is not worth not daring to say where you are going.'[40]

Despite innumerable affairs, Ligne rarely caught venereal disease. In 1777, with Chartres, he watched Doctor Guibert de Preval test a prophylactic against venereal disease, by making love to the most hideous and unhealthy prostitute whom Ligne's footman could find in the rue Saint Honoré. The experiment was successful but the doctor was expelled from the Paris medical faculty, which did not want to lose the customers who came to be cured of venereal disease.[41]

Ligne's passion for sexual conquests did not stop him enjoying the society of old ladies, whom he described as 'impressive ruins like Rome, amiable like Athens and gallant as Versailles under Louis XIV'. The Maréchale de Luxembourg, who after an outrageous youth had become the tyrant of the *ton*, allowing neither familiar expressions nor a single *tutoyement*, and the Maréchale de Mirepoix, so charming that you would have sworn that all her life she had thought of no one but you, were among his early conquests.[42] Ligne also became a friend of another prince of the blood, the Prince de Conti, who, having fallen from favour with his cousin Louis XV, had become a leader of the opposition to the King's policies in the Paris *parlement*, the principal law court of France. He had even planned a Protestant uprising during the Seven Years' War, coordinated with an English expedition. He liked pleasure as well as power and took a ring from everyone to whom he made love. When he died, his executors found 4000 – each labelled with a different name.[43] His principal mistress was another Mme de Boufflers, a friend of Rousseau and Hume. Ligne remembered that she had once been criticised for condemning a woman 'who had a Prince of the Blood'. She had replied: 'I want to restore to virtue by my words what I take from it by my actions.'[44]

Conti enjoyed both the informality of the age and the traditional royal world. Ligne described him as 'affable, ambitious, and philosophical in turn, rebellious, greedy, lazy, noble, filthy, the idol and the example of high society ... the most handsome and majestic of men ... fit for everything and capable of nothing'. Ligne frequently visited Conti at his chateau of L'Isle Adam north-west of Paris and in the Hôtel du Temple in the city. As can be seen in the 1766 picture of Mozart playing at a *thé à l'anglaise* in Conti's salon in the Temple, one of the most famous representations of the *douceur de vivre* of the eighteenth century, Conti entertained on a princely scale. In a gesture of gastronomic patriotism, Ligne once sent Conti a beautiful twenty-five-year-old maid whose face, throat and colouring were worthy of Rubens, buried under mounds of the finest food from Flanders: pigs' heads from Alost, Hainaut cheese, Campine capons, *tripettes*, rabbits from Estambruges, Ostend oysters and Antwerp shrimps. The Prince was delighted for a minute and then forgot about her.[45]

Ligne never yielded to the forces of social compulsion, by which so many people remain in a constricted circle of acquaintances with similar backgrounds, interests or incomes. He liked mixing classes as well as nationalities and in Paris frequented literary salons where writers and nobles had begun to meet on terms of equality. In contrast to Vienna, or the society of his father's generation, in Paris barriers within the elite of power and pleasure were being lowered. An informal group of friends, rather than a formal circle based on rank, was becoming the goal of social life. Conversation and correspondence were regarded as necessities rather than pleasures, and as a means to win a literary reputation.

For an ambitious woman, a salon filled with interesting or celebrated guests whose conversation she could direct and animate could be a substitute for a career or a family. Ligne appreciated the common sense of Madame Geoffrin, a servant's daughter whose well-run salon was one of the literary institutions of eighteenth-century Europe. Her chief rival was the blind, ferocious Mme du Deffand, who called her 'the lard omelette' or, after her visit to her beloved 'son' King Stanislas Augustus of Poland, *la Geoffrinska*.[46]

With Parisian condescension, Mme du Deffand wrote to her friend Horace Walpole that Ligne was 'someone I know, I see him sometimes; he is kind, polite, *bon enfant*, a little mad': she thought him less witty than his friend the Chevalier de Boufflers.[47] Ligne liked her disabused epigrams, such as: 'I do not have one relation whose acquaintance I would have liked to make.' She also said that supper was one of the four purposes of existence, and that she had forgotten the other three. In her effort to banish boredom she often made him talk alone with her until six in the morning.[48] In such salons Ligne met some of the most celebrated writers in Europe, whose works he read as soon as they appeared: Diderot, Beaumarchais and Marmontel.

However, with the exceptions of Rousseau and Voltaire, Ligne disliked most modern French writers of the Enlightenment. Judging them through the eyes of a man of the world, he found that they were too vain and avid for compliments to be truly 'amiable'. Beaumarchais confirmed his view. The author of *The Barber of Seville* (1775), and *The Marriage of Figaro* (1783), whose radicalism and gaiety reflect the spirit of the age, darted ceaselessly between different worlds: he was a music-teacher to Louis XV's daughters, playwright, pamphleteer, secret agent and blackmailer. In 1773, at the request of the Prince de Conti, Ligne collected Beaumarchais at the corner of the rue Colbert and arranged for him to travel in one of his carriages across the frontier to Ghent; Beaumarchais pretended that he was in danger of arrest but eight days later he was in Louis XV's study, discussing the King's secret foreign policy. Ligne also saw him in Vienna, claiming to have survived a murder attempt, and could not believe that the French government employed such a fraud.[49]

Ligne's passion for Paris did not stop him spending time on his estates. Indeed he designed an English garden at Beloeil, which was completed by the end of 1775. Although it continued to expand until 1791, it was simple compared to his friends' parks in France and Austria. In his own he erected a semi-gothic wall and pillars, and a Temple of Morpheus, whose internal decoration resembles a Turkish tent. Built for exhausted voluptuaries, it contained 'enormous round divans where scores of weary beings may lose the last remnants of their vigor in innocent [!] games or find new strength'. He also created the Island of Flora, now a peninsula, connected to the chateau by a trellis bridge, where Ligne loved to read, half dressed and far from unwelcome visitors.[50]

However, Ligne never had the money to realise his wildest plans: for a dairy in the shape of a mosque (the minarets would serve as pigeon lofts); a Chinese bridge; an Indian temple; a

Tartar village; a Mausoleum of Adonis; a statue of Voltaire, a column inscribed with the names of heroes like Lacy and Frederick, or a 'Tableau of Human Life' going from the 'cradle of infancy', through the 'cabinet of philosophy', past the Temples of Truth and Illusion, to the 'sanctuary of death'. They remained nothing but dreams on the pages of his book.[51]

While he was trying to beautify his domain, his staff was lamenting his extravagance. The Abbé Tiroux wrote to Vandenbroucke in horror after a tour of Baudour and Beloeil by the Prince: 'Wherever he went, he thought of something new, improvements here, new decorations there: large plantations whose creation is morally impossible.' When told, in the most respectful tones, that his schemes would be extremely expensive and cause murmurs by 'the people' and 'the total ruin of the village', he replied, with princely insouciance: 'My dear Abbé, all the work had to be done, it is of the greatest utility.' Sometimes he lost his temper, telling one employee who criticised his beloved intendant Vandenbroucke: 'I am fed up with your Beloeil and your Beloeil people, for whom I will have no regard ... and I will not set foot there again.'[52]

The last word on his gardenmania belongs to his despised and neglected wife. The Princesse de Ligne was more perceptive and realistic than the reputation Ligne and their children later created for her. Her Cassandra-like letters to Vandenbroucke provide a realistic counterpoint to the version of events presented in Ligne's memoirs and letters. She never ceased to lament her husband's follies. She wrote to Vandenbroucke on 15 November 1781:

I do not approve, my dear Vandenbroucke, that you should encourage the Prince in his plans for English gardens, Chinese columns, indeed all the follies he wants to commit at Beloeil, where he has been plainly shown that even if he spent a fortune, he would never make it appear natural to see mountains and a river in places where it is physically impossible that they should be. Besides we know from experience that he will only make *capucinades* of which no one approves, which annoys him immensely and would torment him, if it was in his character to be irritated by anything. But if it does not do that to him, it does at least make him sour and bad-tempered.

Please burn my letter ...[53]

When his wife and young family were in residence at Beloeil, Ligne preferred to stay a few miles away, especially in the years 1773-6, at Baudour. It was the stable wing of an old chateau, seventeen windows wide. With many cries to Vandenbroucke of 'quick, quick, I beg you, to work', and the help of a competent and inexpensive architect from Ghent called De Staercke, Ligne transformed it into a house with two large rooms and six apartments. Nevertheless, Baudour remained old and dilapidated. Its Louis XIV furniture and walls lined with the saddlecloths used on Ligne's father's horses amazed Duke Albert of Saxe-Teschen in 1781. No trace of Baudour survives today, since it was pulled down in the 1970s to make way for a football stadium.[54]

The inhabitants of Baudour composed an informal house party. Ligne did not invite his wife, or even like her going to Baudour in his absence. More welcome were Mers, his valet, 'a strange fellow who reads everything, is told everything' and Ligne's favourite secretary, Sauveur Legros.[55] Always ready with a story, or a poem, in *Les Deux Châteaux* Legros wrote that, while Beloeil was the seat of grandeur and etiquette, Baudour was a paradise of pleasure, laughter and friends.[56] In his private notebook he claimed: 'Friendship is like the sunrise. Everybody talks about it and almost nobody enjoys it.' Nevertheless, Legros often implored the Prince to forget thrones and grandeur and return to reign over their hearts at Baudour:

> un ange aimable embellit ce séjour;
> le meilleur maître y tient sa cour.
> Ergo! le paradis s'y trouve.

Ligne, who called him *tu*, thought that he was a good poet and an admirable friend, witty, profound and gay.[57]

Other friends constantly staying at Baudour were old General d'Argout, who had fought against the Turks and the French; the Marquis Desandroins, founder of the first coal-mine company in France; Lord Mulgrave, who had tried, in the Arctic Ocean, to find a route to India; Grétry, master of the comic opera, one of the most popular composers of the day; and a chorus of neighbours, actors, and *abbés*. In the communal *Journal de Baudour ou l'esprit de la campagne à l'usage de ceux qui s'y plaisent par différents auteurs qui ne s'y ennuyent pas* of 1775–6, they wrote or inspired verses sparkling with *joie de vivre*, and love of Ligne.[58] The librarian was an amiable elderly priest, recruited by Ligne in Paris, called the Abbé Pagès, who enjoyed cooking waffles in the library, as well as cataloguing its books. In one poem to 'our beloved prince', he wrote:

> What gold is among metals
> Ligne is among his peers.
> The gods are his only rivals
> and his charity equals his birth.[59]

The resident goddess was a professional actress (therefore social and legal inferior), Angélique d'Hannetaire. Born in Toulouse in 1749, she was daughter of the director of the Grand Théâtre in Brussels and, since an early age, had been much admired in roles of *amoureuse*, on and off the stage. She had previously been a mistress of the Marquis Desandroins, by whom she had three children, while Ligne had had a seven-year-long affair with her sister Eugénie, who had given birth to a stillborn child.[60] In his light, simple style, Ligne wrote:

> Charming goddess of Baudour,
> You permit us everything.
> Nothing equals your power
> Except our hearts and our intoxication.

In another poem to Angélique d'Hannetaire:

> Tout à l'amour
> Dans une paisible retraite,
> Notre félicité parfaite
> Est à Baudour.

Ligne ordered from 'my dear little Belanger' (the great neoclassical architect François-Jean Belanger), at great cost, what he called 'our little pagan follies' for the park at Baudour: a labyrinth; a cave spouting water; a hermitage on an island in the middle of a wood; a circular temple, a kiosk, and a fountain beside an antique column surmounted by 'a bust which is not', since it portrayed Angélique (who later placed the Prince's bust beside it).[61]

To please Angélique, he wrote the score of a comic opera *Céphalide ou les autres mariages samnites*, with music by Vitzthumb and Cifolelli, which opened at the Grand Théâtre in Brussels on 39 January 1777.[62] No letters between them have been found. However, they were so deeply in love that in 1778, when he was fighting in Bohemia, they wrote to each other every day: if he missed a post, 'there are tears, worries, messages', according to Leygeb, who looked after 'Mlle Angélique' as well as the genealogy and interests of 'our most serene family'. Her position at Baudour was so well established that the young girls of the district sang couplets praising her generosity and influence over the Prince. The fact that she stopped acting around 1780 may be an affirmation of their relationship. Since it was the eighteenth century, it may never have occurred to Angélique to question Ligne about his adventures in Paris. Like the Princesse de Ligne, she contented herself with incessant injunctions to economise, which led Ligne to call her a *jolie mais térrible princesse*.[63]

In old age, in his best book, his memoirs, *Fragments de l'Histoire de ma Vie*, Ligne wrote that, until his family grew up, the years he spent with her at Baudour were the happiest of his life; the day was not long enough for everything they tried to crowd into it. 'Angélique in name, heart and face ... loved me deeply. It is impossible to love more strongly. Unfortunately', he adds with a heartbreaker's selfishness, 'two other women, the only ones, with her, who have really loved me, chose precisely the same time. I loved all three at the same time, absolutely sincerely. But that cost me many reproaches and embarrassments ... I did not deceive them but I deceived myself.' In retrospect he regretted not having spent more time with Angélique by her fireside.[64] The names of her rivals are not known.

One day, when Ligne was sheltering from rain in a hut, he heard the owner say: 'But where can I see our master? When he is at Baudour, I am looking for him at Mons. At Beloeil, when he is at Mons. How can we arrange to see him?'[65] For the Austrian Netherlands was so small that no chateau or town was more than a few hours' carriage drive from another. Ligne was often in Brussels, which, thanks to what he called the 'gay, sincere, agreeable, mischievous, drinking, feasting, hunting' court of Charles of Lorraine, was, like Paris, becoming a city dedicated to pleasure.[66] Ligne sold the old Hôtel de Ligne and bought a new and grander one, formerly the Hôtel d'Epinoy, where he gave suppers every Thursday in winter. Charles of Lorraine frequently came for supper, cards or a play before a midnight sleigh ride. He adored Ligne, who appeared in masquerades at court as Mars, Apollo, or one of the four kings in a pack of cards. Ligne had so many appointments, and adventures on the way to them, that he was frequently late. Charles of Lorraine said: 'He would always come too late for me, even if he was the first to arrive.'[67]

In Paris Ligne was a constant guest. In Flanders he was a prince of hosts. He was capable of giving a splendid party on the Brussels–Antwerp canal, with illuminations, musicians in Turkish costumes, and 10,000 spectators, in honour of his infatuation of the moment, the Princesse de Bouillon, or a masquerade representing the Tower of Babel, in front of 2000 spectators at the Grand Theatre in Brussels. Marshal Lacy told him he was 'the first man in the world for giving parties'.[68] For some foreigners Beloeil became part of the Grand Tour. Among his royal visitors were King Christian VII of Denmark, in 1768 before he went mad; Chartres in 1773; the Comte d'Artois in 1783; and King Gustavus III of Sweden, 'the Charmer King', a genius who was reviving Swedish prestige and literature, in 1784. In 1768 with *le Condé du Nord*, Prince Henry of Prussia, a younger, more human but equally brilliant brother of Frederick the Great, one of the Prussian generals Ligne had fought against in the Seven Years' War, he visited Mons, Beloeil and the battle-fields on his estates. Ligne compared Prince Henry's war memoirs to Caesar's, and thought his justice and humanity could have made him the greatest king in history. Like his brother, Prince Henry loved men and Ligne wrote: 'He kissed me thirty times a day and ended our voyage, dangerous for my honour, my facility and my gratitude, by contenting himself with my portrait in miniature.'[69]

Ligne's hospitality was not restricted to his royal cousins. He and his family invited all soldiers of the two regiments of Ligne Dragons and Ligne Infanterie, who had fought in the Seven Years' War, to dinner in the Hôtel de Ligne and served them themselves.[70] In 1771, when twenty guests were staying in Beloeil, Ligne ordered balls for their servants in the outhouses.[71] During the carnival season, on 17 January 1775, to celebrate the inauguration of the statue of Prince Charles of Lorraine in the middle of the elegant, cream-coloured Place Royale in Brussels, which the Prince had recently built, Ligne gave a party for all Brussels, from the bargees to Charles of Lorraine himself. *La bonne canaille*, as Ligne called them, danced around the Prince's statue and enjoyed a roast ox stuffed with chicken.[72]

He also gave balls for peasants in the park at Beloeil, parts of which were deliberately left in darkness: 'There were eight or ten thousand masks, or people without masks as they wanted, barrels of syrup and lemonade, mountains of apples and oranges and plenty of fornication.' When the curé at Beloeil complained about the dancing, and young girls wandering late at night in the park, Ligne wrote a letter, which could only have come from an eighteenth-century *grand seigneur*. Repeating: 'Judge not that ye be not judged,' he reminded the curé that Christianity was founded on forgiveness and love of your neighbour: 'I want them to dance because your parishioners, worn out by their work, thereby forget the burdens they have had and begin work the next day with more gaiety. His Majesty the Emperor has never had the intention of abolishing pleasure.'[73]

V

Versailles

Despite the pleasures of Paris, Baudour and Beloeil, they could not keep Ligne away from courts. Courts were his natural habitat, and what he called 'the finest court in the world', the court of courts, was at Versailles. Ligne's European background was a factor in his success. The court of France normally disdained to acknowledge the rival honours of the Holy Roman Empire: independent sovereigns such as the Elector of Saxony were expected to give precedence to distant cousins of the King of France such as the Duc de Chartres or the Prince de Conti, and preferred to stay away. However, Spain was ruled by a Bourbon cousin of the King of France, and was regarded as a family monarchy. Spanish honours, therefore, were respected. The title of Grandee of Spain, which Ligne had inherited from his ancestor the Viceroy of Sicily, gave him the *entrées de la chambre*, the right to enter the King's apartment when he was rising or retiring.

While pleasure drew Ligne to Paris, money led him to Versailles. His travels, building, gambling and women cost a fortune. He was charitable and signed any document put before him. As a result, despite repeated promises to reform, he spent his life in a cloud of debt, and schemes to escape it – like many eighteenth-century *grands seigneurs*, for example his friend the Duc de Chartres. In 1771 there was an uproar when eleven Paris tradesmen met in a lawyer's office to demand immediate payment of the money he owed them. His Paris banker Théaulon relied on his valet Mers to keep him informed of the Prince's borrowings.[1] That year alone he had raised 77,533 florins on the security of his estates.[2] Again in 1772, a tailor and a carriage hirer both felt obliged to threaten lawsuits to obtain payment. Ligne commented in the margin of one such letter: 'The letter is not tender! Make sure to spare us this unpleasantness, my dear Vandenbroucke, I beg you. Le prince de Ligne.'[3]

In 1773 his friend the fashionable neoclassical architect and designer Belanger started work on a salon for the Hôtel de Ligne in Brussels, to the horror of the Prince's agent Vandenbroucke, and Théaulon. Belanger soon discovered, as they already knew, that there was no connection between the orders given by the Prince and the amount of money available for their execution. Belanger lost his temper and wrote that Ligne was the only *grand seigneur* with whom he had had such trouble. There was an embarrassing moment when the cart Ligne had summoned to Paris to collect the panels for his salon, on which craftsmen had been working for thirteen months, returned empty because the panels had not been paid for.[4] In May 1774, after Ligne had signed the workers' invoices, and promised to pay 40,000 livres within two years, Belanger was finally able to put the three crates containing the panels on the cart for Beloeil. Ligne and Belanger were friends again.[5]

Ligne's hopes of restoring his fortunes were based on law suits. He wrote innumerable letters to Spain trying to recover the dowry of his grandmother Jeanne d'Aragon, Princesse de Ligne.[6] His Salm cousins were sued in the principal law court of the Holy Roman Empire, the Reichskammergericht in Wetzlar, over his mother's inheritance. The Austrian government was asked to repay 100,000 écus lent by a Ligne to the Emperor Ferdinand over a hundred years earlier. He conducted fruitless law suits – forty-six at the same time in the 1770s – over feudal dues, tithes, and wills. One law suit came over a claim derived from his distant ancestress Louise de Lorraine to an estate at Koeurs in Lorraine. His most ambitious scheme, dating from 1768, was to demand 50,000 livres a year for twelve years from the King of France in return for giving up his claim to estates sold two hundred years earlier by an ancestor to the Abbey of Corbie near Amiens.[7] In old-regime Europe law suits lasting for centuries were commonplace. To win his, Ligne sought help from the French government and the King's mistress.

An example of the power of the Paris underworld over the highest in the land, Jeanne Bécu was a ravishing convent-bred girl with an 'air of sweetness and honesty'. Starting as a shop assistant, she had soon become a protégée of the greatest procurer in Paris, Ligne's friend the Comte du Barry.[8] He had farmed her out to the highest bidders, including a friend of Ligne, the Duc de Richelieu, *premier gentilhomme de la chambre du roi*.

Richelieu was an ageing debauchee with a face like a wrinkled apple, one of the *rabatteurs* (beaters) who helped drive the finest girls in Paris towards the King. Either Richelieu, or another of the King's procurers, Lebel, *premier valet de chambre*, known as the Minister of Pleasure, had drawn her to the attention of Louis XV.[9] To try to make the King's new mistress more presentable, she had been married to a dim brother of du Barry, who had then retired to the country. In an absolute monarchy such as France, the King's personal life could not be isolated from politics. Mme du Barry rapidly became the figurehead of a party favouring absolute monarchy and opposed to the *parlement* of Paris. In 1770 she had helped to hasten the fall of the King's chief minister, the Duc de Choiseul.[10]

Ligne often went to see Mme du Barry in her apartment at Versailles, above the King's. He charmed her so greatly that in 1772 his banker Théaulon wrote to his intendant Vandenbroucke that she 'recommended' his law suits to 'everyone'.[11] Ligne's attitude to Mme Du Barry and Louis XV shows his originality. Because the King had recently abolished the Paris *parlement*, because of the public scandal of his love for a former courtesan, above all because the French elite was disabused with absolute monarchy, it had become fashionable to mock Louis XV. Paris friends of Ligne like Mme Geoffrin and Mme de Boufflers spread stories against the King that reveal their contempt for the truth as well as the monarchy.

Ligne saw in Louis XV and Mme du Barry only an ageing monarch and the woman he loved. Ignoring the different standards (of discretion at least) expected of a King of France and a *grand seigneur*, he sprang to the defence of pleasure: 'It is outrageous that those who did what he did condemned it; and the base courtiers of Mme de Pompadour, a little bourgeoise snatched from her husband, cried out about the corruption of morals for one more mistress, who had a much better heart and did not decide questions of war and peace.'[12]

In April 1774 Louis XV caught smallpox, which rapidly became fatal. With his love of events and historian's instinct, Ligne continued to frequent the salon of Mme du Barry when other courtiers were abandoning it. On 4 May 1774, Ligne whispered to his old friend and neighbour the Duc de Croÿ in the King's apartment, seven days before the King died, that 'the lady' was leaving court and that 'the catastrophe is going to take place'.[13] At the same time he told her brother-in-law the procurer: ' The farce is over; you can leave now.'[14]

Lack of money forced Ligne to leave Versailles on 8 May, two days before the King's death. Nevertheless, he sent a superb account of the last days of Louis XV to Voltaire, whom he now called 'my god':

> Versailles provided the most bizarre magic lantern ever seen here. The *camera obscura* [a reference to the darkened royal bedroom] had not been forgotten. How can the land of graces be that of horrors? It was raining bishops and enemas. People were rushing to the death of the King as to the death of a stag. It was enough to make you die from laughing or crying: there was so much that was ridiculous, or touching or horrible.
>
> Poor Mme du Barry was very moving there. She was almost the only person who was not acting. She is the only Minister who can perhaps flatter herself that she is leaving her post without having done any harm.[15]

As Ligne wrote, the curtain had fallen, and the scenery had changed: the King's grandson ascended the throne as Louis XVI.[16] Ligne enjoyed the new reign even more than the old one. He was particularly fond of the King's youngest brother, the young Comte d'Artois, 'handsome as Apollo and as proud as Mars' and the epitome of elegance. They had first met when Artois visited French garrisons near Beloeil in 1775. Artois's captain of the guard, the Prince d'Hénin, known as 'the pimp of princes', was an old friend of Ligne from the salon of Sophie Arnould, and Ligne wrote, 'we drank, we gambled, we laughed'.[17] Artois invited Ligne to Versailles.

There he was presented to the Queen, Maria Theresa's youngest daughter Marie Antoinette. Twenty years old, she was desperate for amusement and applause; Ligne had watched her arrival in Paris from Vienna in 1770, when hundreds of people were crushed to death on the Place Louis XV. Able to find something comic even in the worst tragedies, he noticed a young man desperately searching among the disfigured corpses for the body of a rich uncle from whom he hoped to inherit, and exclaiming in dismay, 'He is not there!'[18]

Cultivating Marie Antoinette as enthusiastically as he had Mme du Barry, Ligne rapidly became one of the Queen's favourites. His love for Angélique d'Hannetaire was at its height. When he was at Baudour he wrote that people at Versailles were heartless, that it was the seat of falsity and treasons, that the fine court ladies who gave themselves so easily could not compare to the genuine sentiments he found at Baudour.[19] But such protestations did not stop him taking the road to Paris and Versailles time and again (he once estimated that he had made the journey sixty times each way). He loved being able to exchange, in twenty-four hours, the company of Mme Gauthier, a local peasant with a strong Walloon accent, for that of Marie Antoinette, Queen of France. From 1776 he spent five months a year at Versailles rather than Paris.[20]

In August 1776 his banker Théaulon wrote: 'The King has conferred an outstanding favour which had been refused to the hereditary prince of Brunswick and all nobles in foreign service … [Ligne] will be able every time he is here to follow the King on all his journeys' – that is, the frequent royal visits from Versailles to the other royal palaces and pavilions in the Ile de

France. After a dash back to Baudour for a few days, no doubt in order to see Angélique, Ligne joined the court for its autumn journey to Fontainebleau – when it was particularly relaxed and agreeable, hunting by day and watching the latest plays in the evening. In November the Imperial ambassador the Comte de Mercy-Argenteau wrote to Maria Theresa that Ligne was in 'the highest favour with the Queen' and had been given the special uniform worn by favoured courtiers at the royal hunting lodge of Choisy, as well as the blue coat of the royal hunt. ' The Queen treated him with particular kindness and distinction...He supped very often in the private apartments, was in a way on a footing of intimacy with M. le comte d'Artois. His frivolity and fondness for teasing made me fear his rise to favour with the Queen'; but Mercy admitted that there had been no ill consequences. The Queen wrote to her mother that Ligne was 'very amiable and very much liked here'.[21] Ligne felt so much at ease that he installed a small folding seat for himself beside the orchestra in the palace theatre. He joked to the King that it was the only place at his court that he could or desired to have.[22]

An observer of the court of France in its silver age, Ligne recorded obsolete traditions such as the escort of bodyguards provided for the Queen's money chest as it moved from one palace to another, even if there was nothing in it; or the daily delivery of a chicken to her apartment because a Queen of France had once requested one for a pet dog and it had become a servant's perquisite.

Ligne also noted that, in contrast to the Habsburg court in Vienna, Versailles cut off the royal family from its subjects. Whereas the Habsburg court connected the Emperor to every level of society in the Austrian monarchy, Versailles and Paris were, as Joseph II noted, 'two objects entirely separate'.[23] Larger and more luxurious than Schönbrunn, Versailles gave the King an enormous domestic household and a social life restricted to the small class of ancient or well-connected nobility that had been presented at court. It provided no special recognition for the officials and officers who served in the government and armed forces. Many nobles 'killed themselves and their horses' to arrive from Paris on the chance of receiving an invitation to sup in the private apartments with the King, but usually returned uninvited and, as Ligne wrote, 'with chagrin in their heart and dared not show themselves'.[24]

Ligne had no doubts about Marie Antoinette. She was Austrian, frivolous, and susceptible to his charm: in his opinion the Queen of France deserved to be Queen of the world. Indeed, he claimed in his memoirs that he had briefly been a little in love with her, for he remembered crying when he had to leave for two weeks to be with his regiment. His jokes about her brother the Emperor or her sister Maria Carolina, Queen of Naples, sometimes led to a frost, but they were soon reconciled. They were so familiar that one day, when she had run out of her allowance for the month, he begged the valets waiting in her antechamber for 25 louis for her to give to a poor woman.[25]

Marie Antoinette wanted her own group of friends or 'society' as keenly as Mme du Deffand or Mme Geoffrin. Ligne became part of what was known as 'the Queen's society', or just 'the society', whose leading figure was her intimate friend Comte Jules de Polignac. He had supported Mme de Polignac's rise to favour with the Queen in 1776 and considered her lover the Comte de Vaudreuil, formerly his companion in the pleasures of the *petites maisons*, a brilliant courtier who could sing, write and act better than many professionals. Mme de Polignac is often dismissed as an idiot. Yet she was clever enough to remain the Queen's favourite for thirteen years, to win the key position of Gouvernante des Enfants de France and to acquire a duchy for her husband as well as official positions for friends and relations. The Polignac family exploited its positions for every financial benefit, making money even out of the hay supplied for the Queen's horses. Ligne, however, saw Mme de Polignac through the same besotted eyes with which he viewed the Queen. He wrote that there was nobody more virtuous or disinterested than *tous ces Jules* and that she detested the court.[26]

A friend of Voltaire and Ligne called the Chevalier Delisle, whom Ligne considered a master of the epigram and the witty poem, was on the fringes of the Queen's society. If Marie Antoinette had dined in Madame de Polignac's apartment, he would be the first guest to arrive after dinner, before the flood of 'the most illustrious bores of France', in order to make his friends think that he had dined with the Queen of France. Nevertheless Ligne was fond of him, Delisle helped write legal briefs for him over his law suits, and they often travelled together. When Ligne was at Baudour or Beloeil, the letters Delisle addressed him from Versailles reveal the level of conversation in the Queen's society. They discussed the turkey they were eating for dinner, Gruyère cheese, the Spanish Inquisition, Paris actresses, the progress of the War of American Independence, the death of Mme Dillon or the marriage of Mlle de Mérode. Ligne's replies were read by the Queen – he had to be begged not to include too many dirty stories – and made her laugh. Laughter was the secret of his charm.[27]

The Queen's *pavillon* of the Petit Trianon in the park of Versailles, where the servants wore not the blue, silver and red livery of the King but her own red and silver livery, seemed to Ligne like a magic world ruled by a goddess. He wrote that, in the famous English garden she created there, 'one breathes the air of liberty and happiness; the lawn seems finer, the water appears clearer'. An old friend from the Brussels theatre, the actor Dazincourt, whose return to Paris Ligne engineered, taught Marie Antoinette how to act servants' parts in the plays she put on in her theatre at Trianon.[28] It is understandable that Ligne wrote: 'It is a charming life for me at Versailles. *Une vraie vie de château*'.[29]

Artois and the Queen competed for Ligne's company, although Ligne generally preferred riding with the Queen to hunting with her brother-in-law. After Artois had fallen ill while staying at Beloeil, Comtesse Diane de Polignac, the Duchess's ugly, witty sister-in-law, arranged for the Queen's society to perform a parody of a *fête de la convalescence*, to tease Artois. The Duc de Polignac and Comte Valentin Esterhazy, another

Austrian favourite of Marie Antoinette, disguised as Cupids, tied Artois to a chair. Ligne appeared in his customary role as Pleasure (the role he had played at Beloeil in 1749), wearing two wings like a choirboy. The Queen, Mme de Polignac, her daughter the Duchesse de Guiche (known as Guichette), and Mme de Polastron (Artois's mistress), dressed as shepherdesses, sang ridiculous songs in Artois's honour. Ligne remembered: 'I never saw anything in better taste than this fête in bad taste.'[30]

Ligne, however, was sufficiently independent to continue to see the Queen's former enemy Mme du Barry, in the convent east of Paris where she been exiled on Louis XV's death. At a time when the fallen mistress had few friends, he intervened on her behalf, for her return to her neoclassical pavilion at Louveciennes. It is true that he had a personal motive. He wrote in his memoirs that he often stopped at Louveciennes on his way from Paris to Versailles, and claimed that she was 'very beautiful to look at and very good to have'.[31]

Ligne was on such good terms with the Queen and the royal family that they helped his sons' careers. Two of his sons, Adalbert-Xavier and François, had died young. Of Adalbert-Xavier, who died at the age of four in 1771, Ligne wrote: 'The maids did so much to straighten him that they made him a cripple; and the doctors so much for his health that they killed him with experiments.'[32] Ligne wrote an 'Ode à la Mort', while listening to the bells tolling for François's funeral in 1777; but he still had two elder sons to establish, Charles and Louis. Ligne's boast that he never asked the Queen for favours was untrue. He persuaded Marie Antoinette to ask Maria Theresa for permission for his second son, Louis, to settle in France and enter French service (as other Ligne younger sons had done in the past).[33] Although Maria Theresa and her trusted chief minister Kaunitz disliked the idea, they felt unable to prevent it. They agreed after forcing Ligne to reapply through the proper channel, the Governor-General in Brussels. In 1781 Prince Louis de Ligne became a second lieutenant in the Regiment des Dragons de la Reine.[34]

Ligne's favourite child was his charming, studious, eldest son Prince Charles de Ligne, who had been educated in Paris, and then at the Artillery School at Strasbourg, where his father would visit him for an hour or two when dashing between Paris and Vienna. His mother and a French cousin, the Princesse de Ligne *née* Bethisy, arranged for him to marry Princess Hélène Massalska, a fellow-pupil of his sister Christine at the fashionable Paris convent school, the Abbaye aux Bois. Another nation entered the Ligne genealogy. The Massalskis were an ancient Lithuanian family, which had recently risen to prominence as protégés of the Czartoryskis, the most powerful of the noble families that dominated the vast and decaying Kingdom of Poland. The head of the family was the bride's uncle the Bishop of Vilna, an unscrupulous intriguer who had stolen plate and property from the Jesuits when the Order was suppressed in 1768. He was also interested in new economic ideas. As Vandenbroucke later recalled, he intoxicated the Ligne family with the prospect of the millions to be earned by trade between Poland and the Austrian Netherlands. Hélène Massalska's dowry included land, two palaces in Cracow, one in Warsaw and the prospect of the payment of 1,800,000 Polish florins owed her by her mother's family, the Radziwills. As an exceptional sign of favour, the French royal family signed the wedding contract on 25 July 1779.[35] The Lignes were moving towards France: later that year Ligne and his son were given the right to use their cousin's apartment in the Tuileries Palace in Paris, in return for a rent of 3000 livres a year.[36]

The celebrations that summer at Beloeil included fifteen days of maneouvres by the Prince's soldiers, performances by magicians, tightrope walkers, villagers dressed as Watteau shepherdesses, parties in the park at night, regattas on the lake and a performance of the Prince's play *Colette et Lucas*, a one-act comedy about the love of two villagers. The word 'pleasure' is in the first line. Ligne wrote that the bride looked so contented, especially when over a thousand local peasants came to pay her homage, that she made him die of laughter.[37]

The new princess, however, said that none of her fellow-boarders at the convent would embark on marriage if they knew what it meant. Charles de Ligne was in love with a Countess Kinsky of Vienna. His wife preferred Paris to Vienna, and made fun of her husband for being too serious and German. The difference in tastes between Paris and Vienna led to the deterioration of the marriage.

As Ligne spent more time at Versailles, his debts increased – despite repeated claims to Vandenbroucke or Théaulon: 'I am giving no fêtes or sledge parties or masquerades'; 'I am not gambling or spending'; 'I am not gambling. I am practising the strictest economy.' At Fontainebleau, during one autumn visit by the court, one of his servants wrote to the Austrian ambassador the Comte de Mercy-Argenteau, asking for 25 louis as soon as possible because the prince had spent all their money as well as his own.[38]

Below his smiling façade, and airy injunctions to his staff to stop prophesying doom, he could be ruthless – or dishonest – in the pursuit of money to pay for his pleasures. He sold bills of exchange worth 10,000 livres, lent by an adventurous cousin called the Prince of Nassau-Siegen, who had sailed round the world with the great French explorer Bougainville: Nassau-Siegen had to repay them although he had not received any of the money. In 1775 the furniture and some of the farms at Beloeil were impounded because of unpaid debts. In 1776 his Paris tailor obtained an order for his arrest because he had not paid his bills. As he had already been obliged to do in 1774, Ligne left for Brussels in a hurry, after a warning from a lawyer concerned to prevent 'a distressing scandal which would no doubt have mortified a prince of your rank'.[39]

In 1777 Ligne handed control of his financial affairs, including collecting rents and signing receipts, to his wife. Although he found her 'great zeal' excessive, he depended on her more than he cared to admit. By her domination of her husband's household the Princess could console herself for her exclusion from his heart. Despite Ligne's continued extravagance, the threat of penury or bankruptcy receded.[40]

One reason for Ligne's cultivation of Marie Antoinette, as of Mme du Barry, had been the hope that she might use her assumed influence over the ministers to hasten a decision in the Koeurs and Corbie law suits. In his first months of favour in the autumn of 1776, when he was not hunting with Artois or making jokes with the Queen, he was attending legal conferences with the Keeper of the Seals and the Minister of Foreign Affairs, the anti-Austrian Comte de Vergennes. His banker and secretaries were so insistent that he ask for favours that Théaulon wrote: 'The Prince, who is not made for such worries, is very upset.'[41]

However, the Queen's friendship for this Austrian officer gave rise to hostile French gossip. In order to avoid criticism, neither the Austrian ambassador in France, the Comte de Mercy-Argenteau, nor the Austrian governments in Brussels or Vienna, would make an official demand to the French government on Ligne's behalf. At a supper party at the end of the year Louis XVI's anti-Austrian leading minister, the Comte de Maurepas, told the Princesse de Ligne, who was visiting France to check on her children's education, that the case would be evoked before the King's council to prevent Ligne winning it in the *parlement*.[42] For the next fifteen years the two law suits continued to occupy Ligne's secretaries, without nearing resolution.

While Ligne was under attack from creditors, Marie Antoinette was under attack from pornographers. Exploiting her conspicuous femininity and the traditional French hatred of Austria, Beaumarchais among others wrote obscene pamphlets against the Queen, with titles such as 'Fureurs Utérines de Marie-Antoinette', depicting her as a voracious bisexual whose children were bastards. Taking them less seriously than many subsequent historians, she showed them to her friends in fits of laughter. There were so many that Ligne once said to her that he was convinced 'that Your Majesty takes fifty per cent of the profits'. Ligne saw how such libels could start from her inner circle. Madame de Polignac and the Queen were weeping in each other's arms because of an intrigue to drive the former from court, when the Comte d'Artois came into the room. He laughed, said: 'Do not let me disturb you,' and went around telling everybody that he had disturbed two lovers.

Ligne always defended the Queen, and helped to propagate the White Legend of Marie Antoinette 'the beautiful and unfortunate Queen, always calumniated, and whom one can reproach only for having a soul without reproach and as white and beautiful as her face', 'a thousand times too good'. It is as far from the truth as the Black Legend of the pamphlets. The Queen surrounded herself with some of the most luxurious furniture and objets d'art ever made, and, as was expected of the Queen of France, spent a fortune on jewels and clothes; unlike previous Queens, she also had her own palace and *gardemeuble*. Yet Ligne wrote that every minister's mistress or maid lived in greater luxury. He denied that she had lovers and claimed that 'there was never any of us who had the good fortune to see her every day and dared to abuse it, by the slightest impropriety; she acted the Queen without realising it, people adored her without thinking of loving her'.

Ligne wrote that she could not put a foot right. If she laughed, she was called *moqueuse*. If she was welcoming to foreigners, it was a sign that she hated the French. If she had dinner with Mme de Polignac in her apartment, she was *familière*. If she gave parties at the Petit Trianon, she was *bourgeoise*. If she walked on summer nights with her sisters-in-law on the terrace at Versailles, she was *suspecte*. When she stopped being frivolous, she was accused of being *intrigante*.[43] With his courtier's eye for the surface of life, Ligne also pointed out that, parallel to her private life with her own friends, she maintained the traditional ceremonial surrounding a queen of France.

The Queen did not neglect one public dinner; her extremely boring public card games on Wednesdays and Sundays; the ambassadors and the foreigners on Tuesdays; presentations; the ceremony known as *les révérences*; the morning court which was called the *toilette de la reine* before going through the gallery to mass, every day; dinners in state; visits to the theatre

in state; *soupers dans les cabinets* on Tuesdays and Thursdays
with boring and prudish grandees; great splendour, decency
and magnificence at great entertainments; dignity and elegance
at her carnival balls; supper every day *en famille chez Monsieur*,
etc.[44]

Nevertheless, even at court, Marie Antoinette inspired dislike
and disrespect. Foolish and selfish, she had learnt to write cor-
rectly only at the age of thirteen. She ignored etiquette, leaving
her lady-in-waiting far behind when she went riding with Ligne
and throwing her guests' hats into the lake after dinner at the
Petit Trianon. In Mme de Polignac's salon Artois and Mme de
Polignac would criticise her behind her back, for lack of dignity
and excessive attachment to the Habsburgs.[45] Ligne even saw
Delisle pick up a corner of the Queen's dress, in front of her
court of Marshals and Knights of the Holy Spirit, and say: 'I was
right. It is embroidery. How good such work is now!'[46] Ligne
later wrote to his daughter Christine that he was perhaps the
only person who genuinely liked the Queen.[47]

Invitations to the pavilions at Marly had been so coveted
under Louis XIV that courtiers lined his way to mass, pleading,
'Marly, Sire?' Under Louis XVI, Delisle wrote to Ligne, since
only four ladies had inscribed their names on the list for Marly, a
visit there by the court was cancelled.[48] By the beginning of the
1780s people who tried to cheer her at the Paris opera were
hushed by the rest of the audience. Ligne's solution, printed in
1783, might have temporarily strengthened the monarchy. The
distance, the climate and the 'gloom' of Versailles were oppressive. 'The court of gaiety' should move to Paris and live in a
restored and enlarged Louvre, which should face on to a magnificent square stretching as far as the Tuileries (a building programme finally realised by Napoleon III). 'Let Paris see, love
and get to know its sovereigns.'[49]

Despite the intoxications of Paris and Versailles, Vienna
remained one of the three poles of Ligne's world, with Brussels
(he kept boxes in theatres in all three).[50] Like Marie Antoinette,

Ligne never forgot that he was Austrian. They were both pawns in the great game of Europe and in the 1770s they were increasingly affected by the ambitions of Marie Antoinette's eldest brother Joseph II, co-Regent with Maria Theresa since the death of his father Francis I in 1765. Under Louis XVI France was a satisfied power, without interest in territorial expansion in Europe. Austria was a power on the make.

Forceful and unscrupulous, Joseph II has been more successful at capturing the imagination of posterity than the hearts of contemporaries. He was a cynic whose distrust of humans was increased after the death of his beloved first wife Isabella of Parma, and his rejection by Ligne's sister-in-law Princess Charles Liechtenstein. When he fell in love with her, she said that he reminded her of a lion about to devour its prey.

Like Frederick the Great, Joseph II preferred military parades to operas and court ceremonies, and slashed the number of gala days and church services at court. Just as Marie Antoinette spent as much time as she could in the Petit Trianon, so Joseph II often lived in a simple villa in the Augarten rather than in the splendour of the Hofburg. Despite her specific request in her will, he closed his mother's favourite palace Schönbrunn.

Ligne was a favourite of Joseph II and one of the thirty-six chamberlains out of the total of 1500 whom the Emperor chose to continue in his service. When he was in waiting, Joseph II told him to admit whomever he wanted; Ligne says he tried to select officers and people from the provinces. Ligne admired the Emperor and believed that, without the agitation and anxiety that drove him to an early grave, he would have been the best monarch in the world: 'He was everything by halves, nearly good, nearly amiable, nearly a great sovereign. Nature had not finished him.' Like a child, Joseph II wanted to touch everything; one day Ligne met in the antechamber a priest sent to ask the Emperor if his church could sing psalms through the nose, as they had before the Emperor had forbidden that style.[51]

As eager for amusing society as Marie Antoinette, Joseph II

was the first monarch to go out in the evening like a private person. He visited, among others, Princess Esterhazy, Princess Kinsky, Countess Harrach or Countess Tarouca, in their palaces near the Hofburg. With Princesses Clary, Kinsky, Charles and Francis Liechtenstein, and Countess Kaunitz, he also formed a coterie, known as *les dames* but including Lacy, the Grand Chamberlain Rosenberg and, occasionally, Ligne. Ligne found the Emperor so human that he could be teased, or told disagreeable truths, in front of his friends. If one of them attacked the Emperor, he would laugh and say to Ligne, 'They have the devil in them today.'[52] In 1772, adding yet another nationality to the multinational monarchy, Joseph II obtained the lion's share in the first partition of Poland, winning more population than Russia and Prussia combined, in part owing to his unscrupulous interpretation of the agreed frontier limits. This unprecedented division of an independent country by three aggressive neighbours shocked opinion so much that, while discussing a thief who had just been hanged, Ligne heard one of *les dames* say to the Emperor: 'How could Your Majesty have condemned him, after having stolen from Poland?'[53]

Joseph II told Ligne that in order to avoid temptation, before visiting a lady to whom he might be able to make love, he had a prostitute. Ligne always yielded to temptation. On one occasion, having met a beautiful Croatian woman at a ball and not had time to deal with her petition, the Emperor told Ligne to investigate. Ligne went to her apartment and, although they had no language in common, stated his mission. From kissing her hands he began to embrace her. All she could say was: 'Fürst' (Prince), then another 'Fürst' in a more friendly tone, then an angry 'Furst', then a fearful 'Fürst', then a tender 'Fürst', then twenty more in every note of the musical scale, between sighs of passion, until finally she uttered a last 'Fürst' of gratitude and friendship: the Emperor did not learn the result of the interview.[54]

Joseph II was only co-regent. He had vicious disputes with his mother, who tended to disagree with him on principle, even when he adopted policies previously advocated by herself. Having given him direction of the army, she corresponded about it behind his back with Marshal Lacy – using especially cheap-looking writing paper in order not to arouse suspicion. Ligne remembered that she liked giving money to soldiers during manoeuvres and watching them sing and dance, while Joseph disliked any irregularity. Although most people found him charming and approachable, 'quite easy and chatty', and a good listener, to his mother he could be teasing and brusque.

In the end she paid more attention to the advice of her beloved State Chancellor, Prince von Kaunitz. Glacial towards foreign ambassadors and the Pope himself, Kaunitz liked Ligne and often pinched his cheeks or stroked his chin. Kaunitz was a vain man who cleaned his gums after dinner in front of his guests and told a Russian presented to him by Ligne: 'I advise you to buy my portrait, Monsieur, for in your country people will be pleased to know the face of one of the most famous men, the best horseman, the best minister governing this monarchy for fifty years, a man who knows everything, understands everything.'[55] Disagreements between Joseph II and his mother were so disturbing that, like many other people at court, Joseph often prophesied doom and wrote to his brother Leopold in 1772: 'Things are bad in every way... No system. No plan... intrigue and cabals and therefore complete stagnation which will result in the death of the state.'[56]

In reality this was a sign of the pessimism of the Habsburgs – a family trait which served to mask their power and ambition. More realistic was the judgement of the French ambassador in Vienna, the Baron de Breteuil, who wrote to the Foreign Minister, the Comte de Vergennes: 'that the throne of the House of Austria has never been occupied by a prince more dominated by the invariable maxim that it is a loss not to increase territory'.[57] In part because of the unprecedented size and ability of the dynasty – Maria Theresa had ten adult children – the 1770s were a miraculous decade for Austria, when it acquired reserves of power and respect that were to help it survive the storms to come.

Joseph II reasserted imperial suzerainty, and raised imperial revenues, in both Germany and northern Italy: the number of cases heard in the Reichshofrat in Vienna rose from 2088 in 1767 to 3388 in 1779.[58] In 1771 his younger brother Ferdinand married the heiress of the ancient Duchy of Modena in the Lombard plain, thereby securing a third Italian domain for the Habsburgs in addition to Tuscany and Milan. In 1775, while protesting friendship for the Ottoman government (from whom it had just extracted a subsidy), Austria occupied Bukowina, a small Ottoman province linking Galicia and Transylvania; the Austrian representative in Constantinople, Baron Thugut, hoped it was a step towards Austria becoming mistress of the Balkans and 'the true Roman empire'. In 1780 the youngest son of Maria Theresa, the Archduke Maximilian, was elected co-adjutor or successor of the Elector of Cologne and Bishop of Munster, thus becoming eventual master of an important state with a large army in north-west Germany. Even excluding such subsidiary family monarchies, Austria's population – a measure of strength often used in the eighteenth century – rose by fifty per cent, from 15 million in 1750 to 23 million in 1787. In the same period the population of France rose from 24 to 26 million.

Internally Austria was also becoming stronger. Whereas the French elites resisted attempts at general reform, in Austria reforms such as the General Education Act of 1774, 'the first comprehensive system of primary education in Europe', which made it in theory compulsory in the monarchy outside Hungary, and limits imposed on the independence of the Church and the number of monasteries, were far ahead of their time. In 1775, for the first time in the history of the monarchy, the budget was balanced. Maria Theresa, who said that she did not want to go to hell for the sake of a few great lords, was even more radical than Joseph in her attempts to alleviate the wretched condition of the peasants: a start was made with the Robot Patent of 1775. In the 1770s conscription was introduced in most Austrian provinces, while, thanks to Marshal Lacy, the Austrian army had become one of the most formidable in Europe. Ligne was not the only person who believed that it was Austria's destiny to dominate Europe.[59]

Marie Antoinette was part of the programme of Austrian power. While Ligne was making Marie Antoinette laugh, Maria Theresa and Joseph II hoped, as their ambassador Mercy-Argenteau wrote, 'to make the Queen reign'. They wanted her to dominate Louis XVI and impose ministers of her own choice – as one of her older sisters, Queen Maria Carolina, did in Naples. In 1776 Maria Carolina, declaring that she would show her husband King Ferdinand IV who she and her family were, sacked his chief minister and entered the council: Naples moved out of the Bourbon and into the Habsburg sphere.[60]

At Versailles Marie Antoinette was supported, and used, by what was often called *le parti de la Reine*, which was anti-Bourbon and pro-Habsburg. Its most important figure was the Imperial ambassador the Comte de Mercy-Argenteau. However, for Mercy-Argenteau, who had a party of courtiers, priests, journalists at his orders, Ligne was too unconventional and uncontrollable to be useful: he helped ensure that Ligne was not allowed to accompany Joseph II on his visits to his sister at Versailles.[61]

Mercy-Argenteau, who came from the Bishopric of Liège, was a mendacious and manipulative diplomat who paid trumpeters to advertise, in the Palais Royal, the Queen's role in choosing ministers. His role in undermining the French monarchy was so well known that, years later, in the midst of the Reign of Terror, on receiving news of his death, a French diplomat, the Marquis de Bombelles, wondered in his diary whether, 'if he had not been born, the King of France Louis XVI would perhaps still be seated secure on his throne'.[62]

Reverting to the present tense, because the memory was so intense, Ligne wrote in his memoirs that at Versailles 'everyone is drunk' – on ambition as well as pleasure: Ligne's own intoxication is shown by the superlatives he lavished on Marie Antoinette. Traumatised by her desire to please her overpowering mother and brother, Marie Antoinette tried to assume a role for which nothing but her contempt for what she called the King's 'weakness' or 'apathy' equipped her. But Louis XVI was not Ferdinand IV.

Intelligent, reserved, indifferent to his public image, Louis XVI is one of the most indefinable monarchs in history. Whereas Maria Theresa evoked a personal reaction by her impulsive, occasionally theatrical manners, Louis XVI created a void around himself by his armour-plated righteousness. He preferred to succour the poor rather than to flatter the nobility, and had no friends. When Ligne was being cruel, he wrote that the King's conversation was that of a lunatic or a hunting bore; at his own *coucher* he fooled around trying to catch Ligne's earring with the blue riband of the Order of the Holy Spirit. Ligne even wrote that this athletic young king was 'the ugliest and most disgusting of all men'.[63]

When Ligne was more benign, he acknowledged the King's 'brusque and kindly gaiety' and repeated some of the jokes he made at supper – that French economists, with names such as Turgot or Mirabeau, sounded like hunting dogs. Louis XVI could arouse extremes of adoration as well as exasperation. In a poem about the King's *lever*, Ligne called him the image of a God on earth, the best of kings, the enemy of intrigue and flattery and scourge of the wicked.[64]

Louis XVI's marriage was as ill-assorted as Ligne's. He loved his wife, gave her the Petit Trianon and applauded loudly when she appeared on the stage. Partly because a precedent was set if he awarded them, he also allowed the Queen to be the channel through whom promotions, pensions and favours were awarded, even to princes of the blood. Although she was so weak that the beneficiaries never formed a solid block of supporters, her role as distributor of favours made her appear important. Croÿ believed that she influenced the choice of ministers and wrote, 'so everyone rushed to her and her society'. Ligne himself thought she could help him win his law suits.

In reality, neither the Queen nor her society had great influence over what was called *les affaires* – policy – or the choice of ministers, despite the opinion of the public and, at the beginnning of the reign, of many politicians. Ministers who were said to be in her party, such as Breteuil, ignored her devotion to the Habsburgs and pursued anti-Austrian policies. She admitted to Joseph II that she had to use cunning and deceit to make the public and the ministers believe that the King told her 'everything'.[65] In the end Mercy-Argenteau and Kaunitz admitted that the Queen was so 'desolating by her frivolity and her little indiscretions' that she had no political influence: Austria could not rely on her.[66]

Ligne himself believed that 'one does more business in a salon than in a study'.[67] This may have been true of the literary world of Paris, where reputations and careers could be made chez Mme Geoffrin and Mme du Deffand; but in Versailles the salon of Mme de Polignac was less important than the study of the anti-Austrian Foreign Minister Vergennes. Far from being a puppet of his shy, childish wife, Louis XVI governed through his ministers.

Despite, or because of, his Austrian wife, Louis was less pro-Austrian than Louis XV. He felt no admiration for what he called 'the ambitious and despotic character of the Emperor'. During his reign, partly because of the growth of Austrian power, France resumed the tradition of hostility to Austria, and friendship for Prussia, which had been in abeyance since the treaty of 1756. Vergennes was so anti-Austrian that he wrote to Louis XVI in 1784, while France and Austria were in theory allies: 'If it becomes necessary to opt between the conservation of the branches of the House of Bourbon in Italy, and that of Prussian power in Germany, we should not hesitate to abandon the first and maintain the other.'[68]

The hostility between France and Austria affected Ligne, as it had his ancestors. Respecting French culture, he had his children educated in Paris. Yet envy and resentment dominated his attitude to France as a state. He told Vandenbroucke: 'I am as certain to beat the French at war as you are in business.' Ligne was delighted that the rise of Austria, Prussia and Russia had diminished France's relative importance: in a note on a book boasting of the pre-eminence of the French army, he wrote that France was only one-twentieth of Europe and Austria, Prussia and Russia laughed at its expense.[69]

In 1778 Joseph II showed his ambition by his plan to exchange the Austrian Netherlands for most of Bavaria.[70] Bavaria, as much as Prussia, was a barrier to Austrian expansion and this scheme would have increased what Kaunitz called the *arrondissement* – the geographical unity – of the monarchy, its weight in the Empire, and its German character. Although the Elector of Bavaria agreed, his heir, a friend of Ligne serving in the French army called Prince Max de Deux-Ponts, and most German princes, led by Frederick, were horrified. Maria Theresa herself, disapproving of her son's 'Prussian methods', showed no desire to exchange her prosperous Flemish subjects for Bavarian peasants. On 5 July 1778 a Prussian army again invaded Bohemia.

Ligne was present, in command of a *corps détaché* consisting of his regiment, a force of light cavalry and 4300 'excellent and handsome' Croats – from the ultra-loyal Kingdom of Croatia in the south of the monarchy, which had long supplied some of the toughest soldiers in the Austrian army. Despite promises not to become the maître d'hôtel of the army, he took a staff of twenty cooks, grooms and valets, and had twenty to thirty people to lunch every day. To his son Charles, who was serving as his aide de camp, he wrote that Joseph II, whom he could see from his window, 'has been very amiable for me. He is always afraid that people will lecture him. He was pleased with my troops and said so many nice things to me about you, my dear Charles, whom he had seen working marvellously.'[71]

For six weeks in Bohemia Ligne did not speak a word of French. In terrible weather he passed the time in marches and inspections, or writing longingly about the pleasures of Paris. His son Charles had become his intimate friend, whom he called the best brain and the warmest heart he knew: original, kind-hearted and sensitive, he was so wild and funny that his father could not think of him without laughing.[72] The warmth of their relations and Ligne's love of war are shown by his remark to Charles, as they galloped hand in hand during one of the few skirmishes of this indecisive campaign, that 'it would be amusing to have a little wound together'. With a heartlessness which would have horrified his pacifist idol Voltaire, he called another skirmish 'a very pretty, and amusing little business'. His major-domo Jean Baptiste Grisset wrote that neither Ligne nor Charles feared any danger and that he feared for their lives at every skirmish.[73] Ligne's attempt to surprise a Prussian force stationed in a convent by an attack through the refectory windows was betrayed by local peasants and easily repulsed, with the loss of a brave Croat officer.[74]

Loyal to Lacy, Ligne thought the Austrian commander Marshal Loudon too slow and said that it was the saddest moment of his life when he learnt there was to be no pitched battle. He was convinced he would have had the pleasure of defeating his friend Prince Henry of Prussia; but Joseph II, with characteristic Habsburg pessimism, was too frightened for the survival of the monarchy to risk a pitched battle. Moreover, behind Joseph II's back, the Empress began peace negotiations. After much expense, by the Treaty of Teschen of May 1779 the monarchy won nothing but a small district of Bavaria with about 120,000 people.[75]

Ligne had his share of glory. On his return to Brussels, the first evening he went to the theatre he was cheered as he entered his box. Finally receiving public office at the age of forty-five, he was appointed Governor of Mons, an important fortress and capital of Hainaut, with the third highest official salary in the country, 19,200 florins a year, a useful sum for an improvident prince. On 19 August 1779 Ligne was again wildly applauded when, to the sound of church bells, he entered Mons, surrounded by soldiers from his regiment, aides de camp and hussars dressed in Ligne pink. Like a wary and suspicious headmistress, Maria Theresa had refused to give him a more important position, and wrote to Joseph II: 'Ligne is young, can still wait for many vacancies, he has made his way quickly.'[76] At the age of forty-five, however, Ligne felt his ascent had not been rapid enough.

Russia

Like making war, or love, travel was one of the principal occupations of Ligne and his friends. Count Zinzendorf covered all Europe, from Spain to Sweden; Joseph II spent much of his reign on the road. Unlike most eighteenth-century travellers, Ligne resisted the lure of the Grand Tour to Rome and Naples. Preferring modern courts to classical ruins, he heard the call of what was called *le Nord* – Prussia, Poland and Russia (then regarded as a northern rather than an eastern power, since its capital was St Petersburg). At their cultivated, French-speaking courts visitors like Ligne were always welcome.

As with his attendance on Mme du Barry and Marie Antoinette at Versailles, there was an additional, financial motive for Ligne's visit: the need to extract the money the Radziwills and the Bishop of Vilna owed his daughter-in-law Hélène. Dreaming of Polish riches, he had written to Vandenbroucke: 'Of all affairs the most essential is to exploit the marriage.' Curiosity was another incentive. He had already 'acquired' the celebrities of Paris and Versailles. Why not exercise his charm on such living legends as Frederick the Great and Catherine the Great, who would provide excellent material for letters or books? In June 1780 he left Paris, from the *hôtel* of the Duchesse de Polignac, 'who had just had a baby and at whose house I had dined with the Queen. I promised them to return there at the same hour in six months' time; and I ordered a hired carriage and footman in consequence.'[1] Bearing his son Charles, now his companion in his travels as well as on the battlefield and at the printing press, and his two favourite writers, Delisle and Sauveur Legros, his carriage sped across Europe like a moving salon, through Munich, Vienna, Prague and Dresden until it reached Berlin.

Prussia was then regarded as an enlightened modern monarchy, whose fame was enhanced by the fascination of Frederick the Great. Ligne had dreamt of returning to Berlin since his visit as a conqueror in the Seven Years' War. In *Préjugés Militaires* he wrote: 'Berlin has the same glory with regard to arms as Versailles with regard to the graces.'[2] Contemporaries like Boswell, the great military reformer the Comte de Guibert, and La Fayette, and many others, also revered the Prussian army and made the pilgrimage to Potsdam.[3] Ligne had expressed his admiration for the ruler he called 'the King of Kings' in a verse he had written under a portrait of Frederick the Great at the Prussian Minister's residence in Vienna:[4]

> Du plus grand des Mortels, des Soldats et des Rois!
> Peuples, voyez ici l'image.
> Lisez ses Vers, ses Combats et ses Lois.
> Admirez tous, les traits d'un Vainqueur et d'un Sage.[5]

In 1780 Ligne announced his arrival in advance, for the sake of a letter from the great 'Fédéric', as the King always signed himself. Eager not to miss such an amusing visitor, whom he had not seen since they had both attended Austrian manoeuvres in 1770, Frederick wrote Ligne three replies, sent to Vienna, Dresden and Berlin. Ligne was presented to the King on 11 July.[6]

Frederick was the only monarch of the day to live away from his court. In the relatively small gilded rococo pavilion of Sans Souci, set in a magnificent park of beeches, statues and fountains outside Potsdam, the Hohenzollern *Residenzstadt* ten miles west of Berlin, Frederick lived among guards, secretaries and army officers. Partly to shield his homosexuality, the Prussian court and his wife the Queen were kept at bay in Berlin. Ligne and Charles (but not Delisle, considered neither sufficiently well born nor sufficiently well mannered) were invited to dinner every day.

Ligne later described his encounter in one of his most brilliant memoirs, the fifty-six-page *Mémoire sur le Roi de Prusse Frédéric le Grand par Msgr. le Prince de L*****, published in French in Berlin in 1789. It begins with the disclaimer, particularly hypocritical from Ligne: 'Je n'aime point à parler de moi et le Je m'est odieux à moi-même, à plus forte raison aux autres à qui il me déplait aussi beaucoup quand ils le prononcent.' The King and the Prince talked for five hours at a time, during and after dinner, about everything under the sun: art, literature, history, Voltaire, religion, the mistakes of the Georgics of Virgil as a gardening manual, the introduction of Prussian drill in the French army, and Joseph II's recent journey to Russia to see Catherine the Great (Frederick pointed out that he was not the first Holy Roman Emperor to travel so far: Charles V had been to Oran).[7]

An underlying theme in the *Mémoire*, as in European politics, was the conflict between Austria and Prussia. Frederick was now so old that he could remember the War of the Polish Succession in 1733 between France and the armies of the Empire under Prince Eugène of Savoy, in which he had fought because his father, King Frederick William I, had been loyal to the Empire: ' "Do you know," the King said to me one day, "that I have been in your service? I first bore arms for the House of Austria. My God how time passes!" He had a way of putting his hands together while saying that "My God" which made him look completely kindly and extremely gentle.'[8] Much of the conversation dwelt on the battles and sieges during the Seven Years' War between Austria and Prussia. Ligne writes: 'Je mourais de peur qu'au milieu de ses bontés il ne se souvient que j'étais Autrichien.' Recalling the Seven Years' War, Frederick praised the Austrians' campaigns of 1758 and 1759, called Marshal Lacy 'a man of the greatest merit' and remembered his relief when Lacy had been replaced in 1760. Frederick called the 'Potato War' of 1778, in which Ligne had commanded an Austrian regiment, 'un procès pour lequel il venoit en huissier faire exécution'. However, Ligne noted, as a sign that the Prussian army could have done better, that this was one war about which the King did not like talking.[9]

Ligne remembered that the King was *un peu babillard* ('a bit of a chatterer') and that his eyes, hardened by war and work, softened when the conversation interested him. As gently as he could, the King broke the news of the death on 4 July of Prince Charles of Lorraine, Governor-General of the Austrian Netherlands. This hardened despot said:

> Poor Prince Charles is no more. Others can perhaps replace him in your heart but few princes will replace him for the beauty of his soul and of all his virtues ... his crossing of the Rhine is very fine, but the poor prince depended on so many people! I have only depended on my brain, sometimes too much for my own happiness. He was badly served, often disobeyed: neither one nor the other has ever happened to me.[10]

On learning that Charles de Ligne had married, using one of his favourite turns of phrase, he said, 'May I dare to ask you with whom?' When told 'a Polish woman, a Massalska', he remembered that her grandmother had also fought in the War of the Polish Succession, and had turned a cannon on the enemy at the siege of Danzig.

Many years earlier, when Mme de Pompadour was still mistress of Louis XV, Ligne had written a ribald poem about Frederick's homosexuality. With such fine men as his guards, who serve Priapus as well as Mars, and are full of fire, it is best to yield:

> In France for large sums
> Louis is between two legs ...
> In Berlin you economise,
> Using soldiers for everything.[11]

Despite a reference to a statue of the Emperor Hadrian's favourite, Antinous, in the garden, this aspect of the King's private life is not openly mentioned in *Mémoire sur le Roi de*

Prusse Frédéric le Grand; but he does say that they laughed a lot
about the nickname *Madame Chimon* given to Prince Eugène of
Savoy when he was young and effeminate: 'It is true, added the
King, laughing even more, we have Caesar, Alexander –
Vendôme and Catinat. Conversation became very gay.'
Showing his extraordinary knowledge of French court memoirs,
Ligne also mentioned, in veiled terms, an incident in the youth
of Louis XIV, when one of Cardinal Mazarin's nephews had
tried to seduce him.[12]

Prussia was considered a 'barracks-state', different from the
other monarchies of Europe. The Hohenzollerns were a mili-
tarist dynasty, determined to transform their small, infertile
monarchy into one of the great powers of Europe. As another
admiring foreign visitor, Mirabeau, said a few years later, it was
not a monarchy that had an army but an army that had a monarchy. 'Everything is forced, even nature, in the dominions and
gardens of the King of Prussia,' wrote Ligne. Frederick himself
complained of the climate, and his orange and lemon trees dying
of hunger. Although Ligne admired the picture gallery, he disliked the parks and gilded statues around Sans Souci and the
elaborate red furniture inside. However, his head was turned by
the King, even more than it had been by Voltaire. For Ligne,
Frederick ennobled everything. 'An old sorcerer who understood everything and whose tact was the finest there has ever
been', he was 'le plus grand homme qui ait jamais existé'. The
opposite of Jesus Christ, he was not a god who became a man
but a man who became a god.[13] He did not blame Frederick for
his attacks on Austria in 1740 or 1756. In Ligne's opinion he had
only done what was necessary to safeguard his 'petit trône du
Nord et de sable', and after his victories had always offered
peace.[14]

Frederick was also enchanted. Normally grudging with
praise, he wrote: 'We have here the Prince de Ligne who is on
his way to Russia; he has wit and little patience with fools; he is a
severe Aristarchus whose domination extends from the cedar to
the ysope' (a reference to the Book of Kings, 5:13). The King

could sense Ligne's infatuation and remarked: 'You only see my good side; but you only have to ask the Herr Generals about my obstinacy and my temper, then you will hear another song.'[15] Indeed the day of Ligne's departure, learning that Ligne was secretly observing Potsdam garrison manoeuvres *en frac*, Frederick cancelled them in order to prevent his Austrian guest learning more about Prussian troops.[16]

After a week in Potsdam, and a visit to another of his heroes, the King's brother Prince Henry of Prussia at his palace of Rheinsberg north of Berlin, Ligne moved on to St Petersburg, where he arrived on 6 August. He found a court totally different from that of Vienna. Just as the uniform mass of the Winter Palace, unlike the warren of the Hofburg, reduced neighbouring nobles' palaces to insignificance, so Russian nobles were more dependent on the Tsar than Austrians on the Emperor. Yet their relationship was punctuated by palace coups and murders unknown in Vienna. Two Tsars, Peter III and Ivan VI, had been murdered by nobles in the service of Catherine the Great in the last twenty years. Catherine concentrated on keeping the nobility happy while reforming her empire: she thought the Habsburg habit of public audiences a waste of time.

Ligne's visits to Versailles had been in the interests of his own finances and amusement. His arrival in St Petersburg in 1780 had an additional semi-political motive: to help Austrian expansion. The map of Europe was about to be redrawn: Joseph II had just visited Catherine the Great, because he needed Russian help to realise his ambition to humiliate Prussia and divide the Ottoman Empire. Although it still ruled the entire Balkan peninsula, from the Danube to the Dardanelles, after its defeat by Russia in the war of 1768–74 the Ottoman Empire appeared close to collapse. Joseph II and Catherine the Great planned to conquer as much as they could. Yet Catherine had been allied to Austria's greatest enemy, Prussia, for twenty years; her chief minister Count Panin was pro-Prussian; and Frederick William, Prince of Prussia, Frederick's nephew and heir, a blond giant for whom Ligne had once hidden a pregnant mistress in Ghent, was visiting St Petersburg.

Ligne cultivated a façade of frivolity. He wrote to the King of Poland: 'I have a horror of anything political or ministerial.'[17] In reality the course of his life was governed by his desire to serve Austria and advance himself; his career shows both the uses and drawbacks of frivolity in politics. Like Marie Antoinette, Catherine yearned to be amused and to be considered amusing; no one could satisfy such desires better than the Prince de Ligne. Like Voltaire, who had visited Frederick the Great with the approval of the French government in the 1740s, Ligne was an unofficial envoy whose charm and wit were used by his government for political purposes.

When Ligne was presented by his host Count Louis Cobenzl, the witty, ugly Imperial ambassador, he charmed the susceptible fifty-two-year-old Empress, whose current lover, Count Lanskoy, was said no longer to be fulfilling his duties. She wrote to Baron Grimm, the German Parisian who supplied her, and many other sovereigns, with regular bulletins of the literary and social news of Paris: 'Here there is still the prince de Ligne, who is one of the easiest and most agreeable beings I have ever met; he is truly original, thinks profoundly and performs follies like a child.'[18]

While the Prince of Prussia endured rudeness and neglect from the Empress, who considered him a bore, Ligne dined or supped every day at her table, in the private apartments in the Winter Palace, known as the Hermitage, from which etiquette was banished; they then played cards or billiards. Catherine gave him the right to wear a green Russian uniform with red facings, which he called 'the livery of honour'. Ligne and Catherine were so at ease in each other's company that one day she said, 'Let us strangle Monsieur Narishkin,' her master of the horse – a remark that convinced Ligne that she had not been guilty of ordering the death of her husband Peter III, strangled a month after she usurped the throne from him in 1762.[19]

Ligne enjoyed the 'wild dissipation' of St Petersburg and its ring of palaces, which make the Habsburg palaces of Schönbrunn and Laxenberg seem small and domestic. The

massive blue and white baroque rectangle of Tsarskoe Seloe, the
Romanovs' principal country palace, was surrounded by a
natural 'English' park laid out by Catherine, filled with what she
called 'caprices', built in the 1770s. These included the Grotto
Pavilion, where a system of 'flying tables', hoisted through
openings in the floor, enabled guests to sit down to a formal
dinner without servants; a Chinese opera house; a neogothic
gate; a Palladian bridge; a bridge of Siberian marble; the Orlov
Arch; and the Victory Column and Kagul Obelisk, erected to
commemorate victories over the Ottomans. Ligne was
impressed by what is possibly the largest 'English' park of the
eighteenth century. In *Coup d'oeil sur Beloeil*, he would write:

> The legislator of the greatest of empires, the support or the
> terror of her neighbours, sows her own lawns. The homage
> her great spirit renders to those who have extended her glory
> even to the gates of the Orient is as great an honour for her as
> for her glorious generals. Tsarskoe Seloe which contains what
> the Empress calls her fantasies presents on all sides the most
> charming of pictures. These fantasies, so called, are water and
> optical effects, well imagined and varied, such as a bridge of
> Siberian marble in an architecture styled by Palladio, baths, a
> Turkish pavilion, the Admiralty – a sort of town that has been
> set up – iron gates, a ruin, monuments to the victories of
> Romianzov and Orlov, a superb rostral column in the middle
> of the lake to commemorate Chesme [a victory over the
> Turks], agreeable contours everywhere, quantities of flowers
> and exotic shrubs, lawns as well kept and as fine as those of
> England, Chinese bridges and kiosks, a temple with thirty-two
> marble columns, a colonnade and above all the grand staircase
> of Hercules on the garden side, all of which makes this the
> most interesting park in the world. It is here that the great
> princess, the honour of her sex, dropping for a moment the
> reins of government, takes up a pencil, a rake, a pruning
> hook ...[20]

Ligne also admired the nearby gothic house and English
garden of Prince Potemkin, a cultivated giant who had helped to

assassinate Peter III. From being Catherine's lover (addressed as 'my beautiful Golden Pheasant', 'darling husband', 'my marble beauty'), he had become her secret husband and chief political and military adviser; like the Empress, he advocated expansion south into the Ottoman Empire and opposed Count Panin's policy of friendship with Prussia.[21] Cobenzl thought Ligne's warm welcome was above all due to Potemkin. Potemkin liked Ligne so much that he persuaded him to stay longer and offered to make his son Charles a colonel in the Russian army. When he left, Potemkin said he could not get used to his absence.[22]

Another friend Ligne made in St Petersburg was the sophisticated, cosmopolitan British ambassador, Sir James Harris. Although Joseph II was allied to France, which was fighting Britain in the War of American Independence, he also wanted a rapprochement with Britain. In the eighteenth century the business of politics was allowed to interfere as little as possible with the pleasures of society. An Austrian officer, and unofficial diplomat, Ligne had dined with Frederick the Great. A friend of Marie Antoinette, he helped the ambassador of a country with which France was at war. On 9 September Harris wrote: ' The prince de Ligne is in the highest favour and is in every respect more distinguished and caressed than His Royal Highness [the Prince of Prussia] ... he certainly does, tho' without pretending it, more service than count Cobenzl.' He later added: 'He has been of the greatest use to me on this occasion, and I shall if possible prevail upon him to stay a week longer as he has the talent, under the mask of pleasantry, of conveying to the Empress the most important truths ... His talent for Humour and Ridicule has certainly done both the French and Prussian Party irreparable harm here.'[23]

In an age that, unlike Ligne, believes in fundamental economic and political forces, it seems incredible that the realignment of Russian foreign policy could have been affected by the charm of the Prince de Ligne. His influence was certainly less than that of Catherine, Potemkin and Joseph II. Yet a French diplomat, the Chevalier de Corberon, agreed with Harris. He reported, with the venom increasingly marking Franco-Austrian relations:

> I believe that among the reasons which prevented the enter-
> tainments which the Prince of Prussia should have found here
> are the intrigues of the Prince de Ligne. This Austrian, very
> close to Cobenzl, who lodged him, paid court to the Russians
> in a base fashion; the affected praise he lavished on the King of
> Prussia at the beginning, made it easier for him to speak in
> favour of the Austrian party subsequently. What is certain is
> that he was very well received by the Empress, who had
> several private conversations with him, and he even, it is said,
> stayed several times alone with her until eleven at night ... the
> Prince de Ligne did not finish as well as he began. His *ton de
> polissonerie* did not seem decent to the Russians; Count Panin,
> always laughing and applauding, sometimes shrugged his
> shoulders at the sight of a *grand seigneur* of fifty-four [in reality
> forty-five] playing *broche en cul* [a card-game] and having bits
> of paper stuck in his behind.

Delisle and Charles made an even worse impression. Delisle asked embarrassing questions about the possibility of the imperial guards deposing Catherine and putting her son the Grand Duke Paul on the throne. Charles had 'the bad tone of a German garrison', and spat in his father's plate when he thought there was something Ligne should not eat.[24]

Ligne subsequently wrote many portraits of his new friend the Empress of Russia. She was a colossus supported by four pillars: spirit, common sense, elevation and energy. She was easily hurt by any reflection on Russia, and jokes had to be simple, or she missed the point. She once said to him: 'It is true, isn't it, I would not be amusing enough for Paris? I am sure that if like the ladies of my country I had travelled there I would never have been invited to supper.'

The Empress preferred to listen and reward, rather than to scold and punish; sometimes she lit the fire in the morning herself in order not to wake her servants. She frequently referred

to her debt to Count Orlov and Prince Potemkin and kept with
her a snuff box with a portrait of Peter the Great in order to
remind herself to keep asking what he would have done. Ligne
claimed that she did not allow him to talk about policy.
'Everything must pass through her ministers, who are simply
canals leading to her ocean of wisdom, for her head is her
cabinet.' In Ligne's opinion, although Catherine had less magic
and powers of seduction than Maria Theresa, being a woman
was just as much of an advantage for her; she did not feel the
temptation to act the hero, her subjects were amazed and
impressed, and she could use her charm and beauty to make
herself obeyed. In 1780 she was still attractive.

> One could see that she had been beautiful rather than pretty:
> the majesty of her face was tempered by a pleasing smile and
> eyes … One did not notice that she was short … her three
> bows like a man, in the Russian style, on entering a room were
> always made in the same way, one to the right, one to the left,
> and the other in the middle. Everything about her was
> measured and methodical.

She called the Russian Empire *mon petit ménage*.[25]

On 5 October, after a stay of two months, Ligne left with
Potemkin, who wanted to show off his regiment, sped by a letter
from Catherine to Joseph II, expressing the hope that he was 'as
pleased with us as we are with him'. He had every reason to be,
since she had given him horses, 'men' (in other words serfs) and
what she called a 'wretched box' – a superb snuff box decorated
with diamonds and her portrait – then a common reward from
sovereigns, since, in case of need, the diamonds could be
removed and sold. Henceforth bearded Russian *mujiks* were
added to the hussars, footmen in Ligne pink and musicians in
Turkish costume, who accompanied Ligne in public processions
in the Austrian Netherlands.[26] However, his daughter-in-law's
dowry was no nearer payment, since he had preferred not to
press the Empress in person. As he was to write when he had lost
his fortune, 'It is easy to be delicate when you are rich.'[27]

The first letter he sent Catherine after his departure shows Ligne's skill in flattery.

> Madame,
> I believe that I have had the most beautiful dream in the world. I had only come to St Petersburg for a fortnight to admire Your Imperial Majesty and to tell my grandchildren that I had had the good fortune to see the finest object of worship and celebrity. She deigned to permit me to leave this circle of admiration, in order to convince me that proximity is an advantage when one has the superiority of every kind which only Your Majesty possesses.

He compared himself to Saint Simeon after seeing Jesus Christ, saying: 'Now I can depart in peace for mine eyes have seen the Lord.' Still pushing Austrian ambitions, he added that he hoped to wake from his dream to hear cannon being fired for the glory of 'the two empires'. In the correspondence which developed between them – more abundant and intimate than that between Ligne and any Habsburg – he praised Russia as the first throne in the world. The reason why the sun so rarely showed itself in St Petersburg was its jealousy of its rival – Catherine the Great.[28]

On his way back from St Petersburg he stopped in Warsaw. Always open to new nationalities, Ligne appreciated the capital of Poland, and its combination of 'the best manners of France' with oriental hospitality. He visited superb but badly lit noble palaces, swarming with servants of every class, and was delighted by women who in his opinion had 'an abandon, an elegance, a liveliness and a charm superior to those of all the women of other countries'.[29] He stayed long enough to obtain naturalisation as a Pole, with the help of Charles's father-in-law the Bishop of Vilna. All other applications, even when supported by the King, had been rejected by the Sejm or Polish Diet; but Ligne, who said in Latin: 'I come from several different countries at the same time. I want to be of yours!', was as great a success in the Polish parliament as in the Russian court. After five hours spent going from deputy to deputy, one declared, in exhaustion: 'Very well, the Prince de Ligne, but only him!' Thereby he acquired (and occasionally wore) another uniform in addition to the white uniform of an Austrian officer, the blue uniforms of Choisy and the French royal hunt, and the green uniform of a Russian colonel: the blue uniform with crimson facings of a Polish palatinate.[30]

The letters Ligne wrote from Warsaw to Sir James Harris in St Petersburg reveal the wit, occasionally slightly forced, that had seduced Catherine the Great, as well as Ligne's taste for flattery, importunity and malice. Swearing that he would never forget him and would remain his best friend all his life, he requested Harris to ask Potemkin to obtain from the Empress 3000 ducats a year for his son Charles: 'As well as being delighted to be obliged to him for it, I would show our court that it is better to make the sign of the Cross from right to left [in the Orthodox style] than from left to right [in the Catholic style], since it has absolutely refused, despite its piety, to repay me a hundred thousand écus that one of my ancestors had the stupidity to lend the Emperor Ferdinand.' He then gave a malicious description of the Sejm: ' There is a devil of a din in this savage Areopagus. At half past five everyone speaks at once. You would think they were bears about to fight to the death. But at six they hurry to finish, the young in order to go to the opera, the old to the tavern.'[31]

Ligne considered the Polish constitution no more absurd than the English, which would not have survived if, like Poland, it had been bordered by three empires and a kingdom instead of the sea (he called England not *Angleterre* but *Angleeau*). Naturalisation as a Pole enabled Ligne to own property, to marry into the nobility, perhaps even, as the Bishop of Vilna unrealistically suggested, enabled him or his son to be elected King of Poland. Realising his fondness for receiving as well as dispensing flattery, other Polish friends also hinted at the Crown, assuring Ligne that the Polish nation counted on him.[32]

Whereas the Habsburg dynasty had created the Austrian

monarchy, lack of a strong hereditary dynasty was destroying Poland. Its last independent king, Stanislas Augustus Poniatowski was a cultivated charmer who owed his election as king in 1764 to a love affair with Catherine the Great ten years earlier. Ligne, who could not resist a crowned head, lavished sentimental flattery on him, calling him 'the best and hand-somest of Kings', proclaiming that his heart had elected Stanislas its king. But he also called the king 'le Stanislas qui n'est pas auguste', and in 1786 told Vandenbroucke that if King Stanislas died from an attack of apoplexy, he would go to Poland at once: 'I could always get a lot out of it.'[33]

After a glorious year, in which he had conquered three new courts, Ligne arrived in Vienna in time to witness the universal regret at the death of Maria Theresa on 29 November 1780. Descending a staircase of the Hofburg in tears, he heard a Hungarian grenadier ask in Latin: 'Is my King dead?' and burst into tears himself. With Princes Esterhazy, Liechtenstein and Starhemberg, Ligne had the honour of being one of the four chamberlains who escorted her coffin from the Hofburg to its resting place in the Habsburg dynastic vault in the church of the Capuchins. On his return to Paris, the carriage and footman he had ordered six months before were waiting for him. Having crossed a continent without a carriage accident, he had one within a quarter of an hour of his arrival.[34]

Her husband's trip to Russia had put the Princesse de Ligne in a jealous rage. She foresaw that any improvement in the family finances would simply encourage her son and her husband – whom she called 'our young people' – to spend more. 'I do not understand on what he can spend so much,' she com-plained to Vandenbroucke. Ligne admitted that he had no idea where to find the money to pay his taxes, although he had suc-ceeded in getting them reduced from 31,000 to 6000 florins – a striking sign of favour from the normally unbending Joseph II, which may have been a reward for services rendered in St Petersburg. Characteristically he added: 'But it does not matter, I am still carrying on as I please.'[35]

After 1780 Ligne continued his triple life, rotating between Brussels, Paris and Vienna. In 1781 Joseph II, determined to see his Empire for himself, came to inspect the Austrian Netherlands, receiving all officials and officers and giving audiences to anyone who asked. Ligne had already represented the Emperor at his inauguration as Duke of Luxembourg, in a splendid procession preceded by a triumphal carriage bearing musicians, dragoons, and his entire household, including the Russian servants given him by Catherine II. The perfect courtier, Ligne discovered the time of the Emperor's arrival in Mons, waited for him at the gate of the city, then escorted him to the Hôtel de la Couronne Impériale.[36] Joseph supped several times at the Hôtel de Ligne in Brussels: 'He pardoned me for arriving later than him because a certain adventure made me forget the time.' (Ligne liked the idea of keeping monarchs waiting while he made love. He also boasts that he was late for the King of Poland, excusing himself with the words: 'Sire, it is one of your most beautiful subjects who is the cause. Her secret will be well kept for it is impossible for me to remember her name, which has five or six diabolical syllables to pronounce.')[37]

Ever eager to distinguish himself, in 1782 Ligne briefly turned to one of the least exploited of his personalities, that of Grandee of Spain (a title he had bothered to have confirmed in 1778). The Prince, who had helped the British ambassador in St Petersburg, now wanted to fight British troops in Gibraltar, in the company of the Comte d'Artois and a besieging Spanish army. His military patron Marshal Lacy was appalled: 'Frankly, my dear Prince, for a soldier of your rank and your distinction you must be mad, seriously to want to go and break an arm or a leg in order to have the honour of serving under the orders of the Duc de Crillon.'[38] Although Artois went to Gibraltar, Ligne did not. Ligne's desire for action was so great that he also applied, without success, to serve with the French army in America or Corsica, and with the Russian army under Marshal Rumiantsev on the Ottoman frontier.[39]

After 1780 Ligne spent more time in the Austrian Netherlands.

At Beloeil he entertained Maria Theresa's favourite and most intelligent daughter, the Archduchess Marie Christine and her cultivated husband Duke Albert of Saxe-Teschen, founder of Vienna's great collection of drawings, the Albertina, who had succeeded Charles of Lorraine as Governor-General. In 1783 the Chevalier de Boufflers and Mme de Sabran came there and acted in Beaumarchais's *The Marriage of Figaro* – the daring play, forbidden by Louis XVI, in which Count Almaviva is upbraided by his servant Figaro with the celebrated tirade, which applied to many of Ligne's friends but not to Ligne himself: 'Because you are a great lord, you think you are a great genius! Nobility, wealth, a rank, offices; all that makes you so proud. What have you done for so many possessions? You have taken the trouble to be born and nothing else.'

Ligne also stayed in his medieval castle of Antoing, near the town of Tournay, where in 1782 his regiment of 2400 men had replaced a Dutch garrison that had been stationed there as protection against France since 1713. He entertained his own and visiting French officers, drilled and shouted at his soldiers (many of whom were deserters from the French army), and completed his catalogue of the military books in his library; he also worked on a life of the great Imperial general of the seventeenth century, Prince Louis of Baden.[40]

Although Brussels had lost much of its charm for Ligne since the death of Charles of Lorraine, he gave masked balls and organised plays in the Hôtel de Ligne in winter. A French diplomat, the Marquis de Bombelles, wrote:

His house is as extraordinary as his conversation. It is a chaos whose disorder offers bizarre sights. It needs a fortnight to understand how the Hôtel de Ligne works, mechanical stairs [lifts, worked by footmen, very unusual for the time] take you from one floor to another, splendid gilded panels and mirrors are in small rooms without antechambers, portraits of great men in a boudoir devoted to their charming weaknesses, curious models of all the arts in attics, everything looks very expensive and badly maintained.[41]

The mistress of the Hôtel de Ligne, in theory, remained the Princesse Ligne. An outsider's view of Ligne's marriage is revealed in a letter from Count Valentin Esterhazy, a scion of the Hungarian family who served in the French army and had become a friend of Marie Antoinette. In September 1784, the Prince and Princesse de Ligne were staying with fifty other guests in the splendid chateau of Mariemont, the Archduchess Marie Christine's country residence south of Brussels. Count Valentin Esterhazy reported to his wife: the Princesse de Ligne 'is rather old, blonde and insipid when she was young and now white and fat. Encouraged by her husband's example, she has enjoyed herself on her side; in fact they get on well by seeing each other as little as possible. She is in addition extremely boring; but it is true that she is very good about paying her losses at loto.'[42] Yet Ligne and the Princess had reached a modus vivendi.

Angélique d'Hannetaire, who often stayed in one of his minor residences, the Château de Silly, remained at the centre of his life. She received a pension from him, and as late as 1788 knew his travel plans before anyone else. She realised that it was in her interests to show respect to the Princesse de Ligne. In 1780 Leygeb had written, no doubt with a smile, that after appearing in a play in Amsterdam, 'Mlle. Angélique', 'having received from H. H. the Princess Mother a present of a sack of Moka coffee, came to the hôtel to thank her, and was very well received ... In her turn she made a present to the princess of a pound of tea which she had brought for her from Holland'.[43] Yet Angélique now had another rival: since 1779 Ligne had had another mistress, twenty-two years younger than himself, Henriette Countess Auersperg. Her air of virginal beauty touched many hearts, and their affair, which may not have been physical, is known only through some entries in the diary of another passionate admirer, Count Zinzendorf. He records, in 1789, her description of the beginning of her affair with Ligne: 'Completely innocent, she was desperately in love with him; his tears, his poems touched her. She embraced him tenderly. He

did not take advantage of her and restricted himself to the sentiment and the preliminaries.[44] Otherwise, owing to the destruction of the Auersperg archives, nothing is known of their
relations.

His children were becoming as important to Ligne as his wife
and mistresses. Ligne adored his daughter Christine, who in
1775 had married a wealthy Bohemian noble called Count Clary
und Aldringen. He called her 'Christ' and his letters to her are as
passionate as any he wrote. However, she lived in Vienna and
Teplitz, the Clarys' country residence in the Bohemian hills. He
was less interested in his other daughters Euphémie and Flore,
who were still young: when Flore, for example, had smallpox,
he did not bother to visit her.[45] His constant companion was his
eldest son Charles, who three years after their marriage already
wanted to divorce his wife (almost impossible in western
Europe, divorce was easily obtained in Poland): Ligne and his
son were so similar that their handwriting is alike and, like his
father's, Charles de Ligne's letters to Vandenbroucke are a continuous yell for money.[46] Ligne admired his son, who acquired
the reputation of being the most promising Austrian officer of
his generation.

In 1784 Ligne went to Lyons to see Charles go up in the latest
scientific invention, a hot-air balloon; it tore and came down
sooner than expected. Ligne then revisited Ferney and Geneva,
and went to Provence, on his only visit to Mediterranean
Europe. Provence seemed to him to be a favourite of the gods:
its gaiety, freedom and delightful climate made it 'a separate
country which no more resembles the country of which it is part
than those from which it is furthest'. The most surprising garden
in Europe, watered by seventy fountains and decorated by a
genuine ruined castle and monastery, belonged to the Marquis
d'Albertas at Gemnos near Marseilles. Albertas, who, like
Ligne, gave masked balls for thousands in his park, was famous
for his remark, on finding a young man 'in the arms of' his ugly
wife: 'What, monsieur, without being obliged to!' When Ligne
left Gemnos for Vienna to perform his service as chamberlain,

Mme d'Albertas could not believe that he was travelling so far in winter. Ligne said, 'Yes, madame, and without being obliged to!'[47]

In Vienna in 1784 Ligne learnt of Joseph's plan to reopen the Scheldt to shipping, as part of his programme to unify and strengthen the monarchy, and encourage commerce. Fearing the competition of Antwerp, the United Provinces resisted the Emperor: Dutch ships fired on a ship leaving Antwerp flying the Imperial flag. Louis XVI and Vergennes sent French officers to advise the Dutch army, and signed a treaty with the United Provinces which, for the first time in a hundred years, removed them from the British sphere. Joseph II now considered France an ally in name but an enemy in reality.[48] France, whose prestige had risen since its defeat of Britain in the War of American Independence in 1783, again helped thwart Austrian expansion.

Knowing the canals and villages of the area like the back of his hand, Ligne was appointed second-in-command of Austrian forces in the southern Netherlands and from October 1784 headed an army of observation stationed on the frontier between the Austrian Netherlands and the United Provinces. Longing for action, he boasted that he would grill the Dutch like herrings; they said they would make him swim like the ducks.[49] He lived in the Abbey of St Michael in Antwerp, where to pass the time he gave balls and supper parties, in a room lined with statues of saints. Candles and servants were in such short supply that his guests left as early as they could, while he repeated: 'Only I can give a party like this.'[50] Commenting on the presence of Ligne at the head of Austrian forces on the Dutch border, Vergennes wrote to Louis XVI a cutting remark that shows how Ligne was viewed by the King and his ministers, as opposed to the Queen and her friends: 'There is not one decent person who should not shudder when he sees the fate of humanity left in the hands of someone as frivolous (*léger*) as the Prince de Ligne.'[51]

For his part, Ligne was more anti-French than ever, and hoped there would be war between France and Austria within a year. Over French opposition to the opening of the Scheldt he told Vergennes: 'I love the country where I amuse myself most, but less than the honour of my Sovereign, who must for once be Master in his own house.'[52]

To soothe his despair at the lack of fighting, Ligne wrote a history of the campaign, which he called the War of Seven Days, after those of Seven Months (1778) and Seven Years (1756–63). He also entered into negotiations with noblemen from the Dutch province of Zeeland, who, claiming to be discontented with their Stadholder, the Prince of Orange, offered the position to Ligne (this may, however, have been a joke at Ligne's expense). In the end his prophecy to Sir James Harris that, after Maria Theresa died and he ruled alone, despite all his merits Joseph II would always have erections and never satisfy them – that his reign would be a continual priapism – came true. Despite all Ligne's efforts, few shots were fired in anger. French pressure ensured that a treaty gave Austria 20 million livres and minor frontier modifications, but the Scheldt remained closed.[53]

In addition to political resentment, Ligne soon had a personal reason for disliking France. Desperate for cash, he still wanted to add 'one more zero' to the sums he borrowed from 'those dogs of capitalists'. His problems would be solved by victory in his law suits over Corbie and Koeurs. 'The prince puts all his heart in it,' his banker Théaulon had written in 1784, and he appealed to the ministers Breteuil and Calonne, the Queen and the King himself. His wife, who had once threatened to wash her hands of her family like Pilate, was as usual more realistic. Bemoaning 'the fatality of the house of Ligne in all its affairs', she wrote: 'It seems to me that despite the credit attributed to him at the court of France the Prince succeeds in nothing.' She hoped that their son Charles would realise the great truth that 'the greatest *grand seigneur* without money has no more credit than a simple *bourgeois*'.[54] However, Charles de Ligne was almost as extravagant as his father. At the age of twenty-three he had gone to Paris to buy a collection of prints without telling his mother (his collection of prints and drawings, which by the end of his life contained nearly 2000 items, including forty-eight drawings by Raphael, eleven by Michelangelo and seven by Leonardo, was sold after his death to Duke Albert of Saxe-Teschen and is now part of the Albertina collection, one of the glories of Vienna).[55] Tormented by unpaid tradesmen, his mother had burst into tears and blamed Ligne for turning their children against her. Ligne, who disliked scenes, fetched his daughter-in-law to calm the Princess.[56]

In 1786, however, assuring Vandenbroucke that his presence at court would make the Koeurs case 'unlosable', Ligne visited Versailles for what proved to be the last time, going to the theatre with the Queen, strolling in the moonlight to the sound of violins with Artois and the Polignacs, and visiting the Chevalier Delisle, dying in the Hôtel de Coigny while a ball was going on in a nearby room. In the end he lost the case; the support of the Queen and Mercy-Argenteau was less important than the opposition of Vergennes (President of the Council of Finance as well as Foreign Minister), who considered Ligne too Austrian.[57] About this time he wrote a poem 'Mes adieux à Paris', complaining: 'In Paris more than anywhere people know how to dissimulate / No one lives or speaks there with an open heart.' After he left in January 1787, Ligne never saw France again.

Ligne was being pulled east. While his schemes in France failed, those in the Holy Roman Empire were succeeding. This apparently powerless collection of sovereign states still had enough vigour and unity to provide a focus for German patriotism and for Frederick the Great's attempts to oppose renewed Habsburg schemes for acquiring the Electorate of Bavaria. Since 1766 Ligne had been trying to fulfill his ancestors' plan to 'incorporate' their sovereign county of Fagnolles in the Circle of Westphalia (which included part of the southern Netherlands), in order to acquire the right to sit and vote with other Princes of the Empire in the Imperial Diet at Regensburg. He wrote letters to Vienna, capital of the Empire, Brussels, Düsseldorf, seat of the Directory and Chancellery of the Westphalian Circle, and the thirty-eight member states of the circle. Despite Frederick the Great's promise to help, and Ligne's presents of crates of Burgundy, it is possible that the Prussian minister Baron von Crumpipen delayed the application because Ligne was Catholic and Austrian, and Prussia wanted to help the Protestant, anti-Habsburg party in the Westphalian Circle: rivalry between Catholic and Protestant counts in the Circle of Westphalia paralysed the entire Imperial Diet in 1784–5. Finally, having becoming an immediate County of the Empire in 1770, Fagnolle was incorporated in the Circle of Westphalia in 1786 and Ligne received the right to sit in the Diet at Regensburg.[58]

The Russian, as well as the Holy Roman, Empire was drawing Ligne away from France. In 1780, in the first letter Catherine had written to him, she had invited him to come and watch serenades, balls and operas beside the Black Sea – a reference to her plans for southwards expansion. The friendship between Russia and Austria was closer than ever. Panin had resigned in 1781, the year that a secret Austro-Russian treaty was signed. In 1782 Catherine had written to Joseph proposing a division of the Ottoman Empire and the creation of a new Greek empire in Constantinople under her younger grandson Constantine. In 1783 she won a triumph by annexing the Khanate of the Crimea, and most of the north coast of the Black Sea. For three centuries the Khans of Crimea, descendants of Genghis Khan, had ruled their Muslim Tartar subjects as vassals of the Ottoman sultan. From Vienna to Astrakhan their armies had served as an Ottoman spearhead; their slaving raids had stocked the markets of Constantinople. The Tsars of Russia had paid them tribute. However, their power declined after 1650: by annexing the Khanate, a Muslim state guarding the Black Sea approaches to Constantinople, Russia had given the Ottoman Empire a greater shock than its loss of Hungary. Catherine promised Ligne a property on the site where, according to Greek myths (and Gluck's acclaimed opera of 1779 *Iphigénie en Tauride*), Iphigenia had served in the Temple of Diana before being sacrificed to the gods. Referring to the laurels he had failed to win fighting the Dutch, she consoled him by inviting him to 'come and gather some in Tauride where they grow all over the countryside and be assured that I will be delighted to receive you there and to assure you myself of the distinguished sentiments I have for you.'[59]

Writing from Vienna, where he was spending a few weeks in the usual round – service in the Imperial antechamber, visits to Prince Kaunitz, dinners with Prince Rosenberg-Orsini, excursions to the theatre with Prince Louis Starhemberg – Ligne called it 'the letter which has given me most honour and pleasure in my life'. Early in March 1787, bearing a letter for the Empress from Joseph II, Ligne arrived with his two sons in Kiev, the mother of Russian cities, where Catherine was waiting for the ice to melt before starting the journey down the river Dnieper to the Crimea.[60]

Even Catherine admitted that Kiev was 'abominable'. Yet people from all over the world had been drawn to this city of huts and mud by the prospect of a voyage in the train of the Empress of Russia. Among them were old friends of Ligne such as a courtier of Artois known as *le beau Dillon* and Nassau-Siegen; Paul Jones a hero of the War of American Independence; and Miranda, one of the earliest partisans of the independence of Latin America (who found Ligne a nauseating flatterer).[61] Discontented Poles had come to plot with Russia against King Stanislas Augustus who, forbidden by law to leave Polish territory, was waiting for the Empress further down the Dnieper in the miserable town of Kamiev. Another friend from Paris, the Comte de Ségur, who had become French ambassador to Russia at the age of thirty-two, was particularly pleased to see Ligne. He wrote:

> Affectionate with his equals, popular with the lower classes, familiar with princes and even sovereigns, he put everyone at their ease, stood on ceremony with no one, wrote verses for every woman; adored by his family, he lived with his children as their companion rather than their father, seemed to have no

secrets from anyone, and never revealed those which were confided to him ... his frivolity was so varied, so amiable, so amusing and so free of all malice that one loved even his faults.

After a few days, Ligne left to take Joseph II the Empress's itinerary, returning to Kiev on 4 April.[62]

Ligne was happy, because he was in a court at the centre of events; moreover, as he wrote to his staff in Brussels, he was living 'at the expense of the North', so they could economise on his household expenses.[63] He told his beloved Christine that 'it is her [the Empress's] simple manner which is so attractive'. She talked of battles and conquest as other women talked of knitting. In the Empress's intimate society, meeting every evening at dinner, Ségur taught her how to write French verse, while Ligne dashed off poems on the horror and boredom of marriage. Ségur remembered that 'The Prince de Ligne did not allow the slightest dullness ... The only person who said everything that came into his head, he added a dash of politics to his charades and portraits and, although his gaiety sometimes resembled madness, from time to time he threw in among his jokes useful and penetrating aphorisms.'[64]

As in 1780, the need to keep Catherine allied to Austria and hostile to Prussia contributed to Ligne's display of charm. Whereas the Austrian ambassador in France, Mercy-Argenteau, considered Ligne an embarrassment, his colleague in Russia, Count Louis Cobenzl, praised Ligne to Joseph II on 25 April:

Her Majesty the Empress has done me the honour of telling me very often that if it depended on her she would like to have him all her life in her society. She added that in every way he was an extraordinary man and that she believed he had real qualities on the level of the charm of his wit. His presence, and the footing he is on here, can only have a good effect; he lets miss no opportunity to speak of the attachment of Your Imperial Majesty for the Empress, and to launch sarcastic remarks against the new King of Prussia [Ligne's butt of 1780,

RUSSIA   119

who had ascended the throne as Frederick William II in 1786],
which in the present situation go down very well.

With the Empress was the eleventh of her twelve documented
lovers, Count Mamonov, a handsome young guards officer who,
in Cobenzl's words, 'satisfies the Empress in every way':[65] from
the colour of his uniform he was known as 'the red coat'. Ligne
wrote later of 'the Pompadours of Russia': 'Lover of the
Empress of Russia is a court office. I have known almost all of
them ... They are aides de camp: do not give themselves airs in
front of her, and very little or not for long in front of others.
There is not the slightest indecency. Nor even a predilection in
public. I have sometimes been the judge in the quarrels between
the Empress and Mamonov.' Despite the public decency, she did
once say to Ligne, looking tenderly at Mamonov when the
weather was very hot: 'Admit that that rascal has very beautiful
eyes.'[66]

One reason for Catherine's invitation to Ligne was her desire
for publicity for her new conquests. No one else but Ligne knew
or corresponded with so many people. The best record of this
historic journey, half state visit, half house party, comes in
Ligne's letters to a friend in Paris called Mme de Coigny. Born
in 1760, she had been a convent friend of *la petite Charles*, as he
called his daughter-in-law, whom he had got to know at Spa in
1783. Her father the Marquis de Conflans, one of Ligne's com-
panions in debauch – and the first person to wear a plain tail-coat
or *frac* at the Paris opera – was famous for a remark made at her
wedding. The bridegroom's father, the Duc de Coigny, said that
he felt rather shy as he had never been to supper with Mme de
Conflans before. M. de Conflans replied: 'My God, nor have I.
Let us go together and give each other courage.'

Mme de Coigny was beautiful and fashionable. Marie
Antoinette, whom she hated, said that Mme de Coigny was
Queen of Paris; she was only Queen of Versailles. Ligne
thought that at twenty she combined the wit of Mme du
Deffand, the tact of Mme Geoffrin and the taste of the Maréchale

de Mirepoix. To the writer Rulhière, who claimed that he had committed only one bad act in his life, she retorted: 'When will it finish?' Since he knew she would show his letters around Paris, she was a natural correspondent for the Prince de Ligne. He described the splendour of Catherine's half-oriental court at Kiev. 'Ah! Good God! what commotion! what uproar! what a lot of diamonds, gold, stars and cordons, without the Holy Spirit! Chains, ribbons, turbans and red, fur or pointed bonnets!' There were so many Caucasian princes, bearded Russian archbishops, and Polish uhlans that 'Louis XIV would have been jealous of his sister Catherine, or he would have married her, simply in order to have a fine *lever*.'[67]

Once the ice had broken on the Dnieper – which with wistful classicism they called, after its Greek name, the Borysthène – they embarked from Kiev on 1 May, one day before the Empress's fifty-ninth birthday. 'Cleopatra's fleet', as Ligne called it, consisted of four luxurious and elegant galleys, each with its own orchestra. One was for the Empress, Mamonov and her 'tester' Mlle. Protasova; one for Potemkin and his three niece/mistresses; one for Ligne, Ségur, Cobenzl and Fitzherbert (Harris's successor as British ambassador, with whom Ligne had often discussed Shakespeare when Fitzherbert had been British minister in Brussels); one was a dining room; and there were forty other boats for the court. Ségur remembered that every morning Ligne knocked on the partition separating their beds, and 'woke me up to recite to me impromptu verses and songs which he had just composed, and soon after his footman brought me a letter of four or six pages which mixed wisdom, folly, politics, gallantry, military anecdotes and philosophical epigrams in the most original manner'.[68]

Ligne now entered the greatest *jardin anglo-chinois* of all. Wherever they stopped, gardens had been created, and crowds of peasants summoned by Potemkin. Higher than ever in the Empress's favour, he was Viceroy of all Russia south of Kiev, as well as President of the War College and Admiral of the Black and Caspian Sea fleets. In case Catherine died, he was planning his own kingdom in the south, as a vassal of Poland, where he had purchased vast estates, and so had a personal motive for his improvements. Towns, villages and huts were decorated with so many garlands and triumphal arches that they looked like palaces. The weather was wonderful. The Empress was particularly amiable, describing the different peoples of the Empire and constantly taking a miniature of Peter the Great out of her pocket to ask herself what he would have done. She was so relaxed that she proposed they call each other *tu*: Ligne began by calling her *Ta Majesté*. The food was good. Everyone enjoyed themselves, except Fitzherbert. He could not hide his boredom and described the entire journey to London as 'rather tedious'.[69]

Soon they drew near to King Stanislas's court at Kamiew. Despite his efforts at constitutional and cultural revival, using the considerable powers still at the disposal of the Crown, the King of Poland was reduced to behaving as a suppliant. Yet again showing political ambition below the façade of frivolity, Ligne had been sending letters to a minister of Stanislas, with advice on how to behave towards Catherine, based on 'what I have endeavoured to have said to me' by the Empress. The King should talk not of politics but of the pleasure of seeing Catherine again, for the first time since the end of their affair thirty years earlier: 'the grace of his conversation, supported by that of his face, will revive a lively interest'. In order to help the Austro-Russian drive against the Ottoman Empire, and perhaps to further his own Polish ambitions, Ligne presented himself as 'the most zealous of the apostles preaching the true religion': Polish–Russian friendship. The King should offer to join in the forthcoming war against the Ottomans, in order to acquire Moldavia for Poland.

Using the ardent, confident style that had charmed the Empress, Ligne also wrote to the King himself: 'Sire, it is not the self-importance of a busybody which emboldens me to the point of daring to lay my respectful homage at the feet of Your Majesty; it is my heart which sets off and which cannot stop itself from expressing its feelings.' He passed on flattering remarks about the King made by Mamonov or Potemkin, and assurances from foreign ambassadors that the interview with Catherine would be 'as brilliant as it will be touching and triumphant'. Only fear of offending 'one' (Catherine), and letting her believe that Stanislas's court at Kamiev was more amusing than her own, had prevented Ligne from paying court in person.[70]

On 6 May, while cannon were fired and orchestras played, Stanislas finally appeared on Catherine's galley with the words: 'Messieurs, the King of Poland has charged me to recommend to you Count Poniatowski.' But Ligne's prophecies proved vain: after half an hour alone together in a cabin, the King and the Empress emerged looking embarrassed. Their talks had led nowhere: Catherine had rejected the offer of a Polish alliance against the Ottoman Empire. Dinner on board ship was gay; but the King could not hide his distress. At Kamiew he gave a magnificent display of fireworks, followed by a ball; but the Empress did not come, and next day 'Cleopatra's fleet' swept on. As Ligne wrote to Mme de Coigny, the King of Poland had 'spent three months and three millions to see the Empress for three hours'.

Ligne tried to console him, later writing of a conversation with 'le grand homme aimable femme' – Catherine – about the interview. 'She said to me, "I have still forgotten to talk to you about it. Did I not appear really foolish? What does the King think?"' Ligne passed on her praise for the King's grace and merit, and her regrets: 'It is a pity that we were too much in public. Why did Prince Potemkin and you always leave us like that?'

Ligne assured the King that the Empress had left so soon, only 'because she feared a slight embarrassment, of several kinds, and that she would have been annoyed that people could have said that she kept the Emperor waiting because of Your Majesty.' The Empress and Potemkin, utterly seduced, were resolved to uphold the King's authority against his enemies in Poland; Ligne predicted, quite wrongly, a reign of thirty glorious and peaceful years, roses and perhaps laurels after thorns.[71]

On 19 May, in contrast to her indifference to the King of Poland, when she heard that Joseph II had arrived, Catherine left her galley and, accompanied by Ligne, rushed to meet him outside Kayduc near the mouth of the Dnieper. His simplicity was a contrast to the pomp surrounding the powerless King of Poland. Accompanied only by Count Kinsky and two servants, he arrived in Ligne's own travelling coach, made in Vienna, which the Emperor called 'ridiculous', 'a real mess'. He was happy to behave as one of the Empress's courtiers, but complained to Ligne that, much as he wanted to, it was impossible for him to flatter her. 'First my dear ambassador does it at a furious pace and hits her on the nose with great swings of the incense burner. You do it without appearing to, as if you cannot help it: you do not do too badly. Ségur also with madrigals and songs and even that devil of an Englishman, Mr Fitzherbert, with a bored or annoyed or rather exaggerated air: his flattery is even more piquant.'[72]

Ligne remembered rescuing Joseph II from a situation that, at that time, appeared merely embarrassing. Foraging for sex among servants and peasants was common at a time when they were dependent on their masters. The second day after his arrival the Emperor had 'caressed' a serf girl early in the morning. Her master arrived in fury, threatening to complain about this Austrian officer (as Joseph II appeared to be) to Potemkin: the Emperor could understand the Russian's curses because he knew Czech. Ligne went to find the girl, took liberties with her in his turn, threatened her master with Russian swear words and above all the sight of his Russian uniform, and settled the affair. To the Emperor, who had been hurt by Ligne's gesture of independence in wearing a Russian rather than an Austrian uniform, Ligne said: 'See what a Russian uniform can do.'[73]

The cavalcade then moved on by land to the Crimea. Travelling between Catherine and Joseph II in a sumptuous carriage, Ligne heard the two monarchs talk of anonymous letters, assassination attempts and, with especial joy, the failings of their fellow-monarchs. Catherine said of George III's loss of the War of American Independence: 'Rather than sign the separation of thirteen provinces like my brother George, I would have shot myself.'[74]

Ligne's belief that personalities, rather than profound political causes, shape the fate of nations received partial confirmation. It was not nationalism, economic forces, or even pressure from their ministers, but their rulers' personal ambitions that drove Austria and Russia to unite against the Ottoman Empire. Catherine II and Joseph II boasted of the size of their Empires and their armies. 'I need an army of six hundred thousand men from Kamchatka to Riga, counting the loop down to the Caucasus,' said the Empress. 'With half that I have just what I need,' replied the Emperor. They discussed plans for what Ligne called 'a jolly war' against the Ottoman Empire, and wondered which provinces they should annex. On the other hand it was the growing and fundamental political, military, medical and demographic weakness of the Ottoman Empire, never described by Ligne, which enabled Joseph II to raise the question that was to haunt Europe for the next hundred and fifty years: 'What the devil shall we do with Constantinople?'[75]

When they finally arrived at Bahceseray, the former capital of the Khans of Crimea, the sixteen horses pulling their enormous carriage down a slope bolted and were only stopped by the Empress's Tartar escort crying 'Allah! Allah!'; as Ligne wrote, sixty million people almost changed rulers in a minute. After years of travel in the Holy Roman Empire, France and 'the North', Ligne now entered a new world: the Ottoman Empire.

Ligne was seduced. Surrounded by Circassians, Cossacks and Caucasian princes 'whose skin is finer and whiter than that of almost all our duchesses, except one or two', he did not know where or in which century he was. With what pleasure this addict of the exotic wrote to Mme de Coigny, on 1 June:

I am in the harem of the last Khan of Crimea, who was quite wrong to raise camp and to abandon, four years ago, the finest country in the world to the Russians. Fate has destined for me the room of the prettiest of the Sultan's wives and to Ségur that of the first of her black eunuchs... There are in our palace (which is a mixture of Moorish, Arabesque, Chinese and Turkish) fountains, small gardens, paintings, gilding, inscriptions everywhere, among others in the very strange and very splendid audience chamber, in gold letters in Turkish around the cornice: 'Despite the envious the whole world knows that there is nothing in Isfahan, in Damascus, in Stambul as rich as here'.

Over half the population of the Crimea had fled, died or been 'moved', but Ligne admired the politeness, kindness and cleanliness of the remaining Tartars and Turks: it was a change from the noise and insolence in the streets of Paris.[76]

Younger at fifty than Ségur at thirty, Ligne insisted on catching sight of a Tartar woman. They crept up behind a party of women who had taken off their veils to swim in a river but decided that Mohammed was right to want them veiled: they were not even 'passable'. The cries from the outraged women sent them flying for safety, pursued by Tartars brandishing daggers. When Ligne recounted the story at dinner that evening, Catherine, who was careful not to offend her new subjects, was shocked and said: 'You are in the midst of a people conquered by my arms; I want their laws, religion, customs and prejudices to be respected.' For once Ligne fell silent.

On 1 June they saw the magnificent spectacle of sixteen ships of the Russian Black Sea fleet, recently completed on the orders of its Grand Admiral, Prince Potemkin, at anchor in the harbour of Sebastopol, one of the many cities he had founded. Catherine was overwhelmed, and danced for joy in front of Ligne, laughing like a madwoman, clad because of the heat in little more than a shift. When the fleet fired a salute, she rose to her feet and proposed a toast to Joseph II, 'my best friend'. She reiterated that she owed all they saw to Prince Potemkin.[77]

Exhausted by court life, Ligne and Nassau-Siegen decided to break away and inspect the estates Catherine had given them at

Parthenizza and Massandra respectively on the southern tip of the Crimea. Escorted by Cossacks and Tartars, they advanced through magnifcent woods, barely avoiding plunging into ravines. When they finally reached Parthenizza on 4 June, Ligne was enchanted. His new domain included fifty-six Tartar families and groves of vines, figs and palm trees.[78] He composed verses for statues he planned to erect in honour of Catherine and Potemkin. While Nassau-Siegen went on to visit his estate at Massandra, Ligne wrote a letter to Mme de Coigny (extensively reworked when published in 1801), sitting on a Turkish carpet in the shade of two enormous walnut trees.

For once he was away from crowds and conversation. Sitting on a Turkish carpet surrounded by classical ruins, Muslim tombstones and views of the Black Sea, he felt at the edge of his world, outside time and space. Adopting fashionable Rousseauesque attitudes of disillusion and melancholy, and even the literary tradition of hostility to courts (as old as, and perfectly compatible with, attendance at them), he passed judgement on his life:

> I feel a new person ... I ask myself where I am and by what chance I am here. That gives me the opportunity to enter into myself and, without realising it, I go over all the follies of my life ... I ask myself why, liking neither constraint nor honours nor money nor favours, and having everything necessary to ignore them, I had spent my life at Court, in every country in Europe.

He asserted that he preferred repose and an author's life: 'I will be read; it is a way of not ceasing to exist. And so one kills oneself working for posterity which is not in the least grateful.' Seeing the classical ruins surrounding him, he thought that London and Paris might meet the same fate and claimed to share the indifference of the Turks: 'After my children and two or three women whom I love, or think I love, to distraction, my gardens are what gives me most pleasure in the world.' But he was hardly ever in them. Even military glory he pretended to

think 'nothing'; his own, he realised, with characteristic perception, was partly charlatanism. 'I play to the gallery too much. I
prefer the courage of my dear good Charles who does not check
to see that people are watching him.' Like friendship, love and
gardens, ambition led nowhere. His love of the gallery, his rest-
lessness and frivolity left him unsatisfied. Which of the Duc de
Croÿ's prophecies, made when Ligne was nineteen, 'that he
might subsequently either become truly great or, if he followed
his presumption or his imagination, turn out very badly', had
Ligne fulfilled? Then he woke from his moment of truth to hear
the muezzin's call to prayer from a nearby minaret, and flocks
bleating their way home, and rode back to rejoin Their Majesties
at Karassbazar.[79]

Back in the world of courts and careers, they were surprised
to receive news of a revolt in the Austrian Netherlands. Joseph
II left in a hurry for Vienna. The Emperor, who had written to
Lacy: 'Ligne is perfect here, and he is behaving very well for my
interests,' was happy for him to stay in Russia.[80] On the journey
back to St Petersburg Ligne travelled in the same carriage as the
Empress, with Countess Braniska, one of Potemkin's nieces, the
Grand Chamberlain Shuvalov, Cobenzl and Mamonov. Ten
times a day he threw gold ducats out of the carriage window,
which landed on the backs of the crowds of villagers come to see
the Empress: he claims that they stayed lying head down, flat on
their stomachs, for half an hour before she went by and a quarter
of an hour afterwards. Travelling in such intimacy, Ligne sometimes snapped at Catherine. When she repeated stories against
Marie Antoinette, he said: 'People lie in the North about the
West, Madame, as in the West about the North; you should no
more believe the street-criers of Versailles than the coachmen of
Tsarskoe Seloe.' There was plenty of champagne, but he died of
hunger, 'for everything is cold and detestable at the Empress's
table, who does not stay there long enough, and who takes so
long to say something agreeable or interesting that nothing is
hot, except the water we drink'.[81]

The return journey took them to Poltava in the Ukraine,

where they inspected the site of the defeat of Charles XII of Sweden in 1709 by Peter the Great, which had been the foundation of the greatness of Russia. Catherine said: 'You see what empires are made of; one day can decide their future. But for the Swedish mistakes, which you have pointed out to me, Messieurs, we would not be here.' Past Tula, where Catherine showered him with presents of Russian furniture made of steel, they arrived in Moscow, the ancient capital, where Catherine was not appreciated. Ligne claimed that the graces had jumped across the Holy Roman Empire directly from Paris to Moscow and even further. 'We have found women who are charming, wonderfully dressed, singing, dancing and perhaps loving as angels.'

In Moscow in July, as Catherine intended, Ligne continued his career as a Russian propagandist. In western Europe people had been making fun of their journey. The phrase 'Potemkin villages' entered the German language as a synonym for deception, since it was believed, erroneously, because of the decorated façades, that Potemkin had had entire villages transported to line the Empress's route. With his instinctive cosmopolitanism, Ligne never shared what he called 'the low jealousy felt in Europe' for Russia. To Mme de Coigny, he had admitted that some towns 'lack streets, the streets lack houses and the houses lack roofs, doors and windows'. Some of the cries of joy as the Empress passed by might have been produced by the whip. The infantry was unimpressive, famine raged in the Empire and too much had been built in haste.[82]

However, like everyone who went to the Crimea with Catherine, even Joseph II, Ligne was more impressed than sceptical. On 3 July he was happy to send Baron Grimm in Paris a long letter clearly destined for a wide audience; the present quotations come from a copy found in the papers of Gustavus III in the library of Uppsala University, and it was also published in a newspaper. He wrote: 'To reassure so many people well intentioned for Russia, I will say that after a charming navigation on the Boristhène, we found ports, armies and fleets in the most brilliant condition; that Cherson and Sebastopol surpass

Ligne at the age of seven, in front of the chateau of Beloeil, the family seat in the Austrian Netherlands. Symbolising his military destiny, the prince is wearing a sword and fashionable 'hussar' clothes, and holding a massive gun.

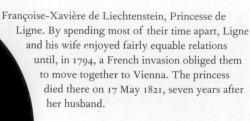

Françoise-Xavière de Liechtenstein, Princesse de Ligne. By spending most of their time apart, Ligne and his wife enjoyed fairly equable relations until, in 1794, a French invasion obliged them to move together to Vienna. The princess died there on 17 May 1821, seven years after her husband.

'The leading *grande dame* of Vienna', Princess Auersperg was mistress of the Emperor Francis I, and of his young chamberlain the Prince de Ligne, in the early 1760s.

The actress Angélique d'Hannetaire was the principal mistress of the Prince de Ligne in the 1770s and 1780s. When he was away on campaign, they wrote to each other every day.

Countess Rosalie Rzewuska, by Sir Thomas Lawrence. Despite or because of her viper's tongue, this Polish Countess, half a century younger than Ligne, held the leading place in his heart between 1808 and 1814.

Young, beautiful, Genevan, Madame Eynard was the last 'enthusiasm' of Ligne in the autumn of 1814, during the Congress of Vienna. Painting by Horace Vernet.

Christine, Princess Clary, the eldest and favourite daughter of the Prince de Ligne,
welcomed him every summer after 1794 in her castle in Teplitz. Both there and in Vienna,
she acted as his secretary, copyist and companion. Her father wrote that he lived only for her.

Prince Charles de Ligne was Ligne's elder son and favourite child,
from the shock of whose death, fighting the French Republicans in 1792,
he never entirely recovered.

Ligne's younger son, Prince Louis de Ligne, ancestor of the present Princes de Ligne, is wearing the uniform of his regiment, the Dragons de la Reine. He served in the French army before deserting to the Austrian army, during the campaign of 1792. After 1803 he lived in Beloeil, which he had recovered from the Republican authorities.

In Vienna, Euphémie de Ligne, Countess Palffy, 'Féfé' to her friends and family, lived close to her parents in a palace in the Wallerstrasse.

TOP: Painted by Bernardo Bellotto for King Stanislas Augustus, this picture shows Warsaw three years before Ligne's visit in 1780. ABOVE: The most elegant city in the Empire and one of the crossroads of Europe, Dresden, painted here by Bellotto in 1765, was frequently visited by Ligne after 1794, in order to see his publishers, the Walther brothers.

TOP: This view of Schönbrunn by Bellotto commemorates the arrival, in Maria Theresa's principal country palace, of news of her army's victory over the Prussians on 16 August 1759: it symbolises the transformation, in her reign, of the Habsburg monarchy into a military monarchy, which Ligne served throughout his life. ABOVE: In 1789, when Ligne and his son helped take Belgrade for Austria, it was still, as its minaret-crowned skyline suggests, a Muslim city, and a bulwark of the Ottoman Empire. This print, dedicated to Prince Charles de Ligne, still hangs in his father's bedroom in the former Clary castle at Teplitz, now Teplice in the Czech Republic.

everything one can say of them; and that every day was marked by a great event' – military manoeuvres, dinners in magnificent tents erected in the middle of the steppe, fireworks, illuminations and balls. Ignoring the deterioration in their condition under Catherine the Great, who did less for her peasants than Maria Theresa for hers, and the Tartars' resentment at the expansion of serfdom into the Crimea, he claimed that Russians 'are serfs only in order not to harm themselves or others but are free to enrich themselves as they often do, as one can see by the richness of the different costumes of the provinces we have traversed. 'The Empress was adored, she had built 237 towns in stone, the Crimea was rich with forests and orchards, and he offered 1000 louis to anyone who could prove that anything he had said was untrue.'[83]

For the following three months, Ligne was established at Tsarskoe Seloe, waiting for war with the Ottoman Empire to break out. He behaved as a Russian courtier, attending the Empress's supper parties, or watching plays in the private theatre she had just built in the Hermitage, with Mamonov, Potemkin, Ségur and a few others. In one play, *L'Amant ridicule*, written by himself, he created a Polish character called Le prince Ridiculowsky, no doubt to please the Empress.[84]

By a miracle of tact and warmth, Ligne managed to be in favour with both Catherine and her son the Grand Duke Paul, the future Paul I (1796–1801) who, on the rare occasions they met in public, found it difficult to conceal his resentment of his mother and Potemkin. Ligne had met the Grand Duke in St Petersburg in 1780, and again in 1782, when Paul was touring Europe as the Comte du Nord. He was already so paranoid that he had believed that some beer Ligne gave him on a barge going from Ostend to Bruges was poisoned on his mother's orders. Ligne wrote to Kaunitz: 'He is extremely changeable; but during the short time that he wants something inside himself, or loves, or hates, he does it with violence and obstinacy.'

Ligne liked Paul and it is a tribute to Ligne that, in his presence, this gloomy and suspicious prince appeared 'gay in society', and revealed some of his inner thoughts. Through his father, the murdered Peter III, Paul was also Duke of Holstein in the Holy Roman Empire and at heart remained a German prince. At Gatchina, the barrack-like palace outside St Petersburg that Paul had turned into a private military haven with guards in Prussian-style uniforms, he interrogated Ligne about the journey to the Crimea and the state of the army.[85]

Ligne told Paul: 'There was deception but there was a lot of reality.' No villages had been transported; the Empress had been robbed but not deceived. Besides, she could not run everywhere and see for herself. 'Oh! I am well aware of it,' replied the Grand Duke, according to Ligne; 'it is for that reason that my bitch of a nation only wants to be governed by women' – an alarming description of his future subjects by an heir to the throne.[86]

Although they both longed for conquests, neither Joseph II nor Catherine was ready for war in the summer of 1787. The Ottoman Empire, a great power allied to France and Sweden, was not as easy to devour as Poland. Fear of the reaction of Prussia, England and above all the oldest ally of the Ottoman Empire, France, held back Joseph and Catherine. As so often, events in Constantinople changed the history of Europe. The people of Constantinople and the Grand Vizier Yusuf Pasha were outraged by the fate of the Muslims of the Crimea and the Caucasus and by what they considered Russian 'insolence', 'insatiable ambition' and 'revolting bad faith'. The loss of the Crimea was an unparalleled shock.[87] Threatened with deposition if he did not act, Sultan Abdul Hamid I declared that so long as Russians remained in the Crimea, the Ottoman Empire was like a house with no doors, which thieves could enter at will. Indeed one of Potemkin's triumphal arches had borne the inscription: 'The Gate to Byzantium'. The imprisonment of the Russian ambassador in the fortress of the Seven Towers in Constantinople on 16 August meant war.[88]

Ligne was overjoyed, for war gave him a chance for glory and fulfilment. As his moment of doubt at Parthenizza revealed, his career had not yet been as impressive as he had hoped. It is true that he had seduced, and recorded, monarchs and writers across Europe (his wife, in exasperation, wondered when he would stop 'playing the Wandering Jew').[89] His rank and open-mindedeness, and the universal acceptance of French, had enabled him to lead a European life, playing a unique collection of roles: Flemish *grand seigneur*, Austrian officer, French writer, Prince of the Holy Roman Empire, Polish noble, Russian courtier and publicist. If he had had his way, he would also have been a Spanish volunteer, at the Siege of Gibraltar in 1782.

Yet the variety of Ligne's successes had also worked against him. His Austrian loyalties had helped to prevent him winning his law suits in France. He had spent so much time in Paris and at Versailles that he had not penetrated the inner circle of power and influence in Vienna. He had written innumerable verses, plays, memoirs, letters, and works of military theory, but had not won fame as a writer. He had the talent and knowledge to write about gardens, but lacked the money to create his own garden at Beloeil. His wildness in behaviour and conversation had made him a person whom people, such as Maria Theresa or Vergennes, found hard to take seriously. Despite Angélique and Henriette Auersperg, was his love life, into which he poured so much energy, satisfactory? Was there an edge of envy in his words to Nassau-Siegen, writing long letters to an adored wife from the Crimea: 'I cannot understand why and to whom you have so much to write'?[90] Above all, because the wars of Joseph II, with Prussia in 1778 and the United Provinces in 1785, had been so short, he had not acquired the military glory that he craved. A war with the Ottoman Empire was the opportunity he needed.

Turkey

The idol dearest to my heart', for Ligne, as for most eighteenth-century nobles, was military glory.[1] The chance to win it might have been provided by the outbreak of war. He was a favourite of his sovereign, Joseph II, and an experienced soldier of fifty-two. However, Ligne was a prisoner of his own charm. His reputation as a courtier overshadowed his qualities as a general. Joseph appointed him not to a major military command, but as Austrian liaison officer with the army of Prince Potemkin, stationed in the Ukraine.

Austro-Russian relations were the key to the course of the war – indeed, until their final breakdown in July 1914, to the fate of eastern Europe. Joseph II instructed Ligne to inform him and Marshal Coburg, the commander of the Austrian army stationed in Transylvania, of 'the real size of Russian forces and not that which is on paper'. Twice a week he was to send an exact record of events and Russian plans to the Emperor in French, on separate pieces of paper marked: 'For His Majesty Alone'.[2] Exploiting their personal friendship, Ligne was to ensure that Potemkin remained full of *bons* [i.e. pro-Austrian] *sentiments*, and that, while Austria stayed neutral, his armies took the offensive. Joseph II ended the first letter of their long correspondence with words of praise, and an Imperial pun, which suggest that while Joseph II used, he also resented, Ligne's intimacy with Catherine: 'Adieu, my dear Prince, I am delighted that your zeal has made you desire an occasion which gives you greater opportunity than would service in the Line [Ligne] to display the full extent of your talents and to justify the confidence you have acquired among this foreign Nation.'[3]

Catherine saw Ligne's new position differently. She wrote to Potemkin on 18 October 1787, in that dismissive tone which Ligne's ambitions often provoked, that despite his desire for an active command and the opportunity to take Belgrade, Ligne was reduced to acting the spy. The Empress was harsh. Since the Ottoman Empire had declared war on Russia but not Austria, Ligne had already, without success, asked Marshal Lacy, in view of his close friendship with Potemkin, to be employed on active service with the Russian army.[4]

Wearing the uniform of a Russian general, eager for action, Ligne left St Petersburg on 1 November 1787. When he arrived at Potemkin's headquarters at Elizabethgorod (now Kirovograd in the Ukraine), only fifty miles from the Russian–Ottoman frontier, his first words, as they embraced, were: 'A quand Ochakov?' A minaret-crowned fortified city between, and controlling, the estuaries of the rivers Dniester and Bug, Ochakov was the main Ottoman naval base on the Black Sea, with about 30,000 inhabitants. It was both a potential threat to Russian shipping and possession of the Crimea and, like Belgrade, a bulwark of the Ottoman Empire.

After the bewitching dream of the Crimea, reality broke in. Potemkin replied that he had no resources and that there were more soldiers inside Ochakov than in his entire army.[5] Ligne wrote: 'Russia really feels the weakness behind its colossus ... All the fine schemes to chase the Turks out of Europe and turn Constantinople into a republic have been forgotten ... The seductive curtain which hid the paucity of real strength is unfortunately raised. Always what is superfluous and never what is necessary.' It was impossible to believe one word said in the armies: Russia was 'a land of fiction'.[6]

Ligne rapidly changed his mind about Potemkin. He wrote: 'I have nothing to tell the War Council for nothing is being prepared.' The Russian army lacked pontoons and bullets, and the siege had not begun. Potemkin had ruined the infantry, and Russian officers were so servile that, if Potemkin dropped anything on the ground, twenty generals bent down to pick it up.

He could conquer his enemies at court more easily than those on the battlefield or behind walls, and spoke of giving back the Crimea.[7] Austria and Russia were as suspicious of each other as the USSR and its Western allies would be in World War II. Ligne soon felt that the Russians were deliberately delaying their offensive until the Ottomans had thrown themselves against Austria.

Lodged in a room so small that he could have opened the door and the window from his bed, if they had worked, Ligne thought wistfully that at the same time at Versailles the Queen's balls were about to begin. His only consolation in Elizabethgorod was the prospect of chasing Tartars across the river Bug. There was no female company. For once, he wrote to Ségur, 'I have nobody; nobody has me.'[8]

When not trying to persuade Potemkin to take the offensive, Ligne spent the time learning Russian, gambling and supping at midnight with Potemkin, in a luxurious wooden palace especially built for him. From Beloeil the Princesse de Ligne, always loyal, sent her husband her own berline or travelling carriage (since Joseph II was using her husband's), horses, four hussars, two *valets de chambre*, a groom and a chef. He felt a melancholy pleasure listening to them shouting to each other in the middle of 'the deserts of Tartary', in the same yelping Walloon patois he had heard as a boy when playing with the village children. With the mixture of trust and condescension that Ligne felt for his wife, he told her to look after the family estates: 'You know the confidence I have in you and the good opinion everyone has of you; so work, my dear good wife, for me, for you and for our children as well as you can.' Since the Princess quoted it with pride in a letter to Vandenbroucke, this is one of the few passages in the correspondence exchanged during a marriage of fifty-nine years that has been found. However, despite a distance of a thousand miles, Ligne continued to conduct another campaign on his own: the law cases over Koeurs and Corbie, over which, indefatigably, he sent a stream of letters to Paris.[9]

Always ready for adventure, Nassau-Siegen soon joined him,

followed in January 1788 by a friend from France, a dashing young officer called Comte Roger de Damas. Desire for action, fear of boredom and the knowledge that 'the dear prince de Ligne, equal in humour, in kindness, in repartee ... never forgot anyone who reminds him of the Paris world in which he enjoyed himself most' had made Damas come to the Ukraine. Ligne was overjoyed to be joined by 'a charming Frenchman, a handsome young man, a nice fellow, *un Seigneur de bon goût de la Cour de France*'. They sang songs from the latest operas together and all three shared a house.[10]

Although it was a small town far from centres of civilisation, in 1788 Elizabethgorod was a political epicentre. It was at the junction of three Empires: Russia, Austria and the Ottoman Empire. The latter's decay allowed statesmen to plan to redraw the map of Europe. Lacy hoped that Austria would stretch to the Aegean. Potemkin and Catherine dreamt that Russia would win Constantinople. Across the Ottoman frontier from Elizabethgorod the Ottoman vassal principalities of Wallachia and Moldavia, in what is now Romania, might become a new state called Dacia under Potemkin, be annexed by Austria, or ceded to Poland.

Ligne was in his element, helping to decide the policy and strategy of both Austria and Russia. He saw Potemkin every day and corresponded with Joseph II, with Kaunitz in Vienna, the ambassadors Cobenzl and Ségur in St Petersburg, King Stanislas Augustus in Warsaw and Marshals Romanzov and Coburg at their headquarters. Sometimes Ligne's correspondence was so important that he used ciphers and his own couriers, but he generally preferred the post. Frequently intercepted and copied, it was a way of being read by the monarch, and thus of conveying approval or discontent while avoiding flattery or satire.

The war against the Ottomans could not be isolated from the struggle for ascendancy in Europe. Europe was dividing into three camps: Russia and Austria; what were called *les bourbons* (France and Spain); and England, Prussia and Sweden. Alarmed by the expansion of Russia and Austria, the last two blocs were trying to help the Ottoman Empire. In the east as in the west Austria was checked by France which, because they were both enemies of the Habsburgs, had been an ally of the Ottoman Empire since the sixteenth century. While Catherine had been on her triumphant progress to the Crimea, Ochakov was being fortified with the help of French engineers sent by Louis XVI and Vergennes. Another French ally, Ligne's friend Gustavus III of Sweden, spurred by the prospect of Ottoman subsidies, launched a daring attack on Russia in May 1788.

For Joseph and Kaunitz the principal aim of the attack on the Ottoman Empire, rather than Balkan expansion, was the destruction of Prussia, 'the greatest enemy of the court of Vienna'. By tying Russia closer to Austria, and winning an increase in Austrian territory unmatched by a Prussian equivalent, Austria would improve its strategic and demographic position before its next war with Prussia. Ligne's Polish connections, as well as his friendship with Potemkin, made him an important player in Austria's struggle with Prussia. As he wrote to Vandenbroucke, he was 'charged by the Emperor' with aspects of Austrian policy in Poland, which since the opening of the Great Sejm in 1788 appeared to be reviving in confidence and hostility to Russia: King Stanislas Augustus hoped that Poland would win Moldavia and control of the trade between the Baltic and the Black Sea. In the same letter begging King Stanislas Augustus for help in his financial negotiations with the Bishop of Vilna, Ligne had again urged him to offer to intervene on the side of Russia and Austria. A victorious Polish army would increase Polish territory and add splendour to his reign.[11]

However, many Poles were seduced by the mirage of a Prussian alliance, and by a Prussian plan for the Ottoman Empire to cede Moldavia and Wallachia to Austria, while Austria returned Galicia to Poland, and Poland ceded two vital cities, Thorn and Danzig, to Prussia. Ligne assured Prince Czetwertynski, and other Poles who had come to Elizabethgorod to see Potemkin, that Berlin thought only of devouring them and that they should trust Vienna. Claiming, quite untruthfully, 'I have no mission nor any talent for politics,' and that he was speaking entirely on his own initiative, without the Emperor's knowledge, he said that Joseph II had told King Stanislas that he wanted not one more tree in Polish territory. Ligne acquired copies of letters from King Frederick William II of Prussia and his ministers offering an alliance to Polish nobles, which he sent to Joseph II. In his turn the Prussian ambassador in Warsaw sent the King of Prussia copies of Ligne's letters urging the Polish nobles to trust Austria.[12]

From this period dates a perceptive and prophetic *Mémoire sur la Pologne* by Ligne. Calling Poland '*belle, grande et superbe* ... your fine nation which I idolise', and himself 'a compatriot who loves you', who had won the trust of Joseph and Catherine, Ligne advised Poles not to regret the last partition but to fear the next. Catherine's policy to Poland was relatively forbearing, because she knew that it was not in Russia's interest to exchange Russian influence over the whole country for territorial expansion in part of it. Poles should feel that it was a sign of trust rather than an insult that Potemkin had received them without his breeches on. Indeed Potemkin, who, like Ligne, had obtained Polish *indigénat*, favoured Poland and its king so much that he had bought them 40,000 guns that might be used against Russia.

Ligne repeated to the Poles Père Griffet's advice to him twenty years earlier: to stick to the throne. While, in 1788, the King of France was making himself into a King of Poland, by summoning the Estates General for the following year, the King of Poland should resemble a King of France in authority, wealth and military power. With a splendid and agreeable court, he could control the great nobles, and, 'by a chain of pleasures and distinctions', stop them spending money on trips to Paris – or, worse, to Berlin, Vienna and St Petersburg. A proper bank should be established in Warsaw, more freedom given to the peasants, provincial diets abolished, the silver ornaments in churches given to the state and Jews allowed to own land.

Always convinced of the importance of appearances, Ligne

also suggested the revival of Polish traditions (except drunkenness), such as the national costume of a long tunic and Polish
bonnet. Women should dress *à l'orientale*, rather than in the
latest models of Mlle Bertin. Above all the Poles should stay
quiet: if they moved they were dead.[13]

The last of the Habsburg–Ottoman wars that had been one of
the leitmotivs of European politics for three hundred years
broke out on 9 February 1788 when, finally honouring his obligations to his Russian ally, Joseph II declared war on the
Ottoman Empire: 140,000 well-equipped Austrian soldiers faced
the Turks. In 1787 Joseph had written to Ligne that he hoped for
a fortunate and short war, but the Ottoman Empire proved
stronger than expected – and its artillery had recently been mod-
ernised with French help.[14] Dreams of Austrian triumph vanished and, like Potemkin, Joseph II stayed on the defensive. He
admitted to Ligne that he dared not undertake the siege of
Belgrade 'so as not to have in such a delicate position all the
Ottoman might against me' – a strange confesssion from a
monarch who had devoted so much energy to improving his
army. The unreformed Ottoman army remained almost as formidable a force as the modern Austrian army. Ligne himself,
despite a screen of flattery, and praise for Joseph II's 'career of
glory', advised the Emperor to avoid adventures, even at one
time to make a quick peace.[15]

That summer the Grand Vizir Yusuf Pasha left Belgrade,
devastated the province of the Banat in Hungary and defeated an
Austrian army on 20 September. His advance was halted not by
Austrian resistance but by the over-extension of his own supply
lines. Roger de Damas believed that Austria's defeats, despite
the excellence of her soldiers and horses, were due to the hesi-
tancy and pessimism of her generals. Joseph II, who commanded the Austrian army in person, was appalled by what he
described to Ligne as the generals' 'unforgivable ineptness', and
fell ill. He blamed the Russians even more, telling Ligne that
they were 'ungrateful and insatiable'.

One of the few Austrian victories had been the storming of

the citadel of Sabatsch, west of Belgrade, which had been built three hundred years earlier by Sultan Mehmet the Conqueror. Bold to the point of foolhardiness, Charles de Ligne was the first Austrian officer to climb over the parapet. He wrote to Ligne: 'Vive la guerre, papa, et vive le Maréchal [Lacy]: me voilà lieutenant colonel et chevalier de Marie Thérèse' – honours bestowed by the Emperor in person. Joseph II wrote to congratulate the proud father, who told Charles that the letter made him cry. It was worth more than all their genealogical diplomas and parchments, which were 'nothing but food for rats'.[16] For Ligne, military success outweighed birth.

Apart from intriguing with Poles, and corresponding with Joseph II, Ligne also spent the long months with the Russian army observing Prince Potemkin. Combining physical details and psychological penetration, Ligne's portrait of Potemkin, like that of Frederick the Great, is frequently quoted by biographers. Ligne described Potemkin as 'the most extraordinary man there has ever been'. A collection of contradictions, he made diagrams with diamonds, had no desk but his knees, no comb but his fingers, and called himself 'the spoilt child of God'. With one hand making signs to women who attracted him, with the other signs of the Cross, he talked theology with his generals and war with his archbishops. Blasé about everything, he could be in turn a sublime politician or a child of ten. He wore either a dirty dressing gown or a superb tunic covered in orders and diamonds as big as fists, and had 'in turn the air of the proudest oriental satrap and of the most polished courtier of Louis XIV; under a great appearance of harshness, in reality at the bottom of his heart very kind; fantastic in his hours, his meals, his sleep, and his tastes, wanting to have everything like a child and capable of doing without everything like a great man'. His secret was genius, more genius and more genius.[17]

Ligne compared himself to a child's nurse: 'but my child is big, strong and rebellious. Just yesterday he said to me: "Do you think you have come here to lead me by the nose?"' If he could not make him act, Ligne was successful in making Potemkin talk. In one of the few contemporary references to the marriage that almost certainly united him and Catherine, Potemkin told Ligne that he could have been Duke of Courland or King of Poland, but 'I am much more than all that'.[18]

Ligne also tried to persuade the other Russian commander, the aged Marshal Romanzov, to take the offensive. Returning from Romanzov's headquarters at Kaminiiecz in Poland to those of Potemkin before Ochakov, Ligne wrote to Charles on 8 June 1788: 'I am constantly running between the armies and the marshals trying to make them do something. But the devil blocks the way, despite all their Russian signs of the Cross.' He had no idea whether they would meet again in Istanbul or Beloeil. Marshal Romanzov proved as unreliable as Prince Potemkin, despite loving letters to Ligne, regretting the 'delicious hours' they had spent together in Kiev. He admitted that he could have stopped the Ottoman invasion of Hungary by invading Wallachia but claimed to be prevented by lack of provisions. Joseph II was so enraged that he described Romanzov, in a letter to Ligne, as 'a damned Prussian and false as Judas as well'.[19]

One consolation was *la belle phanariote*, a beautiful twenty-two-year-old Greek girl bought in the Constantinople slave market by the French ambassador, stolen and subsequently married by General de Witt, governor of Kaminiiecz. Since all their servants were convicts, the Witts' house resounded with the sound of rattling chains. Travelling with her in a berline, Ligne wrote: 'Ah! If I still had a heart! how in love I would be! ... I confess to you that I felt more inclined to reconnoitre her and to find out her weak point of attack than that of the fortress.'

Back in Potemkin's camp, which had advanced from Elizabethgorod to outside Ochakov, they were entertained by his orchestra, directed by the great Italian musician Giuseppe Sarti, and by the 'terrible but beautiful illumination' caused by night-time bombardments, ordered by Potemkin as an after-dinner diversion. Reconnaissance expeditions were another occupation. Once, as Ligne and Potemkin were walking outside the walls of Ochakov, they were nearly killed by cannonballs. On another particularly foolhardy reconnaissance mission, Turkish cavalry almost captured Ligne as he was relieving himself. Using opera glasses as a telescope, he had assured Damas that approaching Turkish cavalry were merely trees waving in the wind.[20] Now that it was summer, Ligne lived under a massive Turkish tent, but found that he was either 'grilled, absolutely grilled' when it was shut or, if he opened it to get some air, was swamped by tarantulas, lizards and snakes.

Ligne's one triumph was to help Nassau-Siegen, rather than the American John Paul Jones, obtain command of an attack on the Ottoman navy. More generous than the Russians, who resented a foreigner's success, Ligne was delighted when Nassau-Siegen's four naval victories in June and July cut Ochakov off from Ottoman reinforcements. He wrote to Ségur: 'Nassau-Siegen by birth has become Nassau-Sieger [German for 'victor'] by his exploits ... His sword is his magic wand.' After these victories both Nassau-Siegen and the great Russian general Suvorov agreed that Potemkin's delay in attacking Ochakov was inexplicable. Ligne believed that with 6000 Croats he could have taken it in six hours.[21]

Ligne was seized by the fury of a middle-aged man who senses that he is missing a chance of glory. So often accused of being a flatterer, he started to be rude to Potemkin, who complained of being 'tormented by you, with insinuations that could be made only to animals or children'. For six weeks they did not speak. Feigning bewilderment, Potemkin wrote: 'My dear Prince, if you have a friend it is me. For the life of me I cannot think how I have let you down.' Ligne also stopped writing to Catherine, although if he had once praised Potemkin to her, he knew that he would have received 'showers of peasants and diamonds'. She would soon learn what he felt by intercepting his letters to the ambassadors Cobenzl and Ségur in St Petersburg.[22]

Despite the tension between Austria and Russia, Catherine, clearly fond of Ligne, asked him to make peace with her and to write to her every six months; she swore she would reply. Ligne did not blame the Empress. He believed, as he wrote to Joseph on 22 October 1788, that 'Her Majesty does not know one word of what is going on'. Indeed both Romanzov and Potemkin acted as they pleased. The Empress had been urging Potemkin to attack Ochakov since October 1787. When she ordered him to cross the Dniester, like many others of her servants, he disobeyed.

The reason why Potemkin hesitated to take Ochakov was his hope that secret negotiations with Turks inside the fortress would enable him to avoid Russian casualties. By the standards of eighteenth-century generals, Potemkin was exceptionally humane towards his own troops. Ligne was more callous. He wrote incredulously to Joseph, 'It is really to spare bloodshed that the prince uses ruses and money so much.'[23]

In October 1788 Ligne left for Marshal Romanzov's headquarters to settle disputes between him and Marshal Coburg over control of Moldavia. From 22 October to 15 December Ligne stayed nearby in the Moldavian capital Jassy, a city of 30,000 surrounded by gardens and orchards. Showing his confidence in the phlegmatic Vandenbroucke, who was in Poland trying to extract money from the Bishop of Vilna, he wrote that he had suffered enough from Russia not to serve in her army any longer. 'Anyone else would have hung himself out of boredom and anger with the Russians; but a book, my pen and a song easily console me. I embrace you just as I am attached to you, my dear Vandenbroucke, with all my heart.' He boasted that he had been extremely economical, had checked his servants' accounts and had achieved much on very little. He could have saved even more money if he had asked the Emperor to pay all his travelling expenses: 'but I wish to be the only person in the whole monarchy who does not deceive or plunder him'.[24]

Ligne was immune from the condescending contempt so often shown towards the smaller countries of Europe. Instead it was the two largest and most confident nation-states, France and England, that aroused his distrust. After a year of frustration at Potemkin's headquarters in the Ukraine, Ligne was enchanted by Moldavia and hoped that 'the tyrants of the Orient' (Turkey, Austria and Russia) would allow such a beautiful country to become independent – as they finally did eighty years later. He praised the 'infinite grace' of Moldavian houses, looking like small palaces, in one of which he lodged. In a late edition of *Coup d'Oeil sur Beloeil* he recommended building a Moldavian house, with one large columned room surrounded by divans and windows, and supporting a domed roof 'in the mosque style' – which he did, with extreme elegance, in the English garden at Beloeil. In Jassy, Ligne met members of the Phanariot elite of Constantinople, such as the Ghykas and Cantacuzenes, who had served as Princes of Moldavia since the seventeenth century, and had adorned the city with churches, schools and hospitals. Although they were vassals of the Ottoman sultan, they were allowed considerable autonomy. They maintained an elaborate Byzantine court and dreamt of reviving the Byzantine Empire. To Ségur he wrote that, although they could have been slimmer, the women were extremely attractive, and had arms of alabaster. They received visitors lying on divans, wearing 'an extremely light, tight and short skirt', and used worry beads, to indicate when and where they could meet their lovers. He was enchanted by their manners, their jewels – one costume had three thousand sequins – and their habit of clapping, rather than ringing or shouting, for their servants. So many of their relations had been executed by order of the Sultan or the Prince that they often had a sad look, but they remained part of the Ottoman world. Ligne noticed that 'Constantinople sets the fashion for Jassy as Paris does for the provinces, and fashions arrive even quicker'. That year yellow was the colour for women to wear and cherry wood instead of jasmine was used for pipes.[25]

Joseph II soon ordered Ligne back to Vienna. After two whole years in Russia and 'Tartary', he arrived in Vienna in January 1789. He criticised Potemkin and Romanzov repeatedly in public and swore that they would not take Ochakov until the next campaign. He was soon proved wrong. On 17 December 1788, after a six months' siege, the Russians had passed the Bug and stormed Ochakov. As Potemkin had planned, Russian losses were slight, but around ten thousand Turks were killed, in massacres that horrified even the assailants.[26]

After 'a very happy and very quiet winter in Vienna', no doubt spent in the company of Henriette Auersperg, Ligne was sent in early May 1789 to Semlin, on the Danube opposite Belgrade (one hundred and twenty-five years later it would be the site of the first gunfire of World War I, when Austrian artillery shelled Belgrade). The year before it had been the site of the Grand Vizier's victories and the 'graveyard of the Austrian army and honour'. Although Ligne caught a fever and almost died, he finally had an important military command. Belgrade was then a city inhabited by as many Turks as Serbs, which the Ottomans called Dar-al-Jihad, the House of Holy War, because it had been the base for so many attacks on the infidel. Ligne was in charge of 30,000 German, Bohemian and Italian troops, under one of his favourite commanders in the Seven Years' War, Marshal Hadik. Overwhelmed by the task of administration, he wrote to his beloved Christine: 'I leave you for a moment to sign my name a hundred times without being able to make one for myself in history.'[27]

Whereas Joseph II and Catherine II underestimated the Turks, Ligne belongs to that tradition of admiring fascination for the Ottoman Empire which, in the eighteenth century, partly because the Empire was still a considerable power, remained extremely strong. Ligne admired the Ottoman soldiers' method of firing and the advantage their lightness and mobility gave them over heavily armed Christians. Their tactics were imbecilic but they would be much worse if they imitated Western armies. They rarely took prisoners and their way of saying *Neboisee* or 'Don't be afraid', as they sliced off prisoners' heads had 'an astonishing effect on the Christians'. With irresistible cynicism he added: 'Anyway this cutting of heads does not do much harm to the dead, sometimes does great good to the wounded, and should stop people surrendering.' However, the opportunities for upward mobility in the Ottoman Empire dismayed him. What would happen to the peoples of Europe, he asked, if a soap merchant could become Prime Minister, a gardener Lord High Admiral or a footman commander-in-chief?

To Ségur Ligne praised the Turks' courage and lack of vulgarity. 'The young favourite of a Janissary, although he and even his master very often have bare feet and legs, and no shirt, is elegant in his own way and has a more distinguished air than the young lords of the courts of Europe.' The instinct of the Turks was often superior to the intelligence of the Christians: he saw captured soldiers refuse money, preferring to die from hunger rather than shame. Two Turkish prisoners, however, called Ismail and Osman, were happy to enter Ligne's household as servants; Ismail stayed with him until his death.

Ligne saw the good and bad in people – and countries – so clearly that he frequently contradicted himself. As a result he liked to construct his verbal portraits – like that of Potemkin previously quoted – through a series of contrasts. For him, although they had more good than bad qualities, the Turks were a people of antitheses. They were 'brave and cowardly, active and lazy, pious and pederast ... clean and dirty, one hand on roses, the other on a cat which had been dead for two days; and sometimes one hand on the charming contours of both sexes and the other on the Koran.' They thought Westerners ridiculous to prefer to be served by trusted old servants instead of having their coffee, pipe or incense burner brought to them in the morning by beautiful youths. With a passion that makes one regret that he never reached Constantinople, where he would certainly have contrived an idyll in the seraglio, Ligne added a manifesto of Orientalism: 'Observers, travellers, spectators, instead of making trivial reflections on the Nations of Europe, which all resemble one another, more or less; meditate on everything which comes from Asia, if you want to find what is new, beautiful, grand, noble and very often sensible.'[28]

Ligne's love for the Turks did not stop him wanting to defeat them. In August 1789 the great general who had beaten

Frederick, Marshal Laudon, replaced Marshal Hadik, while the conqueror of the Austrians, the Grand Vizir Yusuf Pasha, was dismissed for opposition to reform, and later executed. The attack on Belgrade began on 15 September. Under Laudon, whom he now considered the god of war rather than a human being, Ligne commanded the artillery bombardment. He remembered his anxiety that harm might befall his son Charles, who was serving under his orders, and the cries of fright as 12,000 globes of fire descended on the city. Although he still felt weak from his fever and wrote that he had to take quinine to take Belgrade, Ligne proved more successful in attacking Turks with gunshot than Prince Potemkin with arguments.

Like the campaign in Bohemia ten years earlier, the campaign in 1788–9 was one of the few occasions when Ligne emerged, briefly, from his milieu of French-speaking courts and salons. He had used Serbian in secret negotiations with Turks at Semlin, and now from his bedroom window shouted orders in Italian to a flotilla on the Danube.[29] On 8 October Belgrade fell to Austrian forces, followed a few weeks later by Bucharest. Ligne was rewarded with the cross of a Commander of the Order of Maria Theresa, which he described, with habitual hyperbole, as 'what has given me most pleasure in my life'. Laudon wrote to Ligne that he owed 'a large part of the happy end to the active, effective and cooperative action of Your Highness, who certainly greatly contributed by the attack made from the direction of his command'.

Within a few minutes of the cease-fire, Ligne saw Janissaries' turbans beside grenadiers' busbies, as the former enemies began to trade and drink together. While corpses drifted down the Danube, 'there was at the same time a smell of death, burning and rose essence'.[30] A smell of death was also spreading across western Europe. In Silesia Prussian troops were gathering for an attack on Austria. In Vienna Joseph II was on his deathbed. In the Austrian Netherlands, opposition to Austrian rule had developed into a revolution. In Paris the royal family were living as prisoners in the Tuileries Palace, after an infuriated mob had invaded the palace of Versailles, battering down the doors into the apartment of the detested Austrian Queen, where Ligne had so often joked and gambled, shouting that they wanted to cut off her head, eat her heart and stew her liver, and they would not stop there.[31]

Belgium

'But is he a patriot for me?' Joseph II's nephew the Emperor Francis II once asked, when one of his subjects was praised for being 'a good patriot'.[1] As both Emperors knew, and as the fate of Louis XVI and Marie Antoinette would show, patriotism, by placing loyalty to a nation above loyalty to a monarch, was a potential threat to the monarchies of Europe. It could even seduce a courtier like the Prince de Ligne.

Ten years before, in a long *Mémoire sur les Pays-Bas autrichiens*, Ligne had assured the Emperor that his patriotism was sublimated in his loyalty to the monarchy, 'my passion for the service [the Austrian army], and my attachment for him who renders his head-quarters more admirable than the throne' – another swing of the incense burner before Joseph II.[2] A print published in the late 1780s* is a graphic expression of Ligne's Austrian patriotism. Eyes on fire, hair dishevelled, an earring in his left ear, he wears an Austrian lieutenant-general's uniform. The great dynastic Order of the Golden Fleece hangs from a ribbon around his neck. Below is the caption *Pro Patria non timidus mori*: 'Not afraid to die for his country' – apparently meaning Austria.

However, *patria* was about to acquire a new meaning. Joseph II was determined to mould the different nations and provinces of the monarchy into what, with imperial *hauteur*, he called 'one mass directed in the same manner'. In January 1787, while Ligne was in Kiev, he replaced local privileges and traditions treasured since the Middle Ages with a modern, uniform administration. Joseph II even obliged every village fair to fall on the same day.

* Possibly in 1788, at the time of the Austro-Turkish war.

From the Cardinal Archbishop of Malines down, the population of the Austrian Netherlands turned against the Emperor.[3]

The rebels showed none of the lack of identity of which Belgians are accused today. Abandoning the old dynastic term of the 'Austrian Netherlands', they began to claim the rights of the 'Belgian nation' (after the provinces' Latin name). Provincial estates, including those of Hainaut, refused to vote the normal subsidies. In return the Emperor suspended their privileges.[4] In a crucial act of linguistic imperialism, the 'Belgians' appropriated the word 'patriot'. Ligne referred with revulsion to 'this ridiculous name Patriot, once so admirable'.[5] Joseph II himself complained that a 'spirit of turbulent and mistaken patriotism' was sweeping Europe.[6]

Taken by surprise, no friend of priests, Ligne at first denounced the fanaticism of a revolt led by monks, and the 'ridiculous and insolent masquerades of the volunteers' – armed bands beginning to appear in the Austrian Netherlands.[7] Yet in the course of 1789, torn between two worlds, while serving Austria, Ligne began to feel the appeal of 'Belgian' patriotism. He had always been proud of coming from 'the first country in the world', boasting that one was nothing if one was not 'from Flanders, from Flanders, from Flanders'. The Flemish, in his opinion, combined French gaiety and sense of honour with German patience.[8] His glamour, his hospitality and his attempts to open the Scheldt had made him personally popular in the Austrian Netherlands – although, in an aside that astounds at a time when all Belgians are obliged to learn both Flemish and French, Ligne said that he knew a few words of Flemish only because he had bothered to learn a little German.[9]

Ligne did not live in a closed world of courts and salons. Unlike many *grands seigneurs*, he was ready to talk to anyone he met. He had taken market women, in tears because of a rise in the cost of herrings, to see Charles of Lorraine, and had tried to stop a riot over the price of butter. Another tie to 'the Belgian nation' was his membership of the ancient religious brotherhoods characteristic of its Catholic fervour – the Brotherhood of

Saint Dorothy in Brussels, or the Brothers of Mercy in Ath. Equally characteristically, in his mania for uniformity Joseph II had replaced all such brotherhoods by one 'Brotherhood for the Active Love of your Neighbour'.[10]

The Princesse de Ligne helped turn her husband against Austria. By virtue of her marriage and long residence in Brussels and Beloeil, this Austrian princess considered herself *flamande*.[11] In 1789 she too became a patriot for Belgium. She visited her husband's regiment draped in the black-and-yellow colours and lion of Brabant (with Flanders, one of the most violently anti-Austrian provinces). Adopting the language of a Paris sansculotte, she hoped for an end to 'the yoke of tyranny'.[12]

Moreover Ligne himself, like many of his friends, felt stirrings of that aristocratic resentment of absolute monarchy which was one of the driving forces of eighteenth-century revolutions. His stories about keeping the King of Poland and Joseph II waiting (see above, p. 109) suggest a subconscious resentment of his courtier's role. His family strategy was not centred on Austria alone. In February 1789 he wrote to Leygeb that his main motive in making Fagnolles into a free county of the Empire had been to 'try and aggrandise ourselves a little in that direction and to become a bit more free'.[13]

Joseph II formally abolished the constitution of Brabant in June 1789, telling the Estates 'I do not need your consent to do good'. Thereafter the 'patriots' started to raise troops in the Austrian Netherlands. In his memoirs Ligne says that he was approached to join them during the siege of Belgrade, but replied with disdain: 'I never revolt in winter.' However, the journey of one of his adjutants, Captain Dettinger, from Belgrade to Brussels in November 1789, and rumours printed in gazettes, led Joseph II to suspect Ligne of disloyalty. The Emperor wrote him a harsh letter (not preserved with the other Imperial correspondence) and ordered him into 'a sort of exile', with his troops, in the fortress town of Peterwardein, further up the Danube from Belgrade. At Peterwardein Ligne learnt of the violent hostility to the Emperor's centralising measures and new

German-speaking officials raging in another proud and ancient nation, Hungary. The Emperor had even removed the national talisman, the crown of Saint Stephen, to Vienna.[14]

Meanwhile, in Flanders the patriots' army of 20,000 was expelling badly led Austrian troops with remarkably little bloodshed. One prominent patriot was Ligne's younger son Louis. In 'the four Days of Ghent' on 13–16 November, he fought in the 'patriot' army that expelled Austrian troops from the capital of Flanders. Although he soon returned to his regiment in France, the archives at Beloeil contain a testimonial of gratitude from patriots for the help of 'an illustrious House which was long dear to the Nation'. In December 1789 all Austrian regiments, including the Régiment de Ligne, withdrew from the Austrian Netherlands to the sole remaining loyal province, Luxembourg.[15]

Through Lacy Ligne apologised for his son's 'culpable conduct', and received the Emperor's permission to return to Vienna, where he arrived on 30 December 1789. The sight of the Emperor, shattered by news of revolts throughout the monarchy, and dying of cancer, brought tears to Ligne's eyes. Nevertheless, the prospect of a collapse of Austria briefly made 'the Belgian Nation' seem more attractive than the court of Vienna. On 3 January 1790 Ligne wrote to his patriot wife a letter that was printed in the Brussels newspapers: 'I cannot believe it. There has never been in history, and I say more, there will never be such a revolution ... It is certainly impressive for our Nation to have expelled the Austrians with as much humanity as valour and to have covered half a dozen generals with shame.'

He expressed admiration for the 'heart' and 'courage' of the leaders of the revolution, Vandernoot and Vandermeersch, and scorn for the cruelty and stupidity of Austrian officials like the Governor-General Duke Albert of Saxe-Teschen and the Emperor's minister in Brussels Prince Trautmansdorf.

Being almost at the head of the armies, and always in the last two years commanding considerable corps, you will understand that my career is too far advanced for me to quit the service. I will be neither a traitor nor ungrateful: and that would not even please my nation. I will neither serve against it nor with it against the Emperor. But I will serve it to the last drop of my blood against all the other powers of Europe.[16]

Ligne puts his career in the Austrian army before dynastic loyalty or Belgian patriotism, but clearly wants to join the winning side. There seemed no doubt which it was. In January 1790 a 'Sovereign Congress of Belgium' deposed Joseph II and issued a revolutionary constitution modelled on those of France and the United States. On public buildings throughout the land the red bonnet of liberty replaced the black double-headed eagle of the Habsburgs.

Ligne's letter, which he later called *une sottise*, is so uncharacteristic that for a long time historians denied its authenticity. Ligne may have had other reasons for sending it than simple self-interest. He subsequently claimed to have written it at Joseph II's suggestion in order to learn the rebels' intentions, to safeguard his estates and chateaux from the patriots, and 'make myself useful to my Sovereign and my country by reconciling them'; only Vandenbroucke had made it public. However, at the time the Princess guaranteed his sincerity, adding – another sign of Ligne's disloyalty to his Emperor at his time of need – that 'the P. has refused to the Emperor to come here as negotiator'.[17]

Moreover, a letter from his son Charles to Charles's best friend Pepi (Prince Joseph Poniatowski, nephew of King Stanislas Augustus, formerly an officer in the Regiment de Ligne and aide de camp of Joseph II, who had taken part in the storming of Sabatsch with Charles de Ligne) on 4/5 January 1790 confirms that the Ligne family – who were talking politics day and night – were planning to turn 'patriot':

my country is calling me and I am leaving in two or three days with my father: God knows if I can stay in the Service; God knows if I should do so; God knows if my country will be a republic, if we will give ourselves to the Prussians or the Austrians. If I leave and make war on the Austrians I seem like a deserter. If I stay in the Service I seem like a traitor to my fatherland; if I leave and stay doing nothing my blood will boil in my veins to see others fighting and fighting for the good cause and I would seem like a fool[?].[18]

Ligne's threatened disloyalty to the Emperor who had favoured him shows that his 'restless flutter' could affect his political, as well as his personal, loyalties. He liked to worship the rising sun, whether it was another monarch or a successful revolution. The flexibility of mind and tastes that made him love both Vienna and Paris, books and battles, Mme de Coigny and Marie Antoinette, and won him friends and lovers wherever he went, also led him, for a few weeks, to sympathise with a revolution. However, Ligne was more loyal to Austria than most Belgian nobles. Headed by his d'Arenberg cousins, he rallied to the revolution with enthusiasm. The Duc d'Ursel even returned his chamberlain's key.[19]

Moreover, the umbilical cord connecting Ligne to the Habsburgs could not be severed in a month. He belonged to that aspect of European culture which derived force and identity from courts not nations, tradition rather than revolution: in the end he remained a patriot for the Emperor. After a month of admiration for 'the fine revolution which had been so fortunately accomplished', he wrote to Vandenbroucke, who continued to support it: 'seeing that the low country [le plat pays] was not taking part, that you only had a few adventurers at the head of your armies [in other words that they would lose] I found that you were not making a national war and that it was all a matter of the personality of a few individuals'.[20] Ligne chose Austria rather than Belgium. Reverting to his courtier's personality, on 14 February 1790 he wrote to Mercy-Argenteau asking for the post of Grand Bailli (Governor) of Hainaut, promising that he would not permit the slightest change in its traditional constitution.[21]

Feeling that he had failed in everything, Joseph II finally died on 20 February, in the middle of the Vienna Carnival: the sound of the public masked balls, or *redouten*, in the Hofburg reached him on his deathbed. Ligne wrote that before he died Joseph II had muttered to him: 'Your country has killed me,' and kept repeating the word *avanie*, or affront. But he also said things so touching that Ligne would never forget them. He was succeeded by his younger brother Peter Leopold, Grand Duke of Tuscany, who reigned as Leopold II.

One of the ablest rulers of the eighteenth century, Leopold II had turned Tuscany into a model state of the Enlightenment. In 1790, he was to be responsible for one of those miracles, like the defeat of the Ottomans in 1683, or Maria Theresa's appeal to her subjects in 1740–41, by which the Habsburgs confounded their enemies and restored their fortunes. In most of his dominions discontent began to subside as he suspended his brother's reforms and returned to the situation in 1764. On 7 April Ligne wrote to Vandenbroucke: 'There has never been a finer start to a Reign. Every day is marked by a new benefaction or by the righting of an injustice.' Cursing the names of aristocrats and democrats, he would return to Beloeil only if the Austrian Netherlands returned to Austrian rule – though he still refused to fight to ensure that outcome.[22]

The monarchy's external position remained perilous. Dismayed by the Austrian victories over the Ottomans in 1789, Frederick William II of Prussia, a monarch with vast ambitions, was encouraging the rebellion in the Austrian Netherlands and plotting to depose the Habsburgs from the throne of Hungary. As tension between Austria and Prussia rose, Ligne was forgiven his flirtation with revolution, and received an important command under Marshal Laudon, the conqueror of Belgrade, in the army stationed on the Austro-Prussian frontier. War did not break out, but at Alt Titzseten in Moravia, Ligne watched the death agony of Marshal Laudon. 'What an occasion to watch die and suffer a great man whom one has seen so often make light of death and who at last falls into its hands like an ordinary mortal!

In truth Marshal Laudon had been longing for it for eight days because of the terrible sufferings caused him by a surgeon's incompetence.' In his bad French, the old hero said: 'Cher prince de Ligne, je suis terrible!' and died on 14 July.[23]

Soon afterwards peace negotiations began between Austria and the Ottoman Empire. Despite Austria's victories in the Balkans, Leopold was so eager to avoid a war that he made peace (finally signed in August 1791) on the basis of a return to Austria's frontiers before the outbreak of war in 1788. With fateful consequences for Austria's future control over its South Slav subjects, and for its ability to act as a Slav alternative to Russia, he even agreed to return Belgrade. Ligne, for whom the expansion of Austria was an article of faith, was furious. He wrote: 'Everything our blood and our struggles, above all mine, at Belgrade, had won for the glory and size of our monarchy was absolutely lost.'[24]

Ligne and Joseph II had had much in common. They were both cultivated, strong-willed men of the world, and the Emperor had found relief from his own seriousness in his chamberlain's frivolity. Both were Austrian expansionists. However, the cautious and secretive Leopold II had distrusted Joseph II both as a man and a monarch. This distrust had been increased by the violence of Joseph's reforms and extended to the late Emperor's friends. After 1790 Ligne no longer benefited from the motor that had driven him through the 1780s: the Emperor's favour. He disliked Leopold II and wrote that the new Emperor had imbibed in Italy the milk of dissimulation.

Leopold further annoyed Ligne in October 1790 at his coronation as Holy Roman Emperor at Frankfurt. Enraged because he was made neither Marshal nor Governor of Hainaut in the coronation honours, Ligne resigned all his commands, even his regiment. Leopold pretended to have lost the letter of resignation and wrote a meek reply, promising him 'your desired, deserved and promised promotion', future employment, 'and we will be good friends as before'.[25]

Despite his lack of rapport with Leopold II, in 1790, for the first time in his life, Ligne became Viennese. That year, or possibly earlier, he rented a house in the west of Vienna, on the Moelkerbastei, one of the *basteien* or ramparts around the old city, which had been built in the Middle Ages and strengthened to withstand the Turks.[26] The house was so small that it had only two rooms on each floor, connected by stepladders instead of stairs. 'Each room was furnished with a few straw chairs, a pinewood table and a few other small objects of equal magnificence,' wrote an incredulous visitor from Paris. His friends called it 'the parrot cage'.

From the Moelkerbastei Ligne had a splendid view over the empty land between the ramparts and the suburbs. He could also see a vine-cloaked hill towering above Vienna called the Kahlenberg, where, possibly at the suggestion of a favourite cousin, Prince Ludwig Starhemberg, who lived nearby, Ligne had, some time before 1790, acquired a country residence. It was the equivalent, for him, of Sans Souci, the Hermitage and the Trianon – a retreat from the obligations of society and marriage. While Romantic poets were celebrating the beauty of deserted monasteries, Ligne lived in one. He rented communal buildings, and eight monks' cells (in reality small houses), which had been part of a monastery of the Kamaldulensian Order dissolved as a result of Joseph II's religious reforms in the 1780s. Ligne loved the Kahlenberg so much that in 1790 he entered into possession, for life, of buildings in another disused monastery, a quarter of an hour's walk away on the neighbouring mountain of the Leopoldsberg, which he called *mon réfuge*.[27] With his love of the exotic, he soon transformed his new residences, adding Egyptian, Turkish and gothic rooms on the Leopoldsberg, a theatre and more Turkish rooms on the Kahlenberg. Inscriptions in Latin, French and Turkish appeared on the walls – including the Ligne motto, especially resonant in time of revolution: *Quo res cumque cadunt, stat semper linea recta.*[28]

Like Beloeil, the Kahlenberg is at a geographical and historical crossroads. As Ligne wrote, it is 'at the head of the Alps', at their easternmost point, where they meet the most European of

rivers, the Danube, on its way from its source in the Black
Forest to its mouth on the Black Sea. Below the Kahlenberg lie
Vienna and the Marchfeld, the plain where in 1278 Rudolf of
Habsburg had laid the foundations of the Habsburg monarchy,
by defeating Ottokar, King of Bohemia. The Kahlenberg is also
the site where in 1683 John Sobieski of Poland heard mass
before leading his army to victory over the Turks besieging
Vienna.

It has views not only over Vienna but far into the hills of
Moravia, the plains of Hungary, and the mountains of Styria.
The fashionable portrait painter Mme Vigée Lebrun, a favourite
of Marie Antoinette and friend of Ligne, who stayed there in
1794, was entranced: 'I floated above the Danube, divided by
islands beautified by superb vegetation, and above countryside
as far as the eye could see; *enfin c'était l'immensité.*'

Ligne himself wrote:

> Here I am alone. It is truly my refuge. I would defy even the
> cleverest artist to know more about decorating this site than
> Nature, my gardener. You never tire of the wonderful spec-
> tacle of Nature. It helps to expand the mind which is limited
> because of the sense of sight ... Storms and the rising and
> setting of the sun or moon restlessly renew the same
> tableaux ... Depending on the weather or the light, I look on a
> Claude Lorrain, a Poussin or a Vernet.[29]

There have been greater writers than Ligne, but none has
chosen a more dramatic place in which to write.

Love was one reason for Ligne's move to Vienna. Vienna had
the advantage of distance from his wife, and certain phrases in
Zinzendorf's diary suggest that Ligne's love affair with
Henriette Auersperg was at its height. Her husband, fully occupied with her maid, was no obstacle: in September 1790, again
according to Zinzendorf, Ligne told Henriette that in the eyes of
God they were man and wife. The Princesse de Ligne, always
realistic, assumed that a woman was behind her husband's installation on the Kahlenberg: he would give it away, 'when a new

inclination will replace that which at present keeps him so constantly in that country'. His love for Henriette means that Angélique's name now disappears from Ligne's correspondence – as it does from other sources. All that is known is that the ageing actress went to live in Paris.[30]

Public events and private decisions were inextricably intertwined in Ligne's life. Vienna had greater appeal for this Austrian courtier than the two revolutionary capitals Brussels and Paris. Leopold II and Mercy-Argenteau had skilfully exploited a split in Belgian revolutionary ranks into two violently hostile camps, of 'aristocrats' and 'democrats',* known from their leaders' names as Vandernootistes and Vonckistes. In December 1790, Austrian troops recovered the Austrian Netherlands as easily as they had lost it. The Princess, who had remained an enthusiastic patriot, was furious. Thenceforth, Brussels was a divided and embittered city, to which Ligne felt no desire to return.

France, the other focus of Ligne's life, was even less appealing. After the attack on Versailles on 6 October 1789, violence continued. Ligne wrote to Kaunitz: 'Louis XVI in the Tuileries is on the road to the scaffold.' Ligne's friend the Marquis d'Albertas, one of the first nobles to offer to give up his privileges, was murdered in his garden at Gemnos on 14 July 1790, in the middle of a fête held to celebrate the revolution.[31] Ligne wrote to Mercy-Argenteau that autumn: 'I think without ceasing of the unfortunate Queen and am more afraid than ever for her at the hands of all the monsters whom I will never see, for I will never set foot again in either Paris or Brussels.' He intended to visit Beloeil for only four months a year.[32]

Ligne's attitude to the Revolution confirms that books do not cause events, that support of the Enlightenment did not necessarily lead to support of the Revolution: indeed Ligne linked the Enlightenment and the counter-revolution. His radicalism of the

---

*The terms indicate not social origin – each side included both nobles and non-nobles – but political beliefs. 'Aristocrat' meant defender of the traditional, 'democrat' supporter of a modern, constitution. Ligne's cousins the Arenbergs were enthusiastic democrats.

1760s, when he had attacked God, kings and his own class, had continued in the 1780s. In *Mélanges de Littérature*, printed in 1783, he had advocated full civil rights for French Protestants, the expulsion of monks and the application of the wealth of the Church to the relief of the poor in Paris – five years before such measures began to be put into effect. Ligne himself was generous to the poor throughout his life. With characteristic honesty, he wrote: 'I give very often but it is almost always to defend myself against importunities or out of weakness. I suffer too much when I see suffering. I deserve little credit for it…' In 1782, travelling through a village in Lorraine, he saw a family whose house had been burnt down. On arrival in Paris, a servant ordered the Prince's banker to send them fifty louis d'or 'and told him above all not to enter the sum in his accounts in order to hide knowledge of this good work'.[33]

However, at the first signs of revolutionary violence, like hitherto radical monarchs such as Catherine II and Leopold II (and most surviving writers of the Enlightenment – Raynal, Rivarol, Marmontel – except Condorcet), Ligne turned conservative. Three days after the opening of the States General at Versailles, when France was convinced it had broken with the past and entered a new era of Liberty, Equality and Fraternity, Ligne wrote from the banks of the Danube in contempt of 'the three orders without order and the constitution discussed by so many people whose brains are ill constituted'. The people were now for him nothing but 'a maddened animal'.[34] The anger, hunger and poverty behind much of the popular violence, the hatred for the *ancien régime*'s unworkable complex of privileges and feudal dues, left him indifferent.

The 1789 Revolution was completely unexpected. Looking back several years later, Ligne wrote that everyone explained it in their own manner. *Dévots* blamed it on the *philosophes*; libertines on the absence of a royal mistress; ministers on the King's refusal to trust them completely; the *parlements* because they were not like the Parliament of England; peasants on their taxes; soldiers on the requirement to be noble to become an officer (because he was not born noble, Marshal Laudon would not have become a Marshal in France). Presenting himself as an 'observer and man of the world', Ligne saw the Revolution, as he did most historical events, in personal and emotional terms.

For him 1789 was the result of a change in mood, and an unsatisfactory court. A courtier, not a political or economic analyst, he defined it as:

LES SOTS, LES SCÉLÉRATS, LES GENS D'ESPRIT
ERREURS HORREUR STUPEUR.[35]

For Ligne it was a portent of revolution that, after 1780, the love of pleasure that had devoured the Paris of his youth began to lose its appeal: 'people saw each other too much and too early...Elegance consisted in not having any.' Public affairs, which would have bored men fifteen years earlier, interested them more than deciding what clothes, scent, and wigs to wear. Men were becoming less amiable and, above all, more oppressive to women. His friend the Maréchal de Richelieu, who had spent a lifetime being disrespectful to women in private, was the last man truly polite to them in public. Instead of love letters stating the hour at which they would be at their mistress's feet, men wrote *mémoires* on freedom. In 1782 Ligne had prophesied: 'I hardly see any more desire for amusement. People accept a uniform pattern of life, an unbearable monotony. Is the world coming to an end?'[36]

Ligne had a courtier's explanation, both at the time and later, for the outbreak of the Revolution. The monarchy could have been saved if France had had a different king and a more satisfying court. Ligne had written in 1787, only two years before the court was driven from Versailles by a popular uprising: 'Never has a People been more made for a Court.' It had not been created in order to think but to obey while amusing itself, being responsible for nothing. 'A king of France who could have provided his nation with fêtes, victories and gratifying successes of every kind would never have had to face a revolution. France has only become ungovernable since it most regrettably ceased to be frivolous.' The violence and egalitarianism of the revolutionary leaders were caused by disputes over words rather than things, wounded vanity rather than outraged principles: 'To ridicule the first bourgeois author who wrote against the Nobility, he had to be made a baron ... the wit would become the proudest of barons.'*

If Louis XVI had been less indulgent, if he had made his court more splendid, if, like contemporary monarchs, he had been 'a military king' who inspected and exercised his troops in person, and was not ashamed to wear their uniform, he would have given his subjects emotional satisfaction and secured their loyalty. Ligne, who believed that magnificence was a natural support of monarchy, also wrote that Louis XVI's disbandment of part of the traditional royal guard, the Maison Militaire du Roi, was a disaster: 'This people at once ferocious and frivolous, was impressed by this magnificent body of men.' Ligne's main criticism of Louis XVI was that he was not Maria Theresa.[37]

Ligne's courtier vision limited his perception. In his portraits of Joseph II or Catherine the Great (and later of Napoleon), he described their characters and their manners, rarely their reforms, ideas or system of government. In 1789, it was not simply human failings in the King and his court, but also desire for a new society and constitution, based on citizens' rights, not feudal privileges, reason rather than tradition, and equality before the law, which led, in France, to the most drastic break with the past Europe had yet seen. No longer would Frenchmen endure a system so confused and archaic that, to take an example from Ligne's life, the lawsuits he pursued over Koeurs and Corbie could last for decades. Ligne could not understand revolutionaries' passion for Liberty, Equality and Fraternity, since before 1789 he had enjoyed all three: Liberty to do what he liked, Equality with the crowned heads of Europe, Fraternity in the hunt for pleasure. Indeed Ligne later called Liberty and Equality 'a mystification'.[38]

*Indeed the Abbé Siéyès, author of the incendiary pamphlet of 1789, *Qu'est ce que le Tiers Etat?*, would accept the title of Count from Napoleon I after 1808.

Yet Ligne's belief that the French Revolution was caused by the human factor was not absurd. Chance events, such as the personality of Louis XVI and mutiny in his remaining guards' regiments – personal emotions like fear, or desire to join the winning side – did affect its course. If Louis XVI had kept the support of the army, he might have survived. Aspects of his reform programmes resembled those of the National Assembly. The Revolution was a product of, as well as a break with, the old regime. As Claude Arnaud has written, every future revolutionary had had some connection with the old regime and every future counter-revolutionary had espoused the prevailing liberal ideology before 1789.[39] They could have gone either way.

For example Vandermeersch, a leader of the Belgian revolution, had been an officer in Ligne's regiment: it is said that anger at lack of promotion fuelled his readiness to fight against his former comrades.[40] Most of Ligne's French friends were royalists who also favoured radical reform. The Abbé de Périgord, Narbonne, even the epitome of frivolity the Chevalier de Boufflers, supported the early stages of the Revolution. Inspired by a mixture of weakness and ambition, the Duc d'Orléans opposed Louis XVI and began to call himself Philippe Egalité. Orléans's chief adviser was Laclos, who now pursued 'dangerous liaisons' of a political rather than a sexual kind. Ligne wrote that his old friend had become 'an execrable, cowardly, vile and cruel monster', without even *les honneurs de la scélératesse*.[41] He should be burnt and quartered.[42]

After Ségur returned to Paris from St Petersburg in 1790, he also rallied to the new regime. In his letter severing contact with 'Louis Ségur', Ligne proved a good prophet. He warned that there was bound to be a throne even if the Bourbons were replaced by a dictator or a daring young prince. France would be governed by a 'sceptre of iron'. 'That is the result of liberty. You will become slaves and you will deserve it.' In Ligne's opinion, Ségur's radicalism was caused, not by frustrated ambition – he had been an ambassador at thirty-five – but by too much time spent in his study instead of salons or antechambers.

He noticed revolutionaries' corruption of the French language: 'So farewell verses and songs!... Farewell love affairs and gallantry... You will all be very boring... What horrible expressions! *Necessity of crime, individuals' misfortunes leading to the general good, to the lantern.*'[43]

Driven by loathing of Marie Antoinette, Mme de Coigny, with whom Ligne still corresponded, also supported the early stages of the Revolution. She wrote that the Queen was 'too insolent and too vindictive not to take pleasure in putting her in her place and taking her from the King's, which she would like to usurp'.[44] In reality, far from being put in her place, Marie Antoinette intrigued in secret with both left and right, to save her life and win power. The Revolution did not kill the Queen's party. Through a friend and cousin of Ligne, a Belgian 'democrat' called the Comte de La Marck, she subsidised the leading orator of the left in the National Assembly, Mirabeau. She also maintained a network of agents outside France, under another friend of Ligne, a former French ambassador to Vienna and royal minister, the Baron de Breteuil. Using forged letters of Louis XVI, they worked to persuade foreign powers to intervene in France. Hatred of the Austrian Queen helped to make French patriotism revolutionary and anti-monarchical.

While the Queen was plotting in Paris, Ligne put his counter-revolutionary views into practice by acting as unofficial agent for the leader of the French *émigrés*, his old friend the Comte d'Artois. His distrust of the French monarchy disappeared when it was in trouble. Artois's chief adviser, Calonne, 'le plus loyal et le plus aimable des hommes', had been a friend of Ligne since the years 1778–83, when, as intendant of French Flanders, he had visited Beloeil so often that Ligne called him his *co-seigneur*. As controller-general of finance between 1783 and 1787, Calonne had been no help over Ligne's law suits. Nevertheless, after Calonne passed through Vienna in January 1791, they became political allies.

They met by chance during a masked ball. Ligne promised Calonne to try to persuade Leopold II, whose chamberlain he was, to make war on France. With a frivolity that needs no comment they prepared a code whereby Ligne's amorous successes with women would signify political successes of the *emigré* government with Austria: 'So my dear prince, speak to us of your *conquêtes galantes* as soon as possible,' wrote Calonne. If people talked about their long conversation at the ball, 'confuse the chatterers by saying, with your usual seriousness, that I am a very pretty boy with whom, to vary your tastes, you were occupied'. Ligne was 'in the intoxication of pleasure, of hope, of horror, of despair' – for him high praise – and wrote to 'my charming apostle' (Calonne) of the 'certainty of success if the Queen escapes all danger (which I believe she will) of putting her back on the throne'. Ligne's hostility to Louis XVI was such that he does not mention putting the *King* back on the throne. Ligne was excited by the thought of 'carrying the standards of Austria or the Empire to the banks of the Rhine and the Scheldt, [and] to go to cut the monsters' throats on the charming banks of the Seine'.[45]

Such language helps explain why Artois and his *émigrés* acquired a reputation for bloodthirstiness, frivolity and self-delusion. However, Leopold II, like Louis XVI and Vergennes, distrusted Ligne. The Marquis de Bombelles, ambassador of both Louis XVI and (in secret) the Comte d'Artois in Venice, wrote to Calonne: 'He was annoyed that you discussed your mission with the prince de Ligne because he considers him excessively indiscreet.'[46] Leopold II remained dedicated to peace and distrustful of the *émigrés*.

On 20 May 1791 Leopold II appointed Ligne Grand Bailli or Governor of Hainaut, the post for which Ligne had been hoping since 1790. The ceremony of installation, rather than a desire to revisit Beloeil, led him to leave Vienna for the Austrian Netherlands.[47]

Ligne travelled with his son Charles, who had been living with his father in Vienna since his return in 1790 from the siege of Ismail, an Ottoman fortress near the mouth of the Danube, where he had covered himself in glory serving in the Russian army. Catherine had written him a superb letter of congratulation, combining flattery of his family with disdain for revolutionary ideals, which his father said was worth more than all the Lignes' titles and genealogies:

Monsieur le Prince de Ligne,
   In vain people tell me that all men are equal: when experience proves to me daily that they are not, and that there are the strong and the weak: so I will never believe anything except what I observe, but what convinces me even more is that I know families in which military courage and virtues perpetuate themselves from father to son: such is yours, Monsieur le Prince de Ligne![48]

Since Charles de Ligne and his father both worshipped pleasure and disliked their wives, they were an ideal couple. In 1788 Hélène de Ligne had returned to Warsaw, where she had fallen in love with the Grand Chamberlain, Count Vincent Potocki. As the Princesse de Ligne wrote with her acid pen, Charles had received from his marriage nothing but 'the honour of being cuckolded' (and a daughter, Sidonie, born in 1786). Hélène de Ligne soon asked for a divorce – something her husband had been contemplating since 1782.[49]

Ligne behaved as the defender of the family honour rather than as an apostle of personal freedom. He wrote his daughter-in-law a freezing letter refusing his consent and assuring her that she was 'dead to us and to our little Sidonie'.[50] Whereas Ligne adored his elder son, he was outraged that his younger son Louis supported the French as well as the Flemish Revolution. In the summer of August 1791, while the royal family was in prison in the Tuileries after the failure of its flight to Varennes, Louis de Ligne resumed service in the French army. Like many families, including the Bourbons themselves, the Lignes were split by the Revolution. When the Princesse de Ligne (who still had revolutionary sympathies) saw her husband in 1791, for the first time in five years, she did not dare discuss Louis, 'because I do not want to disturb our harmony'.[51]

More than most European *grands seigneurs*, Ligne continued
to work for the *émigré* cause. In the summer of 1791, he sheltered
sixty-four French *émigrés* in his chateau of Beloeil. To a letter of
thanks, he replied in terms that suggest the international appeal
of the *emigrés* as defenders of the social order: 'I also have rights
to your friendship as your Comrade. I also have the honour to
be a French Gentleman and I find that at this time it is the finest
of titles ... Beloeil and I were proud to possess so much honour,
virtues, patience, moderation, discipline and delicacy' – qualities
that few others attributed to French *émigrés*.[52]

On 8 August Ligne made a state entry into Mons as Grand
Bailli, in a six-horse carriage, under a burning sun, to the sound
of pealing church bells. The Prince de Ligne and the province of
Hainaut were reunited in mutual love and devotion to the
Habsburgs: it seemed as if there had never been a Belgian revolution.* Ligne was escorted by soldiers, musicians, servants,
villagers from Beloeil and Baudour dressed as hussars, twenty
household officers, twenty footmen, the bearded Russians given
him by Catherine II, his Turks Ismail and Osman, and a Tartar
leading two camels brought back from Ligne's Turkish campaigns.† Charles de Ligne was in the carriage beside him: the
Princess and their daughters watched from a balcony.
According to a local diarist M. Harmignie, using the torrid
language of the age, Ligne wept for joy at the applause of

> an immense crowd which was driven to enthusism at the sight
> of him and the thought of his rare qualities and which endeav-
> oured to prove him its love by all imaginable means; it was all
> the more surprising because, their Royal Highnesses [Duke
> Albert of Saxe-Teschen and his wife, the Archduchess Marie

---

* However, Ligne noticed that some soldiers in his regiment were wearing new uniforms. When he asked why, he was told that they had deserted to the 'Belgian' revolution the previous year, and had had to be reclothed when they rejoined the colours.
† These camels were later confiscated by the French revolutionary armies and placed in
the Jardin des Plantes in Paris. When the Princesse de Ligne saw them on a visit to
Paris in 1804 and said, 'Oh those are my husband's camels,' Parisians thought she
was the wife of a Mameluke.

Christine, Governors-General of the Austrian Netherlands]
having been very coldly received at Mons on 11 July, many
people had tried to disparage the Prince de Ligne and to
discourage the people from rendering him honours.

Even the Princess reported that they had been received like gods
and that it came from the heart.

Ligne had often advised Joseph II, without effect, to win
hearts in the Austrian Netherlands by attending public banquets
and festivities. His own state entry was followed by four days of
public ceremonies, balls, dinners, and concerts. At a supper in
the Estates building, according to another local diarist, 'there
were very cordial and heart-felt toasts to the prince who each
time rose and expressed his thanks with deep emotion'. Ligne
also gave dances – for 'the people' on the Place St Jean, which
he watched from his carriage, and for the well-to-do in the local
theatre.[53]

As Grand Bailli, in September and October, he showed that
he could charm the deputies of Hainaut as easily as kings and
empresses. For the first time in his life he also, as a peer of
Hainaut, attended meetings of the province's Chamber of
Peers.[54] According to the Archduke Charles, a younger son of
Leopold II who was to become one of the greatest soldiers in the
history of Austria, Ligne behaved like a hero: 'He says the
harshest truths and knows how to direct everyone.' On 10
October, after the Estates had voted subsidies by unanimous
acclamation, 'The Prince de Ligne, Grand Bailli of the
province, eager to unite his feelings to those of the assembly,
came after the session to mix the expression of his sensibility to
the transports of joy of the general assembly.' However, the next
day he wrote to Count Metternich, the Emperor's minister in
Brussels, that while the Estates would always rally to the government through fear of 'the French disease', 'the reports I
receive from the flat country are terrifying, people talk there
only of the national assembly and the neighbours' happiness' – a
rare admission, by Ligne, of the popularity of   French

Revolution reforms, such as the abolition of the feudal system.[55]
Ligne then set off to spend the winter in Vienna, leaving behind,
as a memorial of his last happy summer at Beloeil, a triangular
obelisk erected in the park in honour of his adored son. On one
side are the words: 'A mon Fils Charles pour l'assaut de Sabatsz
et Ismail. L'an MDCCLXXXXI', between the cross of the
Order of Maria Theresa and the Ligne arms; on another *Nec te
juvenis memorande silebo* '(Your youth will live eternally in my
memory'); on the third: 'Sa gloire fait mon orgueil, son amitié
mon bonheur'.[56]

On the way Ligne stopped at the city of Coblenz on the
Rhine, in the Electorate of Trier. The Archbishop Elector of
Trier was an uncle of Artois and Provence (Artois's elder
brother, who had escaped from Paris in June) and had allowed
them to assemble their own army and administration in his
Electorate. From Coblenz, Ligne sent Catherine his condolences
for the death of Potemkin, 'this rare and extraordinary genius',
with whom he had recently been reconciled: 'He wrote to me
above all about Charles, whom he called his son, letters so full of
sensibility that I would almost wish not to have known him. He
reminded me of our disputes, our passing quarrels, our touching
reconciliations and the need we had to see and love each other.'
Ligne added: 'I am leaving for Vienna to tell the truth about the
Low Countries and France.' He arrived on 24 November.[57]

At the Emperor's request Ligne submitted a *Mémoire sur l'état
présent des Pays-Bas autrichiens*, in which he advocated strict
censorship, and a limited amnesty – ultra-reactionary views he
also proclaimed in the salons of Vienna. After one evening at the
salon of the Baronne de Reischach, whose husband had been an
Austrian official in Brussels in the 1780s, Zinzendorf, always
critical of Ligne, wrote: 'The Prince de L, declaiming against
the house of Arenberg, complained that the rebels were not
being punished … he forgot the letter he wrote at the beginning
of the revolution to his wife.'

While Ligne was preaching counter-revolution in Vienna, his
wife went to Paris to prevent Louis de Ligne making an

unsuitable marriage to a Mlle de Berghes. Owing to Louis XVI's sanction of a radical constitution in September 1791, the city was experiencing an interlude of calm. The Princess found it enjoyable and perfectly safe.[58]

Indeed, to Ligne's dismay, in the winter of 1791–2 Leopold II showed no desire to lead a crusade against the French Revolution. Leopold believed that the true counter-revolution could only come from within France, not through violent measures from outside. Ligne, on the other hand, pressed for war. He remained so sympathetic to the *émigré* cause that he was one of the few observers to affirm that Coblenz was a serious military headquarters and not 'a nest of intrigues and a real court and a hundred such stupidities'.[59] He claimed that 8000 (in reality many more) French officers had joined the Princes, that they represented a substantial force, and that the Archduke Charles was wrong to denounce Coblenz. Had Ligne been blind to the chaos in the Princes' army, and the waste in their households?[60]

On 1 March 1792 Leopold II unexpectedly died and was succeeded by his eldest son Francis. In the new reign Ligne was occasionally consulted on policy in the Austrian Netherlands. The Estates of Brabant, for example, less malleable than those of Hainaut, appealed to him to act as an intermediary with the Emperor over their rate of taxation.[61] In reality Ligne remained out of favour. Only twenty-four at his accession, lacking in self-confidence, Francis II was a reserved, apparently colourless sovereign with whom Ligne had little in common. He felt that he had died with Joseph II.

The drama of Austria was that, like Ligne himself, it tried to play too many roles: Imperial and Hungarian, German and Italian, anti-Ottoman and anti-French. Within one year of the end of the last of the wars with the Ottoman Empire, which had lasted three centuries and absorbed much of its energy, Austria adopted the role of leader of a crusade of dynastic Europe against the French Revolution – though Louis XVI, on the advice of Jacobin ministers, was the first to issue a declaration of war. The hidden hostility that had marked Franco-Austrian relations since 1756 was out in the open. Fear of what Ligne called 'the general epidemic' and desire to save Louis XVI led to an unexpected rapprochement with Prussia. In the summer of 1792, Austria and Prussia prepared to invade France.

In a memoir written in 1808, Ligne suggests that one of the great sorrows of his life was his failure to be employed in the war against France, 'although I never stopped asking to... Unfortunately I have never served since the year 90.' However, a confidential letter from the Princess again contradicts Ligne's later statements. She wrote that it was his unwillingness to serve under a general as incapable as Duke Albert of Saxe-Teschen, commander of troops in the Austrian Netherlands, that deprived him of a military command in 1792.[62] Ligne had wanted the supreme command for himself.

As a result of his overambition, in 1792, for the first time in his life he was a spectator rather than an actor in the great game of Europe. From Vienna he wrote to his cashier Claus to excuse his absence from Beloeil: 'This summer will be too turbulent, my dear Claus. So many troops and troubles on every side would deprive me of all tranquillity at Beloeil, as would so many visits of one sort or another ... if they decide to send our uhlans as far as Paris everything will be over in four or five months.' He expected 'the French farce' to finish as easily as 'the Flemish farce'. Ligne made the error of judging France by Belgium. His wife, who had seen revolutionary France for herself and detested the émigrés, was, as usual, a better prophet. She wrote: 'Whatever people say the foreign armies will never enter Paris.'[63]

While Ligne remained all summer in Vienna, Charles had left to fight in the Austrian army. Hoping that the shots of these *jean foutres* would be no worse than those of the Turks, he wrote to Prince Joseph Poniatowski: 'I am leaving to bring back to reason these wicked arch-wicked *bougres* of French revolutionaries.'[64] Soon he was joined by Louis de Ligne. Horrified by the prospect of fighting his own brother and the hatred for Louis XVI and the royal family growing inside France, on 16 June he had deserted to the enemy – precisely the kind of action that, within France, was bringing suspicion of the royal family and noble officers to the point of eruption.

On 10 August, as Austro-Prussian forces entered France to 'save' Louis XVI, revolutionaries stormed the Tuileries Palace. Three days later the royal family was imprisoned in a tower in the grounds of the Hôtel du Temple, where Ligne had so often supped with the Prince de Conti. French armies fought the foreign invaders with increased determination: they were no longer patriots for the King but for the republic. Charles de Ligne wrote his father a letter, which was intercepted and read in the French Convention: 'We are beginning to tire of this war in which MM. the *émigrés* promised us more butter than bread. We are fighting troops none of whom desert and national guards all of whom hold their ground ... I do not know how we will perform or what will become of us.'

The fall of the French monarchy led to a cataclysm for Ligne. As Charles's exploits at Sabatsch and Ismail had shown, he loved military glory as much as his father. On 14 September, shouting *Courage, braves Wallons!* while leading a cavalry charge on an artillery position near Beaumont, he was killed by a French cannonball, the only Austrian officer killed on that occasion. Even Francis II was moved to express his regrets for the young prince 'whom I esteemed infinitely for his rare merit'.[65] Years later his father wrote:

Everything I most loved, two thirds of myself, the most perfect of beings was taken from me. The newspapers which resounded with his praises, (for never was a loss felt more acutely throughout Europe and even, their ambassador told me, in Turkey) have said how. I can still see the spot where Marshal Lacy told me that my poor Charles was no more. I can see my poor Charles himself arriving every day at the same time with his good and cheerful face looking for mine ... It was on 25 September 1792, a Friday, that I learnt this terrible news which would have made me desire the end of my existence, if another more precious than my own, that of my perfect Christine, was not attached to it.[66]

Ligne's agony must have been sharpened by the knowledge that he had himself encouraged his son's love of war, and the particular war in which Charles was killed.

In his will Charles left his heart and some drawings to his mistress, 'since she always had my heart during my life'; personal legacies to Viennese friends; most of his money to an illegitimate daughter called Christine and Norikos, a Turkish orphan he had adopted during the war, with a plea that they should marry; pictures of his victories and his orders to his father, 'because it is to the example my father has given me that I owe having won them'; his horse and his sword to 'mon bon ami Poniatowski'; and a portrait of his wife to their daughter Sidonie, 'in order that she should remember not to imitate her'.[67]

Ligne and Christine remained grief-stricken, the latter like a statue, almost insensible to those around her, the former experiencing 'terrible moments'.[68] When he heard that, to mourn their son together, his wife might arrive in Vienna, Ligne commented: ' That is a fine consolation in this sorrow.' He considered that she had the anger of her Kinsky sister and the wickedness of her Waldstein sister, and deflected the threatened visit by claiming that he was going to Naples.[69]

After the defeat of Valmy on 20 September, the allied retreat from France turned into a rout. In her letter of condolence Catherine wrote to Ligne that Charles's loss was one of the events that had caused her most sorrow that year. She feared that Germany itself was now threatened by a volcano of incalculable woes: 'Alas! Alas! Alas!' The armies of republican France under General Dumouriez advanced in triumph into the Austrian Netherlands. On 6 November another village near Beloeil, Jemappes, became the site of another battle between French and Austrian armies. Duke Albert of Saxe-Teschen proved as incompetent as Ligne had foreseen, and French revolutionary élan won Dumouriez a great victory. Five days later

Republican troops were enthusiastically received in Brussels, which had not forgotten its year of 'liberty' in 1789–90. For the second time in two years the bonnet of liberty replaced the double-headed eagle on public buildings.[70] The Princess remained in Brussels and, thanks to her efforts and to the relatively mild regime of General Dumouriez, Beloeil was not confiscated. The estate suffered less from what Ligne called *les Carmagnoles*, or *la canaille*, than from the Austrian army the previous summer.

While the Austrian Netherlands was under French occupation, a second revolution was taking place in France itself. Louis XVI had been opposed to the political emigration, with which he had no contact after the autumn of 1791. However, the intrigues of the Queen and the princes had convinced many of his subjects that the King desired the invasion of his kingdom. In Vienna in October, in the house of a brilliant *émigré* writer called Senac de Meilhan, a friend of Ligne since he had been intendant of French Hainaut in the 1780s, Ligne again showed his hostility to Louis XVI, saying: 'That the King is very guilty, and recognised as such, his correspondences with the Princes, with M. de Breteuil, with M. de La Fayette, in part through the Comte de La Marck, directly contrary to his repeated oaths, are all discovered and can very well lead him to the scaffold.'[71] Ligne was right in his prophecy, but wrong in his facts. Revolutionaries neither found nor required proof to condemn Louis XVI to death. He was guillotined on 21 January 1793. The Queen and their children remained in the Temple.

In the long duel between France and Austria for preponderance in Europe, Austria was a resilient and formidable foe. On 18 March 1793 at the battle of Neerwinden, twenty miles east of Brussels, the Austrian army under Marshal Coburg defeated the French under Dumouriez and recovered the Austrian Netherlands. Ligne returned to spend the summer at Beloeil; the day of his arrival, when he saw his son's tomb for the first time, was 'almost mortal agony'. Charles's death further diminished Ligne's interest in Beloeil. He had already written that Louis should be instructed about every aspect of the estate: 'It should concern him more than me, who more than ever no longer wants to discuss business.' He would be quite happy to draw 24,000 florins a year from the estate, which, with his general's salary of 8000 florins and his salaries as Grand Bailli of Hainaut and Governor of Mons, would enable him to live in comfort in Vienna.[72]

That summer, while the Reign of Terror spread across France, Ligne enjoyed his last months of glory as master of Beloeil. Every day there were fifty people to dine or sup, including his old friend Roger de Damas, who was fighting what he called 'our criminal fatherland' in the ranks of the Austrian army. Another émigré called M. de Laval Loubrerie has left a portrait of Ligne, which shows that Ligne's sorrow over Charles did not affect his behaviour in his salon: 'His eyes on fire, his attitude proud and grand, his bearing noble and majestic ... his left hand in his belt, gesticulating with his head and above all his right hand', Ligne dominated the conversation. He was 'the only general who could talk about war without boring me to death'. Full of outrageous jokes, puns and anecdotes, equally happy to play games with the children or make declarations of love to the ladies, 'he is what I call the most amiable, the most perfect gentleman and the one best suited to our age, although he would have been worthy of that of Louis XIV, and if you ask me his secret, I will tell you it is grace, and then grace and then more grace'.*

For the first time in Ligne's life he was spending some time with his younger daughters Euphémie and Flore, and Laval Loubrerie noticed that Ligne was 'more of a friend to his children than any [father] you have known'. The war was so near that while the young princesses were playing music in the salon, the sound of cannon fire from the Austrians' siege of Valenciennes (24 May–24 July 1793), a few miles inside France, could be heard in the background.[73]

Having served at the sieges of Ochakov and Belgrade as a

---

* Possibly a reference to Danton's call, in September 1792, to French revolutionaries to display 'de l'audace, de l'audace et encore de l'audace'.

general, Ligne had to watch the siege of Valenciennes as a spectator.[74] It reminded him of the sieges he had witnessed as a boy, and he wrote bitterly: 'I laughed to myself to see my career finishing as I had begun it, and I shrugged my shoulders that events led me to witness the glory of others instead of making them witnesses or collaborators in mine.'

His observation thirteen years earlier in *Préjugés militaires*, that 'Europe, the more civilised it becomes, is more barbaric than the barbarians,' was confirmed by events. Ligne and his guests at Beloeil read in the gazettes that Marie Antoinette had been separated from her children, confined in a prison cell and brought to trial. The accusation of incest, prised out of her son by the prosecution, was a last revenge by the sexual underworld of Paris on the court of Versailles. She was guillotined on 16 October. Ligne always defended her after her death. A typical phrase is: 'the beautiful and unfortunate Queen, always calumniated, whose only fault was to have a soul without reproach and as white and beautiful as her face'. For years he kept a box decorated with her miniature in his pocket.[75]

In Ligne's words, the guillotine was now queen. Even early enthusiasts for revolution such as Mme de Coigny and Narbonne emigrated. Most of Ligne's friends who remained in France were doomed to the scaffold: 'Philippe Egalité' in 1793, in 1794 Mme du Barry and the Prince d'Hénin, the former 'pimp of princes'.

Ligne's reaction to the slaughter of so many friends and of his French world was to advocate a restoration of the 'happy and old regime'. The new King, with a severe and frugal court and a largely foreign guard, should inhabit the palace of Compiègne, north-east of 'that great prostitute', the city of Paris. Every province should have a governor, a bishop, a *parlement* and an intendant, guarded by a garrison of 10,000. The idea of a constitutional king made Ligne shudder.[76]

In the autumn of 1793 Ligne again attended meetings of the Hainaut estates and obtained a healthy subsidy. Although he had no official military position, he suggested to Marshal Coburg, and the Archduke Charles, that the local peasants, who all had guns, should be used to defend the frontiers of the Austrian Netherlands. They would have 'the courage of fear', and would free the Austrian army to strike into France – an excellent idea at a time when the royalist revolt in the Vendée was winning success after success. However, the Austrian high command rejected the plan.[77]

The Austrian Netherlands had little to offer Ligne, and in February 1794 he made the last of the thirty-four journeys between Brussels and Vienna that had punctuated his life since he had first gone to Vienna, in 1751, at the age of sixteen. For once he travelled with his wife who, having spent seven years in Brussels with her younger daughters, wanted a change. Ligne wrote back to Metternich in Brussels that he had 'reassured all Vienna on the interior of the Low Countries'.

The interior might be reassuring, but the exterior soon collapsed. The Austrian defeat at Fleurus on 25 June 1794, thirty miles east of Brussels, which Ligne attributed to the failure to give him a command in a country he knew like his own bedroom, led to the reconquest of the Austrian Netherlands by the French.[78] For the next twenty years the ancient province of Hainaut would be a French *département*. The 'patriots' had won. Later that year, at a time when he had no idea what had become of it, Ligne wrote a long lament, 'Mes Adieux à Beloeil':

> Hélas il n'est plus pour moi ce cher Beloeil
> Où chaque moment caressait mon orgueil
> Où les beautés de diverses contrées
> Venaient suivre l'amour dans mes grandes allées
> Et j'étais bien traité par le dieu des jardins.*

In reality the loss of Beloeil was a liberation already planned by the Prince himself.

---

* Alas it is no longer mine, my dear Beloeil,
Where every moment caressed my pride,
Where beauties from different countries
Came to follow love down my long avenues.
And I was well treated by the god of gardens.

Vienna

After 1794 Vienna was the right city for Ligne. For, during the turmoil of the Revolution and the Empire, Vienna replaced Paris as the unofficial capital of Europe. An Englishman called John Morritt, who visited Vienna during his Grand Tour in 1794 (and became a dancing partner of Ligne's daughters), praised it in terms that explain why foreigners found it so compelling: 'Perhaps of all the great towns I ever was in Vienna is the very pleasantest, particularly at this time of year. The number of people of fashion who reside here, the ease with which we were introduced and the many places of public lounging are beyond those of any town we have seen on the continent.' Language was no problem, since 'Vienna is a perfect Babel and you meet with many men and women who can speak five or six languages, and almost all three – French, German and Italian.' Having travelled throughout Italy and the Empire, he concluded that Vienna was 'the only capital fit for a gentleman to live at'.[1] Another friend of Ligne, the Comte d'Escars, one of the first French *émigrés* to arrive in Vienna from Paris in 1789 (bringing with him the young Alexandre de Laborde, son of Marie Antoinette's banker, who entered the Austrian army and later became Ligne's most intimate friend), confirmed Vienna's appeal: 'Vienna then had no equal in Europe, for the choice, the number and the attraction of its societies.'[2]

It was an international city of 230,000 inhabitants. The streets were brightened by the different costumes of the Balkans, while there were so many Turks that cafés put out cushions for them, so that they did not have to use chairs.[3] It was also the principal centre of commerce, literature and newspapers for the Greeks of the diaspora.[4]

Vienna was pleasant for the people as well as the elites. In the Austrian countryside many peasants were miserable and close to starvation, but in the city even the beggars appeared well fed and well dressed. It was said that in Vienna people lunched until dinner and dined until supper. The Irish tenor, Michael Kelly, noticed that the great public park of the Prater was frequented by 'people of all ranks in the evening who *immediately after dinner* proceed thither to regale themselves with their favourite dish, fried chickens, cold ham, and sausages; white beer and Hoffner wines, by way of dessert; and stay there until a late hour: dancing, music and every description of merriment prevail ... nothing could exceed the gaiety of that delightful place.'[5] Plentiful supplies of food at low prices helped keep the Viennese, at least in appearance, contented. Beethoven, Ligne's neighbour on the Moelkerbastei, wrote a few years later: 'So long as an Austrian can get his brown beer and sausages there will be no revolution.'[6] Mme Vigée-Lebrun wrote: 'As for the people, nowhere have I seen it have that air of happiness and ease ... one realises at once that they are living under a paternal government.'[7]

In Vienna after 1794 Ligne started a new life. No longer constantly travelling, he inhabited Vienna more fully than he ever had Paris or Brussels. Both the physical and the emotional parameters of his life changed. The modesty of the Moelkerbastei and the Kahlenberg replaced the grandeur of Beloeil. Above all, he began to live with his own family.

The Princess and their unmarried daughters Euphémie and Flore lived with him in the Moelkerbastei, where he now rented three contiguous houses. Five minutes away, in the elegant, unpretentious Palais Clary, on the street of noble palaces called the Herrengasse, lived the member of his family he loved most, his daughter, secretary and confidante, Christine, Princess Clary. He continued to regard her as 'a masterpiece of perfection, kindness, charming naivety, gaiety, good temper and friendship for me. It is not friendship I have for her, I think, it is I whom I love in her and it is he who is me. She has a superb brain. And what a heart!' His letters to her are ecstatic: 'Be certain, dear Christ, that without you even if I amuse myself there is something telling me: "you are not happy." I no longer adore anything in the world except you. You are my Monarchy, my everything.'[8] Unkind friends said that father and eldest daughter were two eccentrics lost in mutual admiration.

'Very fat and ... stuffed with good nature', according to an English friend, wild and odd to the point of childishness, Princess Clary spent the day reading, playing music, gossiping about love affairs, and cutting out bizarre prints and drawings to paste on screens or in albums. Another favourite pastime was to watch buildings being pulled down. So that she would not miss a minute, the Emperor would give her advance warning of each impending demolition.[9]

On 11 September 1798 Ligne's second daughter Euphémie, known as 'Féfé', married her cousin Count Jean Palffy, an invalid described as 'the most tediously ill man in Hungary'. Her mother had worried that 'in the age we are in girls without money rarely find husbands'. However, the Palffys, one of the few noble families in Hungary to remain constantly loyal to the Habsburgs, were so rich that Count Jean could afford to marry a princess without a dowry. By her marriage Féfé Palffy became mistress of one splendid palace in Vienna, in the Wallnerstrasse next to the Herrengasse, and of another Palais Palffy, fifty miles from Vienna in Pressburg in Hungary (now Bratislava in Slovakia). Féfé Palffy was popular in Vienna for her kindness, her manners and her cook, and she was devoted to her husband. However, like her sisters and father, she was in a state of constant agitation, and had a 'passion for amusement expressed as naively as the necessity to drink or eat'.[10]

Féfé Palffy was particularly close to her younger sister Flore, who was said to be the wittiest of the three: when they met, they giggled together like schoolgirls. Flore's conversation was so ironic and incisive that, like her father, she could be alarming: 'It is so easy to appear stupid beside her that one naturally becomes so,' wrote a French *émigrée* friend called Mme du Montet.

Admired by Baron Spiegel, a Lutheran from the Empire who was an ADC of the Archduke Charles, for years she laughed at his German accent and absurd face. However, in the end she weakened and, having won her father's reluctant consent, they married in 1812, when she was thirty-seven.[11]

Ligne adored his daughters for their wit and grace and beauty: he called them 'three perfections in completely different styles'. He also had two granddaughters, both born in 1786: Sidonie the legitimate, and Titine the illegitimate, daughters of Charles de Ligne. Sidonie, who had been rescued after the fall of the monarchy from the Paris convent where she was being educated, was brought up thereafter by the Princesse de Ligne. She had an even sharper tongue than her aunts and grandfather, and was not generally liked. Her sister Titine, Charles de Ligne's daughter by an actress called Adélaïde Bernardy-Nonès, had been described by her father as 'cette petite illégitime de ma façon ... elle est gentille à manger et est reconnue comme telle par tout le monde'.[12] After his death she was brought up by her aunt Princess Clary. Inevitably Ligne said she was a Ligne but not a *Ligne directe*. He adored her because her mannerisms and humour reminded him of his son. Even the most disdainful Viennese princesses – even her own sister – liked her. Mme du Montet wrote: 'Titine permits herself to say anything that comes into her head and one must admit that strange things pass through it, above all *polissoneries* that would scandalise if they were not so funny; she makes the pious and the prudish laugh as well as high society.'[13]

Innumerable writers of memoirs or diaries record meeting Ligne and his family in Vienna. To most the Lignes appeared irresistibly cheerful and united. Countess Anna Potocka, for example, praised their '*charmante bonhomie* ... indulgent, easy-going and kind, he was adored by his children and loved them because they were amiable ... one could say that he had gained in gaiety what he had lost in fortune ... in Paris I have never found such an agreeable reunion ... what frank and amiable gaiety!'[14] However, one sharp-penned Viennese countess, 'Lulu'

Thurheim, wrote in her memoirs that 'Féfé' Palffy had told her of hidden tensions in the Hôtel de Ligne: 'It seemed so harmonious at the time the old Prince de Ligne was alive, and yet how little real warmth bound its members to each other. What a family! The old Prince, thoughtless and frivolous, loved only himself.' His sons-in-law felt so frightened of the sharp tongues and endless jokes that they stayed away. Christine Clary was said not to have spoken for seven years to her niece Louise Chotek, who married her son Charles in 1802 and was said to have been so dim-witted that she needed a quarter of an hour to understand a joke.[15] Whatever the truth about strains in the family, Ligne kept it united until his death.

The main problem was 'the zero in the Hôtel de Ligne', the Princesse de Ligne. The realism and directness evident in her letters were missed by most visitors, to whom she seemed bitter and unkind – perhaps because she was ignored by her husband and children. Anna Potocka wrote: 'Husband and wife seemed to speak different languages and never to have said anything to each other.' The Princess loved Ligne but also felt: 'He is mad! On my honour he is mad! He will ruin his children.' On his side Ligne enjoyed teasing her. When new guests arrived, he would keep them so busy that they forgot to pay their respects to the Princess. She would sulk in a corner for the rest of the evening, sewing hideous pieces of embroidery, and muttering about the rudeness of the modern age.[16] Partly to escape his wife, Ligne spent several weeks every summer with Princess Clary on the Kahlenberg, the refuge, where, in 1794, he added a Belvedere surmounted by a golden ball, baptised *mon petit Beloeil*.[17] His wife did not come because 'The Princesse de Ligne hates the country.'[18]

Below the Kahlenberg, at the village of Nussdorf on the Danube, Ligne rented another retreat, which he called 'my fisherman's house'. Walking along the same path he used to take fifty years before from his father's house nearby at Klosterneuburg, he concluded: 'Life is a circle. It ends more or less as it starts, the two childhoods are proof.' As in his youth there were pets in his bedroom: a fox, a lamb, and a dog called L'Ami, which shared his breakfast and had 'the most direct mind I know'.[19] His antechamber had less welcome visitors: creditors.

They were there because Ligne was ruined. Austria's loss of the Austrian Netherlands in 1794 led to the sequestration of all Ligne's property by the French Republic. He received no more money from his estates, or from the governments of Hainaut and Mons. Until Catherine II came to his help (see below), all he had was a military salary of 4000 florins a year, half of which was absorbed by payment of the debts of his son Charles. His fall from wealth and grandeur taught Ligne not to rely on the charity of friends and relations. His comrade from the Seven Years' War, Prince Louis of Württemberg, who had become Duke of Württemberg in 1793, said he could do nothing. Referring to the Princesse de Ligne's nephews Prince Liechtenstein and Prince Esterhazy, Ligne wrote in his memoirs: 'Two nephews with a million a year each: Marshal Lacy with so much friendship and ready money, so many other so-called friends, never offered to help when I only had four thousand florins for my wife, a son, two daughters and me.'

Ligne is being slightly dishonest, since Prince Liechtenstein did give the small sum of 650 florins a year to each of his cousins, Euphémie (until she married) and Flore de Ligne, thereby saving them from the fate of their aunts, and many other impoverished noblewomen: relegation to a convent.[20] Moreover, like other intendants of dispossessed noble families in France and the Austrian Netherlands, Vandenbroucke managed to send money and possessions to his exiled masters, and even to extract rents from certain farmers. The French Republic could not extinguish the House of Ligne overnight. The Hôtel de Ligne in Brussels, which had been submerged by a tide of taverns, coachmakers, and stables, was cleared out on Vandenbroucke's orders in 1797.[21] Angélique d'Hannetaire, with whom he still corresponded, returned him a picture he had once given her, worth 20,000 florins, which enabled him to live for two years.[22]

Thereafter Ligne continued to live off borrowed money. He wrote that he would be delighted if, after his death, a surgery school bought his corpse from his surviving son Louis: 'I have nothing to leave him but me.' It was through Louis, however, that Ligne eventually recovered a degree of financial security. Louis de Ligne was rarely in Vienna, since he served in the Austrian army until he was captured in the Tyrol in 1800. As an officer who had deserted the French army eight years earlier, he was in danger of being shot. However, by one of those courtesies across the political divide that recurred throughout the Revolution, he was protected by the enemy commander. His name was General Ney. Louis de Ligne had made him an adjutant in his regiment the day before he abandoned the French army. Ney said: 'Prince, you began my fortune ... I will show my gratitude despite the order and habit of shooting ... I will try to have you exchanged as quickly as possible.'

Louis returned to Vienna in 1801. That year he resigned from the Austrian army and left Vienna for Brussels, which was still under French rule. As Ligne had predicted to Ségur, in 1800 France had again become a monarchy in all but name, under the 'iron sceptre' of the First Consul, General Bonaparte. Order was restored: hostility to nobles and émigrés was on the wane.[23]

Six years earlier Ligne had worried about Louis's failure to marry, and the possibility that the House of Ligne might be extinguished. He had pressed on his mild and dutiful son-in-law Prince Clary 'the project to make only one House of those of Ligne and Clary', whereby Clary's second son, Count Maurice Clary, would assume the name and arms of Ligne. However, for once Clary had stood up to his father-in-law, and refused. In the end Ligne's fears proved groundless. On 27 April 1803 Beloeil, which still contained much of its furniture and pictures, awoke for one week from a ten years' sleep, without official authorisation, to celebrate Louis's marriage. In a sign of the changing times, Louis had chosen, instead of one of the foreign princesses previously favoured by his family, a local heiress called Countess Louise Vandernoot de Duras, a relation of the leader of the 'aristocrats' in the Belgian revolution. There were cheering peasants, illuminations, a ball where the new Princess danced with everyone 'indistinctly'. Familiar faces resurfaced: at the wedding banquet Ligne's old librarian the Abbé Pages, who had survived by taking every oath required of him, showed that he had lost his hearing but not his appetite (he died three years later at the age of ninety-two). Finally, on 29 October 1803, a special decree of the First Consul lifted the sequestration order on all properties of the Ligne family, including Beloeil. On 28 January 1804 Louis de Ligne became father of a son called Eugène. Ligne had the joy of knowing that his name would be perpetuated. His great-great-grandson Antoine, twelfth Prince de Ligne, is the present master of Beloeil.

Although Beloeil returned to the Lignes, Ligne did not return to Beloeil. In accordance with his plan of 1793, he formally ceded Louis all claims to his estates, except Fagnolles, which gave him an 'existence in the Empire'. A good son and efficient administrator, Louis was soon able to send his father 9000 florins a year. Two years later Louis dismissed Vandenbroucke. In his last letter, after thirty-six years of collaboration and protestations of gratitude and friendship, Ligne showed his cruel side. He reproached Vandenbroucke, at length, with having profited unduly from his post of intendant, and the failure to have the sequestration order lifted earlier, like those of other nobles: 'You only reappeared to work for the ruin of my house.'[24]

In addition to his family, Ligne was surrounded in Vienna by a large household (this suggests, although details of his financial arrangements are not available, that he was not as impoverished as he claimed). Since many of them were Walloon, they provided a living link with Beloeil. His secretary, Sauveur Legros, had followed Ligne to Vienna and saw him continually, addressing him loving letters and poems, praising his ability to defy time, the only tyrant who had taken nothing from him, occasionally reminding him of arrears of salary. However, he returned to Belgium in about 1806.[25]

Ligne's coachmen were called Ghislain and Léonard, while sitting behind his carriage, resplendent in Turkish dress, was a Turk, his former captive Ismail. Ligne's last valet, Louis

François d'Albertenson, came from near Valenciennes. So much
of the day was spent with servants that Ligne felt there should be
schools for them to learn how to think, serve and talk well. The
'Dialogue entre Léonard et Moi', written in 1814, shows how
relaxed their relationship could be. As Ligne's last love, Rosalie
Rzewuska, leaves Vienna, Léonard* says: 'I am very sad myself
when I see His Highness so sad.' Ligne relishes his Walloon
slang – *drôle* for sad, *dedans là* for drunk – and notes that,
because the Countess remembers his name and gives him ducats,
Léonard admires her very much.[26]

Ligne also had a military household, for the Régiment de
Ligne had survived the end of the Austrian Netherlands. It was
stationed five hundred miles from Vienna at the large but primi-
tive town of Leopol in Galicia. From Walloon it became Polish
in composition: however, its Colonel was too fond of life in
Vienna to visit it more than twice, in 1800 and 1806. Emile
Legros, son of Sauveur, became one of Ligne's adjutants in
1800, at the age of nineteen, and remained with him until his
death; Ligne wrote to his father of 'our son Emile ... always
good natured, excellent, punctual and born to be loved'.[27]

His family and his regiment were not enough for the Prince
de Ligne. He yearned for an active military career. However, his
relations with the Emperor Francis II had not improved. Ligne's
patron Joseph II had been a confident and aggressive monarch.
After eight years on the throne, Francis was described by his
closest adviser, his Grand Chamberlain and former tutor Count
Colloredo, as 'confused, even apprehensive, and indecisive'.[28]
Young and serious, he was so thin that he looked like his own
ghost.[29] 'I do not think I ever saw as thin a man,' wrote Michael
Kelly.[30]

Nevertheless Francis had an attractive side: Metternich later
described him as 'gold with the outward appearance of brass'. For
Francis loved, and was (with few exceptions) loved by, his own
subjects. At his weekly public audiences, standing from six in the

---

*Like many servants he used a name given him by his masters. His real name was
  François Baudelet.

morning until two in the afternoon even when the temperature was 93°, he saw over a hundred people of all ranks, from princes to washerwomen. Saying that he was only a man, he refused to let them kneel, and usually gave sound advice over such matters as their daughters' marriages or their grievances against his government.[31] After every defeat, his loyal subjects continued to cheer him on his return to Vienna. Francis II shows that absolute power does not always corrupt absolutely.

Francis was so simple that, apart from official receptions after mass on Sunday and religious services, court life or entertainments barely existed. The Emperor had no taste for luxury (he ordered furniture out of a wholesaler's catalogue) and never went into society. The Swedish ambassador Count Armfelt, a friend of Ligne known for his charm as the 'Alcibiades of the North', wrote: 'No court in the world has ever existed which had less influence on the life and habits of the people inhabiting the capital. You see the whole court out for a walk and everywhere without guards, without any apparatus of splendour.'

Despite the contrast in their tastes and characters, Ligne saw the Emperor's good qualities. With the condescension of a sophisticated *grand seigneur*, he wrote:

Francis II has the right impulses of heart and head. All he lacks is to be well, or not at all, surrounded. He is inclined to justice and even charity and thinks and wants to have firmness. I often saw him at the beginning of his reign. I found good ideas in him. He is unfortunate and interesting, generous and benevolent with discernment. He shows and has kindliness in his maxims and his exaggeratedly Austrian dialect. He writes well and clearly on political matters. He pays them too much attention, reads useless papers and gives too many audiences which become so also. But it is out of kindness and to console or satisfy. He has a good memory, is a good son, good father and good husband.

Ligne claimed: 'I like him more than do those who have driven me away from him.'

The man who kept Ligne away from the Emperor was *le grand vizir*, Baron Thugut, Director of Foreign Affairs since March 1793. The son of a minor, non-noble official from Linz, constantly supported by Colloredo, he was energetic, unpopular and unprincipled. Thugut's immorality, combined with Francis's inexperience and Colloredo's mediocrity, created, in the opinion of one German historian, 'one of the most unfortunate political constellations in history'.[32]

Under Thugut's influence, Austria fought longer against France than any other continental power. Between 1792 and 1814 Britain fought against France for 240 months, Austria for 108, Prussia for 58 and Russia for 55.[33] In contrast, after 1794, Ligne like Lacy, Kaunitz, and the Emperor's brothers advocated peace. Charles de Ligne's death had spoilt his father's appetite for war. Since Prussia and Spain made peace with the French Republic in 1795, why not Austria? However, 'Thu-nicht-gut', or the 'Baron of War' (as Ligne called him after the King of Spain's favourite Godoy had been made 'Prince of the Peace' for signing peace with the French Republic), wanted war.

Ligne hated every aspect of Thugut – his twisted smile, his presumption, his quarrels with Prussia, Russia and Britain, his isolation of Francis II from the Archduke Charles and nobles like Princes Kaunitz, Starhemberg, and Ligne himself.

> His eyes are very intelligent, his conversation is not distinguished but nor has it anything definitely common ... He has been thought proud; he is only contemptuous. He cared neither for honours nor honour. A bachelor, without friends, relations, society, neither estates, nor consideration, coming from humble origins, shut up at home for fear of being understood, he preferred to hate men rather than to see them.

Above all, the sin of sins for Ligne, Thugut did not realise that 'one does more business in a salon than in a study', and refused to entertain.[34] This was the same error as had led Ligne to overestimate the influence of the Polignacs and underestimate that of Vergennes at the court of Versailles. Ligne forgot that efficiency and judgement, as well as bons mots and knowledge of human nature, were needed to succeed in politics.

On his side Thugut was one of those cold, conventional officials like Mercy and Vergennes for whom Ligne was nothing but a wit who wasted his talents. Thugut called Ligne a 'chatterbox', Colloredo labelled him 'a scatterbrain'.[35] Their contempt ensured that after 1794, instead of commanding an army, Ligne was condemned to inactivity. Grimly he wrote to Catherine the Great: 'My kingdom is not of this world.'[36]

Another reason for his failure to win a military command may have been the habit, at once his strength and weakness, of riding too many horses at the same time. In 1795, to try to recover Beloeil, he declared to the Republican authorities that he had never served against France, praised their mildness and justice, and also asked help of Frederick William II of Prussia, who had just made peace with France. Prince Dietrichstein told him: 'What have you done ... You have addressed yourself to Prussia! The baron was going to give you an army; he is furious. You will never have one.'

Although he was a brave and conscientious officer on the battlefield, and had helped Austria win Belgrade, Ligne's reputation for recklessness was a third reason why he was ignored. With inbuilt pessimism and caution, Austrian commanders put the preservation of their armies even above victory in the field. Rilke expressed their priorities in the words: 'Who speaks of victory? Survival is all.' Thugut claimed that Ligne would have got the Austrian and Piedmontese armies exterminated in one campaign.[37]

Ligne, who records Thugut's remark in his memoirs, concludes: 'I was not his man.' Instead of Ligne, Generals Alvinczy, Wurmser, Clerfayt and Ferraris, 'four feeble idiots or invalids whom I have had under my orders and to whom, except Clerfayt, I would never have given three battalions to command', were chosen to command Austrian forces against the French in Italy. Even Thugut admitted they were 'utterly incapable'.[38] Against such commanders, in 1796 and 1797, General

Bonaparte won a series of famous victories that drove Austria out of northern Italy and brought French armies within 140 miles of Vienna. Ligne could not have done worse.

The peace of Campoformio between France and Austria on 17 October 1797 was negotiated by Ligne's old friend Louis Cobenzl, former Austrian ambassador to St Petersburg and one of the few Austrian diplomats who was a match for Bonaparte. Austria ceded the former Austrian Netherlands to France, and the Duchy of Milan to a French satellite, the Cisalpine Republic. In return Austria received the former Venetian Republic – two and a half million inhabitants for a loss of four and a half million. Compared to France, Russia and Prussia, Austria was slipping in the balance of power.

Ligne could not hold his tongue. He expressed disdain for the Austrian government and admiration for General Bonaparte so openly that in late 1797 Francis II briefly banished him outside the boundaries of Vienna. Naturally he made a joke and said that, having for so long been the Prince *de* Ligne he was now, by the grace of the Emperor, the Prince *hors Ligne* (the prince outside the line). He consoled himself by starting a new love affair and giving dances on the Kahlenberg, and was soon forgiven. On 1 March 1798, as a gesture of reconciliation, he had the honour, as chamberlain in waiting, of carrying the Emperor's latest daughter, the Archduchess Marie Clementine Amélie, at her baptism.[39] Yet even on the rare occasions he went to court, Ligne found ways to show his discontent. If he rode behind the Emperor's carriage in a procession, because he felt he should be a field marshal, he refused to wear his lieutenant general's uniform and wore his regimental uniform instead.

Persistence was a Habsburg quality and Francis II and Thugut did not give up in the fight against France. The size and loyalty of Austria's population made it easy to raise new armies. In March 1799, Austria, allied to England and Russia, again declared war on the French Republic, and at first won a series of victories. When Lord Mulgrave, whom Ligne had known in Brussels and Baudour in the 1770s, came on a mission to Vienna from the

British government, he wanted Ligne to be employed in the Low
Countries, regarding him as 'the most likely person to hold
the Brabançons together and to hold that country against the
French'.⁴⁰ However, the tide of war soon turned in favour of the
French Republic, and Ligne missed another chance.

Having failed with Britain, Ligne turned to Russia, with
whose rulers he had better relations than with his own.
Catherine the Great had proved a true friend. In 1794, when
Ligne was at his financial nadir, she had ordered Count Valerian
Zubov, whose brother had replaced Mamonov as her lover, to
buy the estate she had given Ligne in the Crimea. As a result
Ligne received an income of 1500 florins a year. Gratefully
recalling previous presents of furs, rings, snuff boxes, Ligne
wrote to her: 'If all my agents served me as well, I would be
twice as rich as I am.'⁴¹

Her son Paul I, who succeeded her in 1796, was equally kind.
The new Tsar assured Ligne of his 'very special good will' and
granted him a pension of 1000 ducats in consideration of his
claims on the Massalskys. Ligne knew that, contrary to a widespread opinion, Paul I was not mad, simply an 'extraordinary
being who was driven mad' – by his own nobles. In 1800, a year
before a group of nobles murdered the Tsar with the connivance
of his own son, Ligne wrote to Paul I, 'the restorer of chivalry
and the upholder of honour', in the hope that Russian pressure
on Francis II would win him command of an army, or the post of
chief Austrian liaison officer with the Russian army. As in 1788,
Ligne felt that he had a special vocation as a link between the
two Empires. He promised to avoid what he called 'the bitter-
ness, the insolence and the jealousy of our generals', which poisoned Austro-Russian relations. With the help of an *émigré*
friend, the Comte d'Antraigues, who sold European governments false news bulletins 'from Paris' – in reality composed by
himself – Ligne hoped to bring the two governments back
together. Again his services were ignored.⁴²

Deserted by Russia, in 1800 Austria suffered two more
devastating defeats, at Marengo on the Lombard plain and

Hohenlinden near Munich. Panic spread in Vienna, and Ligne
sent plans of defence for the city, and an offer of service to the
Emperor. Count Colloredo passed back the crushing reply:
'The August Master is aware of your zeal, your attachment and
your desire to offer him your services; he is keeping them in
reserve.'[43]

After Marengo, Thugut's bellicose policy had few defenders
and in January 1801 he was dismissed, wrongly blaming his fall,
in part, on a conspiracy by Ligne and Prince Trautmansdorf.
The peace of Luneville in 1801 confirmed the preponderance of
France in the Empire and Italy but led to little direct loss of
Austrian territory. Thereafter, Louis Cobenzl and the Archduke
Charles were in charge of foreign and military affairs respectively. The Archduke, long a friend of Ligne, proved an excellent
reorganiser of the Austrian army.[44] Like many Austrians, Ligne
admired him more than the Emperor and, referring to his epi-
lepsy, wrote: 'If the Archduke Charles had had better health, his
application, his intelligence and his firmness would have been
doubled. He would have equalled Condé and Eugène.'[45]
Nevertheless, Ligne was still ignored – proof that it was the
Emperor himself, not Thugut, who blocked his military career.
Escaping to the Kahlenberg – 'my mountain' – helped to soothe
Ligne. On a wall with a view of Vienna, he wrote:

> From this mountain I see the path to glory,
> Favours, pleasures, the grandeur of the court.
> My heart and my health, far more than history,
> Occupy my time in this delightful place.

This was fantasy: Ligne never forgot history and always
yearned for the court.[46]

Rejected by the court, deprived of a military command, Ligne
turned to an alternative career: social life. Poverty did not affect
his social position – as it might have done in the twentieth
century. Rank was what mattered in 1800. Since the lady of
highest rank was the only person permitted to sit beside her

hostess on a sofa, one of the few joys of the Princesse de Ligne was that the antiquity of her husband's title of Prince of the Holy Roman Empire, which dated from 1602 (older than that of Prince Liechtenstein or Prince Schwarzenberg), meant that she nearly always 'had the sofa'.[47]

Making the most of the fact that 'circumstances have rendered me only too indigenous and indigent', Ligne treated Vienna as his drawing room. Every morning, whether in Vienna or at his summer residence in Teplitz – and earlier at Beloeil – however late he had been out, he wrote in bed from eight to a quarter past three. He often dictated to Christine or Titine, rather than writing alone. For someone with his energy writing had become a necessity: 'the uncertainty of how to occupy the day makes me unhappy', he wrote. 'Literature is a port in the storms of the heart and the Court' – those storms for which he yearned.[48] He then dressed and went out.

In the words of a Russian friend, Count Ouvaroff: 'The most indefatigable of strollers, the Prince de Ligne was everywhere, at the theatre, in taverns, in the Prater, much in the salons and rarely at court. In Vienna everyone, people and grandees alike, saluted him with pleasure.' His progress through Vienna was clearly a remarkable sight. Another friend, the French *émigré* Senac de Meilhan, describes him as having 'the expression of a poet in the exaltation of his verve, or that of a painter in the heat of composition. He has a noble air, his manner is either distract-ed or affectionate; he tenderly embraces a man whose name he would sometimes be embarrassed to remember. He walks past one of his friends and does not see him.'[49]

Nevertheless, Ligne's most regular destination, at 6.30 on most evenings, was the palace on the Herrengasse of his kind, virtuous, but now old and deaf, sisters-in-law, Princesses Charles and Francis Liechtenstein: he called them *les princesses du soir*. Their salon was, with the Hôtel de Ligne, one of the last places in Vienna where French was the first, rather than the second, language. To Ligne's regret, in most other houses, in part because of the revulsion felt for the French Revolution,

German had become the first language again, as it had been before the reign of Maria Theresa. At his sisters'-in-law Ligne met 'the remains of the society of the Emperor Joseph, who went there every day. I perform there the office of the dead, as I replace him, Marshal Lacy and Rosenberg [who died in 1801 and 1796 respectively]. It is gentle, reassuring and calm, without being lively.'[50]

Despite occasional aridity on the part of Lacy, they had remained friends, until the Marshal died, as Ligne waited outside his bedroom. Lacy had been not only the last great general of Maria Theresa, but also the last of the giants Ligne had known in his youth. Voltaire had gone in 1778, Frederick in 1786, Catherine in 1796; half his French friends had been guillotined. Thanks to his longevity, Ligne now had, for the young, the fascination of being a survivor from a lost world: the fabled era of pre-revolutionary *douceur de vivre*. He was living history or, as Astolphe de Custine would write, one century watching another.[51]

In addition to his sisters-in-law, Ligne saw cultivated Viennese nobles such as Count Zinzendorf. He played in amateur theatricals with Louis Cobenzl and his sister Mme de Rombeck, known because of her sharp tongue as *Caquet-bonbec*. Outside Vienna he maintained a routine of visits to *grands seigneurs* who lived in greater splendour than the Emperor, with their own guards, miniature courts, and theatre companies (playing to audiences of princes and peasants): Prince Lobkowitz at Raudnitz, Prince Liechtenstein at Feldsberg and Prince Esterhazy at Esterhaza.[52]

However, Ligne was in, but not of, this world. He found going out in society both physically and mentally disagreeable. You went from the cold of an uncomfortable carriage to an overheated palace where you were tempted to overeat, and 'You have said fifty foolish things and heard a hundred and fifty, thirty calumnies, forty malicious remarks, twenty lies and seen ten injustices. The next day everything begins again, and that is the variety, the reliability and the gaiety of high society.' One link with the Vienna nobility went with the death of his friend the Baronne de Reischach in 1800, after a period of ill health. Ligne began to refuse assemblies and the dinner parties for thirty, served by fifty footmen, beloved by the Vienna nobility. If his wife and daughters dined with Prince Joseph Lobkowitz, whose dinners were so succulent that he was known as Joseph 'Lucullus', or Prince Trautmansdorf, Ligne simply looked in beforehand.[53] Even at the Baronne de Reischach's, Ligne had usually arrived at 9.30 when the crowds had left and, in the company of a few intimates, conversation became extremely candid.[54]

A sign of Ligne's independence of the Vienna aristocratic world – and of his self-confidence – was his willingness to break its conventions. Friends such as Lacy, Zinzendorf and d'Escars complained that he looked like a gypsy, dishevelled and dirty. Sometimes he smelt. He himself wrote that his fleas jumped for joy at the approach of his friends.[55] His house was in a similar state. In 1796 Count Fersen, the former admirer and agent of Marie Antoinette, had there 'a very bad dinner, the house was dirty and it bore all the signs of disorder and discomfort; it pained me to see'. The contrast with the Palais Liechtenstein or the Palais Schwarzenberg could not have been more marked.[56]

Ligne turned to Vienna. Like Grillparzer, who called Vienna 'a Capua of the mind', where life was so pleasant that intellectual effort became impossible, and Zinzendorf, who complained of the 'softness and frivolity for ever in vogue in Vienna', Ligne believed that the Viennese lacked enthusiasm and elevation. He wrote: 'There is material here but it needs to be shaped. There are brush strokes but they need colouring. There is a body but there should be an electric machine to strike sparks out of it.'[57] However, Ligne did succeed in striking sparks out of Vienna. Most Viennese nobles had so little contact with what was known as 'second society' – bankers, writers, or people with less than sixteen quarterings of nobility in their coat of arms – that they did not even make jokes about it.[58] Ligne, on the other hand, never a prisoner of his own milieu, made a friend of a writer from a relatively humble background, an orientalist called Joseph von Hammer-Purgstall, whose forty-four-volume history of the Ottoman Empire, based on Ottoman sources, has yet to be superseded. They had met in 1792 in the Imperial Library in the Hofburg.

Below the stupendous ceiling (described by Friedrich Heer as 'art drunk with victory') glorifying the conquests and piety of the Habsburgs and Vienna as 'the new Athens', Hammer saw 'an elderly gentleman notable for his powdered hair taking notes from a book'. Told that it was the Prince de Ligne, Hammer wrote Ligne a poem in French, which he sent down the long table they were sharing between the pages of a Persian manuscript. Ligne looked up and sent back this answer the same way, which demonstrates his gift for the impromptu:

> Etant dans l'âge des amants,
> Et soutenu par ton génie,
> Tu ne peux qu'embellir ces contes galants,
> Et leur donner une nouvelle vie.*

Ten years later, after long periods in Constantinople and Egypt, Hammer returned to Vienna and revived the friendship. While dreaming of the East, and writing works on oriental history and literature, he enjoyed dining at the Hôtel de Ligne, despite being wedged against other guests because the table was so small. Ligne loved the 'torrent of enlightenment' provided by his books and conversation, praised the 'charming sweetness of your character', and called him not Joseph, but Youssuf.[59] Hammer was his main contact with the East. Possibly because of the expense, Ligne failed to follow his own advice (see above, p. 145) and never travelled to the Ottoman Empire.

In 1802 Ligne met another writer from a modest background,

---

* Being of the age of lovers,
  Upheld by your genius,
  You can only add beauty to these amorous tales,
  And give them a new life.

called Friedrich Gentz (later by his own decision, *von* Gentz). He had been born in Silesia and originally served as a Prussian civil servant, but in 1802, leaving an unloved wife and a mountain of debts in Berlin, he went on a journey to Vienna that 'decided my fate and decided it for ever'. Cobenzl and Colloredo imposed him on a reluctant Emperor as an Imperial Councillor with 4000 florins a year and no duties except to 'write for the Good Cause' – which, since he was the ablest political journalist in Europe, he did very well. Prussian ministers joked that he was Prussia's indemnity to Austria for the loss of Silesia.

Gentz arrived with a letter from an old friend of Ligne, the British minister in Dresden Hugh Eliot, asking Ligne to show Gentz not only his grace and frivolity but also the superiority and solidity of his genius, to allow Gentz 'to lift the veil of the temple and enter the sanctuary'.[60] Gentz was surprised to find that, far from being a debauchee bent by age, Ligne was a handsome man looking no older than Gentz himself – who was thirty years younger. Ligne owed his air of youth to his excellent health, his mental alertness and the fact that almost all his friends were younger than himself.* He was charmed by Gentz, calling him 'sublime in his language and luckily very amiable in ours'. At first Gentz was slightly overawed in the Hôtel de Ligne; as he rose in the Austrian service, until he became Metternich's *éminence grise*, he acquired the dismissive official view of Ligne, and wrote of his 'unlimited intelligence, superficiality and foolishness'. However, 'my excellent Gentz' was part of Ligne's life until the end of his days.[61]

In Vienna Ligne also remained in contact with French *émigrés* – a diaspora which, despite its political defeats, had a cultural influence as great as that of the Huguenots a hundred years earlier. Ligne remained resolutely counter-revolutionary. In 1797, referring to the first *émigrés* returning to France, he wrote: 'Grace, good taste, the Fine Arts, literature and the charm of life are *émigrés* which will never return there.'[62]

---

* Hammer, for example, was born in 1774.

Ligne's two chief links with the French *émigrés* were hospitality and literature. Most Austrians, as one *émigrée*, the Baronne du Montet (née Mlle de la Boutetière), complained in her souvenirs, felt for French *émigrés* 'a pusillanimous distrust ... a result of ancient national hatreds'.[63] Ligne, however, showed more sympathy for French *émigrés* than he had for French nobles in their days of glory before 1789. Moreover, he could identify with them since he too had lost his inheritance and, since the Austrian Netherlands was now part of the French Republic, was also in theory a French *émigré*: in a letter to the Marquis de Bombelles he talks of *nous autres ruinés*.[64]

With relief French *émigrés* hailed the Hôtel de Ligne, despite the bad food, as a corner of France. The Comte de Salaberry even said: 'You feel you are in your homeland when you are in his house.' For the Comte d'Escars, who spent part of almost every evening at Ligne's, 'He was linked to all those serving those unfortunate princes and thought only of their misfortune ... He welcomed the French everywhere with eagerness.'[65] Proving his sympathies by acts as well as words, Ligne employed two French *émigrés*, Comte Auguste de Ségur-Cabanac and M. de Mussey, as adjutants in his regiment. The former drew an idealised map of the lost paradise of Beloeil, showing temples and mosques Ligne had not built. Mussey, however, was later dismissed by the Austrian government for having, at Ligne's instigation, gone to a party disguised as Louis XVI's nephew the Duc d'Angoulême.[66]

Literature was a more lasting link between Ligne and the French *émigrés* than hospitality. One of Ligne's closest friends in Vienna was a writer called Sénac de Meilhan, author of the celebrated novel *L'Émigré* (Brunswick, 1795), and many counter-revolutionary works (*Des Principes et des Causes de la Révolution Française* (London, 1790); *Du gouvernement, des moeurs et des conditions en France avant la Révolution* (Hamburg, 1795)). In 1795 Ligne helped to obtain an official residence permit for him to live in Vienna.

In the past Ligne had been too peripatetic, too obsessed with

women and himself, to be a good friend. In letters to new friends
– of whom his rank, warmth and charm always ensured copious
supplies – and in his works he frequently proclaimed his need
for intimate friendship with someone he saw every day.[67] Many
of his friends responded equally warmly: for example, Prince
Louis of Württemberg had written to him: 'I know nothing so
charming nor so tender as you. You are such an amiable and
loving creature that it is impossible to refuse oneself the happiness of being tenderly attached to you.'[68] However, after an
initial explosion of heat, his relationships often cooled rapidly.
Friends, such as Lord Malmesbury (whom, on first meeting he
called 'cher chevalier de mon âme', the best Englishman and best
ambassador, to whom he swore to be 'the best of your friends all
my life'),[69] disappear from his correspondence within a few
years. When his beloved friend, the Prince of Nassau-Siegen,
had fallen ill on their journey to the Crimea, it was the Prince of
Anhalt who took care of him; 'Ligne had the same concern, but
he could not take it on himself. I suffered and he could not bear
my moans.'[70]

In Vienna Ligne had more time for his friends, and was
extremely kind to Sénac. When this impoverished sixty-year-
old *émigré* was ill or tired, Ligne frequently climbed the stairs to
his third-floor room (all *émigrés* in Vienna lived on third or
fourth floors, as they were cheaper), and begged Sénac to take
more care of himself and go out more often. They saw each
other so frequently that, after Sénac died, Ligne wrote that,
although he had sent few *letters*, he had sent more than 1000
notes 'from my bed to his'. A footman would wait outside
Ligne's room to ensure he sent a reply: when Ligne was out of
Vienna, and his letters went by post, Sénac complained, as
Ligne's friends always did, that they were not as frequent as they
should be.[71]

Sénac wrote Ligne moving lines on the 'harvest' he could
derive from the loss of Beloeil, which could apply to many other
émigrés forced to turn from careers in the army or at court to
literature. Ligne had lost an immense inheritance but:

Il lui reste des biens à jamais affranchis
de la démocratique rage,
des rigueurs des saisons et des fureurs de Mars.
C'est son esprit, son coeur, riche et brillant domaine,
que l'amitié, l'amour ainsi que les beaux-arts,
comblent de fruits, de fleurs, qu'il moissonne sans peine.*

Indeed, the loss of his estates enabled Ligne to concentrate on his passions: literature and love. The mental harvest that Ligne reaped in the years away from Beloeil would fill many volumes.

Despite their close friendship, however, there is a cold note in Ligne's single sentence referring to Sénac's death in 1803, in a letter to another *émigré*, the Marquis de Bonnay: 'The death of him who had already long been defunct nevertheless pained me, although my legs are truly rejoicing.'[72] A literary portrait of Sénac by Ligne is equally cool, talking of his 'fatiguing' and 'extinguishing' wit: one always left his presence feeling discontented both with him and with oneself.[73]

Bonnay, whom Ligne called *mon cher bon*, was a former royalist deputy in, and three times President of, the National Assembly. Ligne and he had first met in Paris in 1768.[74] In 1798 he arrived in Vienna as an agent for the Bourbon pretender in exile, Louis XVI's younger brother, known to *émigrés* as Louis XVIII. Like Ligne, he was a former admirer of the Enlightenment who had turned to the counter-revolution. His white face and freezing manner gave him the name 'the spectre of the ancien regime'.[75] He looked so pale that when he was drinking a glass of red wine, a young woman shrieked 'he is swallowing his own blood!' Ligne and Bonnay shared a taste for scandal, word games, and forging other people's letters. Bonnay treated the Hôtel de Ligne as his own, and his letters to Ligne

---

* He still possesses goods for ever freed
  From democratic rage,
  From the rigours of the seasons and the fury of Mars,
  His spirit, his heart, rich and brilliant domain,
  Which friendship, love and the fine arts
  Cover with fruits and flowers, which he harvests with ease.

are loving and perceptive. When Ligne was out of 'our Vienna', Bonnay missed 'the charm of your malice' and 'the flexibility of your character and your mind':[76] 'You are for me the good half of Vienna.'[77] Their correspondence forms a chronicle of Vienna full of word games, parodies, literary allusions, gossip about mutual friends such as Nassau-Siegen, Armfelt and Countess Lanckoronska. Like Sénac, Bonnay complained that Ligne's letters were so rare that he felt 'in the crowd of the unlucky women whom you have exploited and abandoned'.[78] Bonnay's 'passion' for Ligne was strengthened by his feeling that he did not know Ligne by heart, that there were always new discoveries to make: 'You are a strange Prince. You do not give a f... about anything or anybody and yet suddenly, from time to time, one finds you have a heart where we least expected it.'[79]

While Bonnay kept Ligne in touch with French royalism, through another *émigré*, Charles-André Pozzo di Borgo, Ligne could observe the struggle against Bonaparte. The first and most relentless enemy of Napoleon Bonaparte, Pozzo di Borgo is confirmation of Ligne's belief in the importance of personality in history. Pozzo and Bonaparte came from Corsican noble families convinced of their superiority over the others. Originally revolutionary, in 1793 Pozzo chose to stay in Corsica and support counter-revolution while, perhaps for that reason, Bonaparte continued to serve the French Republic. Having been chased, in 1796, from Corsica, where he had been President of the Council of State during the British occupation, Pozzo came to Vienna on a mission with Lord Minto in 1798. Henceforth the political clash between dynastic Europe and France was paralleled by the personal duel between Pozzo and Bonaparte. Ligne said: 'Pozzo wants revenge on Napoleon for having taken his place.'[80]

Despite an unpolished manner and a Corsican accent, Pozzo became a star of the Vienna salons. Ligne admired him as 'one of those men who has the most fire and eloquence. He starts on any subject whatever, without knowing what he has to say: and insensibly it becomes luminous, profound, new, and often

reasonable.' In 1804 he left Vienna to enter Russian service, recommended by their mutual friend Count Razumovsky, the
Russian ambassador. Ligne wrote Pozzo a farewell letter saying
how much he would miss Pozzo's *beaux yeux noirs* and the white
teeth that lit his salon better than the guttering candle on the
Princesse de Ligne's loom: 'The ice of the Neva will never
extinguish the Vesuvius of your heart and spirit.' Ligne was fascinated by Pozzo: one of the last things Ligne wrote, after
Napoleon's fall, was an imaginary conversation between Pozzo
and Napoleon.[81]

For Pozzo's patron, the millionaire Russian ambassador
Count Razumovsky, Ligne professed a 'tender and eternal
attachment'. They corresponded about war and peace, and
Ligne attended the Count's Sunday dinners in the Palais
Razumovsky, a neoclassical masterpiece in the suburbs of
Vienna that combined Asian magnificence with European
luxury. Ligne could not resist mocking the ambassador's sense
of his own importance, declaring: 'I know a means certain to
make him perfectly happy.' After much questioning by friends
he replied: 'Yes, if it was possible that in all Vienna only he
knows what time it is.'[82]

The Palais Razumovsky was at the heart of Viennese musical
life in its golden age. Razumovsky maintained one of the last
private orchestras in Vienna; he was a friend and patron of
Mozart, Haydn and Beethoven, some of whose works were
dedicated to him and first performed in his palace. For Ligne,
however, music was little more than a soothing balm at church
or the opera. He described Mozart as 'this excellent and charming composer' but preferred Gluck. From 1804 to 1814
Beethoven lived on the Moelkerbastei, in a fourth-floor flat,
where he composed the fourth, fifth, seventh and eighth sym-
phonies. Yet it is possible that they never met. Among the hundreds of names mentioned in his memoirs, Ligne never refers to
the genius next door.[83]

In the tolerant atmosphere of Vienna, Ligne revised his
opinion of the English. He wrote: 'The migration of the English

is like that of the swallows and the woodcock. You see them at a certain season of the year and then no more ... the least amiable among them always have something rather remarkable about them. Even fools from that country never say anything vulgar and the wits have a cutting tone which does not resemble that of others.' In 1799 Ligne met Pozzo's patron Lord Minto, in Vienna to plan the next war against the French Republic. Lady Minto wrote: 'He is very constant to us, very clever but too odd to be understood at first by everybody. I like the whole family, especially Madame de Clary ... He has now nothing to live on but his pay; but they bear their misfortunes gently, and never grumble or complain.'[84]

In addition to French, English and Germans, Vienna attracted visitors from central Europe and the Balkans. Among Ligne's Hungarian friends in Vienna were Count Szechenyei, founder of the Hungarian National Museum, and Prince Louis Batthyani, with whom he had long conversations about the nature of liberty. After the third partition and extinction of Poland in 1795, Warsaw had become a Prussian garrison town. Paris was uninhabitable; therefore many Poles settled in Vienna. Ligne frequented two Polish salons, that of his neighbour the Princesse Maréchale Lubomirska, who lived in a splendid colonnaded palace in the Moelkerbastei, moving from room to room, or table to table, 'always pursued by inexorable boredom'; and that of Countess Lanckaronska, whose palace in the suburbs of Vienna was a second home for Ligne and his greatest friends, Bonnay, Pozzo and Armfelt.[85] Ligne was now so counter-revolutionary that he had congratulated the Russian commander Marshal Suvorov for destroying the country of which he had once dreamt of being king.[86] However, he was more broadminded culturally than politically. He wrote in praise of the Slav language, as 'the oldest because it is the most widely spread in the world although that is not a complete proof. It is *slavon* and not *esclavon*; and slav means glory.' In the early nineteenth century, at a time of general contempt, this passage was quoted with gratitude by Slavs trying to revive their culture.[87]

Vienna was also beginning its glorious and tragic destiny as a Jewish city. Despite Joseph II's edict of toleration of 1782, formidable restrictions remained on Jews' numbers, professions and property rights: they were not allowed to enter government service or own land. Nevertheless, a few thousand were allowed to live there, principally because the Imperial government needed them as bankers who helped finance the war effort.[88] Like the Emperors Joseph II and Francis II (who both visited synagogues) and unlike most of their contemporaries, Ligne was immune from anti-Semitism. Indeed Ligne liked Jews. As early as 1780 he had paid for the upkeep of a Jewish child staying with one of his staff in Brussels. In Teplitz, to the horror of Gentz, who had a vicious anti-Jewish streak, he turned up several evenings with 'this young Jewish boy from God knows where'.

Ligne especially liked the cultivated Jewish women who, barely out of the ghetto, opened salons that would be as important, for German literature, as those of Mme du Deffand and Mme Geoffrin had been for French. What Ligne called their 'excellent conversation', the freshness of their views and the depth of their culture, attracted an exhilarating mixture of actors, writers, diplomats and princes.[89] Among Ligne's friends in the Jewish literary sisterhood were Sophie, Baronne de Grotthus, whose vanity reached the proportions of a disease, and Regina Frohberg, a novelist whose real name was Rebecca Friedlander. In his letters he compared her to the Pope, asking her to give him her feet and hands to kiss as often as the Pope gave his to the faithful, claiming that the touch of her little finger had more effect than 'the complete favours of other women'.[90]

Ligne's views on Jews, expressed in *Mémoire sur les Juifs*, written in about 1798, show that Vienna could be a city of tolerance. He wrote: 'They have never been in fashion since God abandoned them ... a quarrel of 1800 years seems to me to have lasted long enough.' Even Voltaire, who preached tolerance, had been anti-Jewish and Ligne quoted his incredible remark: 'Nevertheless, they should not be burnt.' Ligne, on the other hand, praised Jews' morality and lack of drunkenness and, on

both practical and human grounds, criticised Christian governments for doing nothing to help alleviate their poverty and
living conditions. He was shocked that in many countries they
still had to wear distinguishing marks on their clothes. Instead,
he averred, they should be allowed decent quarters in towns,
land to cultivate, and freedom to conduct any business they
wanted. Before any other Christian, Ligne foretold the birth of
Zionism. If Jews continued to be ill-treated in Europe, in return
for helping the Ottoman Sultan to regenerate his Empire, they
might restore the Kingdom of Judea and rebuild the Temple of
Solomon. A new Garden of Eden would be 'the finest English
garden in the world'.[91]

Whatever their nationality or religion, Ligne's friends
flocked to the Moelkerbastei. Instead of being a guest in the
palaces of the nobility, Ligne preferred to be a host in his own
'parrot's cage'. Even more than before, hospitality became a
career. He wrote:

> My little house, the colour of roses, like my ideas, is on the
> ramparts and is the only open house in Vienna. I have six
> dishes for dinner, five for supper. *Arrive qui veut. S'asseoit qui
> peut.* Sometimes when the sixty people who frequent it arrive
> or meet there, there are not enough of my straw chairs; people
> stand in flux and reflux, like in the stalls, until those most in a
> hurry leave.

Vienna was obsessed with its stomach, and was said to consume
more food than any city of the same size. However, at supper at
the Prince de Ligne's there was so little to eat that guests fought
for a chicken wing. If he gave a tea party, tea, and nothing else,
was served.[92]

Ligne's conversation was the attraction. The most detailed
description comes from a former *Kapellmeister* of Frederick the
Great called J. F. Reichardt, who was so entranced by the
Prince's talk at dinner in the Moelkerbastei that he forgot to eat
or drink: 'Every event, every move, every word that occurs in
conversation lights a spark in him which flares up brightly, and

these sparks often follow each other so quickly that they appear to create a continuous circle of fire. In his presence one is wittier than usual and he often seems to me like a steel that strikes bright sparks from every flint.'[93] Unfortunately Reichardt recorded the Prince's style, not his words.

However, some of Ligne's jokes, which were called 'the stinging nettles of society', and terrified the Viennese, have been written down.[94] His old friend Prince Henry of Prussia – who did not die until 1802 – talked so much about the Seven Years' War that Ligne said it sounded like the Thirty Years' War. When a banker called Nathan Arnstein, who had made generous contributions to the Austrian war effort, became the first unconverted Jew in Vienna to be made a Freiherr in 1798 (almost a hundred years before a Rothschild was admitted into the House of Lords in England), Ligne called him 'the first Baron of the Old Testament': Ligne was a friend of his wife, Fanny von Arnstein, who held a rival cosmopolitan salon in Vienna. Some of his jokes are untranslatable.[95] When Pius VII succeeded Pius VI as Pope in 1800 Ligne said, 'Le Saint Siège va de pis en pis' ('The Holy See goes from bad to worse'), a play on the assonance, in French, between 'Pius' (*Pie*) and 'worse' (*pis*). He still talked about anything that came into his head – for example, the bare bottoms, several hundred in each regiment, that were seen when soldiers relieved themselves while waiting before a battle.[96]

Ligne also enjoyed what he termed 'white malice', claiming that like white magic, it gave so much pleasure that it was not harmful; of his dear cousin Louis Starhemberg, Ligne said that he had just enough ambition to be envious, and just enough conversation to be exhausting. He christened Princess Jablonowska, an agitated Polish woman whose conversation consisted of a rapid succession of unconnected ideas, Princess Confusionowska. When Francis II's third wife had her apartments redecorated, Ligne told Zinzendorf, at court, that they combined bad Italian taste with bad German taste.[97]

Despite, or because of, the sharp tongues of the Prince and

his daughters and granddaughters, everyone wanted to shine in the Hôtel de Ligne. Countess Thurheim wrote: 'The salon de Ligne formed the shrine of good taste. It was an Areopagus at the service of society...the school for good conversation.' Gentz, who in his first years in Vienna went to the Hôtel de Ligne once or twice a week, called it 'the first coterie in Vienna', and found the conversation so witty that it made him feel stupid.[98]

Ligne's friends show the range of his interests: he gossiped with Bonnay, talked history with Hammer, politics with Gentz, Pozzo and Razumovsky, and literature with Sénac de Meilhan and Regina Frohberg. Including Swedes and Corsicans, English and Russians, Poles and Hungarians, Germans and Jews, and French, they confirm that in Vienna in 1800 Europe was a reality. People talked, exchanged ideas, took jobs or mistresses, irrespective of national origin: barriers between races were less than between classes.

This cosmopolitanism was facilitated by a sense of belonging to a common cause: the struggle against France. The events of the Revolution, and the devastation caused by the subsequent French invasions of the Empire, Italy and the Netherlands, gave a moral, indeed religious, justification for the resentment much of Europe, and Ligne in particular, had long felt for France, 'this detestable, execrable and abominable nation which had been so happy for one hundred and fifty years', as Ligne put it.[99]

Ligne's friends were not just counter-revolutionary but royalist as well. Ligne, Bonnay, Sénac, Gentz, Pozzo di Borgo, Razumovsky formed a coterie dedicated to the destruction of the Republic and the restoration of the exiled Bourbons. They corresponded with Artois or Louis XVIII: indeed, at Gentz's request, he was naturalised French by Louis XVIII.[100] When Artois's younger son, the Duc de Berri, passed through Vienna in 1800, Ligne wrote a poem thanking heaven for letting them see a descendant of Henri IV.[101] For him the Bourbons now had the glamour of martyrdom. He wrote panegyrics of Marie Antoinette, corresponded with Artois and Vaudreuil and admired the devotion of Louis XVIII's courtiers the Ducs de Guiche and Duras, passing through Vienna on their way to his residence in Mittau in Courland because it was their year to be in waiting.[102]

Mysteriously, Ligne wrote nothing about the daughter of Louis XVI and Marie Antoinette, who lived in Vienna from 1795 to 1799 – perhaps he was considered one of her mother's unsuitable friends, against whom her teachers warned her. However, his secretary, Sauveur Legros, helped, with the *émigré* government's representative in Vienna the Bishop of Nancy, to compose one of the gospels of the new French royalism: *Journal de ce qui s'est passé à la tour du Temple, pendant la captivité de Louis XVI, Roi de France* by Cléry, a former *valet de chambre* of Louis XVI, who was residing in Vienna. The book was a commercial and political success when published in French in London in 1798: the list of subscribers was headed by the King and Queen and sixteen members of the British royal family.[103]

In the summer of 1803, at Teplitz in Bohemia, Ligne met Marie Joséphine of Savoy, wife of the exiled Louis XVIII. Ligne, who called her *Notre Dame de Mittau*, helped her to find lodgings and wrote to Bonnay on 16 August:

> She is better than twenty years ago when she was obliged to behave well. We talked more in the course of four days ... than during entire evenings when the most beautiful of Queens having taken my arm for the terrace [at Versailles] told me to give it to her sisters whom I dragged in silence and bad temper. Her small household is exactly right, neither splendid nor miserable.[104]

In 1803 Bonnay was summoned to Warsaw, to act as secretary to Louis XVIII: it was from Warsaw, earlier that year, that Louis XVIII had issued a declaration reasserting his right to the French throne and refusing Bonaparte's offers of financial compensation. Bonnay tried to tempt Ligne to come there, perhaps in the hope that Ligne would write a portrait of Louis XVIII as flattering as his recently published portraits of Frederick II and

Catherine II. On 5 October 1803, in a long description of a day at the Pretender's court, Bonnay expressed the wish that Ligne could participate in the conversation, in flattering terms: 'If you were here, dear Prince, you would appreciate the King and would be much appreciated by him; and in total you would spend two hours every day with us with the greatest pleasure. You would be so well understood by the King!' After he read out Ligne's letters to the Pretender, he

> charged me with a thousand compliments and expressions of friendship for you. Good God! how much you would enjoy his society and he yours! I must tell you that he has much gained in amiability since you last saw him ... he joins in everything, understands everything: I assure you that he would be completely at home in the soirées of the Moelkerbastei. (I mean those of *la bonne compagnie* and not those where you have been out at every crossroads to recruit the blind and the lame.)

Ligne, however, limited his relations with the exiled King to expressions of respect and attachment.[105]

Although Ligne was kept from an active career, many of his friends were personally engaged in the fight against the French Republic. Louis Starhemberg and Lords Minto and Mulgrave helped weave the coalitions against the Republic. Counter-revolution was the reason why Gentz and Pozzo first came to Vienna, and why both received pensions from the most persistent enemy of France, the British government. Even Hammer worked against the French, as an interpreter for the British army in Egypt. In these years Vienna was unofficial capital of the crusade against revolutionary France. Years before it formally opened in 1814, the Congress of Vienna had started; one of its centres was the Hôtel de Ligne.

Bohemia

At the end of the eighteenth century the most fashionable spa in Europe was the small town of Teplitz, in the rolling hills on the border of Bohemia and Saxony. It belonged to Ligne's son-in-law Prince Clary; Ligne came there for three to six months every summer. Prince Clary was one of the energetic Bohemian nobles who helped make Bohemia the richest province, and themselves the richest nobles, in the monarchy. While Princes Liechtenstein or Lobkowitz encouraged industry or agriculture, Prince Clary favoured tourism. Following a fire in 1793, Prince Clary had restored the family *Schloss* in Teplitz, transforming it into a large eighteenth-century town palace. Opposite it, he built hotels, bath houses and the first neogothic church in Bohemia. A theatre, a temple and a Turkish pavilion were constructed in his park. In 1801 the English philosopher Crabb Robinson wrote: 'As he derives great profit from the Bathing Guests he is interested in making the town attractive. In his Palace is a small but very handsome Theatre, his Gardens are open to the public and himself and family distinguish themselves by their Courtesy and Affability.'[1]

Ligne enjoyed Teplitz, not for its mineral waters but for its social life (and, no doubt, the opportunity to live at his son-in-law's expense). Just as Vienna seemed more attractive as a result of the eclipse of Paris, so Teplitz owed much of its animation to the decline of the rival watering place of Spa in the Ardennes, after the French occupation in 1794. An island of peace in a war-torn continent, Teplitz attracted German princes, French *émigrés*, Polish nobles, Russian diplomats and Dresden prostitutes (who, Ligne remarked, like the swallows, abandoned the gardens with the approach of autumn). Everyone met at the castle, to watch plays, stroll through the park or, if lucky enough to be invited, eat supper in the great rococo concert hall.

There were so many promenades, lunch parties, supper parties, plays, balls and *petits jeux* at Teplitz that when Armfelt visited it in 1801, with his mistress the Duchess of Courland and her daughters, 'the four richest heiresses in the North', he called it 'Sodom and Gomorrah'.[2] For Ligne:

> Teplitz ou paisible ou bruyant,
> Ou simple, agréable ou brillant,
> Par les fêtes de la soirée
> Varie toute la journée;
> Ou pittoresque, ou pastoral,
> Solitaire, ou sentimental,
> Ou tout en chaque genre abonde,
> Est le premier séjour du monde.[3]

Prince Clary must occasionally have found his father-in-law's company exhausting: his great-great-great-grandson 'Alfie' Clary, expelled from Teplitz with other Germans by the Czechs in 1945, in *Reminiscences of a European*, records a family tradition that Ligne was 'not always easy to live with'. However, Ligne was useful in attracting people to Teplitz, and acting as an unofficial master of ceremonies, like Beau Nash at Bath. In the evening at the castle Prince Clary settled down to cards; Christine cut out prints and drawings for her screens; Ligne played billiards, flirted or harangued swooning German ladies about the rash of suicides caused by the exaggeration of their literature.[4]

At Teplitz, as well as seeing his daughter and old friends such as Prince Henry of Prussia or the Comte de Vaudreuil, Ligne made a succession of new ones: Princess Gallizin, Comte Féodore Golovkine, King Gustavus IV of Sweden. Almost any attractive or high-born lady who arrived at Teplitz received letters, poems and offers of friendship from the Prince de Ligne. Princess Louise of Prussia, a niece of Frederick the Great, writes in her memoirs that in 1799: 'On the very evening of the day we arrived there the Prince de Ligne ... came to beg us to join their circle in the hall where all the visitors to the baths met.'[5]

One new friend Ligne made through his visits to Teplitz was an ageing adventurer, living eleven miles away in the baroque palace of Dux, which belonged to a nephew of the Princesse de Ligne called Count Waldstein. His name was Giacomo Casanova. Worn out by a life of love affairs, financial speculation and secret diplomacy (as well as eleven bouts of venereal disease), in 1784 Casanova had accepted the Count's offer, made over a Vienna dinner table, to be his librarian. Ligne and Casanova met ten years later during Ligne's first summer at Teplitz, through the Clarys: Casanova often went to Teplitz to give readings from his works or to direct plays in the theatre. Ligne and Casanova shared the religion of the senses (although Casanova specialised in nuns, nieces and lesbians), and a love of literature. In the castles of Bohemia, as Europe, in Ligne's phrase, went to the devil, the two ageing debauchees fell into each other's arms.[6]

In Dux, Casanova, at this time famous for his life of adventures (such as his escape from prison in the Doge's Palace in Venice in 1755) rather than his writings, was so unhappy that he thought of flight or suicide. He had transformed the castle into a nest of vipers: he received only 1000 florins a year, plus board and lodging, and senior servants teased and insulted him or had him beaten up. He was grateful for Ligne's 'electricity': 'Your mind, my Prince, is one of those which gives élan to another's.' He admired Ligne as one of the few men who had learnt to know themselves and to despise flattery: the only quality he lacked was patience (what Ségur called his 'restless flutter').[7] He loved Ligne so much that he said that if the Prince recovered Beloeil, he wanted to go and live there.[8]

With Casanova, Ligne dropped his mask of charm and opened his heart. Modest, encouraging and tender, Ligne passed on compliments, reassured Casanova that Count Waldstein and all the Ligne family loved and appreciated him and behaved, not as a Prince to an employee, but as one writer towards another. Casanova was trying to make sense of his life and win fame and fortune by writing that astonishing panorama of the century of frivolity and promiscuity called *The History of My Life*. Ligne was one of the first people to read it, section by section, literally as Casanova wrote. Ligne said that it made him either laugh, think or have an erection. The memoirs' cynicism was their greatest merit, but Casanova should not veil his pleasures. Showing his persistent interest in homosexuality, referring to certain of Casanova's adventures in Constantinople and Venice, he asked, in his mocking tone: 'Why did you refuse Ismail, neglect Petronius and rejoice that Bellisse was a girl?'[9]

No writer could have found a more encouraging reader. In a letter of 17 December 1794 Ligne begged Casanova not to cut his memoirs: 'You have done so well uncastrated. Why do you want your works to be? Leave the *History of My Life* as it is.'[10] Ligne relished the Italicisms in Casanova's French: 'They have more force than ridiculous French grammar: an old woman past menopause.'[11] Referring to his own contract with the Walther publishers in Dresden (see below), he added: 'Do as I do. Sell yourself in your own lifetime to the Walther brothers in Dresden for 100 ducats a year. I can never tell you enough, my dear friend, to what degree I am tenderly attached to you.' At times Ligne wrote to him once a month. The envelopes were addressed, in French, 'A monsieur Casanova, bibliothécaire de Mr le Comte de Waldstein, à Dux près Toeplitz, par Prague'.[12]

Ligne was kind to the man as well as flattering to the writer. He lent Casanova money, interceded for him with Count Waldstein, and tried to dispel his gloom, assuring him that with his stomach, his heart and his genius, no one could be old (Casanova was sixty-nine in 1794, ten years older than Ligne).[13] Ligne showed his esteem by sharing his disappointments, confiding in Casanova his hopes of a command in Italy, claiming that a phrase was as difficult to create as a coalition.[14] With Casanova, Ligne even tried, for the first time in his life, to be a reliable correspondent.[15] An example of their passionate friendship is the end of Ligne's letter to Casanova of 8 December 1796:

> Adieu, my two dear Casanovas,*
>
> I love today's Casanova as much as the Casanova aged 36 and if I was a woman I would prove it to you.
>
> I detach myself with difficulty from your body and your mind and will never detach myself from your heart, mine being all yours, my dear friend.[16]

The two writers laid bare their feelings. Whereas Casanova made a religion of pleasure, Ligne was more disillusioned. His heart had been broken by his son's death. He wrote to Casanova:

> I believed like you in the superiority of the mass of good over the mass of evil. But two years ago today [22 September 1794], the most unhappy day of my life, I learnt that my poor Charles had lost his, and I feel that all my my pleasures together (and I have had a prodigious number of them) have never caused me, either in mass or in detail, the thousandth degree of pleasure that this dreadful loss has caused me pain:
>
> Take away from me this sort of destruction of part of my being. I agree with you. The loss of my finest possessions and of my entire fortune has not caused as much pain as the kiss of a Jewess of seventeen years has caused me pleasure yesterday in the garden of Teplitz. All the pleasures of the body, the soul and the mind are a force for good: and there are only two real ills, illness and poverty to the point of not having enough to eat. So much the worse for the fools who know others.
>
> Can I place the life of my poor Charles beside his death? I adored him for his courage, his character, his naive, funny and expressive gaiety: but he has never given me as much pleasure by living as he has given me pain by living no more. I am sorry, my dear friend. I did not expect to finish so sadly after

---

* The young Casanova about whom Ligne had just been reading in his memoirs, and the old Casanova living in Bohemia.

having begun differently. I am shaking myself. You see the
bad moment is passing.[17]

Goethe called Ligne 'the most cheerful man of the century'.
He had an enviable life, doing what he wanted, conquering
courts and hearts wherever he went. He electrified everyone,
from Frederick the Great to Casanova. In old age he was surrounded by adoring daughters and granddaughters. Since he
was able to add to the Kahlenberg and build *le petit Beloeil*, he
was not as poor as he pretended. Yet a phrase in his memoirs, 'it
was at a sad period of my life and it added to it',[18] like his confession to Casanova that Charles's death had given him more pain
than his life had given him pleasure, suggests that there was, in
some moods, a dissatisfied and disappointed man beneath his
glittering façade. Life had not come up to expectations. He lived
with a wife he found unbearable; he had neither found the ideal
mistress nor won military glory. Even at Teplitz, he was no
stranger to solitude.[19]

Even Charles de Ligne, the most important person in Ligne's
life, had put other people first. He belonged to a group of seven
friends in Vienna who had declared themselves *les indissolubles*.
One of them, Countess Kinsky, was his mistress. Her letters do
not survive; Charles de Ligne's to another *indissoluble* do. Prince
Joseph Poniatowski, the handsome unmarried nephew of King
Stanislas Augustus of Poland, formerly an ADC of Joseph II
and an officer in the Regiment de Ligne, had been wounded with
Charles de Ligne at the storming of Sabacz. Charles wrote to
Poniatowski with an emotional intensity remarkable even by the
standards of the age. In 1790, while Poniatowski had returned to
Warsaw, Charles had remained in Vienna with his father.
Nevertheless, his days and his heart, he writes, were empty
without the most perfect creature who exists,

> *mon bon et incomparable ami, mon unique ami intime, mon cama-*
> *rade de coeur et d'âme, de pensée, de volonté, de désir* ... as for
> love I detest it and if I ever felt myself again infected with such

a frenzy, I think I would go away to America, in fact, *mon garçon*, without you, my heart, my horses, my clothes, my body, my appetite, my member, in fact everything is [?useless], adieu, if anyone tells you that he loves you more than I do, give him a blow from your sword.[20]

In his letters to 'Pepi' Poniatowski, Charles rarely mentions his father.

Ligne's portrait of Casanova, like those of Potemkin and Frederick the Great, regularly receives the honour of quotation by his biographers. Ugly, dark-skinned, built like Hercules, he was vindictive and easy to anger, particularly at Dux, where he could no longer behave like a satyr in a forest, and seduce women.

A day did not go by that he did not have a quarrel in the household over his coffee, his milk, his plate of macaroni on which he insisted. The cook had failed to give him polenta, the equerry had given him a bad coachman to come and see me, dogs had barked in the night; more guests than Waldstein had expected had led him to eat at a small table. A hunting horn had annoyed him by false or sharp notes. The priest had bothered him by trying to convert him. The count had not said good day to him first... The count had lent a book without telling him. A *palefrenier* had not taken off his hat to him when he went past. He had spoken in German, nobody had understood. He grew angry, people laughed. He showed his French poems, people laughed. He gesticulated while reciting his Italian poems, people laughed. He made a bow when entering as Marcel the famous dancing master had taught him to do sixty years ago, people laughed.[21]

At the end of his life Casanova was especially saddened by the French destruction of his ancient and beloved Republic of Venice in 1797. He died in June 1798, saying, 'Great Lord and you, witnesses to my death, I have lived as a philosopher and die as a Christian.'[22] Ligne had been one of his last visitors.

In 1801 and 1802 Ligne saw much of another brilliant memoir writer, an *émigré* called Comte Alexandre de Tilly. Once a pert young page at Versailles, Tilly had become a heavy-drinking professional gambler (he was to commit suicide years later when found cheating at cards). He lived in Berlin, where his French poems and charm won him the title of Court Chamberlain: another visitor to Teplitz, a Baltic baroness who wrote religious novels called Julie de Krüdener, introduced him to Ligne. They continued to correspond and in 1805 Tilly dedicated his memoirs to Ligne as 'one of the men who has best judged Europe and best known France'. As a revelation of debauch and disillusion, Tilly's memoirs are the equivalent among the memoirs of the eighteenth century of *Dangerous Liaisons* among its novels. They suggest that Mme de Balbi, the mistress of the Comte de Provence, future Louis XVIII, went cruising at night in the streets of Versailles.[23]

Teplitz also brought Ligne into contact with German writers. While France was winning victories on the battlefield, central Europe was winning victories of another kind. Karl August Duke of Weimar made Weimar, a rustic city of only 7000 inhabitants, as famous for writers as Dresden for porcelain or Berlin for soldiers. With a smaller revenue than many English peers, living in simple houses and castles, Karl August gave jobs to the geniuses who were giving force and purity to the German language and literature: the journalist Wieland became tutor to the Duke's children, the critic Herder a civil servant, and the playwright Schiller, director of the Ducal theatre.[24] Goethe himself found security and inspiration not in the great trading city of Frankfurt, where he was born, but in Weimar. He became a noble, the Duke's chief minister and favourite, and director of court festivities: they went hunting and drinking together and called each other *du*.[25]

The Duke first met Ligne at Teplitz in 1797. Both were natural, amiable pleasure lovers who were schoolboys at heart: they liked each other at once.[26] The Duke said that he had never felt at ease in his life until he met Ligne.[27] Ligne was invited to

Weimar, the Duke was begged to return to Teplitz. In one letter Ligne wrote to the Duke: 'If only I could pass all my life with Your Highness about whom all our family has talked ecstatically all evening, on account of all the kindnesses with which he honours us and the amiability, gaiety, good temper and simplicity joined to so many qualities which we admire...' Another letter to the 'sovereign of the modern German Athens' ends: 'I beg him to receive with kindness the eternal assurances of my soul *immortal* for Your Highness.'[28]

With Goethe, Ligne's relations amounted to little more than the respect and flattery accorded, from a safe distance, by one celebrity to another. After an exchange of poems in 1804, they finally met in 1807 at another Bohemian spa, Carlsbad, in the salon of a Russian beauty called Princess Bagration, known as *la chatte blanche*, for her amatory skills and alabaster skin. It seemed miles from the wars and troop movements that were then infesting Germany. Goethe found that Ligne lived up to his reputation: 'He appeared ever in good spirits, ingenious, equal to all occasions, everywhere welcome and at home as a man of the world and of action.' They met, talked and gambled again at Teplitz in 1810, 1811 and 1812: Goethe was especially captivated by Titine de Ligne, with whom he went on excursions into the Bohemian countryside. Ligne, who enjoyed Goethe's novel of rustic love, *Elective Affinities*, overwhelmed his *cher, grand, sublime ami* with more poems and greater compliments.[29]

As well as a social epicentre, Teplitz was a place of reunion for the Ligne family. Ligne knew that marriage was principally a property arrangement, and claimed to be outraged by its 'indecency', calling it 'the most sacred engagement of the heart profaned by parents and notaries': after a brutal wedding night, the bride usually awoke in tears.[30] But he enforced conventional marriages in his own family – for example, that of his granddaughter Sidonie at Teplitz in 1807.

In 1806 Ligne had gone to Lemberg to inspect his regiment and drill the men in Polish. On the way there he had a touching interview, arranged by Princess Jablonowska (one of *les indissolubles*), with his daughter-in-law Hélène, whom he had not seen since 1787. After Charles's death she had married her lover, Count Vincent Potocki, who had turned into a despotic and unfaithful husband. She greeted her former father-in-law like a drowning woman in need of help. 'What a touching interview with my former daughter-in-law become, by an error for which she told me she paid heavily, Madame Vincent Potocki! What a lot of sweet, bitter, gay, sad, charming, cruel, consoling and poignant memories!' In the joy of reunion after nineteen years of separation, remembering Charles and shedding so many 'tears of regret or of tenderness', they could hardly speak. They forgot their quarrels and assured each other that neither had changed.[31]

Through Ligne's efforts a marriage was concluded between his granddaughter Sidonie and her stepfather's son by a first marriage, Count François Potocki: the Potockis were one of the richest families in Poland, so Sidonie could count on a grand establishment. Vincent Potocki's role in the break-up of their son's marriage horrified the Princess but not the Prince de Ligne. Ligne wrote to Vincent Potocki: 'I am delighted thereby to reunite interests of family and heart ... By this marriage I feel I am becoming Polish again.' In a letter to Hélène, who had last seen her daughter when she was four weeks old, he wrote: 'Without being beautiful she is pretty, very well formed and agreeable. I do not doubt that she will suit our son-in-law as I already like to give him this name.' With a dig at his wife he added, 'She is at a school likely (between ourselves) to form character.'[32] The marriage took place at Teplitz on 8 September 1807. That evening in the great hall of the *Schloss* there was a concert and a play during which Ligne gave a speech so touching for the new couple that the audience began to laugh and cry at the same time. Afterwards the guests, escorted by torchbearers in full livery, proceeded to Mont Ligne where the Duke of Weimar had organised a supper and splendid illuminations. Much in love at first, the couple soon separated. Living between Paris and Warsaw, Sidonie remained a stranger to the Ligne family, as she had always been.[33]

The Princesse de Ligne had still not forgiven her daughter-in-law and did not attend the wedding. Despite the fact that her brothers and sisters had married some of the greatest nobles in Bohemia, Counts Sternberg, Kinsky and Waldstein, there is no evidence that, after visits in 1794 and 1795, she came to Teplitz.[34] Was she invited?

Ligne summed up Teplitz in his autobiographical notes: 'A life charming on account of my Christine and varied on account of all Europe passing through or bathing there ... Many *passades* with Jewesses or actresses.'[35] Even after he entered his sixtieth year in 1795, love remained one of his principal occupations, and he had more time for it in Teplitz than in Vienna. Christine was his confidante – although Ligne could not believe, and frequently reproached his daughter for, her failure ever to allow an admirer to reach 'the point where she could be pregnant by him'.[36] One of the frankest letters sent by a father to a daughter describes a love affair at Beloeil, when he was about fifty-eight:

> I have abandoned myself to a rustic little penchant, for a village girl, pretty enough to eat, who has the most beautiful eyes in the world, and enough relations and prejudices to ensure that I am lucky enough to be still unlucky for a few days. She is called Lucie, sings wonderfully, [unreadable] wonderfully, and every day comes to the park to inflame me further. I find it charming to decide to love respectfully in the village. I embrace you from afar with even more pleasure than my Lucie close up.[37]

All his life Ligne would continue to bed servants and peasants (no doubt often paying for the experience): Ligne also saw prostitutes or courtesans, whom he found more relaxing than ladies, since he could guarantee spending at least an hour in their beds, undisturbed by a husband or a mother. However, affairs outside his own class did not occupy Ligne for long. As he wrote, in a portrait of himself under the name 'Menippe': 'You had to be at least a baroness to keep the attention of Menippe, whose aristocracy has always been in the heart.' When he arrived in Vienna,

Henrietta Auersperg was no longer in love with him: he had every reason to hunt.[38]

The list of his mistresses is as cosmopolitan as that of the visitors to Teplitz. Among the least transitory were: in 1795–6, in Teplitz, a grand passion with Countess Josephine de Pachta, who left him after two years for a philosophy professor in Prague.[39] From 1797 to 1802 he frequently saw Mme de Crayen, 'the queen of Leipzig', a ravishing and witty woman of Huguenot descent who numbered the Chevalier de Boufflers and the King of Prussia among her admirers. Ligne admired her, calling her a *première consule*, 'because you are in genius and conquest a true first consul capable of taking Egypt and the entire world. I kissed your letter for lack of anything else to kiss.'

Other mistresses, or at least objects of admiration, were: Mme Ventz Losska, 'the most beautiful creature I have had and seen', who owned the feudal lordship of Kahlenberg; and in 1802–4 he was almost in love with a pretty, devoutly Catholic, nineteen-year-old Dutch refugee called Comtesse Josephine de Velderen, who kept him at a distance. He himself wrote, when inscribing a mistress's initials on the wall of the Kahlenberg: 'I always think it is the last one: oh! this time it certainly is.'[40]

While such affairs were entirely sexual, his relations with his other mistresses retain an aura of mystery: in the absence of the ladies' diaries or letters, it is impossible to know how enterprising he was, or what they thought of him. Often the only surviving evidence comes from his memoirs. Some affairs at least were comedies of manners, pursued out of a desire to maintain his reputation as a Don Juan, an addiction to writing love letters and arranging rendezvouses, or simply the need to occupy himself. In Vienna, as Ligne knew, people said: 'I do not love when I love.'[41] Bonnay, who knew him well, did not believe in half his love affairs. However, one surviving love letter in the Decin archives, written in 1799 and begging for an 'infusion of Ligne', suggests that Ligne could inspire passion. 'Come, come here, dear angel prince. I love you too much to repeat to you that I love you. The French language is so poor and my heart so rich.'[42]

As he grew older, his passions became more platonic. In 1805–7 at Teplitz and Vienna he worshipped Princess Basile Dolgoruky, to whom he wrote: 'You are in my head, in my heart and everywhere; you are a mythical goddess, you are a princess out of a novel.' To amuse her he told her – what cannot be found in his writings – that Catherine would leave the room to make love and when she returned he would laugh and say only a quarter of an hour ago Her Majesty was behaving like a private person. However, Princess Dolgoruky also kept him at a distance: she was angry if even his hand touched hers.[43]

Since temples were part of his life, Ligne built his own just outside Teplitz, on a hill with splendid views, which he called Mont Ligne. It was a red-roofed hexagonal neogothic summer house, lined with mirrors and sofas and surrounded by trees. It was inaugurated in 1805 by a mock coronation of Ligne (to parody the recent coronation of Napoleon in Paris), and appointment of dignitaries, lunch for twenty, and guests singing couplets written by Ligne and Princess Dolgoruky.[44]

In 1807 he had another platonic passion for the Princess of Solms, sister of Queen Louise of Prussia, whom he called 'grace and beauty in perpetuity'. He felt for her not love, nor passion, nor friendship, 'too weak and disinterested', but *entraînement*: 'we write to each other two or three times a day; I make little verses. I am very happy.'[45]

Another attraction of Teplitz was its proximity to Dresden. Dresden had 60,000 inhabitants and between 1794 and 1804 Ligne went there, by boat down the Elbe, at least twelve times.[46] Because of its position between Berlin and Vienna, and on the road east to Warsaw and St Petersburg, as well as its own appeal as a court city, Dresden attracted many foreigners, especially Russians and Poles; Dresden had been the principal residence of the Kings of Poland from 1697 to 1763 and Poles felt more at home there than in Berlin. The post of ambassador to Dresden, the first in his long and brilliant career, seemed to the young

Metternich an excellent place from which to observe 'the northern courts'.[47] Ligne, who hoped Metternich would marry either Euphémie or Flore, saw him often, ending letters: 'Come quickly to Teplitz, I beg you, dear Count.'[48]

Time appeared to have stood still at the court of the kindly Elector Frederick Augustus II, known as 'the righteous', where courtiers wore clothes fifty years out of date. Ligne wrote that the Elector had taste, merit, and virtue with a touch of the grotesque. After spending a day at court: 'My God, what nice people they are, that whole family of Saxony! What cordiality! What good conversation with the king [as Frederick Augustus II had become in 1806] despite his shyness! What boredom at the reception! What bad food at dinner!'[49]

However the principal reason for Ligne's visits to Dresden was not to visit the court but to see his publisher and check on sales and proofs. After 1794, to compensate for his inactivity as a general and a courtier, he concentrated on his career as a writer. His principal occupation every day was neither society, nor love, but writing. Even in the 1780s, at the height of his military and political career, he had continued to write: the *Mémoires sur les Campagnes du prince Louis de Bade* were published in Brussels in 1787, the memoir on Frederick the Great in Berlin in 1789. By 1793 he had finished works on the wars of 1756 and 1778.[50]

When he arrived in Vienna in 1794 he brought most of his manuscripts with him. Later that year he signed a contract with the Walther brothers, court publishers of the Electors of Saxony, for the publication of his complete works. Dresden had more writers and larger lending libraries than any other German city, so it was a natural place of publication.[51]

The Walther brothers were the first publishers with whom Ligne had negotiated on a commercial basis. They paid Ligne 100 ducats a year, since he needed the money. Ligne wrote to Casanova that he made 'the presses groan in Dresden, in order not to make my creditors groan in Vienna'. His books paid for his grotto and pavilions on the Kahlenberg, and he was so keen to earn more money that, like some modern authors, he tried to sell copies directly to his friends. Ligne loved the Walther brothers (unfortunately their archives were destroyed in the bombing of Dresden in 1945). They had published an edition of Voltaire's *Oeuvres* in 1752–6 and, although printing in French in Germany, their presses were so accurate that Ligne never had a word or a punctuation mark to correct.[52]

In all, Ligne published thirty-four volumes called *Mélanges militaires, littéraires et sentimentaires*, the first in 1795, the last in 1811. By a remaining sense of princely propriety, his name does not appear on the title page, although the Ligne arms, the bonnet of a Prince of the Holy Roman Empire, the initials 'CL' and the place of publication, 'de mon réfuge sur le Leopoldsberg', made his identity obvious. These volumes show that Ligne had followed Senac's advice to cultivate the 'rich and brilliant domain' of his mind. Indeed they provide a near-complete inventory of its contents, as well as a panorama of his life and times.

A mixture of poems, plays, stories, history and autobiography, the *Mélanges* have an astonishing range. There is no order or structure. They include the 'Discours sur la profession des armes', which he had written at the age of fifteen; reprints of previous works such as *Coup d'oeil sur Beloeil* and *Préjugés militaires*; and accounts of his conversations with Voltaire and Rousseau and military campaigns. The same volume might contain texts on topics as varied as Paris, Cretins, Gypsies and Poland. Ligne even wrote about his lavatory. In *Voyage philosophique à ma chaise percée* (the title is a parody of the recently published and very popular *Voyage autour de ma chambre* by Xavier de Maistre), written on 11 September 1798, he praised his lavatory as a refuge from the importunate and self-important visitors who flooded his bedroom, many of whom begged for money. He described its contents (letters, newspapers, pot pourri jars and sofas), and the people who had received or died on the lavatory such as the Duc de Vendôme, Catherine II, Stanislas Augustus, and, with a remnant of his former radicalism, made fun of his own titles and distinctions.[53]

By their length the *Mélanges* have both preserved and

destroyed his reputation. He wrote too much too quickly, relying on inspiration rather than reflection, so the better pieces are drowned in a mass of lesser works. The Marquis de Bonnay, who claimed to be his only friend to have read all his works, praised his flexibility of style and taste, but added: 'Since nothing is perfect, you are too lazy to correct and as an author you have too much *amour propre* to prune, I would like to charge M. de Meilhan with this task.' His volumes should be castrated: it would make them more vigorous.[54] Ligne replied to *Monsieur le châtreur* that he defended only 'my wars and my gardens'. However, he was sufficiently an author to enquire: 'What effect would the memoirs of my life have on the public?'[55]

As in his correspondence, there is often a sense of trying too hard, too many displays of wit or erudition, too many word games and jokes whose point is now lost. Much is easy to forget. Many of his plays, such as *Don Carlos* a tragedy in five acts, based on Schiller's *Don Carlos*, or *Le Sultan du Congo*, which, as Basil Guy has shown, is copied from Diderot's *Les bijoux indiscrets* (like many of his remarks on women in *Ecarts Posthumes*), have not been performed.[56]

The volumes include poems written to anyone he met: to an ugly woman pretending to be Polish (because Polish women were thought alluring), whom he called *la belle terriblowska*; to his adjutant Lieutenant Dettinger, who had started a law suit against him; to his own capital sins; to a Teplitz friend, Princess Gallizin, returning her handkerchief:

> Sultan, je vous le jetterais,
> Admirateur je vous l'adresse.
> Jeune et beau, je vous aimerais;
> et vous le redirais sans cesse.

or to 'Mlle de.', asking her to make love on his tomb:

> Vous voyez ce gazon dont j'ai couvert ma tombe,
> Qu'au plus charmant objet on y donne le jour;

Qu'au lieu de la tristesse au plaisir on y succombe,
Et que mon tombeau soit un autel à l'Amour.*[57]

The most moving poem is addressed to Angélique d'Hannetaire, who was now living in Paris. Saying that he felt as if he had lived a hundred years, he expressed bitter regret for the number of times he had left her to pursue her rival, glory, in Paris or Vienna: 'laissant les vers et l'amour et la chasse, pour ne trouver ailleurs rien à mettre à leur place.' With her every day had seemed like a minute. He should have listened to his soul: even while travelling he had regretted her fireside. Too late, he realised that he had deceived himself.[58]

Of the thirty-four volumes, thirteen are history, of every kind: personal, philosophical, classical, above all military. Having read extremely widely, he realised that history was often a tissue of prejudice, vanity and partiality. It should only be written by a contemporary or by a researcher who had been through government or family papers. Memoirs were full of lies; diaries were more credible: he himself went through the records of the Hofkriegsrat, presumably with the help of a German-speaking assistant, to write *Mémoires sur les grands généraux de la guerre de quarante ans* in volume XIX, an account of sixty-two of them. He hoped to suck the juice out of everything already written on a subject and make it 'new, piquant, clear and with a moral message'.[59]

However, Ligne did not always follow his own precepts. Much of his history is simply collections of letters and documents from the years he had served Joseph II – which led to protests from the Austrian police on the grounds that he had revealed political secrets.[60] He published dull accounts of the Orders of the Golden Fleece and Maria Theresa. *Petit Plutarque de toutes les Nations*, a catalogue of famous men from all ages and

---

* You see this grass with which I have covered my grave:
  Let it be used for the most charming purpose;
  Instead of sadness, let people yield there to pleasure,
  And let my tomb be an altar to Love.

countries, contains phrases such as: 'The four Erics [of Sweden] are not admired enough.'[61] At least he often displayed an unconventional point of view. For example, while most contemporaries admired Peter the Great's brutal occidentalisation of Russia, Ligne wrote that Europe was so 'civilised' that it was more barbarian than *la barbarie* and 'The Russians were not barbarians when Peter I became so to make them civilised.'[62]

His best historical works are those dealing with the campaigns in which he himself had served, like the Seven Years' War and the campaign against the Turks, or with people who captured his imagination – for example, one of the most unconventional soldiers of the eighteenth century, the Marquis de Bonneval, later known as 'Ahmet Pasha'. Having left both the French and Austrian armies in disgrace, Bonneval had arrived in Constantinople in 1731, exchanged the hat for the turban and begun to help modernise the Ottoman army's tactics and artillery. Instead of Commander-in-Chief of the Imperial army, he became the restorer of the Ottoman Empire. As Ligne relates with glee, he avoided the necessity of circumcision by inviting mullahs to dinner, getting them drunk, leaving the room and then returning brandishing a bit of blood-stained sheep intestine. D'Antraigues, whose uncle the Comte de Saint-Priest had been ambassador in Constantinople, and Casanova, who had met him in Constantinople in 1745, provided some of his stories. Von Hammer-Purgstall translated oriental manuscripts and the inscription on Bonneval's tomb in Constantinople; and Ligne also relied on stories about Bonneval that he had heard from his father and uncle, who had known him in Brussels and Vienna.[63] Ligne's habit of listening to the old and befriending adventurers had enabled him to write a work which is still a source for Bonneval's life.

For their combination of physical details and psychological perception, Ligne's portraits – of Potemkin, Casanova or Breteuil – often disguised under names taken from antiquity – Aventuros for Casanova, Aristophile for his own father – are always quoted by biographers. In 1829, referring to the letters to

Mme de Coigny published in the *Mélanges*, his old friend the Comte de Ségur, who had witnessed many of the events Ligne described, delivered his judgement on Ligne's value as a historical source: Ligne was

> too favourable to all his friends. His happy temperament and happy position made him see all things through a medium *couleur de rose*. He praised everyone and if he was sincere, he must occasionally have been misjudging. He was also, when I knew him in 1786, too young perhaps for his years; it gave him a restless flutter that took from the respect his solid talents and wonderful experience of mankind naturally excited. Still he was charming. The Empress played with him as with a child; and the adoration he expressed for her was perfectly sincere. His manner of giving her conversations and those of the emperor of Germany, during our interesting voyage, is perfect; it is often verbatim; and this is the charm of his letters. With all their wit and affectation of wit, truth lies at the bottom; and without truth there is no good writing.[64]

Ligne still believed in the importance of personalities in history. In an unpublished thought preserved in the Clary papers at Decin, he wrote:

> We judge history with sang froid, because we are not living with Pericles, Solon, Caesar and Cicero. I hazard that the personal feelings they aroused, or private interest, made people judge their actions and speeches with bias. Towards contemporaries there is always party spirit, envy, frustrated ambition. Vengeance for not having a part to play. Cabals. Admiration for fools. Pandering to the powerful. Taking the opposite side. And no profound convictions because we do not dare to interrogate ourselves profoundly.[65]

In his youth, describing his visit to Rousseau, he had written: 'Even if I could be profound, I would not make the effort to be so.' He often gave the impression of being too rushed and too confident to want to see below the surface. After 1794, however, he was eager to distil the experience of a lifetime for the reading public. The best of his epigrams, which he called *Mes écarts*, show that frivolity and profundity can be two aspects of the same appetite for life, as compatible as love of war and gardens, or love for two people at the same time.

Among his hundreds of epigrams, some are worthy of comparison with La Rochefoucauld or Clausewitz. 'Politics is the art of making war without killing anyone' anticipates the maxim of Clausewitz: 'War is politics pursued by other means.' For him political skill was a matter of instinct: 'Tactics are taught to young officers. But there is no school for young ministers. One is suited to politics or one is not.'

'I would like to see a School of presence of mind and a Professor of firmness, prudence, foresight and expediency, rather than of Law and History, which can be learnt without a guide.' Always convinced of the importance of private emotions in public life, he wrote: 'The passions of the wicked are stopped by the executioner. But those of the virtuous are much more dangerous. Lovers commit crimes; zealous ministers start wars; and pure but blinkered men are not afraid of revolutions. Any passion, even for the good, is something dangerous.'[66]

Many of his 'outbursts' make one speculate that Ligne's love affairs lacked intensity:

> In love only the beginnings are charming; I am not surprised that one enjoys beginning again often.

> Jealousy lasts longer than love … It is because amour propre is the last to die.[67]

> There are symptoms of love as predictable as symptoms of illness. You feel hot or cold at the time. You share the same attitudes. You agree in your opinions.

This last anticipates Stendhal in *De l'Amour*.[68]

His cynicism about friendship is expressed in the following epigrams:

One thinks one greatly regrets one's old friends, whom one has seen die with sang froid. It is oneself whom one regrets.

It is as difficult to find a real friend as a wife or mistress.

One should ask permission to help; for if one receives favours from a man for whom one does not care, one is obliged to feel obliged.[69]

Some of his remarks anticipate the medical discoveries of the twentieth century. People should pay more attention to colours: 'They have, I am sure, much more authority and analogy with our feelings than we imagine. I bet that the inhabitants of a town painted white and pink, in green, in yellow and in light blue, would be much happier than those of an Imperial city of Swabia with black houses.'*

'I would like to know if there are no physical means of improving the soul and regulating the mind... Who knows if there is not a food which influences thinking? ... Doubtless it is to their type of nourishment that Nations owe their character.'[70]

In the end, introspection was his recipe for happiness. Casanova had been right to say that Ligne belonged to the very small number of people who knew themselves. Quoting a famous line from *Cinna* by Corneille, he wrote: 'I always say: *Look inside yourself, Octave*. It is not in order to become wise, as that seems to me impossible; it is in order to realise that one is not, and that one must be proud of nothing.'[71]

In addition to the thirty-four volumes of *Mélanges militaires, littéraires et sentimentaires*, there are two collections printed posthumously, *Mémoires et Mélanges historiques et littéraires* (five volumes, 1827–9), and *Oeuvres Posthumes Inédites* (five volumes, 1914–19). In Belgium two reviews entirely consecrated to Ligne, *Annales Prince de Ligne* (eighteen volumes, 1920–38) and *Nouvelles Annales Prince de Ligne* (edited by Jeroom Vercruysse, one volume every year since 1986), have published many other works and letters by the Prince. Nevertheless, there still remain

* He himself had planned to build a blue village at Beloeil.

many unpublished letters, diaries and early and obscene works in
the archives of Beloeil, Antoing and Decin. Considering that
letters from Ligne can be found in practically every archive in
Europe (see Bibliography), his fecundity attains the proportions
of a disease.

However, if Ligne wrote one masterpiece after *Coup d'oeil sur
Beloeil*, it is his memoirs, which he called *Fragments de l'histoire
de ma vie*: 1200 pages in forty-seven notebooks, written in bursts
between 1797 and 1814, they were judged by the Prince himself
to be his most 'piquant' work, more piquant than, if not as well
written as, the *Confessions* of Jean-Jacques Rousseau.[72] Like
Chateaubriand in *Mémoires d'outre-tombe*, he knew his memoirs
would not be published in his lifetime (not, in fact, until 1928),
so he wrote with exceptional frankness, to 'amuse the inquisitive
and interest amateurs of the history of their own period'. As a
memorialist, Ligne is remarkably accurate: his secretary Leygeb
had recorded Ligne's movements before 1793 in a diary and he
used it (as Saint-Simon used the diary of his contemporary
Dangeau) and some of his own letters, to provide a factual
framework.[73] This author has found errors of omission and bias,
but not of fact. For example, Ligne describes how, fifty years
earlier, Francis I and Maria Theresa had dressed him up, at the
age of twenty, as a rich young lady of the court called Mlle de
Turheim. The staffs of the Imperial kitchens and stables staged a
mock battle for his favours; he kissed everyone he met; even the
lady's suitor, M. de Saint Julien, was deceived. The same events
are recorded, with little difference, in the contemporary diary of
the Lord Chamberlain von Khevenhüller, which was not available to Ligne.[74] The fidelity with which Ligne claims to have
continued to visit Mme du Barry during the last days of Louis
XV, while other courtiers had abandoned her, is confirmed in
the diary of the Duc de Croÿ.[75]

As in *Coup d'oeil sur Beloeil*, or *Préjugés militaires*, he used his
favourite form of separate fragments – hence the title – often
several pages long, separated by black lines. There is a vague
chronological structure: they begin with his childhood and end

in 1814. Nevertheless, it is a labyrinth, containing letters, speeches, love affairs, reflections on strategy and Christianity: sometimes he jumps from country to country on the page as freely as he had done in his life. In four pages taken at random, he moves from Antwerp in 1784 to Belgrade in 1789 and Venice in 1763. At one moment he remembers having stolen a mistress from his son Louis; at others he gives portraits of Joseph II and Catherine the Great, and the golden years of Charles of Lorraine in Brussels and Marie Antoinette in Versailles.

Often rereading, he or his secretary, Sauveur Legros – who did much of the physical process of writing – corrected themselves, cutting or adding as they went. Nevertheless, Ligne did not reread consistently. As he claimed: 'My publishers do not give me the task of eliminating my repetitions if there are any. I never read myself.' [76] In his memoirs he frequently repeats his own jokes – for example, his remark to Lord Malmesbury about Joseph II's priapism, or a story about making love in the Prater while a herd of deer made a noise like thunder jumping overhead, with the punchline: 'It was enough to stop the most *hardened* sinner.'[77] A typical aside is: 'Have I not written, for as I never reread myself and am only writing many years later, I am afraid of repeating myself?'[78]

Nevertheless, with these memoirs Ligne himself attains a distinguished rank among the array of memoir writers in French who had enchanted him when young. It is a gold mine, sixtynine years related in a hard, frank, frivolous style. The flavour of his style and the range of his experience are given in this evocation of the courts of his youth:

I have seen in their brilliance the countries and the Courts where no one amuses themselves any more. For example, that of the last Saxon, King of Poland, or rather of the Count of Brühl. I have seen the last splendours of this satrap who, to go a hundred paces on horseback, was accompanied by one hundred palatines, *starostes*, castellans, *cordon bleus* and quantities of princes related to the House of Saxony. I have seen

Louis XV still with an air of grandeur like Louis XIV, and Madame de Pomapadour with that of Madame de Montespan ...

I have seen three weeks of enchanting fêtes at Chantilly, plays and visits at Villers Cotterêt, where the most amusing people were gathered. I have seen magical visits to L'Ile Adam. I have seen the delights of the Petit Trianon. Promenades on the terrace, music in the Orangery, the splendours of Fontainebleau, the hunts at Saint Hubert, visits to Choisy, Marly, etc. and I have seen everything shrink and completely perish ... I have seen the last splendours of Europe where in a frozen climate Catherine II had joined Asiatic luxury to that of Louis XIV, and of the Persians, the Greeks, the Romans and the Thousand and One Nights.

I have seen Potsdam, Sans Souci and glory, military rule, at the same time an august Court and a severe headquarters.

I have seen disappear with Prince Charles of Lorraine the Netherlands and a delightful, gay, sure, agreeable, outrageous, drinking, feasting and hunting Court. And to show that I am seeing everything decay, all the Courts of the Empire, large and small, disappear, down to the least, by lack of respect, that of the last Prince of La Tour which although ridiculous, was nevertheless magnificent.[79]

The unconventional syntax and style – the use of etc., the last sentence without a main verb – only increase the impact. He writes in rapid, conversational, highly coloured prose – for example, in this description of his life after 1794: 'Passe-droits, injustices, ma montagne, philosophie, mes ouvrages et ensuite je ne sais pas moi-même: tout ce que Dieu voudra!' The freedom of the style is increased by his habit of using conversational questions: 'Have I said that?' or, anticipating Proust: 'Have I ever spoken of the pain one suffers from memories? The dinner bell of the chateau here [Teplitz] has the same sound as that of the chateau of Beloeil. That has the same effect on me as the cries of some peacocks which are in the Prater ... Oh! God! God! God! ... What is life? How few moments of real happiness there are! And how short they are!'[80]

The omissions in *Fragments de l'histoire de ma vie* are revealing. He consciously suppressed details about his childhood,
probably because it bored him. His daughters are praised, but
there is little mention of wife or sons-in-law. He regrets
Angélique d'Hannetaire but does not mention Henriette
Auersperg or other mistresses – out of respect or resentment?
Events mentioned in a brief autobiographical summary, such as:
'1765 Follies at the head of 10 or 12 young Princes who were
joining the Service', or '1779 Stay with the court and considerable favour at Laxenburg', are omitted.[81] So are such important
occasions, witnessed by Ligne, as the coronation of Joseph II at
Frankfurt in 1764, immortalised by Goethe in *Dichtung und
Wahrheit*; the deathbed of Louis XV in 1774; and the funeral of
Maria Theresa in 1780. He barely mentions his greatest friends,
the Duke of Braganza, Lord Malmesbury, the Baronne de
Reischach, Hugh Eliot, the Marquis de Bonnay and Alexandre
de Laborde: Laborde, a son of Marie Antoinettte's banker, had
served in the Austrian army in the 1790s and Ligne called him in
letters 'since his childhood the best of my friends', 'the most just,
the most loyal, the most generous and the most enlightened man
I know', and entrusted him with responsibility for the book's
publication after his death.[82] Casanova, to whom he had opened
his heart, appears as one name at the end of a long list of writers
whom he had known: Alfieri, Casanova, Ancillon ...

As was typical of his generation, he makes himself appear
more frivolous and impulsive, less ambitious and callous, than in
reality. He twice recounts his attempted seduction by the aged
Countess Gradenigo in Venice. His careers as an Austrian agent
in the court and army of Catherine the Great, as a colonel of a
regiment and governor of a province, are passed over lightly.

On the other hand, he could be extremely frank about his
sexual life. Even in old age, Ligne enjoyed *passades* more often,
he admitted, out of vanity than desire. In 1809, at the age of
seventy-four, he claimed he enjoyed various 'happy and Jewish
little love affairs with Eva, Rachel and Regina. Unhappy with
Fanny. Happy with Wilhelmina, Christina and stormy with

Amélie, a demon who put all my household in a rage.' In the same year in Vienna, by a young governess called Adélaïde, he fathered a daughter, also called Adélaïde, who died a year later in 1810 (her existence is proof that his love affairs are not self-delusions or fabrications). Her coffin was decorated with ribbons in pink, the colour of the House of Ligne. Her father deplored the cost of the funeral as well as the loss of the child: 'My child, this dear child has just died! Mademoiselle her mother has just told me the news in tears and we are settling our accounts for the funeral ... Imagine, my dear readers, what that costs; and disgust yourself with the idea of having natural children.'[83]

Another *passade* took place one morning at four o'clock while he was walking in his nightshirt in the garden of the Kahlenberg:

> I would like to say a shepherdess; but my cook whom I had never noticed, very good-natured, which is a great merit, very pretty, and very clean, for she had got up to wash herself in my fountain, appeared extremely desirable to me. Respect, gratitude for my declaration had probably more effect than my charms. She was guilty; and I was happy. I came back to bed as if nothing had happened. I slept until eight when I woke up enough to write down our poor little crime.[84]

In our age such an episode, and the use of the contrasting adjectives 'guilty' and 'happy', like the episode of the illegitimate child with the governess, can appear a form of heartless sexual exploitation, by a rich and powerful older man, of vulnerable or dependent women. In 1810 such episodes were everyday occurrences. What is exceptional is the honesty – and sense of shame – with which Ligne recounts them, which makes him nearer to writers like Casanova or Boswell than to nobles of his own milieu.

The appeal of *Fragments* lies not only in its account of Ligne's experiences and feelings but also in its observations on his own epoch. Ligne's interest in manners and customs, and his longevity, give him an unusual angle of observation. He is the eighteenth century sitting in judgement on the beginnings of the nineteenth. The shock of the French Revolution had led to a decline in the number, or openness, of love affairs. As a result, Ligne considered that one should bid farewell to the pleasures of society. 'One sees each other without searching for each other. One parts without regret. One talks without interest. One sits down at table next to each other without caring.'[85] Pomposity had become fashionable: 'No one is young any more. People prefer *le genre Caton au genre catin*.'[86] After the individualism of the eighteenth century, even language was becoming uniform. 'For example, everyone now writes their morning notes perfectly.* I like the time when women made spelling mistakes.' He also noted the revolution in men's costume by 1800, which made everyone, master and servant, wear a plain blue tail-coat, whereas in the past even army officers had worn the elaborate silk and lace embroidered *habit habillé*: 'Down to the *cordonnier* everyone is dressed the same. *Frac*, black stockings, shoes like slippers... it is like a funeral.'[87] That stronghold of counter-revolution, the Palais Razumovsky, was the last place in Vienna where men still wore the *habit habillé* and powdered hair with a *queue*.

Ligne's memoirs, like his portraits, also excel in recording the surface of life, what he called 'those little details which seem to be nothings [but which] give pleasure a hundred years later', such as the ways Catherine entered a room, Marie Antoinette ran her fingers through her hair, and Maria Theresa used, as rewards, a nod of the head, a look in the eyes or, if really pleased, a smile.[88]

Ligne's memoirs also reflect the most spectacular of all changes in the spirit of the age: the return to Christianity. As a young man Ligne had been a scornful atheist, or sceptic. As late as 1791 his wife wrote to Vandenbroucke: 'It is incredible all the lies the Prince is told about his son, in which he believes far more than he has ever believed in the Gospel.'[89] His reputation

---

* Many people began the day writing brief notes, often in pencil, quite different in form and purpose from the letters they wrote in ink.

for sacrilege was such that, in a book asserting that the French Revolution was caused by a conspiracy of atheists, the Abbé Barruel claimed that Ligne had corresponded with Voltaire solely to spread irreligion in the Austrian Netherlands. This was untrue; but in 1776 Ligne had refused to build a new church at Beloeil.[90]

As well as pursuing a policy of egalitarianism and confiscation, the French Revolution had killed priests and nuns and in 1793–4 enforced a policy of de-Christianisation. Such events transformed Ligne, like many other traumatised pagans, into a pillar of the Church. He was too honest not to see what was happening. In a remark worthy of Marx, he wrote: 'The irreligious rich noticed that they were robbed by people without religion ... They realised they should have one. One could say they want God to look after their household.'[91]

His evolution from sceptic to Catholic can be followed in the different editions of his books. In the first edition of *Coup d'oeil* published in 1781, he wrote: 'In destroying monasteries one will by the same blow destroy religious prejudices.' In the edition published in 1795, when Beloeil was under republican occupation, he changed his words to: 'Formerly I declaimed against monks, before realising by experience the links necessarily connecting this class to the others of society. Let us respect prejudices in theology.' Similarly the enthusiastic: 'All men are brothers', of 1781, became the disabused: 'All men should help each other', of 1795.[92]

Christianity was a good bargain for Ligne, both spiritually and domestically:

What do you risk to promise to have no more women when desires and opportunities are diminishing, and to go to mass every Sunday when the reason which stopped you has also stopped? It was to see my mornings cut and my literary works interrupted. I have almost stopped them, like my adventures. So I want to, and easily can, be happy in the other world, after having been happy in this.[93]

Ligne even became a proselytiser for Catholicism. A friend
from Teplitz called Julie de Krüdener was a mystical Protestant
who was to be the inspiration behind the Holy Alliance, founded
in 1815 by her admirer Alexander I of Russia. In the summer of
1807 she had long arguments at Teplitz with Ligne and tried to
convert him to Protestantism, while he advanced the case for
Catholicism.[94] Referring to Chateaubriand's *Le Génie du
Christianisme* (1802), which Ligne considered immortal and
sublime in its grace and imagination,[95] Ligne said she had *la rage
du christianisme*. He counter-attacked by trying, in secret, to
convert her friend Mme d'Ompteda to Catholicism. His arguments emphasised Catholicism's role as buttress of monarchy
and aristocracy: Catholics showed greater fidelity to the
Habsburgs; Catholicism was 'the only aristocratic religion, the
others are a breeding ground of Democracy by their independence and their semi-enlightenment dangerous to governments';
could two thousand years of history be wrong?[96]

As he grew older, Ligne became more devout. In 1805, to
please his sisters-in-law, *les princesses du soir*, he went to confession, although he found he had less and less to confess. It was the
first time in years and, when he knelt down, he realised he had
forgotten the words. Soon he was going to church regularly,
although he did sometimes find himself, confused by the sound of
the Latin words, reciting an ode of Horace instead of prayers to
Jesus. The last sections of *Fragments de l'histoire de ma vie* are
almost as Christian as passages in Chateaubriand's *Mémoires
d'outre tombe*, containing remarks such as: 'I thank God for his
mercy ... I love, believe and repose in Him.'[97]

By the summer of 1805 he felt: 'All my achievements as a
body, a heart and a mind are over. I have no one to love any
more.'[98] In reality a greater task awaited him: to observe, and
attempt to thwart, one of the greatest challenges in the history of
Austria; Napoleon.

Napoleon

The Napoleonic era was, on one level, the French revenge for the period after the Seven Years' War, when, as Ligne had written, France was only one-twentieth of Europe, and Austria, Prussia and Russia laughed at its expense. France was now half of Europe: instead of laughing at France, Austria, Prussia and Russia were terrified of it. Ligne was first affected by Napoleon in 1803, when, as part of his programme of French expansion, the First Consul initiated the death agony of the Holy Roman Empire. He decided to compensate Imperial princes who had lost territory to the French Republic on the left bank of the Rhine, with morsels taken from the weakest states of the Empire on the right bank: the Imperial cities and ecclesiastical states. Ligne was one of the princes.

However, Ligne's loathing of the French Republic extended to the First Consul. He was furious when his son Louis, now a French citizen, commanded Bonaparte's guard of honour on a visit to Brussels in 1803: 'A Ligne commanding the Consular guard, composed of those Flemings whose folly it is to make entries!'[1] While other Imperial princes flocked to Paris to beg for favours, Ligne, who always had another country in reserve, turned to Russia. On account of Catherine's 'particular confidence', Paul I's successor, his son Alexander I, instructed Russian ambassadors in Paris, Berlin and Regensburg, seat of the Imperial diet, to defend Ligne's right to a territorial indemnity for his independent county of Fagnolles.[2]

At Regensburg, in 1803, a mass redistribution of territory was made by the Imperial diet in consultation with the French and Russian ambassadors. Bonnay had hoped that, since Louis de

Ligne had restored the family fortunes by marrying an heiress, alone of the Princes of the Empire Ligne would give a lesson to 'revolutionary iniquity' and refuse to act as 'a thief', by despoiling the noble chapters that had been 'the pride of Germany'.[3] Ligne himself admitted to Christine Clary: 'I was tempted myself to consider an indemnity, an indignity – and a secularisation – an abomination. But I said to myself: all that was considered perfectly acceptable at the Peace of Westphalia [which had brought peace to the Empire in 1648] which passes for the finest achievement in the world, that its parody will perhaps be admired.' Ligne was given the minute independent enclave of Edelstetten. Situated in south-west Germany (see Map) between the expanding powers of Bavaria and Württemberg, and said to be worth 15,000 florins a year – considerably more than Ligne had received from Fagnolles – it owed allegiance only to the Emperor. For centuries it had belonged to a convent, like those to which Ligne's sisters had been despatched, which acted as a finishing school for young noblewomen (who were given the temporary title of canoness).[4]

In May, a few weeks after Louis's return to Beloeil, Ligne came to visit his new domain. His week in Edelstetten was an idyll out of Rousseau and Jane Austen. Edelstetten was (and is) little more than a few farms and houses clustered around a great baroque church with stupendous gilded interiors, typical of Swabia and Bavaria. Delighted to report a break in his Vienna–Teplitz–Dresden routine, he kept a journal of his visit for the amusement of his family and friends. Discovered by this author in the Clary archives in Decin, it shows his increasingly simple style and readiness to portray himself as a semi-comic character, to whom love, money and status were a game.

23 May: I enter. Turkish music. I kiss the hand of the Abbess. She faints with joy. She finds me better than my portrait ... Made Sophie de Freyberg smile. It is a good sign ... Supper is served. What a supper! What a sight! And I will even have to pay for it! At least a hundred écus ... I say in

German and French that I am happy to have found this new *patrie*. They are touched. The Abbess weeps ... Talk for a moment with maid. Sophie de Freyberg and I assure her in a hushed voice that I am heartbroken that the Empire had not been partitioned earlier.

24 May: Terrible bed. No sleep. Composed twelve couplets for Madame Freyberg. Prepared a short note to slip into the hand of the little canoness according to the place and opportunity.

Having spent the morning planning what trees to plant and how to beautify the cemetery, he attended a Te Deum organised in his honour. 'I appear. Great cannonade, general salvo. I am presented with holy water and incense. I enter the church at the head of the chapter. Trumpets and cymbals. I feel as if I am making a cavalry charge. My prie-dieu is finer and higher than that of the Abbess. Dispute of courtesy. I win.' After prayers for the new sovereign of Edelstetten, they left for another prolonged banquet, followed by couplets sung by Sophie de Freyberg comparing him to Mars and Apollo. In the evening there was the inevitable *comédie de société* and then 'work in my room with my ministers until 10 o'clock'.[5]

Ligne enjoyed the first days, giving his hand to be kissed by 'my excellent inhabitants of my good fat village', devising a new uniform for the soldiers of his toy 'army' (blue with facings in Ligne pink), and visiting his farms and forests, escorted by a flock of white-robed canonesses. He was amused by the boarding-school atmosphere in the convent, frightening one canoness by sending her a box full of beetles, and laughing with 'my angel canonesses' about the size of the 'empire' he was taking from them. In letters to Bonnay he swore that he had permitted himself no 'word or hand games. I always had a perfect tone ... I cannot put on my modest air that you know. However, Louise Freyberg always sat beside me: and perhaps sometimes squeezed my hand without me noticing.'

Nevertheless Ligne soon longed to be back in Bohemia in the arms of 'my Christ'. After no more than a week, to spare himself tears of farewell, he fled at one in the morning. His last memory of Edelstetten was the sound of the band of 'my army', which had learnt of his departure, playing Turkish music in his honour in the middle of the Swabian night. More worldly in reality than he presented himself in the journal, he took 250 ducats from the Edelstetten treasury, and told Bonnay that he had no intention of returning except to see 'if even more cannot be made out of all this'.[6]

By coincidence, the King of Prussia, Frederick William III, who had succeeded his father Frederick William II in 1797, and his beautiful young wife Queen Louise (born a princess of Mecklenburg-Strelitz) were visiting the nearby baroque town of Anspach, recently acquired by Prussia. Anspach was on the way to Bohemia, so Ligne had an excuse to pay his court. He told Bonnay that he felt a start when he heard the words: 'The King of Prussia is arriving,' since they made him think of Frederick the Great. Instead it was Frederick's great-nephew, a monarch who lacked his genius but pursued relatively mild and tolerant policies. 'But here is the court! I rush to it! Well, I have come back and am enchanted. Dinner was very gay on my side.' Ligne glowed in the proximity of royalty: 'A remark, a joke are passed around the royal family as at Versailles, where everyone recounted in the evening what they had heard in the day ... The uncertainty, idleness and also unpredictability of each day remind me of other courts. Down to the magnificence, sometimes I think I am travelling in Tauride, and sometimes at Edelstetten.'

Three years later Queen Louise's beauty and patriotism were to make her a heroine of Prussia's struggle against Napoleon. Ligne's punctuation betrays his ecstasy:

What a queen she is, the queen of Prussia! What beauty! what grace! How she recalls, with more regular features, those of the unfortunate queen of France! What charming sisters! What a court and what a family! ... The King, rather shy and perhaps not having much to say at the beginning, being rather vacant in society, where he can be interesting and amiable through his simplicity and common sense; where he often walks around alone; I often attacked him in conversation. He then replies very well and talks well on war and the service.

Indeed he said that he liked Ligne's books, which was more than Francis II had done. They also talked, as everyone did in the Empire, about the growing power of Bonaparte, whose troops had occupied the Electorate of Hanover, belonging to George III. Ligne offered to lead an Imperial army against them.[7]

At Anspach the Elector of Bavaria also came to see the King of Prussia. Prince Max de Deux Ponts, whom Ligne had known when he was a young officer in the army of Louis XVI, had inherited the title of Elector of Bavaria in 1799. Ligne found him 'as much of a bon vivant as when he was Prince Max in France, my companion at court, at the hunt and at supper with our demoiselles of the opera'. At dinner with the King of Prussia, he made Ligne writhe with tales of long-forgotten escapades.

Fearing Bonaparte's designs on the Empire, only a year after Ligne acquired Edelstetten, he sold it for 11,000 florins a year (more than Ligne had succeeded in extracting from it) to a cousin of his wife, Prince Esterhazy, the richest man in Hungary. Even in its death throes, the Holy Roman Empire was so imposing that, like Ligne before 1789, Prince Esterhazy wanted a piece of 'immediate' territory in order to be acknowledged as a Prince of the Empire by his fellow-princes. Unfortunately, *Charles par la grâce de Dieu prince de Ligne et du Saint Empire Romain*, as Ligne still signed himself, was not always paid on time and continued to borrow money.[8]

While Ligne was descending from his 'throne', Bonaparte was ascending his. As early as 1801 Ligne had noted what escaped many contemporaries and historians: that the French Revolution, rather than suppressing the French elite, had redefined and expanded it. Even before Napoleon created his own nobility, the generals and prefects of the Republic were beginning to show themselves as proud and power-hungry as the old nobles; on the opposing side, every *émigré*; because he served the cause of Throne and Altar, considered himself the equal of a Montmorency. 'In our time by dint of being democrats, the French have become Aristocrats; and the latter, delighted to be Gentlemen, believed that they became Gentlemen the moment they emigrated. The Revolution has made almost as many as it has destroyed.'[9]

To reassure former republicans that his monarchy would not be a replica of Louis XVI's, and to deter further assassination attempts by royalists, on 21 March 1804 Bonaparte had a cousin of Louis XVIII and Artois, the Duc d'Enghien, the last prince of the House of Condé with the hope of producing children, kidnapped from neutral territory in the Empire, taken to France and shot. Like most princes of the Holy Roman Empire, Ligne felt both disgusted and insulted: 'The Duc d'Enghien has killed Bonaparte. Vanity has killed his glory.'[10]

On 18 May Bonaparte proclaimed himself Napoleon I, Emperor of the French. Ligne's view of the French – 'Never has a people been more made for court life' – began to seem less foolish than when expressed in 1787. The elaborate court formed in July became a power centre of the Empire. The coronation of the Emperor on 2 December, attended by many ex-revolutionaries and marshals who had fought their way up through the ranks of the republican army, confirmed Ligne's contention that the French Revolution had been about vanity and titles, names rather than things. The Grand Master of Ceremonies was one of Ligne's many friends to whom political upheavals had given a new role: the Comte de Ségur. Ségur's pride in his new job codifying the etiquette of the Imperial palace made him forget his former enthusiasm for Liberty, Equality and Fraternity. Unfortunately the break in their friendship during the Revolution deprived Ligne of the opportunity of sending Ségur mocking letters of advice.

Over the years between 1804 and 1814, Ligne recorded his views on Napoleon in a notebook called *Ma napoléonide*. It reflects the fear and hostility widespread in Vienna and central

Europe. Seeing Napoleon through the eyes of the eighteenth century, and of an Austrian accustomed to the simplicity of the Habsburgs, Ligne felt disdain above all for Napoleon's vulgarity: his love of emphatic display and 'inextinguishable priapism of glory'. For once Ligne was horrified by a court. Like his neighbour on the Moelkerbastei, Beethoven, who struck Bonaparte's name off his dedication of the Third Symphony on receipt of the news of the proclamation of the Empire, Ligne felt that Bonaparte had thereby diminished himself. The title of Emperor was a folly. 'If he only took one hundred thousand francs a year for himself, with no splendour except parades, of which I approve, if he listened, if he replied, he would be the greatest man there has ever been.' He should restrict his household to four aides de camp and some servants. There should be no court receptions or presentations of women and he should inhabit his wife's country house of Malmaison, not the former royal palace of Saint-Cloud.[11]

When Napoleon began to hunt in the forests around the former royal palaces of Compiègne and Fontainebleau, as Ligne had often seen Louis XV and Louis XVI do, it made him ill. 'Why does Napoleon act the King of France, being the king of the world? ... When you hunt kings you should not hunt deer.' Ligne was disgusted by the stories he heard of Napoleon keeping people waiting, insulting ambassadors in front of the whole court: ' The bad taste of an Italian noble is everywhere evident. A false magnificence, etiquette and striving for respect remove the rights he would have to admiration.'[12]

Napoleon's personality did not, at this stage, impress the Prince de Ligne: 'Clemency, generosity, military popularity, nobility; everything is contrived and has a purpose ... never sublime because he is not simple; never touched nor touching, because he is not born benevolent; ferocious in his audiences because he wants to frighten or is not master of himself; yet despite all that he is master of Europe.'[13] As in his portraits of Frederick II, Catherine II and Joseph II, Ligne concentrates on style and personality. He did not discuss Napoleon's methods of government or reforms, the Code Napoléon or the 'career open to the talents'.

Ligne did, however, discuss Napoleon's tactics. He did not believe that Napoleon's military glory was due to a 'new method'. Napoleon had invented nothing: his method was

> like that of all men of war to profit from mistakes and to bring together in one point, either in infantry or cavalry, greater forces than those opposed to him. No one admires more than I do the power of his genius. But I think he can be stopped ... I think that with a lot of depth, by many lines which would support or replace each other, and large numbers of reserves, one could conquer him, or worry him, by fortified camps, in good positions [here in part Ligne is anticipating Wellington].[14]

Napoleon's territorial ambition horrified Ligne as much as his bad taste. In late 1804, Ligne and his anti-French coterie, the Emperor's brother the Archduke John (who described himself as 'a good German, heart and soul'), Gentz, and Razumovsky, wanted an alliance between the two great German powers, Austria and Prussia – and war with France.[15] They had an ally in the young Metternich, who had recently become Austrian ambassador to Prussia. On 28 August 1804 Ligne wrote to Metternich from Teplitz, referring to Francis II's recent assumption of the hereditary title of Emperor of Austria, in addition to the elective title of Holy Roman Emperor (to make his family Imperial Highnesses like the Bonapartes):

> To the double minister of the two empires to whom I wish four eagles ... Dear doubly amiable Count whom I love ... open your arms to me shortly to receive me, when I will accompany Princess Louise [of Prussia] back to Berlin from Teplitz ... Have 50,000 Prussians given to my dear Prince Louis Ferdinand who is all heart for us and as many Austrians to me and I promise you that we will de-Charlemagnise the Emperor of all the Gauls and all the Italys.[16]

The verb 'de-Charlemagnise' expresses Europeans' fears that Napoleon's ambitions extended outside the 'natural' border of France – the Rhine frontier – to seize the Holy Roman Empire. In November 1804, while Napoleon was receiving German electors and princes in Mainz (then on French soil), Ligne arrived in Berlin, after an interval of twenty-four years, with Princess Louise of Prussia and her brother Prince Louis Ferdinand, a cultivated young prince, equally admired by Jewish hostesses and Prussian officers. Ligne was received by Frederick William III 'with kindness, pleasure, cordiality and distinction at Potsdam, where he receives no one. How cold it was at the review of his guards and garrison which he showed me!' Like other visitors he was charmed by the simplicity of the royal family. In his study Frederick William III said: 'Come and warm yourself by the fire,' then, 'Let us go and lunch with the Queen.'[17]

Like his visits to Catherine the Great in 1780 and 1787, Ligne's visit to Berlin in 1804 was a foray into unofficial diplomacy, in an attempt to create a united German front against Napoleon.

German patriotism had hitherto been weaker than French or English. The great critic Wieland wrote in 1793: 'I see Saxon, Bavarian, Württemberg and Hamburg patriots, but German patriots who love the entire Reich as their fatherland ... where are they?' However, the influence of the new French ideas of *patrie*, combined with horror for the depredations of the invading French revolutionary armies, helped to strengthen German patriotism. Germans saw themselves as simple, noble, sublime compared to the cruel and immoral French. Even Ligne began to feel German. He wrote: 'I do not know a sweeter, though without amenity, better, more reliable or less cruel nation than Germany.'[18] Having lived so long in Vienna, Ligne claimed that he could now read, write and speak German – though when talking what he thought was passable German, he often received the reply, *in French*, 'Monsieur, I do not understand French.' Fearing the 'despotism' of the French language and ideas, Ligne even wrote that 'German culture' could alone 'regenerate

Europe', referred to Swabia as his new *patrie*, and celebrated Goethe as 'the honour of our Germany'. To the King of Prussia he preached brotherhood between the two greatest German powers, Prussia and Austria, and asked him to hang the first minister who told him that they were natural enemies: 'for where is Germany if it is not you, Sire, and him [Francis II]: same language, same interest, without that no *patrie*'.[19]

However, as Ligne frequently complained, he was 'a voice crying in the wilderness': there was no Joseph II to support his plans for a German alliance and he had as little influence on Austrian policy as Prince Louis Ferdinand on Prussian. Metternich had already tried and failed to form an alliance with Prussia. As Ligne feared, far from supporting German nationalism, Prussia preferred to remain neutral and devour scraps of territory thrown it by Napoleon.

In Ligne's youth the thrones of Europe had been occupied by giants: Maria Theresa, Frederick the Great, Catherine the Great. In his old age, their successors, Francis II, Frederick William III, and Alexander I could be shrewd and well intentioned. However, they could compare neither with their predecessors nor with their enemy Napoleon. Ligne wrote: 'We only see good fathers and good husbands on the throne and not good kings.' They were so suspicious of each other that they did not unite in a coalition against Napoleon until nine years after he had ascended the throne.

Although Frederick William III would not fight France, Francis II was convinced that Napoleon wanted 'universal monarchy'. In 1805 Napoleon crowned himself King of Italy, annexed Genoa to the French Empire and gave Lucca to his brother-in-law, Felix Baciocchi. The anger expressed in the opening sentence of *War and Peace** – 'Well, Prince, so Genoa and Lucca are now no more than the private estates of the Bonaparte family' – was shared in the salons of Vienna: Ligne heard debates whether to put Bonaparte in a cage or on a

---

*In which a particularly hard-hearted character, Princess Hélène, is mentioned as being in correspondence with the Prince de Ligne.

gallows. Francis II had signed a secret alliance with Alexander I
of Russia on 6 November 1804. To command the Austrian
army, the Emperor selected General Karl von Mack – vain,
incompetent, unlucky, later described by Napoleon as the most
mediocre man he had ever met.[20] Intoxicated by illusions of
grandeur, Austria was hasty and overconfident, in 1805 as in
1792 – and 1914. On 7 September 1805 Austrian troops crossed
into the territory of Napoleon's ally Bavaria, while Russian
troops were far away and there was no assurance of Prussian
support.

At first Ligne was exhilarated and told Jean de Müller that,
with speed, 'our successes are certain'. In language considerably
more humble than he had used to Joseph II, he begged Francis II
to be employed wherever the Emperor chose:

> It is the twelfth time that I request it ... The only favour I ask is
> to conquer or die for Your Imperial Majesty ... I await with
> resignation and almost with some hope this first and last sign of
> His graciousness; and am with as much personal attachment as
> respect,
>
>   Sire,
>
>   of Your Imperial Majesty,
>   the most humble and faithful of His subjects
>   Ligne.

Although this plea was issued when the monarchy was fighting for survival, like its eleven predecessors it too was ignored.
By October, partly from conversations at Teplitz, Ligne realised
that Prussia would not fight and wrote to Gentz: 'Everything is
going very badly, everything will go very badly. They are
deluding, flattering, trapping the Emperor.'[21] At Ulm on 19
October Austrian forces under Mack surrendered in ignominy.
The *grande armée* rushed on Vienna.

On 29 October Ligne arrived in Vienna and found the city
like a bad dream, abandoned by the Emperor to the charge of
generals who were incompetent, or worse. The streets were
filled with wounded or dying soldiers; carts piled high with the

possessions of the Viennese and the treasures of the Hofburg headed east to Hungary. An incident Ligne recorded in *Mes Posthumes* reveals the despair sweeping Austria. On 8 November Ligne visited the Augustinian church, the court parish church beside the Hofburg, to see Canova's recently finished masterpiece, the monument to the Archduchess Marie Christine, former Governor-General of the Austrian Netherlands. Thinking of the Archduchess, whom he had known since childhood, of the kindness of her mother the Empress Maria Theresa and the contrast between those happy and glorious times and the present 'horrible tragedy', he began to cry.

At that moment the Archduchess's widower, Duke Albert of Saxe-Teschen, whom he had not seen for two years, arrived looking equally sad. According to Ligne's account the old Duke said:

> 'I am coming to take leave of my wife and of Canova. My horses are ready. I am leaving and I do not know where to.' He sees my pity for him, for the monarchy, for the melancholy masterpiece. He shares it. Mine is doubled. We fall into each other's arms. Mass was being said. All the spectators of this scene of sensibility burst into tears, like us. The Duke embraces me, says to me: 'What a moment, good God!' and I rush away.[22]

Whereas in 1791 Louis XVI and Marie Antoinette had nowhere to flee from Paris except a frontier fortress, because it was a multiple rather than a unitary monarchy Austrians had a supply of emergency capitals: Olmütz in Moravia (where Francis II fled in 1805, as his son Ferdinand would during the revolution of 1848), Budapest and Pressburg, the capitals of Hungary. Ligne arrived at Pressburg on 9 November, to stay with his daughter Féfé Palffy. (His dislike of his wife is expressed by his silence over her movements during these terrible months: presumably she remained in Vienna.) From Pressburg Ligne despatched *mémoire* after *mémoire* on the defence of Vienna, how to use the Danube and fortify the city. It was useless. Paralysed by failure of will, the defenders let the incredible happen. Having resisted Turks and Protestants, the 'imperial capital and residence city', of which Ligne had proudly said: 'Vienna is never taken,' fell to the French on 12 November.[23] Napoleon's marshals were lodged in the palaces of the Liechtensteins and the Esterhazys. Napoleon himself moved into Schönbrunn, the palace of Maria Theresa.

At the battle of Austerlitz on 2 December, near the tomb of Kaunitz, the author of the alliance with France that had led Austria to such eminence in the previous century, Austria and Russia were defeated by French troops. Francis II sued for peace. From his observation post at Pressburg, Ligne recorded a French soldier's explanation of Austria's chain of defeats, which Ligne considered more convincing than any military manual: 'You have some brave soldiers but you will always be beaten ... When we see action is beginning, we rush forward ourselves either to help our comrades or to repulse those who are making them retreat ... As for you ... you wait for orders. If they arrive they are slow and too late. You act on them even more slowly.' Austrians had no élan, and no generals: Pressburg had fallen to the French with hardly a shot fired in anger. Considering the judgement of an Austrian military historian that both preparation and conduct of the 1805 war were so erratic that a psychological rather than strategic explanation is necessary, and Ligne's dash and initiative, Francis II's refusal to give him a command seems incomprehensible.[24]

On 9 December Ligne returned to Vienna. The French occupation horrified him as an Austrian but fascinated him as a writer. Three friends, including Zinzendorf, were made to repeat every detail of Napoleon's behaviour and conversation during an audience. Succumbing to the fascination of the man, Ligne then recorded it in *Mes posthumes*, as eagerly as Napoleon's courtiers were to do on Saint Helena. Ligne's account shows not only the brilliance and lucidity of Napoleon's monologues but also that, in Austria, Napoleon presented himself as the embodiment not of French nationalism or revolutionary ideas, but of monarchy and the nobility.

Passing his snuff box more and more quickly from one hand to the other, Napoleon told an Austrian delegation:

I pity your Emperor for being badly served, badly surrounded! Colloredo, Cobenzl, Collenach! It is pitiable... This bad entourage and ignorance about things and people always come to those who are born sovereigns, although I do not always know everything either. At least the little knowledge of men I have comes from the fact that I have been a private person and that from the rank of simple soldier I have raised myself to the throne where I have established myself. I like to give it splendour and to surround myself with the best from all classes.

The great Maria Theresa, of whose glorious reign I am often made to think by her portrait and the palace I occupy, liked to consult the grandees of her empire and to draw them closer to her. All this would astonish her, if she knew it, and would not have happened.

I have found your Emperor better than I thought: and I believe he has good qualities. But they do not reassure me. Which means, as I have said, that I need a geographical and military guarantee...

I cannot believe that I am here. How astonished I was when at Linz they came to propose to me the capital of a great empire! To yield it to the enemy! To summon us there! Such an event has never been seen before.

Enfin, everything is mine at this moment...

Speaking of conquests and lost provinces, what is there to prevent Austria reconstructing itself a little at the expense of some provinces of the Ottoman Empire? I will not oppose it, for we all need barriers against Russia. It is unforgivable to have partitioned Poland with her and Prussia: it is unforgivable, immoral and impolitic...

My army, so fanatical at present, at the end of ten years will lose this military spirit which makes it victorious. So if I am forced to make war I prefer that it is now when I am still young ... I must tell you that if I start again and if, by chance, I was again fortunate, I would not leave one inch of land to the House of Austria.

Accustomed to the splendour of the Tuileries and Saint-Cloud, he expressed contempt for the Hofburg to Zinzendorf: 'How can the son of so many Emperors be lodged in this hovel? I who am just a petty noble [*un petit gentillâtre*] would like you to see how I am furnished. I could not even find a carpet in that Schönbrunn.'[25]

Warfare did not then extend from the battlefield into the drawing room. The French occupation was relatively orderly, although Vienna was hit by a massive war indemnity. Ligne felt no more shame in meeting French officers than other Viennese like Zinzendorf, although he tried to avoid the marshals. Moreover, an old friend from Versailles and the salon of Sophie Arnould, the Abbé de Périgord, had arrived. Having abandoned his religious vows and the Bourbons, M. de Talleyrand, as he was now known, had become Foreign Minister of Napoleon. Like many committed Europeans (down to Churchill, who hoped to recreate an Austrian Empire, under a Habsburg, in 1945), Talleyrand considered Austria as 'indispensable to the future salvation of civilised nations'. It was a barrier against Russia, and the most sensible way of organising central Europe: Talleyrand helped ensure that peace terms were relatively moderate.[26]

Ligne had a financial motive for wanting to meet Talleyrand: desire for compensation for a confiscated property in Aix-la-Chapelle. On 20 November Ligne wrote Talleyrand a short note, calling himself one of his former admirers and ending: 'I beg you to tell me where and when I could have the honour of seeing you. Without that no peace with me.'[27]

To Frenchmen like Talleyrand Ligne appeared to be the equivalent, among individuals, of Austria among monarchies: cosmopolitan, civilised and wise. Moreover, with his network of correspondents, his mania for writing, he might provide favourable publicity for the new French Empire, as he had for the Russian Empire in 1787. At dinner with General Clarke, the French military governor of Vienna, on 19 December Ligne was 'enchanted and delighted' to meet Talleyrand again. Talleyrand tried to lure Ligne to see Napoleon, as Bonnay had tried to lure him to see Louis XVIII. 'How can you refuse to your imagination, as fresh as if you were twenty, what is bound to please it, what will nourish it in a country where nothing can speak to it? He is sure to enchant you. You are sure to please him.'[28]

To Ligne, a professional author quarrying for material, a courtier eager for monarchs, it was an offer almost impossible to refuse: 'What a wonderful supplement to my conversations with the great Frederick, Voltaire, Catherine etc.,' he wrote wistfully. Moreover, the lost house in Aix-la-Chapelle gave him a pretext for demanding an audience. However, this was one temptation that Ligne resisted. He knew himself too well. In the exhilaration of Napoleon's verbal gunfire, he would go too far and his flattering remarks would be repeated in the gazettes. He replied with words lifted from a poem of Voltaire: 'Willingly at a review, but *I only like sheep when they are mine*. And I have no pleasure in seeing conquerors.'[29]

Talleyrand also pleaded with Ligne to revisit Paris, writing: 'You could desire to close them [Ligne's eyes] for some time about France, and more recently for several months about Austria; but all that is over. There is, as we say, peace and friendship between the two countries. The friendship will be perpetual on the part of those whom you allow to love you and to tell you so.' Again Ligne refused. He did not want his friends to feel remorse for their conduct in the Revolution when they saw him:

> then the memories ... that Place Louis XV* ... the Petit Trianon, good God! ... And then the fear of being questioned by the great man of Italy (but the little man of the Tuileries), who by ignorance or impertinence with the foolish tone of

---

* Where the guillotine had operated.

stupidity of sovereigns, inseparable from thrones, would perhaps have asked me if I had served in this last war ... It would have been impossible for me not to say to him: 'You should, by the position I see you in, realise that I did not.'

Clearly, although he had commanded no army in battle since 1790, he was sufficiently vain to think he might have defeated Napoleon.[30]

In the aftermath of the Austrian catastrophe Ligne wrote to Gentz, admitting: 'the list of my errors is longer than that of my prophecies. I did not believe in the war, then I believed in Prussia, then I believed in our army, then I did not believe in that of the defrenchified French ... I believed in some of our generals ... I nearly believed in a coalition ... I might have been beaten but surely not routed.' No words were too harsh for 'our conceited and dishonourable stupidity ... Europe is in a bad state but it is truly the fault of its leaders.' Indeed in these years of torment, Francis II's defeats exposed him to vicious criticism. Ligne's cousin Prince Jean Liechtenstein, for example, who had distinguished himself both in battle and in negotiations, told the Emperor to his face that he had ruined the monarchy. Their relations were so bad that when two Russian ladies asked Ligne why Jean Liechtenstein had not killed 'this terrible Napoleon' during an interview, Ligne replied: 'It was not his emperor.'[31]

Yet Francis II survived. The great twentieth-century Austrian writer Hugo von Hofmannsthal believed: 'Politics is magic. He who can summon the forces from the deep, him will they follow.' His grandiose sense of mission, and evident concern for his subjects' welfare, gave *Kaiser Franz* that magic. After each defeat he changed his ministers and re-entered Vienna to the cheers of his loyal subjects. Count Philippe Stadion, an Imperial knight, replaced Cobenzl as chief minister; Colloredo, the Emperor's friend and mentor for thirty-three years, was dismissed with a few ill-chosen words. Although the Emperor set agents to spy on the Archduke Charles, he also made his brother head of the War Ministry, with more power than any subject since Prince Eugène.

Within a year of Austerlitz, Ligne lost the right to sign himself 'Prince de Ligne *et du Saint Empire Romain*'. On 22 July 1806 Napoleon told the Austrian ambassador that, unless Francis II abdicated as Holy Roman Emperor, by 10 August French troops would invade Austria. The Emperor was so eager for peace that he obeyed this command to end an empire of a thousand years. The Reichshofrat and the remaining Imperial institutions were dissolved. Francis II, Holy Roman Emperor, became Francis I, Emperor of Austria (although, for the sake of clarity, he will continue to be called Francis II in these pages): for the first time all his hereditary possessions were part of one state, the Empire of Austria. In the Holy Roman Empire some Germans felt abandoned; most Austrians were delighted because, like Turks eager to end the Ottoman Empire after 1918, they considered the Holy Roman Empire had brought them more trouble than benefit. Zinzendorf, by then one of the Emperor's leading ministers, commented in his diary: 'This is one of the numerous results of that fatal coalition, of that imprudent war, in fact of the public and military follies without number which we have accumulated since in 1791 we began to concern ourselves with this unfortunate revolution, which without us would have finished suddenly like all the *enragements* originating in French light-headedness.'[32]

Ligne spent much of the summer of 1806 in Teplitz and Dresden discussing the future of Europe with Gentz, the Duke of Weimar, Prince Louis Ferdinand and Princess Dolgoruky, and filling the pages of *Ma napoléonide* with further analysis of Napoleon. While Gentz considered Napoleon a mixture of devil and charlatan, Ligne resisted the gratification of hatred. He never used terms of denigration common in the salons of Vienna, such as 'the usurper', 'the Corsican'. By 1806 he regarded Napoleon as simply another emperor.

Ligne praised 'the cleverness of Napoleon in mixing old and new'. Combining absolutism at home and aggression abroad,

'Napoleon is the example, the terror, the support and the scourge of kings.' He knew 'the art of using and playing on men as a great musician plays instruments'. While admiring the monarch, Ligne felt no sympathy for the man. Napoleon had genius but no soul.*

> One admires him without loving him ... [He is] the extinguisher of the heart and mind ... He is a prodigious being, but there is not one remark to quote from him showing elevation or sensibility ... He knows everything except how to be moderate ... I accept that that man-demon has made himself a torrent. But earthquake, it is really too much. What a scourge! What turbulence, what movement! He is making the whole of Europe play the game known as *toilette madame* [grandmother's footsteps] where everyone rushes, when his name is called out, to the first vacant chair.[33]

The next move in the game came from Prussia, which was preparing to attack Napoleon on its own. Ligne had learnt the lesson of Austerlitz, and no longer advocated war. He warned his beloved friend the Duke of Weimar, who was also a Prussian general, of the fate awaiting Prussia: 'I truly wish I am mistaken. But I see that for lack of looking on the dark side beforehand, one does so afterwards: and that one never believes the French in such large numbers, nor so rapid, as they are ... again 100 thousand respectful tendernesses to the best and most amiable, whom I would like to see the most powerful, of Princes.'

As Ligne had predicted, on 14 October 1806 the Prussians were crushed at Jena; his beloved Prince Louis Ferdinand died in battle. The King and Queen fled east. Ligne wrote to his old friend Roger de Damas, who had reappeared in Vienna after the Napoleonic conquest of Naples, where he had been serving as Inspector-General of Infantry: 'What came from the magic flute of Frederick the Great is reduced to the drum.'[34]

---

* This view of the Emperor's egotism would be shared by André Malraux, who would define him, to General de Gaulle, as 'un très grand esprit et une assez petite âme'.

On 17 July 1807 Ligne finally saw Napoleon, passing through Dresden on his way back from Russia, where he had just signed the Treaty of Tilsit ending the war with Alexander I and Frederick William III. Ligne 'filmed' Napoleon for *Fragments de l'histoire de ma vie*, as he had so many other monarchs:

> At last I have seen him, this maker and unmaker of kings. Knowing that after his victories, his interviews and his peace, he was going through Dresden on his way to Paris, I went there from Teplitz on 17 July. I placed myself with the Duke of Weimar at the bottom of the Court staircase. The Emperor and the King he has created [Frederick Augustus II of Saxony] climbed it slowly enough, on account of the number and clumsiness of the Saxon courtiers, for me to examine closely the first from head to foot. He had a fine way of holding his head and an air of military nobility. It is not that of parchments or the throne, which gives an air of disdain or impertinence which is often taken for nobility.
>
> His expression was firm, calm and impressive.

Beside Ligne a young lady said: 'How good and sweet he looks! He is a lamb!'

Ligne then followed Napoleon like a lover pursuing his mistress at a dance, not wanting to miss a remark or a look, through the picture gallery, past the masterpieces of Correggio, Titian and Rubens, until Napoleon deliberately stopped in front of a battle picture. Ligne noticed that, compared to Frederick II, Catherine II and Joseph II, Napoleon had a 'grimacing smile of false *bonhomie*, sensitive and protective'; 'he asked some questions and made some observations in staccato style; and what is singular, like the Bourbons, whose way of balancing when walking he also imitates a little. Is it the result of the throne of France? Is it acted?'[35] He admitted that Napoleon was 'the most prodigious being who has existed' but added, with Austrian disdain for an Empire of three years: 'And then how long will this mosaic of the Empire last? One fall from a horse. Everything returns to confusion.'[36]

King of Italy, 'Protector' of the rump of German states in the

Confederation of the Rhine, Napoleon had fulfilled Ligne's fears and become the new Charlemagne. The French Empire dominated, and terrorised, Europe. Nevertheless, whereas almost every other monarch or prince in Europe begged for favours, Ligne did not. The Tsar of Russia declared himself proud to be Napoleon's friend. The Electors of Bavaria, Saxony and Wurttemberg were promoted by Napoleon to the rank of king, as if they were officers in his army. The German princes Ligne saw at Dresden were so deferential that he told them: 'You look as if you are going to the Vale of Jehosophat for the Last Judgement.' One of Ligne's cousins, Prince Prosper d'Arenberg, married a distant relation of the Empress Josephine (who asked for an annulment as soon as she could). But Ligne held out.

One reason for Ligne's refusal to pay court to Napoleon was that in 1807 he finally returned to favour at his own. Almost fifty years to the day since the victory of Kolin, 'as a sign of My total happiness with the many years of constantly faithful devotion to Me and My House', the Emperor appointed Ligne to the important position of Captain of the Trabant Guard and the Hofburg Guard.[37] Francis II was a kind master and the appointment, which Ligne attributed to the influence of his hero the Archduke Charles, may also have been a way of giving Ligne the large salary of 11,691 florins a year. The Trabants, the equivalent of the Yeomen of the Guard in England, were stationed in the outermost antechamber of the Imperial apartments and escorted the Emperor on ceremonial occasions, and every Sunday in winter when he went to mass. The Hofburg Guard was responsible for the outer security of the palace. The trust between the Habsburgs and their subjects was so strong that these two small units (there were 90 soldiers in the Trabants, 177 in the Hofburg Guard), recruited from soldiers who had been especially brave in battle, were the Habsburgs' only foot guards. Every other royal or imperial capital contained regiments of foot guards several thousand strong, entrusted with the defence of the monarchy, such as the Preobrazhensky Guards in St Petersburg, the Grenadier guards in London or the many regiments of Napoleon's Garde Impériale in Paris. Vienna did not.

The position of Captain of the Guard could have been created for Ligne, since it combined military prestige with court duties. Ligne enjoyed appearing in Vienna, in the street, at the theatre or at church, with 'my guards'. He did not mind that 'when I pronounce this word with a certain self-important air my whole family starts to laugh'.[38]

As Captain of the Trabants, Ligne witnessed a 'regeneration' of the court of Austria. Napoleon's need for a court to bolster his regime, and his own personal tastes, had created a new style of monarchy – grandiose, official, military – which rapidly found imitators abroad. The informal royal retreats Ligne had known so well, such as the Petit Trianon or the Hermitage, went out of fashion. Even Francis II, whose tastes were so simple, absorbed the new spirit. In 1807 he added a splendid new ceremonial hall to the Hofburg, by Louis de Montoyer, the architect of the Palais Razumovsky. The renewed grandeur of the Austrian court was displayed at Francis II's remarriage, on 6 January 1808, six months after the death of his second wife Maria Theresa of Naples, to his third wife, a first cousin called Maria Ludovica of Modena (daughter of the dispossessed Duke of Modena, therefore from a branch of the Habsburg dynasty especially hostile to Napoleon).

Standing beside the throne wearing the red and black uniform of Captain of the Trabants, Ligne was impressed by the skill and dignity with which this Italian princess replied in Latin to the Hungarian deputations (it was their official language), in German to the others. 'The court has become a court again. The fêtes of the marriage were superb. One could see more than one hundred millions of diamonds dancing or promenading in the new hall ... Their Majesties talk to us and always have something agreeable to say.' Ligne was complimented on the new uniforms he had introduced among 'my guards'.

The Emperor himself was overjoyed with his new wife and told Prince Trautmansdorf, Grand Master of the Court and a friend of Ligne, that the arrangements had been much better than at his previous two weddings. The only sombre note came from the sight of the French ambassador, in a dark diplomatic uniform, surrounded by other ambassadors, all of whose masters his own Emperor had wholly or partially dethroned.

The previous Empress, Maria Theresa of Naples, had kept the Emperor away from his courtiers, and had shocked her own mother, Queen Maria Carolina – no prude – by her reckless behaviour with handsome young singers. The new Empress preferred talking with Goethe and Mme de Staël. She was charmed by Ligne, whose conversation was so much livelier than other courtiers'. Soon she brought the Emperor and the archdukes to visit the Kahlenberg, where they behaved like schoolboys on holiday. When they went on to the Leopoldsberg, Ligne shared the Empress's carriage and wrote with a courtier's glee: 'I think it is the first time that one has been in a carriage with one of our Empresses. What a pity I told her … that my two mountains are so near to each other!'

Ligne was a favourite at court with whom, according to Zinzendorf, the Emperor practised how to behave at ceremonies of the Order of the Golden Fleece. Ligne filled his day not by writing books but by sending memoirs on finance to Archduke Rainer, books on fortifications to Archduke John, a survey of European armies to the Archduke Charles and demands for a chamberlain's key to the Emperor.[39]

The 'regeneration' of the court was also evident in September 1808 at the Empress's coronation as Queen Consort of Hungary, in the church in Pressburg where her husband had been crowned King sixteen years earlier. It was a rare moment of harmony in the turbulent relationship between the Habsburg dynasty and the Hungarian nation. Ligne went to Pressburg, by boat down the Danube with a detachment of his guards, and again stayed with his daughter Féfé Palffy.

During this Hungarian interlude, Ligne rode beside the Emperor's carriage in processions or stood like a caryatid beside his throne: 'Ah! How beautiful I looked on the most beautiful

horse of the Court and in the world, and so superb that the
Emperor rode it the day of the coronation ... My God! how the
Empress was beautiful and touching when, a minute before com-
municating, she felt faint on the steps of the altar! ... What heat!
How heavy my helmet was!'[40]

There was a startling contrast with his last visit to Pressburg
in 1805, when he had been a 'poor devil' with only one uniform,
afraid to be taken prisoner by drunken French soldiers.

> Instead of the conditions of which I have just spoken, I am
> sparkling with gold beside Prince Esterhazy,* sparkling with
> diamonds, at all our cavalcades, parades and magnificent cere-
> monies and harangues. The last was very touching. The
> Emperor and then the Empress, when he descended from the
> throne, replied to the harangues in a manner so eloquent, so
> simple and so loyal that I still have tears in my eyes as I write
> this two hours after everything is over.[41]

To heighten his happiness, on 7 September 1808, the day the
Empress was crowned and anniversary of Ligne's attack on
Holzberg near Görlitz in 1757, the Archduke Charles told him:
'Thank the Emperor who has just made you a Field Marshal.' He
owed this supreme favour, for which he had been hoping since
1790, either to the Archduke or (in Zinzendorf's opinion) to the
Liechtenstein princesses. With her skill at pleasing, the Empress
said: 'I would never finish if I told you all the pleasure given me by
this act of justice on the part of the Emperor, as much for him as
for you.' Showing the mock-simplicity that enchanted the
Viennese, the Emperor asked: 'How will you manage with two
batons, that of Captain of the Guard and that of Field Marshal?'
Ligne replied: 'I would throw them both away ... to seize a gun if
Your Majesty is attacked.' His military career had not been the
blaze of glory of which he had dreamt, but at least he was now the
Marshal Prince de Ligne.[42]

During this second Hungarian visit he made an unsuccessful

---

* Captain of the Hungarian Noble Guard, a small unit of horse guards.

attempt, by demanding *indigénat*, or naturalisation as a Hungarian, to found a second, Hungarian, branch of the House of Ligne, in favour of Louis's second son, his grandson Jules-Louis. (He had already in 1791, been given an estate in Hungary, since sold, as a reward for his role in the fall of Belgrade.)[43] Distrust of the boy's French nationality led to the rejection of this demand. Nevertheless Ligne's links with Hungary explain why he was able to boast, in *Fragments*, of a unique plurality of nationalities: 'I have six or seven *patries*, Empire, Flanders, France, Spain, Austria, Poland, Russia and almost Hungary.'[44]

The strands in Ligne's life were coming together in his triumphant old age. At the age of seventy-three he was a court favourite, a field marshal and a European celebrity. Beloeil had returned to his family and there was a grandson to assure the succession. Ligne was also much richer. He now had 12,000 florins a year military salary; 11,000 florins a year from Prince Esterhazy, the purchaser of Edelstetten; 9000 florins a year paid to him by Louis de Ligne; and his pension of 1000 and revenue of 1800 ducats a year from Russia. Henceforth no visitors to the Hôtel de Ligne record the filth noticed in less prosperous years by visitors such as Zinzendorf and Fersen.

Ligne also had someone new to adore. Her name was Countess Rosalie Rzewuska. Married to a grandson of his old friend the Princesse Maréchale Lubomirska, she was only nineteen. Ligne called her 'one of the first beauties in the world, ravishing rather than seductive and all the more amiable, when her coldness or laziness does not prevent her from being so, for having the reputation of being disdainful'. Despite an age gap of fifty-four years, they shared a love of Viennese gossip, French culture, and European royalty. Ligne said he was not in love, but enchanted: 'We appeal to each other; it is what suits us best; and is a continuous pleasure with no drawbacks.'[45] 'Madame Rosalie', as Ligne called her, soon took the place of the Princess of Solms. Her unconventional husband Count Wenceslas Rzewuski, known as 'the Emir', was no hindrance: he preferred travelling in the Ottoman Empire, or rearing his celebrated stud of Arabian horses in the Ukraine, to living with his wife in Vienna.[46]

Ligne was still an attractive man. At the time he began to see Rosalie, he was described by his grandson-in-law, Count François Potocki:

> The prince is tall and well built, his face majestic, his manners noble and natural. His white hair, curled and lightly powdered, frames a handsome face with hardly a wrinkle. A charming smile, an expression of kindness mixed with *finesse* and malice, like his features. His mouth is large and graceful, his wide, intelligent forehead radiates serenity. His expression is lively, sometimes his eyes seem to be on fire; everything about him expresses frankness. He is not loved but adored by his friends, his family has a real cult for him; no one can resist the seduction of his person and his wit. He always wears the uniform of Captain of the Trabants, the rank he has just received: on his chest the cordon of Maria Theresa and the Order of the Golden Fleece are intertwined.[47]

Despite his personal seductiveness and excellent health, for Ligne, as for many amorous old men, a physical relationship was less important than having someone to visit, to worship, and to receive his letters – like Asquith's to Venetia Stanley, they were sometimes four pages long. Ligne wrote: 'I need a house to go to after dinner until quarter past ten.' Almost every day he visited Mme Rosalie's blue salon, filled with caged songbirds and pots of hyacinths, on the third floor of the Jacoberhof on the ramparts.[48]

For once we know the woman's point of view, since at the end of her life, in her seventies, Rosalie Rzewuska wrote her memoirs. She thought Ligne was an 'enchanter', whose company and conversation spread a form of magic around him; but her friendship was not blind. With the precise analysis of emotion that, like 'white malice' and espionage, was characteristic of Vienna, she wrote of Ligne:

Far from being afflicted by the evil he saw, or even disapproving of it, he regarded it as an amusing necessity, attached to the
human condition ... Indulgent, easy-going, always ready to
oblige, he sympathised so acutely with others' sufferings that
they became for him real torture, and to escape it his kindness
often degenerated into weakness. He was reproached with
having little discrimination in his social relations. He was often
accused of having more softness than sensibility in the heart
and of being more interested in the attraction of pleasing than
the happiness of attaching [*de tenir plus à l'agrément de plaire
qu'au bonheur d'attacher*]. Nevertheless, he put a touching
fidelity in his dealings with old acquaintances ... I think I can
still see him, slowly climbing the staircase, greeting all the servants, entering the salon, extending his left hand, rearranging
his dishevelled hair, and crying 'God, God, God, dear
Madame Rosalie, how can one live on the third floor?'[49]

Her reference to kindness degenerating into weakness probably
reflected her disapproval of the sums of money Ligne gave
away. Her remark about Ligne being more interested in pleasing
than attaching shows that she too had noticed the indifference of
which Bonnay had complained.

Despite her indifference to her husband, Mme Rosalie's relationship with Ligne remained no more than a passionate friendship. Brought up by a prison laundress after her mother had
been guillotined in Paris, she was a cold woman, whose wit was
one of her main attractions: many of Ligne's most malicious
remarks were addressed to her. Mme du Montet, who had
clearly suffered at her hands, compared her disdainful, ironic
regard to that of a snake about to strike. Moreover, she was a
pious Catholic with two young children. She went to church
every day and had no intention of taking lovers – although she
liked elderly adorers so much that Bonnay, who in 1808 returned
to Vienna as Louis XVIII's representative, came to visit her as
often as Ligne; presumably at a different hour.[50]

'Enchanted', a favourite at court, Ligne was also about to
become a famous author. On 27 December 1807, just before the

Emperor's wedding to Maria Ludovica of Modena, an invader from France considerably more appealing than Napoleon had arrived in Vienna: Mme de Staël. The author of celebrated emotional novels called *Delphine* and *Corinne*, she was in search of material for a new book, on Germany and its writers – a subject chosen in part because of its implicit reproach to the war-loving Emperor of the French. Her red shoulders, and restless twitching fingers (when she wore sandals, people saw that her toes twitched as well), aroused derision in the salons. Moreover, her enthusiasm for the early stage of the Revolution had led Ligne to make fun of her and her father Necker, a finance minister of Louis XVI, in his *Mélanges*.

However, in the soothing ambiance of Vienna they became friends. They agreed not to talk about the Revolution. On other subjects they spoke each other's language – both were consumed by the pursuit of love and fame, fascinated by the new Germany, and enemies of Napoleon. Moreover, when not devouring a new lover, or striving for effect, with her intellectual curiosity and knowledge of human nature, Mme de Staël could be excellent company.

She fell under the charm at once. To her former lover Benjamin Constant she wrote: 'He touches chords of my soul which I cannot admit to myself and of which he has no idea' – because he reminded her of another benevolent eighteenth-century grandee, who had been the love of her life: her own father.[51] Ligne was delighted by this human volcano, but thought she was her own worst enemy.

> Her Christianity makes one want to be pagan, her mysticism makes one prefer dryness; and her love of the extraordinary gives one a taste for whatever is most simple and most vulgar, so often do exaggerations produce the reverse effect... This devouring flame of sensibility and this love story without a subject make her unhappy and slightly ridiculous; but it is compensated for by so much that is unexpected, rapid and inspiring that you forgive her what would be unbearable in

anyone else ... she is not completely a man, she is not completely a woman, she is the most distinguished person.

Soon they saw each other every day, at parties at the Palais
Liechtenstein or the Palais Lobkowitz, at *comédies de société*, or
at dinner with selected intellectuals such as August von Schlegel,
the translator of Shakespeare, Sismondi, the Italian historian,
and Hammer-Purgstall. Another guest, the Dutch ambassador
van Hogendorp, felt that in conversation Ligne tried too hard 'in
order always to find new and piquant ideas', but was natural and
gay compared to Mme de Staël, who strove to appear learned
and profound. Ligne gave her an open invitation, as one of the
family, to the Hôtel de Ligne after ten in the evening. Many of
her notes to her lover of the moment, an Austrian noble of Irish
origin called Count Maurice O'Donnell, end: 'I must go and
dine at the Prince de Ligne's,' or, 'We are supping at the Prince
de Ligne's, are we not?'[52]

Maurice O'Donnell was clever and self-absorbed. Many
Viennese felt that he saw Mme de Staël simply in order to earn a
few pages in her biography. Although she was fourteen years
older than her lover, she dreamt of marriage, and they often
quarrelled. One night at the Princesse Maréchale Lubomirska's,
Mme de Staël was so jealous of the attention O'Donnell was
paying Flore de Ligne that she started to eat the leaves of a laurel
tree: footmen had to come and take it away. Ligne was as gentle
over her love affair as he had been ten years earlier with
Casanova over his quarrels with the staff at Dux. After he found
her in tears, he urged her not to expect 'the beautiful, the pure,
the sublime' in one person, and to reason with herself: 'I always
say, *Rentre en toi-même, Octave!*' He also helped her with her
book. Unlike many modern experts, he did not believe in the
'German national character', and in his notes emphasised the differences between Bavarians and North Germans, Austria and
Weimar: 'As for nations, you can no longer make generalisations
about them.'[53]

Mme de Staël, for her part, possibly in return for his advice over her book on Germany, offered to publish a selection of his works in Paris. Ligne turned to a friend called Caroline Murray. Known as *la muse belgique* in her youth, she had taken refuge in Vienna during the Revolution. Ligne had often helped his *chère excellente et aimable amie, chère aimable Clio*, with money, accommodation and other favours: he called her poverty *le comble de la gloire*. They frequently corresponded in prose and verse. At his request she copied out extracts from his *Mélanges* – epigrams such as: 'A battle is an ode; there are few Pindars or Condés but many authors of fugitive pieces' – so that Mme de Staël would miss disobliging references to herself and her father, and would not have to read all thirty volumes.[54] Ligne showed his desperation to please Mme de Staël in his notes to Caroline Murray: 'Do you not have a few more less foolish little *pensées* to send to Mme de Staël, without verses. *Chère amie*, even if there were only about thirty passable ones on delicacy or envy, give them to me this evening at the theatre.'[55] To Mme de Staël herself he even offered to write a eulogy of her father and forged a letter from himself to Catherine II, praising Necker: she wisely refused to use them both.[56]

Mme de Staël left Vienna on 22 May 1808. Thereafter letters flew between Coppet, her chateau on Lake Geneva (she was known as Our Lady of Coppet), Vienna and Teplitz. Napoleon overshadowed their correspondence: Ligne warned her that Gentz 'does not do honour to wickedness' and underestimated Napoleon. Mme de Staël prophesied that Austria would not have war 'this year', and lamented the horrors of the war in Spain. They also discussed her forthcoming selection of Ligne's works. Mme de Staël chose his letters to Mme de Coigny and Ségur, his portraits of Voltaire, Rousseau, Frederick II, Joseph II and Catherine, and many detached *pensées*. She shampooed his text, rewriting extensively, removing some originality as well as grammatical errors. He bowed to the power of his editor, calling her his master, working like a devil to send her corrections and selections, saying that if she had been an empress, he would have liked to be her Potemkin.[57]

Lettres et pensées du Maréchal Prince de Ligne (he had finally abandoned the pretence of *M. le P. de L.*****, or *un officier autrichien*) was published in Paris and Geneva, *chez J. J. Paschoud*, in January 1809. Mme de Staël's preface remains one of the best explanations of his charm. She praised his simplicity and courage, his youthfulness of spirit and independence of mind.

> Men, things and events have passed in front of the Prince de Ligne. He judged them without plan and without goal, without wanting to impose on them the despotism of a system; that is what they were like, or at least that is how they appeared to him that day ... You see before you the person the Prince de Ligne describes for you; he gives life to everything because he puts art in nothing.[58]

The book was at once a critical and a commercial triumph. Already in the 1780s Ligne had begun to win a reputation as a writer, even though works like *Coup d'oeil sur Beloeil* and *Mélanges de Littérature* had been privately published. On 21 August 1783, the famous journalist Metra had praised his gaiety and *style serré et concis*: referring to the author of some of the most famous and licentious memoirs of the early eighteenth century, the *Mémoires du Comte Hamilton*, in 1789 a Hungarian friend, Count Janos Fekete, had called Ligne 'the chevalier de Grammont of our age'.[59]

However, the revolutionary wars had cut off Ligne from his public in France. The *Mélanges militaires, littéraires et sentimentaires*, published in French in Dresden, had received little publicity: the difficulty of finding copies in France today shows how few were sold there. In 1809 alone, however, there were seven editions of *Lettres et pensées du Maréchal Prince de Ligne* in French (including three published 'à Soho Square à Londres' by a famous *émigré* publisher, B. Dulau et Co.); one in English, and one in Russian. They were followed by Italian (1811) and German (1812) editions. Mme de Staël had helped arrange publicity with old friends who wrote for Paris newspapers, such as

Benjamin Constant, Elzéar de Sabran and his stepfather the Chevalier de Boufflers. They praised Ligne's combination of grace, verve, imagination and truthfulness, which were an agreeable contrast to the pomposity of the Empire. Some compared his letters to those of Mme de Sévigné, his epigrams (for example, 'It is easy to be generous when you are rich') to those of La Rochefoucauld.[60] The appeal of the eighteenth century at the beginning of the nineteenth was such that a lady-in-waiting of the Empress Josephine wrote that she enjoyed Ligne's books precisely because they reminded her of 'the style of the conversation of a salon thirty years ago'. A sign of Ligne's new-found popularity is that three other selections from his works, *Mémoires et lettres du Maréchal Prince de Ligne faisant suite aux Lettres et pensées de même auteur* (two volumes), edited by M. Malte-Brun, *Oeuvres choisies, littéraires, historiques, et militaires du Maréchal Prince de Ligne* (two volumes), edited by the Chevalier de Boufflers, and *Oeuvres choisies*, edited by M. de Propiac (who called his selection 'flowers' that the 'too delicate hand' of Mme de Staël had not considered appropriate to gather), were published in Paris and Geneva later in the same year. Thus the best of his works were easily available in France.[61]

In England Ligne was also praised for his liveliness, charm and gaiety. The Whig *Edinburgh Review*, however, while praising his 'grace and ingenuity', deplored what it called his 'profound ignorance of the true constitution and progress of society' and his 'entire disregard of the rights and feelings of the inferior [*sic*] orders'. Other English critics complained that the origin of the work was the author's vanity.[62]

Nevertheless Ligne now had what he wanted: he was a field marshal in Austria and a famous author in France. Two years later he wrote to Mme de Staël words that came from the heart: 'I thank you again thousands and thousands of times for having taken me out of the dust of Dresden and of the world which without you would not know that I exist. One can make kings [a reference to Napoleon] but only you can create reputations out of a phrase or a line [Ligne].'[63]

War and Peace

At the beginning of 1809, while Paris was acclaiming the works of the Prince de Ligne, Vienna was dreaming of war. High and low, all were united in hatred of the new Genghis Khan: Napoleon. News of the first French defeats in the Peninsula War in Spain sharpened Austrian hopes of revenge. The imminence of war gave special excitement to the carnival season. At one court ball in February there were so many uniforms that it looked like a military camp. Zinzendorf lamented that the anti-French coterie of 'Gentz, Pozzo di Borgo and Razumovsky govern the city'.[1]

Austria prepared to attack in the spring. Metternich, by then Austrian ambassador in Paris, maintained secret relations with Talleyrand and encouraged Austrian hopes of victory. On 13 March 1809 the Empress Maria Ludovica presided over the blessing of new army flags at St Stephen's Cathedral, in a state of such exaltation that she seemed like a 'soul on fire'. When she followed the flags on foot through the streets of the capital, cries from the crowd hailed her as the new Maria Theresa. According to a French diplomat, in 1805 only the government had been eager to fight; in 1809 government, army and people were equally keen.[2]

Ligne was one of the few people in Vienna to remain detached. He still considered Napoleon the enemy of Austria. In 1808 he had given him a new name: Satan I; but Austerlitz had convinced him Satan I was such a genius, commanding such overwhelming force, that only a European coalition uniting Berlin, Vienna and St Petersburg could defeat him: 'Each power would be destroyed separately if the three were not united.'

Meanwhile Vienna should remain neutral. Moreover, embroiled in the Peninsula War, Napoleon did not represent an immediate danger. In a letter to Mme de Staël, Ligne condemned 'that superb stupidity of believing ourselves always about to be crushed, that it is our turn etc., that it is imminent'.[3]

In contrast to Gentz and Mme de Staël, he had no confidence in the power that funded every anti-Napoleonic coalition, 'scornful, proud, disdainful England'. In *Ma profession de foi sur les anglais*, he described them as arrogant, drunken, badly brought up and ignorant of everything happening on the Continent. In tragedy they only had Shakespeare, in warfare only Marlborough. In 1807 the bombardment and occupation of Copenhagen, a neutral capital, in time of peace by the Royal Navy (in order to prevent the Danish fleet being used by Napoleon), seemed to him particularly odious: 'If the French had attacked Denmark as unjustly as the English and killed 2000 civilians by the bombardment of Copenhagen, how we would cry against them. What monsters we would say. But the English are angels.'[4]

'I have left the *jeu*, *cercle* or *appartement*, whatever one wants to call it,' wrote Ligne in April, 'and seeing the tranquillity of the Empress who was more amiable than ever and the confidence and good nature of the Emperor, I could not restrain my tears, fearing that it might be our last day at court.' Without consultation or coordination with Britain, as overconfident as in 1805, Austria declared war on 9 April 1809. Austria had some grounds for confidence. Although preferring a policy of peace, the Archduke Charles had reformed and reorganised the army, whose idol he was. Excluding the national guard, the Landwehr, Austrian forces comprised 281,000 men, compared to 170,000 in the French armies in Germany. Moreover, the quality of the Austrians had improved, while the French had begun that long decline that Napoleon had prophesied four years earlier in Vienna – and many of their best troops were fighting in Spain.[5]

In an order of the day to his army on 11 April, Archduke Charles proclaimed Austria's European mission: it was fighting 'to give Germany back its independence. The liberty of Europe has taken refuge beneath your banners.' Ligne, on the other hand, reverting to his dream of 1788–90, thought it was not the French Empire but the Ottoman that Austria should attack. Spread out from Warsaw to Trieste, Austrian forces were in a catastrophic position: 'The more we recognise the satanic spirit, the infernal soul and the diabolic power of Napoleon, the more we should show prudence and lack of touchiness towards him ... we are *en permanence de suicide* ... we have wanted war for a year. We have it. Please God it will not be disastrous within two weeks!'[6]

If he admitted the value of German patriotism as a link between the Emperor of Austria and the King of Prussia, Ligne despised the patriotism of the street. While Vienna resounded to the sound of war songs – 'When she wants it, Austria is above all others! / She wants it, she wants it, long live Austria!' – Ligne commented with a disdain, both traditional and prophetic: 'They do not realise that this false enthusiasm leads to cruelty. To make a nation political and instruct it in its affairs is a strange idea.' Again he was a voice crying in the wilderness. The Emperor did not take him as a captain of his guards when he left on campaign.

On 10 May French armies entered Austria and Ligne left Vienna for Pressburg. (Again he fails to mention what happens to his wife.) From a distance he could see flames rising on the Leopoldsberg, where French soldiers were burning the *petit Beloeil*. On 13 May, after a resistance almost as feeble as in 1805, Napoleon entered Vienna, three and a half years after the previous French occupation. He told a delegation from the city that 'the Habsburgs were as ill-suited to reign as the Bourbons'.[7]

On 14 May Ligne arrived in Pest, the half-German commercial city on the other side of the Danube from the Hungarian capital Buda. The Empress, as bellicose as ever and reproaching the Archduke Charles for his slowness, lived in the palace constructed for Maria Theresa on the hill of Buda overlooking the river. However, Ligne did not cross the Danube to pay his court to her and he avoided 'four or five places where I could have met people who displease me because of the war', probably members of the war party like his friends Gentz, Pozzo and Roger de

TOP: The Emperor Joseph II in a circle of friends, to which Ligne was admitted when in Vienna. From left to right; Countess Leopoldine Kaunitz, Count Orsini-Rosenberg, Princess Clary, the Emperor Joseph II, Princess Kinsky, Princess Charles Liechtenstein, Marshal Lacy. Conversation could be very free in the Emperor's circle of friends. Marshal Lacy was Ligne's principal patron in the Austrian army. ABOVE: A parade of Walloon grenadiers in the presence of Joseph II during his visit to the Austrian Netherlands, 26 June 1781. Ligne is standing beside the Emperor, his constant patron, to whom he would owe his highest military commands. Eight years later the Austrian Netherlands would rise in revolt and drive out Austrian troops.

Prince Potemkin in the uniform of Grand Admiral of the Black Sea and Caspian Sea Fleets. From their meeting in 1780 until Potemkin's death in 1791, Potemkin was a patron of Ligne and a partner in the 'grand design' of a partition of the Ottoman Empire between Austria and Russia.

Catherine II in travelling costume, during her voyage to the Crimea in 1787. Catherine II loved Ligne, to whom she talked freely, and on whom she bestowed estates and pensions.

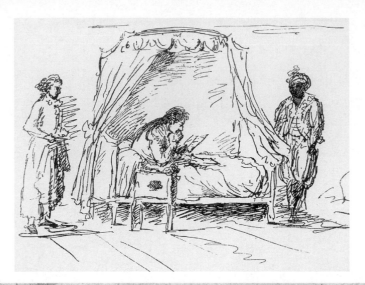

TOP: The Prince de Ligne in bed at Beloeil, 22 September 1793, drawn by his secretary, Sauveur Legros. As was his habit, Ligne is reading and writing in bed in the morning. On the right is one of his Turkish servants, captured during the Balkan wars. ABOVE: Interior of the Hôtel de Ligne on the Moelkerbastei, Vienna. The prince is sitting on a chair facing his illegitimate granddaughter Titine de Ligne. On the sofa are his daughters Flore and Euphémie. On the right the Princesse de Ligne is, as usual, working on a piece of embroidery. The interior of the Hôtel de Ligne in this drawing by Ligne's secretary, made between 1794 and Legros's departure from Vienna in 1803, appears more elegant and less dilapidated than it is described in visitors' accounts.

A page of the manuscript of *Fragments de l'Histoire de Ma Vie*. Contrary to the prince's claims, this page, and many others, show that, like the professional author he was, Ligne corrected his own and his copyists' manuscripts.

A view of Mont Ligne outside Teplitz. In this rustic temple built in 1805, inaugurated by a coronation of Ligne parodying that of Napoleon in Paris in 1804, and destroyed by Russian troops in 1813, Ligne entertained vistors to Teplitz, at a time when it was the most fashionable watering place in Europe.

Marshal Berthier requesting the hand of the Archduchess Marie Louise in marriage, on 6 March 1810. Like the slightly distant observer he was, Ligne stands on the far left, wearing the uniform of Captain of the Trabant Life Guard. Prince Trautmansdorf is to the left of the Emperor Francis. Metternich is second to the right of the Emperor.

The Prince de Ligne in 1812, at the age of 77. Ligne is going to court: he is wearing the uniform of Captain of the Trabant Guard, the Order of the Golden Fleece and the Grand Cross of the Order of Maria Theresa. The artist, Emile Legros, son of his secretary Sauveur Legros, was one of the prince's adjutants and a witness at his deathbed.

The Prince de Ligne driving in the Augarten in 1814. Ligne was not so poor that he could not afford to keep a carriage, coachman and postilions. In his will he ensured that his widow could continue to keep a carriage after his death.

The knight in armour who followed the funeral procession of the Prince de Ligne on 15 December 1814. This symbol of the chivalric values which guided Ligne's life accompanied the funerals of all Austrian Marshals and generals who died in Vienna. He is heading for the Kahlenberg, where Ligne is buried.

Damas. Politics had come between them like a sword. He preferred to lodge in the house of a Jewish lady called Judith: he played cards with the family in the evening and he 'did not miss one synagogue day'.

On 21 and 22 May, before the delighted eyes of the Viennese crowded on the ramparts and the church towers, Napoleon suffered his first defeat at Aspern, in the plain below the Kahlenberg, at the hands of the Archduke Charles. Throughout the battle the Archduke displayed immense courage, rushing into the fighting and himself seizing the flags of the Fifteenth Infantry Regiment. The German nationalist writer von Kleist hailed him as the conqueror of the unconquerable. Thereafter, with the fatal hesitation of Austrian generals, the Archduke lost the advantage: he waited for Napoleon to commit the first mistake and for national uprisings which – except in the Tyrol under the heroic Andreas Hofer – did not occur.

From Pest, Ligne inundated Francis II and his own notebooks with battle plans and prophecies of apocalypse. Aware of the genius of Napoleon and the weakness of the Austrian army, he was sceptical about the prospects of Austria: 'The most brilliant victory, the greatest glory of our arms is useless ... may God ensure that this plain, cradle of the house of Austria, does not become its tomb!'[8]

As Ligne had feared, at Wagram on 5 and 6 July, on the same corpse-strewn plain, Napoleon defeated the Archduke Charles. On 12 July, without consulting his brother, the Archduke signed an armistice. Furious, the Emperor replaced him with Jean Liechtenstein, whose diplomatic and military skills ensured that his outspokenness was forgiven. Austria was defeated but, in contrast to Prussia after Jena, had preserved a strong, well-disciplined army.

For five months, while the French and Austrian armies observed each other from opposite banks of the Danube and central Europe held its breath, Ligne adopted a new way of life. He stayed writing in bed until half past three as usual, then rose and dined in the company of his aide de camp Emile Legros.

Dinner was followed by a walk until 6.30, when he went to a German-language theatre installed in a former Ottoman mosque. The plays were so cheaply mounted that the gods of Olympus appeared on stage dressed as Hungarian hussars. Thereafter, Ligne went not to the court or a salon but to a café, where he drank lemonade while watching funeral processions and herds of animals crossing a square in front of him.

As usual he showed his ability to escape from his milieu and adopt the sensibility of another epoch. Like other writers of the nineteenth century such as Stendhal (who visited the Kahlenberg in 1809 as an official of the French occupying forces) or Baudelaire, although with more *joie de vivre*, Ligne recorded the sensation of urban solitude.

> I have counted a hundred and fifty hours I have passed in the same seat in the German theatre without having said a single word or got to know my neighbours who changed every day, and I said to myself more than ever that one can do without society, speaking or listening. Elsewhere I have shown that man is the only animal that is not sociable. But I like society and crowds when I know nobody, I like to find myself in the middle and to be alone there.[9]

Presumably sitting alone in a Pest café, the silver-haired field marshal wore neither his Golden Fleece, nor the black and red uniform of the Captain of the Trabant Guard, but a simple tailcoat.

In the middle of his café life Ligne received the visit of the most warlike of the war party, his old friend Friedrich von Gentz. 'I have renewed my former links with the Prince de Ligne,' wrote Gentz in his diary. 'This old man, or *ce vieux radoteur*, as our great diplomats like to call him, has seen and judged the situation better than we have. I am ashamed to have sacrificed him for the vain chatter of coteries. However, he received me as if there had never been a break between us, and we got on better than ever.' Gentz, who called the Emperor nothing but a puppet moved by stupid routine, shared Ligne's rage at the catastrophe. Even the intendant-general of the Austrian army, Radetzky, the future saviour of the monarchy during the revolutions of 1848, at this time talked to Gentz of 'the incapacity of the Emperor and the advantages which could result from a total change of dynasty'.[10] Perhaps Radetzky wanted a Bonaparte in the Hofburg.

Napoleon himself thought of demanding the Emperor's abdication, giving independence to Hungary and, as he had threatened in 1805, abolishing the monarchy; as if the Habsburg monarchy was defunct, in a characteristic gesture he founded the Order of the Three Golden Fleeces to replace the Habsburg Order of the Golden Fleece. Many art treasures and manuscripts were taken to Paris from the Imperial collections. To avoid catastrophe, the Empress and Jean Liechtenstein persuaded the Emperor to sign a treaty of peace on 14 October. Liechtenstein had negotiated the terms. Austria lost its remaining coastline, Carinthia, Carniola, Dalmatia and three and a half million subjects; it had to agree to pay an enormous indemnity, and to limit its army to 150,000 men. Ligne judged that his nephew had won for Austria better terms than had been considered possible and had preserved Francis II from the fate of the Bourbon pretender Louis XVIII; 'At least we exist.'[11]

Despite the catastrophic peace, the Viennese welcomed their Emperor with delirium on his return on 27 November 1809. At this stage nothing could shake the rock of dynastic loyalty on which Austria had been founded. In 1918 it would require the conjunction of total defeat, after four years of total war, an emperor who inspired little respect, and famine, for the Austrians to cut their ties with the Habsburgs.

Ligne had returned to Vienna on 24 October, having written a farewell poem to what he called the aptly named city of Pest:

> Adieu ville d'ordure
> De crotte et de poussière,
> Ou j'entendis parler si mal
> de paix et de guerre.

On his return some letters addressed to him in September by Comte de Grünne, an aide de camp of Belgian origin of the Archduke Charles, unleashed a scandal worse than that which had been caused in 1790 by Ligne's own letter to his wife. Like many of the letters of the period, these letters, sent from one house in Pest to another, were in reality pamphlets destined for public consumption. While the Empress and the war party accused the Archduke Charles of 'strangling' the monarchy by his indecision, the correspondence between Ligne and Grünne was an attack on the war by two partisans of the Archduke. To make the attack more public, Ligne authorised Gentz and others, including Prince Esterhazy and Count Zinzendorf, to take copies. The letters were soon circulating throughout the monarchy and were published in foreign newspapers.

Ligne judged that the Austrian campaign had been the result of 'an imbecilic policy and of a plan without a plan'. Grünne denounced Count Stadion, Chief Minister of Francis II, who had dared attack a power as strong and as united as France. Showing the real purpose of the correspondence, and Ligne's relentless ambition, Grünne wrote to Ligne that he hoped that 'the supremacy of your genius will preside in our Councils, that you will indicate the means to save the fatherland and to keep for the reigning dynasty the throne of its ancestors'. Austria had proved its vitality by surviving four wars against Napoleon, and was about to promulgate a modern and relatively enlightened legal code, the *Allegemeines Bürgerliches Gesetzbuch*. However, Grünne described the monarchy as 'an antique edifice which the force of inertia stops in its fall but which is crumbling by morsels and which the first tremors will cause to fall into ruins'. The cruellest cut was reserved for the Order of the Golden Fleece. Grünne wrote that it was a suitable symbol for the highest order of a country whose government showed itself so sheep-like.[12]

These letters hit Austria like a declaration of war. For the government, any open criticism, particularly in such a moment of crisis, was an act of disloyalty. One of the most voluminous dossiers in the archives of the ministry of police (before they went up in a fire in 1928) concerned the attempts made to prevent the letters' circulation. Ligne received a 'terrible *Handbillet* [manuscript letter] from the Emperor'. He wrote a humble but mendacious reply, admitting that 'this publicity despite him, despite me, is a horrible abuse of confidence', and promising 'the greatest circumspection' in the future, but not revealing the number of people whom he had authorised to copy the letters. The Emperor put him under house arrest for a day and expelled him from a meeting of the chapter of the Order of Maria Theresa. Grünne was dismissed from the army and appointed grand master of the household of the Archduke Charles.[13] French newspapers also criticised Ligne for his *excessive légèreté*.[14]

Ligne was soon forgiven. In a few days the Emperor spoke to him again at court. Ligne resumed one of his favourite occupations, that of unofficial diplomat. That winter many Napoleonic officers passed through Vienna on their way back to France. Ligne dined with Marshals Berthier, Masséna, Oudinot and Davout at the French embassy. He was not impressed: 'Why spoil their glory by ravages, pillages and stealing, by generals two thirds of whom are as coarse as those of Attila?'

General Comte de Narbonne, however, whom he had met before 1787 in the salon of Sophie Arnould, became an intimate. With the profile of Louis XV, whose illegitimate son he was said to be, Narbonne had been one of the last Ministers of War of Louis XVI. After the disgrace of his friend/enemy Talleyrand (whom Ligne called *le prince à tout vent* when he was named Prince de Bénévent in 1808), Narbonne had become one of Napoleon's favourite aides de camp. Narbonne had much in common with Ligne, including intoxicating charm. Hence the remark by Mme de Staël, who had been in love with Narbonne twenty years earlier, that Ligne 'had the manners of Narbonne, with a heart!'[15]

In December 1809 Narbonne spent most of his days at the Hôtel de Ligne, often accompanied by his young aide de camp Victor de Broglie. To avoid meeting servants of 'the usurper',

Ligne's former intimate friend, the Marquis de Bonnay, representative of the exiled Louis XVIII in Vienna, no longer attended: a similar coldness occurred with another royalist friend, Roger de Damas. Ligne, who considered that the Bourbons had no more partisans and no more hopes, joked that, in the new atmosphere of enthusiasm for Napoleon, the remaining royalists resembled the early Christians during the persecutions of Diocletian.[16]

If Ligne's memoirs often give the impression of the eighteenth century judging the nineteenth, Broglie's show how Ligne appeared to nineteenth-century eyes. Broglie was stupefied by the simplicity of the Hôtel de Ligne.

> The evening and often even the afternoon was spent in interminable conversations during which all the events of the court of France, under Louis XV and Louis XVI, were recounted in a tone suitable for the character of that frivolous time, during which the Prince de Ligne compared the battles of the Seven Years' War to those of the Revolution and the Empire, and everyone, even a very young man like me, was constantly provoked to take part or make a contribution for good or ill.

To Ligne, in 1809, Broglie appeared as arrogant as he would twenty-five years later, when he was Prime Minister of Louis-Philippe, to the members of the Chamber of Deputies in Paris: 'He speaks only out of charity ... lacking all graces, he never tries to make any other merits shine except his own.'[17]

Soon the principal subject of conversation was not memories of Versailles but the marriage of the eldest daughter of the Emperor, Marie-Louise, with the man she had regarded as anti-Christ, who had twice driven her father out of Vienna. In his determination to create his own version of the *ancien régime* and father a son and heir, having recreated a court, a monarchy and a nobility, Napoleon decided to marry an Archduchess.

On 1 January 1810 Prince Trautmansdorf, probably acting on the orders of the Emperor, let Ligne know that his master would not oppose such a union. Ligne then wrote to Narbonne, in his presence, a letter that was sent to France to serve as the basis for a proposal. The marriage agreed upon in February was followed by a new Franco-Austrian alliance. Ligne felt that he had contributed to a marriage that had saved Austria. In reality his initiative was part of a general diplomatic offensive launched by Francis II and his new Minister of Foreign Affairs Clemenz von Metternich (who at this stage had the reputation of being simply an instrument of the Emperor's will). Since Austria could not defeat Napoleon, Metternich believed she should ally herself to him as closely as possible. 'It is better that an archduchess should be *foutue* than the monarchy,' commented Ligne.[18]

The war had ruined the Emperor, who had even been obliged to sell part of his silver. Nevertheless he organised sumptuous ceremonies to impress Napoleon's proxy Marshal Berthier. A painting commissioned from the court painter J. B. Hoechle represents the official demand in marriage on 8 March. In the new reception room of the Hofburg, facing Austrian courtiers, including Metternich and Ligne with their powdered hair, Berthier with his natural brown hair and blue embroidered cloak and the members of his suite (including Ligne's friend Alexandre de Laborde) seem to come from another planet. On one side of the throne, plump and willing, stands the girl about to be sacrificed to the Minotaur, the archduchess Marie-Louise. In the picture her father, who in reality looked like a man reduced to a quarter of himself, is shown as larger and taller than the courtiers surrounding him. The wall hangings, carpets and candelabra are of a simplicity that would never have been tolerated in the palaces of Napoleon. On the steps of the throne, looking wilder than other courtiers, standing slightly apart, Ligne, in the red and black uniform of a Captain of Trabants, observes the scene. Austria was far weaker in 1810 than in 1770, but the court of Vienna had preserved its pride. 'The French admired our remains of magnificence and high nobility,' wrote Ligne.

They only found that we made too much noise and did not

show sufficient respect to the Imperial family. At their court of parvenus, where there is only an artificial éclat instead of the solid splendour of which I have already spoken, where everything is froth and overheated with ceremonies, it is not the sovereign whom they respect: it is the great man, the great general who impresses them. And, ill-suited for reflection, they do not know how to seize these nuances. In truth the *criaillerie de synagogue* of our antechambers does not come from a lack of veneration but from this cursed German idiom which necessitates an uncouth tone and forms of speech, for example, women's habit of calling each other *du*. A *du* which a pretty Austrian woman sends another, from one end of a salon to another, deforms her in my eyes.*

Only Ligne could have compared the court of Vienna to a synagogue.

Ligne was happy in Vienna. He loved his family, Rosalie and the court. However, at seventy-five years of age, as the correspondence with Grünne had shown, he was still tormented by ambition. Now that the two Empires were allies, he saw no reason not to meet Napoleon. His request to Metternich to be sent on a mission to Paris is a demand as revealing of the man within, and his vanity, as his letters to Casanova on love and loss:

> *Clementissime et Amabilissime ministre*, if you need a compliment-bearing commissioner, a diplomatic courier or jockey, I am not afraid to meet the savage whom I would tame better than another, since he has said several times that he would have liked to know me, and much regretted that I had not wanted to see him at Dresden and twice at Vienna ... Still admiring your fine bearing in appearance and intelligence, *dixit*. Good day, dear and very dear count to whom I am very tenderly attached.

---

* This use of the second person singular in German created a linguistic barrier around the high Viennese nobility, more impenetrable than any accent. *Du* was used between nobles of the same sex, even if they had never met before. Until a relatively recent date, people outside that class had to be content with *sie*.

In a postscript he added with the naivety of vanity, 'If he has learnt that what I most desired in the world was to command against him, even with a sort of confidence in myself, that can only give a form of consideration; and everything together will make him grant more faith to my words than to those of another.' However, Ligne feared, rightly, that he had lost the Emperor's respect since the Grünne affair and that his offer would be rejected.[19] Like the Archdukes Charles and John, Ligne was too critical and original for Kaiser Franz.

It was another chamberlain, his own grandson Count Charles Clary, known in the family as 'Lolo', who left for Paris with a letter from the Emperor for his new son-in-law. Elegant, handsome, easily bored, Lolo had achieved little in life except to invent a piece of furniture designed to avoid the fatigue of holding heavy books: with the same motive, he often cut books into two or three segments.[20] However, the letters he wrote from Paris to his wife and his mother were masterpieces of malice.

He saw the second marriage of Napoleon through the eyes of an Austrian chamberlain. During the civil ceremony in the Palace of Saint-Cloud, the sight of the Bonapartes in glory, including *Madame Mère*, made him think of the surprise which *Monsieur Père* would have felt if he had climbed out of one of the massive Sèvres vases adorning the Imperial apartments. Only a grandson of the Prince de Ligne could have compared the Empress Marie-Louise, approaching the altar during the religious ceremony in the Louvre on 2 April, her train of purple velvet held by her sisters-in-law, to 'the silver-pawed tortoise of Baron Strogonof'. The Emperor seemed in a bad mood throughout the ceremony, because his sisters and sisters-in-law, considering their duty to bear the train of the Empress unworthy of their new rank, had sulked all day: 'So nothing was more comic than to see the manner in which they acquitted themselves of their task: one made a *moue*, another holding her smelling salts under her nose seemed about to faint, the third let the train fall and it was even worse because she had to pick it up.'[21]

As a good Austrian, Lolo was dismayed to see so many

monuments in Paris erected in celebration of victories over his own country. However, he was delighted by Parisians' lack of enthusiasm as the wedding procession drove from Saint-Cloud to the Louvre. A footman said of Marie-Louise, seated beside the Emperor, 'Oh! she is a beautiful princess, truly beautiful and then it was so touching to see her in the carriage with her old governess!'[22]

Thanks to his grandfather, Lolo enjoyed the city of Paris more than the Napoleonic court. When he was introduced as Count Clary, people showed themselves polite but cold. But when the magic words 'the grandson of the Prince de Ligne' were added, then 'all faces smile and overwhelm me with questions to know the date of his arrival'. Napoleon I himself had asked, at Lolo's first audience: 'Are you related to the Prince de Ligne?' to which he had replied: 'He is my grandfather, Sire.'

'How is he, the Prince de Ligne? His property near Vienna was a little damaged by us?'

'Yes, Sire, a little.'[23]

Ligne's Paris friends had emerged relatively unscathed from the traumas of the Revolution and the emigration. Covered in rouge, Mme de Coigny, the former 'queen of Paris', had become an admirer of the Emperor. The Chevalier de Boufflers and Mme de Sabran had finally married. Clary found the former older, the latter fatter than he had imagined. Even Talleyrand, normally 'very cold and disdainful', with his air of wanting to eat people alive, often invited Lolo Clary to dinner. When he was not trying to make an impression, and was in good humour, he could be 'very amiable … he has a dry and monotonous way of speaking without changing his expression which sometimes becomes rather *piquante*'.[24]

Lolo saw everything in Paris, including the collection of antiquities of Baron Denon, director of the Louvre and the Emperor's pillager-in-chief: 'After the antiquities of Denon, I went to see an antiquity of another sort, Angélique, who received me as well as possible, talks and talks, loves you all to madness, all the family in Vienna. She had a dinner for fifteen, wanted me to stay for it and claimed that I resemble the Prince de Ligne and Maman like two drops of water.' This brief encounter was, as far as is known, the last indirect contact between Ligne and the woman who had been his greatest love. Angélique d'Hannetaire lived comfortably in Paris until her death there in 1822.[25]

Instead of visiting Paris, Ligne returned to Teplitz. The summer season of 1810 was particularly brilliant. The Archduke Rudolf, patron of Beethoven, played the harpsichord in the casino. Louis Bonaparte, whom his brother had just deprived of the throne of Holland in order to annex it to the French Empire, was staying in the same house as Goethe. Féfé and Flore de Ligne were there too, teasing their father who, they said, would not have time to see them. For not only his brilliant friend Rahel Levin, whom he called 'an angel for her heart, Robert le diable for her wit', but also the Empress Maria Ludovica herself had arrived.

Ligne and the Empress had forgotten the disagreement of 1809. Gay, gracious and intelligent, she impressed Ligne: 'She has the prettiest little majesty in the world and so much dignity that we do not notice it... she enchanted all Europe because people rushed from all sides to see her. One look, one remark seduced in the semi-circle of two or three hundred people who everywhere she went always surrounded her.' She had the gift of repartee. Once, noticing Metternich particularly elegantly dressed at a reception for princesses, she had asked him: 'Count Metternich, what is your rank as princess, and by what permission do you present yourself here unannounced?' When Princess 'Nani' Schwarzenberg had said she could not receive the Empress as she had her period, the Empress had asked out loud 'if Nani took her for a lover'.[26]

Writing continued to occupy the greater part of Ligne's time. He produced a number of letters stupefying even by the standards of the period, when writing and reading letters were a favourite pastime. He was so prolific that in one night he could write a twelve-page letter to his ex-daughter-in-law, although she was staying in the same hotel. Although he often denied it, he and his 'familial secretaries' (Christine and Titine) kept many copies of his letters, with a view to publication, as well as the letters addressed to himself: as he knew, some people were afraid to write to him for fear of seeing their letters, or embarrassing replies, in print.[27] Some of his letters to Mme de Coigny, Catherine II, Ségur, Prince Kaunitz and Joseph II had been published in volumes of *Mélanges militaires, littéraires et sentimentaires*. These were not the actual letters sent, but like other famous eighteenth-century letters, for example those of Lady Mary Wortley Montagu, versions edited to entertain the reader – and to throw the author into a more favourable light. (The German writer Varnhagen von Ense, for example, would edit the letters of his wife, Ligne's friend Rahel Levin, in order to give a more aristocratic and less Jewish image of her circle of friends.) Ligne's letters to Ségur in 1787–8 had been expanded to incorporate portraits of Potemkin or the Moldavian court.[28]

In October 1811, fourteen years after having been first invited there, Ligne finally went to Weimar from Teplitz, to oversee publication of a new collection of his letters. Already in 1809 Ligne's life of Eugène of Savoy, and in 1810 his military works, had been published in Weimar by the Duke's press. With characteristic impertinence Ligne had written to the Duke, 'the best of booksellers', with complicated instructions on the method of printing his letters, *toujours à linéa*, interspersed with exhortations to seduction.[29] In 1811 he met the wife and mistress of the Duke, as well as Goethe, discussed plans for a German Academy and a universal dictionary with Wieland and pronounced the Duke 'adorable ... a good sovereign, good general, good soldier, good friend'.[30] Thanks to these publications, and to the Duke's friendship, he could proclaim himself, like Goethe or Schiller, a citizen of the 'modern German Athens'. His book was called *Nouveau Recueil de Lettres du Feld-Maréchal Prince de Ligne en réponse à celles qui lui ont été addressée*.

The letters describe incidents in Ligne's life, such as the funeral of Maria Theresa in 1780, or his flight to Pest in 1809, and speak of the latest works of Goethe or Mme de Staël.

Despite the second part of the book's title, those addressed to the dead such as D'Alembert or King Stanislas Augustus are literary creations. The real letters he sent to King Stanislas, kept in the King's papers in Warsaw, bear no relation to those Ligne published. The first deal with political matters such as war with the Ottoman Empire, or Polish relations with Catherine II. The latter describe Ligne's personal experiences, such as his visit to Frederick II.

Even those letters addressed to living people, such as Mme de Staël or Alexandre de Tilly, are revised and corrected versions of the originals. He admitted as much to Mme de Staël: 'I am removing everything which can compromise us and am inserting many things which I have said, or perhaps not, in the originals. You will see some which the post, surely, has prevented from reaching you' (i.e. they were invented).[31]

Vanity even made him introduce changes in what should have been a sacred text. In his letter of 1788 announcing his success at Sabatsch, Charles de Ligne had written: 'Vive la guerre, papa, et vive le maréshal [sic]. I am a lieutenant colonel and a knight of Maria Theresa.' When Ligne printed it in his volume on the Turkish war, it became: 'We have Sabatsch. I have the Cross. You can well imagine, Papa, that I thought of you when rushing first to the attack.'[32]

In 1811 Ligne was also occupied by the future of his grand-daughter Titine, with whom Maurice O'Donnell, the former admirer of Mme de Staël, had fallen in love. Skilled manipulators of the human heart, Ligne and Titine kept repeating to O'Donnell that his family would never forget Titine's illegitimate birth (although Francis II had legitimised her in 1810). To show his scorn for convention, O'Donnell became determined to marry. The ceremony took place on 6 December. Thereafter Ligne took great pleasure in referring to 'my granddaughter Countess Maurice O'Donnell'. However, since Princess Clary and Lolo found Maurice boring and pedantic, one more victim had entered the Ligne family, in addition to the other in-laws, Prince Clary, Count Palffy, Baron Spiegel and Countess

Charles Clary. Since Titine and Flore supported their husbands, the Hôtel de Ligne resounded to the sound of quarrels.[33]

In 1812 Napoleon decided to attack the last independent great power in Europe, Russia. On 6 June, as French forces crossed into Russia, Mme de Staël arrived in Vienna for the second time, on her way to London to continue her crusade against Napoleon. Ligne came to see her at her inn, and offered her hospitality on the Kahlenberg. She would, however, have been horrified if she had known that on the same day, Ligne had asked Metternich for command of the Austrian corps (which included his own regiment), accompanying the Napoleonic troops into Russia. Like the Maréchal de Villars who, at a similarly advanced age, in 1709, had reinvigorated the French army, he would give back the Austrian army the good luck that it had not known since the epoch of Prince Eugène: 'I could be given whatever regiments, generals and general staff are considered suitable; for I will know how to use them and I have no need for a governor.'[34] His ambition made him forget the gratitude he owed the memory of his protector Catherine II, and to her equally generous successors.

Ligne and Metternich had much in common: both were servants of the Austrian monarchy who loved women, salons, and French culture. Metternich was what Ligne could have been if he had concentrated on politics and diplomacy instead of also trying to be a general, courtier, writer and rake. Divided between envy and admiration, he showered the minister, who was half his age, whom he claimed to know better than anyone, with unsolicited flattery and advice. However, their resemblances hid profound differences. Ligne was indiscreet. Metternich, in Ligne's words, was like 'a beautiful slab of white marble, impenetrable and uninfluenceable'. Ligne invited anybody he met. Metternich considered the company in the Hôtel de Ligne 'very mixed'. The minister practised a prudent diplomacy committed to peace and the balance of power in Europe: he believed in the value of a strong France, Prussia and Bavaria. Ligne, like Joseph II, believed in Austrian expansion.

In 1812 he sent Metternich a geo-political fantasy, an extreme expression of the old Austrian proverb 'AEIOU' (*Austriae est imperare orbe universo*: 'Austria should rule over the entire world'); 'Popo (as they say his wife calls him) is immortal only for history. If the God of Mohamet, of Israel or our own takes him, I think that it would be easy to give back our Monarchy its former splendour.' Leaving the left bank of the Rhine to France, 'We could have everything to the Vistula, the Black Sea or the Adriatic: we will inherit without having the odium of everything that Napoleon has done.' The Emperor of Austria would become Emperor of Germany and King of Italy, master of Stettin, Belgrade and Rome, more powerful than Charles V; the Pope would be reduced to 'his palaces and his croziers'.

Also shared by some senior officers, this vision of empire was not totally absurd. All the great powers had dreams of imperial expansion. Britain was creating an empire in India. The French Empire extended to the Baltic and the Adriatic. Russia still yearned to conquer Constantinople, Prussia to conquer north – or all – Germany. This letter, however, confirms that Metternich and Ligne did not speak the same political language. Like Thugut twenty years earlier, Metternich judged Ligne unemployable. He had offended the Emperor and was too old. It was a general half his age, Prince Charles Schwarzenberg, who was chosen to command the Austrian auxiliary corps.[35]

In June 1812, as the *grande armée* and its allies headed to disaster in Russia, the Empress Marie-Louise came to Prague to visit her family. Prince Clary was responsible for her reception. Many people, including Lolo Clary, judging her by her awkward public manner, believed her to be frigid and stupid. In reality she was intelligent, artistic and one of the few people to stand up to her husband. Ligne admired her almost as much as her great-aunt Marie Antoinette: 'What magnificence at this court of France that I have just left in Prague where I have been for fifteen days,' he wrote. 'Kind, sensitive, generous, the empress is so well made, so much freshness, such pretty feet, such a beautiful neck that with the air of representation in addition to that, she is almost pretty. It was a little bit of Paris that I met ... Down to the chamberlains, equerries, pages, they were all *fort bien*. They have become French again.'[36]

That is the version of her visit that Ligne recorded in his *Fragments*. The same events, and Ligne's assiduity as a courtier, were recorded through unforgiving youthful eyes in a letter from Lolo Clary to his wife:

> The Prince de Ligne is in a seventh heaven of happiness. He spends three hours every morning and three hours every evening with the French, he patiently waits for their return to their apartments in the room of Mde Seraphina, the hunchbacked maid of Madame de Brignoles. He breaks their jaws with his swings of the incense burner, he makes witticisms, he writes Mde de Bassano folio size letters without a's* and above all without common sense.[37]

From Prague Ligne proceeded to Teplitz, where he spent his last summer. He gambled with Goethe, gave a tea party in honour of Empress Maria-Ludovica on Mont Ligne and cooked buttered potatoes for the King of Prussia, an inconsolable widower since the death of Queen Louise in 1810. When Frederick William III came to say goodbye to him one morning, Ligne had the joy of seeing a king sit on his bed (as, forty-nine years earlier, Voltaire had done in Ferney).[38]

He was convinced that if Napoleon was not killed in battle, he 'will date a decree from Tsarskoe Seloe to have a street cut through Paris. That is what he likes. He has capitalomania.' The retreat from Moscow surprised Ligne as much as most Europeans. In gratitude for their services, Alexander I should, he thought, make generals Oktobreskov and Novembreski princes. Nevertheless, almost alone in his milieu, perhaps influenced by Polish friends for whom Russia remained the principal enemy, Ligne continued to believe that the salvation of Austria

---

*Ligne wrote this *dame du palais* of the Empress, whose beauty he admired, a letter, now lost, containing only words without 'a's.

lay in alliance with Napoleon. His enthusiasm was reinforced in March 1813 by the return to Vienna of his old friend the Comte de Narbonne, as French ambassador.

During the retreat from Russia, Narbonne had shown the vitality of the roué of the eighteenth century. As thousands died of cold, he had his hair powdered every morning, 'as if he was in the most agreeable boudoir'. In Vienna Narbonne had to endure not the horrors of the Russian winter but the malice of the Austrian nobility. The only place where he was received as a friend was the Hôtel de Ligne. In contrast, Ligne's former intimate Bonnay, Louis XVIII's representative in Vienna, who had once regarded the Hôtel de Ligne as a second home, is never mentioned.[39]

Even in the Hôtel de Ligne Narbonne suffered the hostility of Titine O'Donnell, who showed him that she wore on a ring the enamelled portrait of a cossack. 'So these cursed cossacks follow us everywhere,' he commented. Narbonne and Ligne went out at night in search of amorous adventures. They were followed by an agent of the Emperor's secret police, whose reports signed '**' were always noted, in the sovereign's own hand, 'Taken into consideration, Francis.'

Years later, on Saint Helena, Napoleon would say: 'Narbonne saw with the help of the old Prince de Ligne, who was precious, knew everything, talked.' Nevertheless Narbonne's mission to Vienna failed because his master refused to be 'de-Charlemagnised'. Napoleon would not be content with the Rhine frontier – the one conquest to which French public opinion was attached – although, as Metternich pointed out, it would have made him three times more powerful than Louis XIV. He was determined to keep his protectorate over the German states on the right bank of the Rhine.[40] Napoleon himself was ensuring the reduction of French influence in Europe.

Ligne was as bewitched by Narbonne as Narbonne was by Napoleon. Like his ancestors, Ligne had passed his life in opposition to French power, under Louis XVI, the Republic and the early years of the Empire. Nevertheless, when Europe finally united against the French Empire, and Francis II and Metternich succeeded in leading Austria from a position of armed neutrality to an alliance with Russia and Prussia, Ligne inexplicably remained a solitary advocate of peace. He sent Metternich a letter underlining the Austrian army's lack of talented officers, of horses and ammunition, expressing the fear that, as in 1805 and 1809, the first cannon shot would annihilate Austria's hopes, and advocating neutrality. Scrawled across the top of this letter is an exasperated comment by Metternich: 'I replied to this letter by the entry into Paris nine months later.' Ligne did not exaggerate Austrian military weakness: many soldiers had no shoes.[41] But he underestimated the superhuman efforts of which it was capable, as well as the cumulative might of the allied coalition – the coalition that he himself had for so long advocated.

Even before Austria entered the war, 1813 was a year of mourning for Ligne. On 10 May 1813 his son Louis died, one of the few people in Ligne's world to have caught a fatal venereal disease. 'Why did this stupid little *flamande* do so much harm to the brave Louis?' Ligne had written to their cousin the Duke d'Arenberg. 'Could he not still try some more baths?' Other deaths followed – Zinzendorf, Mme de Romberk and, to his 'inexpressible chagrin', Princess Charles de Liechtenstein. Conscious of having failed in his mission, Narbonne left Vienna in June to die in battle three months later as the Napoleonic Empire collapsed around him. Ligne wept for him, regretting his wit and gaiety: 'Every evening I look at the place he used to occupy on my bench near the fireplace. What a difference from those who sit there!'[42]

For his part, Ligne continued to enjoy excellent health. As soon as it was clear that Austria was going to attack Napoleon, in a final bid for glory, Ligne asked Metternich for the command of the Austrian forces. At seventy-eight he had not lost hope of defeating Napoleon. 'There is no one in your army who has made war in Bohemia, where I have fought in two,' was one of his arguments. The wars in question (the Seven Years' and seven-week wars) had taken place fifty and thirty years earlier respectively. At least he could make fun of his own ambition. A few months later, when asked why he had hoped for the supreme command, he replied: 'Because I am the only general of his rank whom Napoleon has never defeated.'[43]

Formerly islands of peace in a war-torn continent, Bohemia and Saxony were now at the centre of the storm. Teplitz was the scene not of concerts and love affairs but of a battle and, on 9 September, of the signature of the treaty between Russia, Austria and Prussia by which Austria joined the war against Napoleon. Soon the roads leading to the city were deep in dead and dying soldiers. The temple on Mont Ligne was destroyed by Russian troops. (However, it was commemorated in a vase painted with a view of the vanished temple, which he was given by the King of Prussia.)[44] The ballroom of the Clary castle was used for amputations – for those soldiers who could afford to pay for them.

This clash of empires, with more than a hundred thousand men fighting on each side, marked the triumph of Ligne's world over France. Despite the immense contribution of Russia, Metternich was leader of the political coalition and Schwarzenberg was commander-in-chief of its largest army. Gentz had become the confidante of Metternich, Pozzo di Borgo of Alexander I, whom he urged to march on Paris and depose Napoloen. All the friends of Ligne, though not Ligne himself, were helping to realise the dreams they had discussed in Vienna in 1798 to 1805.

Ligne's reputation of being a 'fervent Karlist' – that is to say, a partisan of the Archduke Charles (who also did not serve in the campaign 1813–14) – made the Emperor fear a new attack on his war policy. Ligne had a doctor, Dr Putterman, 'who enjoys the full confidence of His Highness', whom he saw every day and who loved him so much that he requested to be buried at his feet. This did not stop Putterman, like other Viennese, from acting as a police spy. He promised to report all Ligne's remarks about the war and to warn the police in case Ligne prepared a repetition of the Grünne affair.[45]

Soon, however, Ligne had nothing to criticise. In the Battle of the Nations at Leipzig – on 16 to 19 October 1813 – at the head of forces twice as large as the French army, Prince Schwarzenberg defeated Napoleon. As the allies prepared to cross the Rhine and enter French territory, Schwarzenberg asked Ligne for his blessing. 'It is Prince Eugène who from his tomb in St Stephen's sends you his,' Ligne replied. He complimented Schwarzenberg for his loyalty, his simplicity, 'your taste for union, in fact what in music is called perfect accord, has added to your military talents to make you triumph over so many obstacles. For example, this is the first coalition which succeeds despite having so many crowned heads in one bonnet. Perhaps you are winning a battle at the moment I am writing to you,' he added with envy.[46]

While others were winning glory on the field of battle, Ligne's battlefield was his salon. With the end of the Napoleonic alliance, the Hôtel de Ligne had again become a rehearsal for the Congress of Vienna. 'The moment a distinguished traveller arrives, he sends him a general invitation to come to his evening parties,' noted a German traveller. Ligne himself compared his house to the Collège des Quatre Nations in Paris; having been French, it had become Russian, then Neapolitan; finally, with the admission of Austria into the anti-French coalition, English. In autumn 1813 John Cam Hobhouse, the closest friend of Byron, witnessed a clash between Ligne and a Russian diplomat who had drunk a toast 'to the death of the Emperor Napoleon'. Ligne's reply showed that he had not forgotten the assassination of Tsar Paul I in 1801: 'We drink healths not deaths; moreover, in this capital we are not used to the death of Emperors.'[47]

Schwarzenberg continued to win victories over Napoleon until 31 March, the day when, with the Tsar of Russia and the King of Prussia, he led the allies' triumphant entry into Paris. Thereafter, Pozzo and Talleyrand helped ensure the deposition of Napoleon and the return of the Bourbons. On 12 April, the day the Comte d'Artois re-entered Paris, Napoleon abdicated unconditionally at Fontainebleau. Roger de Damas, who had been accompanying the Comte d'Artois, and had been appointed royalist military governor of Alsace and Lorraine, could now forgive Ligne his weakness for the Napoleonic alliance. He sent his old friend the following *cri de coeur* from Nancy on 11 April 1814. With tears of joy in his eyes, Damas thanks Ligne for the happy days spent in his company in Vienna and – like Talleyrand nine years earlier, and with a similar motive: to publicise a monarchy – implores him to revisit France. Returning *émigrés* are being received in France like consoling angels, he wrote in triumph:

> *vive le roi* ... you know that there are different nuances of happiness, that there are forms of it of every kind, but you have never imagined or dreamt of one which equals mine. All of France is as filled with it as I am ... I give you my word of honour that there is no more question of *Buonaparte* among the nations than of *Pougatcheff** in Russia *without the slightest exaggeration* ... Leave Napoli on his island with his alimentary pension and the general execration. O classical man, triumph of good taste and good society, come to the Bourbons.

Damas ends with the magic phrase, the realisation of so many dreams of the emigration: *je suis français, je suis en France*.[48]

Ligne, however, was less concerned by the return of the Bourbons to France than by the departure of Rosalie Rzewuska from Vienna. Their intimacy had continued to grow during the last year. 'There is mysticism in this last love and a sort of magnetism,' wrote Ligne, who even went to mass to please her. She had visited him every day and had even stayed with him on the Kahlenberg – which few other women outside his family had done. On 4 May, the day after Louis XVIII's entry into Paris, she left Vienna in tears for her Polish estates. Years later she remembered: 'the Prince de Ligne accompanied me as far as the Danube bridge: he stopped my carriage, took my hand and held it against his heart without speaking.'[49] They never saw each other again.

---

* The peasant rebel against Catherine II in 1775.

Europe

Vienna in 1814 was a city in triumph. European princes and diplomats were converging on the Austrian capital to attend the congress destined to organise the peace of Europe after the fall of Napoleon. By the end of September their number was said to be 16,000: the Viennese felt like people in a foreign country. Among the crowds of royalty were the Kings of Denmark, Bavaria, and Württemberg. Lord Castlereagh, most European of Foreign Secretaries, represented England, the Prince de Talleyrand France. Finally, on 25 September, under a blazing sun and to the sound of cannon fire, escorted by the finest regiments of the Austrian army, Tsar Alexander I and Frederick William III of Prussia made their ceremonial entry into the city.

Ligne, who said he would not have missed the congress for a hundred thousand florins, was living in a dream. Hardly seeming sixty, overflowing with energy, he had spent a quiet summer on the Kahlenberg in the company of the O'Donnells and Christine Clary, writing poetry and recovering from the departure of Rosalie Rzewuska. Féfé Palffy was nursing her husband in Baden. Flore Spiegel had followed hers to Milan, again an Austrian city, where he commanded a regiment. The Princesse de Ligne had stayed in Vienna.

An anonymous correspondent wrote to a cousin of Ligne, Prince Auguste d'Arenberg: 'As for our own good Prince de [Ligne] he is younger than ever, for his wit in bed in the morning, and for his character in society in the evening.'[1] The congress concentrated into one time and space much of what was important to him: courts, unofficial diplomacy, pretty women, social life. Many of his friends were there: Talleyrand,

Pozzo (one of the Russian delegates), Gentz (official secretary of the congress) and the Duke of Weimar who, partly to save on living expenses, frequently took up Ligne's offer to take all his meals at the Hôtel de Ligne.[2]

The anonymous correspondent of d'Arenberg could not believe the number of people Ligne had met in one day – which he had ended, at midnight, by attending the re-opening of a popular dance hall, the Apollo Saal.[3] A typical day began with a lunch at quarter to two at the house of the Princesse Maréchale Lubomirska. He drank a bottle of champagne and tasted all the dishes, exclaiming: 'But it is an assassination! I am being presented with everything that is most delicious; there is no way to resist.' At quarter to three he looked at his watch and left the table in a rush, saying that he only had a quarter of an hour to reach the King of Bavaria – where another meal awaited him.[4]

The hospitality offered by the Emperor of Austria has never been surpassed. The court of Vienna functioned as a European institution. Ligne remarked that it was more brilliant than that of Louis XIV, who had only welcomed the King of England (the exiled James II), while Kaiser Franz lodged and nourished half the crowned heads of Europe, as well as three exiled courts – of Saxony, of Naples and of his own daughter, the ex-Empress Marie-Louise.[5] The number of princes lodging in the Hofburg was such that in one afternoon alone the guards stationed in the inner court had to present arms fifty-three times.[6]

They were not only lodged but fed as well. Every day the Imperial kitchens supplied six hundred rations of coffee and fifty-five tables, in addition to those of the monarchs, who could invite whom they wished. Since every guest received a carriage from the Imperial stables, there were soon more court carriages than private carriages on the streets of Vienna.[7] The Austrian nobility was mobilised to serve the Emperor's guests. In Ligne's family alone, Prince Clary served as grand master of the Tsar, Lolo Clary as chamberlain of the Tsarina, Maurice Clary as chamberlain of the King of Denmark and Maurice O'Donnell as chamberlain of the King of Prussia.[8]

Accustomed to their Emperor's simplicity, the Viennese were impressed by the scale of his hospitality. 'Everything the court does here is always grand and on a large scale,' wrote one witness.[9] If an Austrian, Lolo Clary, provides one of the most vivid accounts of the court of Napoleon, two Swiss, M. and Mme Eynard, are among the best chroniclers of the Congress of Vienna. They were astonished by everything and noted what they saw. Eighteen years younger than her husband, pretty and elegant, Mme Eynard was much admired; she would be one of Ligne's last attachments. To the delight of her husband, people asked: 'Have you seen *la belle Eynard? la belle suisse?* How pretty she is, how fresh she looks!' They were invited everywhere, until one day, to her stupefaction, Mme Eynard found herself dancing in the same quadrille as the Tsar of Russia.

The ball that took place on 10 October in the gallery of the Hofburg is typical of those that Ligne attended during the congress. The gallery, a masterpiece of Fischer von Erlach that today houses the Spanish Riding School, was decorated in white and silver. 'The view was dazzling,' noted Mme Eynard. 'It was as bright as if there were several suns at midday. The room was more than immense, it was infinite and the entire space was so packed that you needed half an hour to advance a step. Everything was so brilliant one could have believed oneself in one of those fairy-tale palaces of which the Thousand and One Nights have left us so many beautiful descriptions.' From the principal hall the guests could reach, through innumerable corridors and antechambers, the ceremonial hall, where they found another orchestra, banks of flowers, candles burning like fireworks, and buffets laden with food, around which activity was often more intense than on the dance floor. Mme Eynard continued:

> At ten o'clock the orchestra started playing a fanfare and by its redoubled noise announced to us the arrival of emperors, empresses, kings and queens; the Emperor Alexander arrived first giving his arm to the Empress of Austria, then immediate-

ly afterwards the Emperor of Austria giving his arm to the Empress of Russia, then the King of Prussia, the Queen of Bavaria, the hereditary princes, the Grand-duke Constantine, etc. The entire cortège went three times round the hall before taking up its reserved places ... I was able to have such a good look that the physionomies of these monarchs will be engraved in my memory all my life.[10]

They were hard to forget. In contrast to Alexander I and his empress, who looked amiable and distinguished, the Tsar's brother the Grand Duke Constantine made Monsieur Eynard think of an 'enraged hyena'. The King of Denmark resembled an albino goat; of the King of Württemberg, Napoleon had said that he had been put on Earth to see how far human skin could stretch. Of Kaiser Franz M. Eynard wrote: 'It is impossible to have less the outward manner of a sovereign: he resembles a good little bourgeois of a provincial city.' As for the Empress, the true organiser of these festivities, who said that the congress had taken ten years off her life, she had the air of an exhausted tadpole.[11]

After the traumas of the French wars, the Congress of Vienna was designed to efface the memory of French hegemony in Europe and to consecrate the triumph of Austria and its allies. One of the problems that had dominated Ligne's life – the disproportionate size and power of France in Europe – had been resolved. By the Treaty of Paris of 30 May 1814 France had been reduced to its frontiers of 1789 (with a few minor additions in the southern Netherlands and Savoy). Compared to its rivals Austria, Prussia and Russia, France had become even weaker than in the eighteenth century. She had lost territory: their territorial gains would be confirmed by the Congress of Vienna.

After twenty-two years of warfare, the congress constituted the first occasion when the world to which Ligne belonged – European court society – could feel free from the threat of a French invasion. The guests' pleasure was increased by the fact that 'the French ... rendered justice to the magnificence of our fêtes', as Prince Leopold of Saxe-Coburg, formerly an abject courtier of Napoleon, wrote to his uncle, old Marshal Coburg, the victor of Neerwinden; 'The court is so brilliant that I could not have imagined such splendour and the former French court does not come anywhere near it.'[12]

Love as well as dancing was one of the congress's principal occupations, as is confirmed by the reports of the Emperor's secret police. Like extra linen and carriages, extra police agents had been hired for the duration of the congress, among whom were servants in the Hofburg and perhaps Josef von Hammer. The Viennese were skilled in copying letters found in desks and waste-paper baskets, reconstituting them from half-burnt fragments recovered from bedroom stoves, or simply using their eyes and ears. The reports, published in a masterpiece of erudition called *Les dessous du congrès de Vienne*, are more informative about Vienna in 1814 than many official documents or memoirs.

Thus, while eating his breakfast Francis II could learn that the King of Prussia had gone out the evening before dressed in civilian clothes with a hat pulled over his face, accompanied only by his Grand Chamberlain Prince Wittgenstein, and at ten in the evening had still not returned. The Russian guests in the Hofburg had disgusting habits and 'constantly' invited back prostitutes. Alexander I said to Countess Szechenyei: 'Your husband is away, it would be very agreeable provisionally to occupy his place,' to which she had replied: 'Does Your Majesty take me for a province?'[13]

While continuing to correspond with Rosalie Rzewuska, Ligne took a close interest in a ravishing courtesan of twenty-two from Pest, called Sophie Morel. The police noted the visits he paid her, as well as those of a young rival, the Grand Duke of Baden. The report of an agent attending a masked ball in the Hofburg on 6 November signals: 'The beauty of Madame Morel has yet again produced a great effect. She talked with Counts Schoenfelt and Narischkin, then it was the Prince de Ligne who took her under his protection and stayed beside her for a long time. The Grand Duke of Baden did not dare show himself with her in the hall, but he did not cease prowling around her and never lost her from sight.'[14]

Ligne 'protected' another courtesan, a beautiful Greek woman called Mme Panam, the repudiated mistress of the brother of Prince Leopold of Saxe-Coburg, Duke Ernest. Ligne was magnetised. On summer nights he had walked along the ramparts of Vienna, late after a ball, in the hope of meeting her. With his habitual kindness, he gave her advice about her son's future, wrote a letter of recommendation to Metternich on behalf of her husband (see Appendix, letter 25) and presented her to his family.'[15]

There were also non-professional courtesans, such as Ligne's friend from Teplitz, Princess Bagration, whose apartment was compared to a brothel. Ligne attended her twice-weekly suppers, where the food was so good that no one had the heart to criticise the hostess. Like everyone else, he was amused by the struggle for social and sexual hegemony between the Princess and her rival the Duchess of Sagan. The Duchess, born Courlande, had taken Metternich from the Princess, as thirteen years earlier she had taken Armfelt from her own mother. Neverthless, they both lived in the same building, the Palais Palm (on the site of the present *Burgtheater*): each occupied an apartment on opposite sides of the grand staircase. They were called the right side and the left.

Princess Bagration was uncontrollable. The Prince d'Arenberg was told that

our good Pce de [Ligne] claims that our little pcesse B[agration] is ill from an in-growing duchess, that is to say growing into the heart, or her rights, with M. de M[etternich]. For compensation the little princess has charged herself with the education of a headquarters and a college. She has collected all the aides de camp and school-boys she could find. Cannot you say that they are the small change of M. de M.? And to judge the coin by the quantity necessary to replace it, one must believe it to be of a great value.

Soon the police were reporting that the Tsar had spent three hours alone with Princess Bagration in her dressing room, that she had treated his venereal diseases, or that, enraged by his desertion to the Duchesse de Sagan, she had taken the Crown Prince of Württemberg as her lover: he did not leave her apartment until three in the morning.[16]

The Hôtel de Ligne welcomed almost as many visitors as the Palais Palm. When Ligne was not supping with Princess Bagration or attending a court ball, he held open house. For Madame Eynard, 'the most agreeable house in Vienna without contradiction and where there was the most conversation', which she preferred to the palaces of Prince Metternich or Prince Razumovsky, was the Hôtel de Ligne. 'You were received there with a charming welcome and they took care to say to you as you left "come back soon" ... it is true that you felt so much at ease in his house that you were more amiable than you were elsewhere.'

Madame Eynard had met Ligne at a grand dinner where she was seated between him and Talleyrand. Most other people would have trembled at their proximity to such devastating conversationalists; but her beauty and naivety enchanted the enchanters. 'I spoke almost all the time with the Prince de Ligne who is a great admirer of Switzerland and he suggested that I often go and sup in his house after the theatre.' Two days later she received two notes from Ligne inviting her to supper.

So we went to his house after a few visits. There were not many people but a well-chosen society composed of princes, dukes, etc. The only women present were the Princesse de Ligne and two daughters of the Prince, Princess Clary and Countess Palffy; conversation was sometimes general with much simplicity, the prince gave me his arm to go in to supper and while crossing his little apartment pointed out to me its simplicity. In effect it is horrible, a staircase like a ladder, a more than exiguous salon and all the rest in proportion. M. de Talleyrand had given me a description of it which I believed exaggerated, but I saw that it was not, and I understand why the Prince de

Talleyrand does not like this staircase, he who is obliged to
balance himself while walking in order to keep his equilibrium.

Ligne was soon so smitten that he told her (as he had told
Bonnay, Mme de Staël, the Duke of Weimar and many others)
that she formed part of his family, that he would not let her leave
Vienna.

Relating another evening at the Hôtel de Ligne, Madame
Eynard again noted that 'conversation was general and very
amusing'. Princesse Jeanne Liechtenstein described the
diamond-encrusted costume that the Duchesse de Sagan had
worn at a carousel. Since she did not have enough diamonds for
herself and her friends, she persuaded Metternich to lend her
those of his Order of the Golden Fleece, and had one of her
diadems cut up. When she was told that some of these jewels had
been lost, she had replied: 'That has no importance, they are
only small stones.' Conversation then moved on to the coarse-
ness of the British. The worst example was their ambassador:
Lord Stewart had dragged the Empress of Austria by the hand,
in order to introduce her to a friend. One guest remarked that, if
the English had been separated from the Continent for twenty
years more, they would have become 'worse than the
Iroquois'.[17]

Nevertheless, the diary of M. Eynard shows that, even at the
Hôtel de Ligne, questions of power rather than gossip dominated the conversation. Throughout the evening diplomats came in
to discuss the future of Saxony or Naples. Pozzo di Borgo, who
was now Russian ambassador in France, made an appearance
and reassured the company on the popularity of the Bourbons.
Féfé Palffy asked M. de la Tour du Pin of the French embassy:
'Well, Monsieur le comte, they say that the affairs of the congress are being settled, and that the Emperor Alexander is
becoming more reasonable?'

Her remark shows that Alexander I was voracious for territory as well as women. To the horror of other powers, and his
own nobility, he wanted to re-establish a Kingdom of Poland,

truncated but autonomous and with a liberal constitution: it would be linked to Russia in a dynastic union like that of Hungary with Austria. In exchange for losing some of its Polish territories to the new Kingdom of Poland, Prussia would receive Saxony, whose King Frederick-Augustus had, longer than the other German monarchs, remained an ally of Napoleon (prompting Talleyrand's celebrated remark: 'Treason is a question of dates').

The perspective of such an increase of Prussian power in Germany France and Austria and brought about their reconcili- ation. However weakened, France remained a great power and possessed in Talleyrand the cleverest of ambassadors, who pre- sented himself as 'a good moderate European' (as, in his efforts to limit Napoleon's expansion, he had tried to be since 1808). With few friends in Vienna, he found the Hôtel de Ligne a useful place to meet other diplomats and re-establish France's European contacts. He was normally silent and scornful. However, in the Hôtel de Ligne he showed himself 'very talka- tive and very amiable'.[18]

Ligne liked Talleyrand more than he trusted him. One day the latter tried to justify himself for having served Napoleon by saying: 'Prince, for seven years I have been suspected by Bonaparte.' Ligne replied: 'What ... only seven years ... And I have been suspecting you for twenty years!'[19] However, his dis- trust was less than his fascination for the political game and his pleasure in seeing Talleyrand take the side of the King of Saxony. According to a police report Ligne declared: 'I have the pleasure of having in my house three very great brains, three very dangerous and very wicked brains: La Harpe, Talleyrand, Jomini.'* He was again part of the world of unofficial diplomacy as in the 1780s during the reign of Joseph II. Even if he could not make high policy, he could discuss it with Talleyrand, the Tsar, the King of Bavaria or the King of Denmark.

His old age, like his youth, was affected by the rivalry

* La Harpe was a former tutor of the Tsar, Jomeni a Swiss general in Napoleon's army who had changed sides in 1812.

between Austria and Prussia for domination of Germany. According to a police report, he declared to Talleyrand, La Harpe, the Duke of Weimar and Humboldt, the last two of whom were in Prussian service: 'Prussia still has a great appetite.' It already wanted to unite Germany. Now apprehensive of 'that nice king of Prussia who at Teplitz sat on my bed', he sent Talleyrand long letters of political advice.[20]

In October the conflict between France and Austria, soon joined by Britain on one side, and Russia and Prussia on the other, grew fiercer. On 24 October a violent quarrel took place between the Tsar and Metternich over Poland and Saxony. Metternich wrote to Francis II that the rage of the Tsar reminded him of that of Napoleon at his worst moments. Adding insult to injury, the Tsar tried to buy Metternich with a million florins. Ligne saw this as proof that the handsome Emperor, so charming when he wanted to be, was drunk with success and planned to create a second capital in Germany.[21]

While Russia and Prussia were bent on expansion, Austria concentrated on diplomacy. Francis II could have realised certain of Ligne's dreams of empire. As a symbol of peace and moderation, he had become popular in Germany. In Fulda the previous year people had knelt before him in adoration for the 'true heir of Charlemagne' (as opposed to the false one, Napoleon). At Frankfurt he had been better received, by a hundred thousand people delirious with enthusiasm, than when he had been crowned Holy Roman Emperor there, twenty-one years and five wars earlier.[22]

Francis II, however, was too modest and too practical to desire European pre-eminence. He put geography before history, Austria's Italian before its German role. He preferred to recover Lombardy and Venetia, which were contiguous with his other possessions, and strategically useful in case of the next war with France, rather than strengthening Austria's position in Germany by acquiring former Habsburg territory in the west or south-west of the Empire. To delegates from the former Austrian Netherlands who asked to become Austrian again, he replied: 'Messieurs, I bear you all in my heart, and I am going to put your address in my pocket.'[23] That was the end of the connection between Belgium and Austria, of which Ligne had been the most celebrated incarnation. To form another barrier against French power, Belgium was united with the northern Netherlands in a kingdom under the Prince of Orange.

On 22 October the Emperor signified his refusal to revive the Holy Roman Empire. Receiving a delegation of former Imperial princes and knights, led by Metternich's father, he declared to them: 'I would do it if this arrangement could be compatible with the interests of my possessions' – that is to say Hungary, Bohemia and the other hereditary provinces.

Like many other former Imperial princes and Austrian generals, Ligne was disappointed to see Austria realise proportionately fewer territorial gains, since 1789, than Russia or Prussia, and Francis II refuse to become Emperor of Germany. Nevertheless Austria gained one diplomatic victory in which Ligne took part. In November he wrote to Talleyrand suggesting an alliance against Russia and Prussia between France, Austria, Bavaria and Württemberg, who would receive large portions of German territory: 'Move your troops, my Prince, towards Alsace. Publish an alliance of Austria and of all the Empire with you. The north [Russia and Prussia] will know what that means.'[24]

On 16 November a police report revealed that Ligne had denounced to Alexander I in person Prussia's plan to annex Saxony. The exasperated Tsar had interrupted him by saying: 'I cannot continue the conversation as people are waiting for me.' The celebrated remark by Ligne, ' The congress dances but does not advance,' was aimed at the Tsar, an enthusiastic waltzer, whom it greatly irritated. On 25 November relations between participants had reached the point where Ligne feared that the congress would end in war. If Britain refused to fund Russia and Prussia, he knew who would win.[25] Finally, thanks to the determination of Francis II to save Saxony and the influence of Britain, France and Austria won. The Tsar retreated: the King of Saxony recovered the greater part of his kingdom; the new

Kingdom of Poland was much smaller than Alexander I had hoped. By the final treaties of June 1815 Prussia won extremely important territories on the Rhine; but until its defeat in the Austro-Prussian war in 1866, the principal power in, as well as the president of, the new German Confederation was Austria. Saxony was among its most faithful allies.

Despite this near war, thanks to European statesmen such as Metternich, Talleyrand, Castlereagh and Alexander I, the Congress of Vienna enshrined a new principle of international relations. Henceforth changes in Europe should be made by agreement between the great powers at congresses and conferences. This principle, which would have seemed alien to Ligne's heroes Joseph II, Frederick II and Catherine II – but not to Louis XVI and Vergennes – enabled the monarchies of Europe to survive relatively unscathed until the breakdown of peace in 1914.[26] The principal exception was the period between 1852 and 1870 when another Bonaparte, Napoleon III, launched the Crimean, Franco-Austrian and Franco-Prussian wars and Bismarck the Austro-Prussian war.

The other matter that occupied Ligne during the congress was the fate of the Emperor Napoleon on the island of Elba. The Emperor's former admirers had turned on him. The King of Bavaria spoke of sending him to St Helena. Talleyrand described him as coarse, brutal, insolent and cowardly. Ligne, however, who called him 'Robinson Crusoe', considered it outrageous that Napoleon had not been paid the money promised him by his treaty of abdication of 12 April 1814. Ligne was one of the few Viennese, except for members of her own family, to be kind to 'this unfortunate Empress Louise', who had enchanted him two years earlier in Prague. He regularly went to see her at Schönbrunn; she visited him on the Kahlenberg. He took a particular interest in her four-year-old son, the former King of Rome, who one day welcomed him with the words: 'Is he one of the marshals who betrayed Papa?' Ligne had model lead soldiers made for him representing the Trabants and the Hofburg Guard. Throughout his short life Napoleon's son, who like

Ligne combined loyalty to Austria with a strong attraction to France, venerated the Prince's memory. On his deathbed the Duke of Reichstadt, as he had become, would ask to have Ligne's military works read out loud to him.[27]

Death came for the Prince de Ligne in the middle of the congress. That summer on the Kahlenberg he had sometimes talked of death with Titine, but in October and November he had been in excellent health. On 31 November he ended his last poem, seventy-six lines dedicated to *ma bonne patrie, ma Belgique*, keeping in his heart the seductive hope of revisiting it, with these lines: 'J'avance dans l'hiver à force de printemps, / ne désespérant point d'arriver à cent ans.'[28] The following day he fell ill.

In Ligne's case, Oscar Wilde's phrase 'each man kills the thing he loves' should be reversed. Ligne was killed by the thing he loved: court life. In his moving account of his grandfather's last days, Lolo Clary wrote: 'In the last days he greatly tired himself: visits, staircases, kings, the court corridors, fêtes where he stayed four or five hours on his legs, and above all the desire to be everywhere and not to admit that he was tired may have contributed to his illness.' On 1 December, after a sleepless night, he insisted on attending a reception given by the Empress of Russia: 'He had a terrifying appearance, a terrible shiver: he stayed there only a moment and then went to bed.'

It was his last night out. Nevertheless, he still felt well enough to get up for a few hours and on 3 December he gave a last supper party in the Moelkerbastei, at which he spoke with adoration of Mme de Staël to Eynard, who noticed nothing abnormal. The following days he fell victim to a fever and an erysipelas that turned his skin red. 'He had always said: "I want to die like the cats without anybody seeing me,"' continues Lolo Clary. 'From the moment he was in danger, he hardly saw any of us, not even Maman. When he spoke to her for a moment, it was without turning his head to see her. He was afraid of being moved.' On 6 December, in addition to Dr Putterman, who was his personal doctor, Dr Malfatti, the most celebrated physician in Vienna, was sent to see him. Ligne only agreed to receive him when Malfatti told him that he had been sent by the Empress's mother, the Archduchess Beatrice.[29]

Dr Putterman, who stayed with him until the end, describes his last days. On 10 December he received the Holy Sacrament with a noble and courageous air that astonished everyone. 'Lying on his bed and repeating the prayers with the priest, with an air of admirable contentment, he received communion with veneration and deep devotion.' The Princess was so delighted that she rushed to kiss his hand, provoking a final *mot* that sped around Vienna: 'Ah, I am not yet a saint.'

Then he entered into a state of semi-delirium. Learning from the Princess that all the sovereigns had sent messages enquiring about his illness, he replied: 'Let them go to the devil, they are the cause of it.' He often made the sign of the Cross, putting his hands together and praying to God. He asked to see Titine, but his aide de camp Emile Legros pointed out to him that it would give pain to the rest of the family. 'Let them all come,' he then said – wife, daughters, grandchildren. Seeing the Duke of Weimar, the most devoted of his friends, among them, he cried out: 'Vivat le duc vie.'

In his delirium certain preoccupations haunted him. 'He believed he was commanding an army corps and said that he had four battalions of erysipelases whom he called the red-legs.' He often assigned parts in imaginary plays and 'very often he asked for news of the fêtes of the court, and then he said: "I don't give a damn about them, I had no desire to go there."' He also praised his daughters and repeated that his wife would have enough to live in a grand fashion and as she wished. At the end he began to sing, then he said: 'C'est fait.' These were his last words. He died on 13 December at 10.30 in the morning.[30]

His funeral took place on 15 December, a day of spring-like weather. 'Doctor, do you think that the funeral of a marshal would divert the sovereigns?' he had joked: 'Then I will do my best.' He succeeded. The ceremony was both military and European. The coffin, which had been taken to Ligne's parish church, the Schottenkirche, received benediction there. Detachments of 'my guards', of infantry, cuirassier, fusilier, uhlan and grenadier regiments, the flags bordered by black mourning ribbons, lined the streets. The only sound was the beating of drums. The coffin then left the church borne by eight grenadiers. On it had been placed the Marshal's hat, sword, baton and decorations. It was followed by a figure who symbol-ised both the sense of chivalry whose ideals had guided Ligne's life and the sense of ceremony of the Viennese: a knight in black armour with lowered visor escorted the Prince to his tomb, as he did every Austrian marshal. At the head of the funeral cortège were Austrian, Russian, Prussian, Bavarian, French and British officers, among them Charles de Ligne's friend the Duc de Richelieu, Field Marshal Prince Schwarzenberg and Leopold of Saxe-Coburg, sixteen years later appointed, by the great powers of Europe, first King of the first independent Belgian state.

Behind them came Ligne's servants, leading a horse draped in black, at the sight of which Mme Eynard burst into tears. The Tsar, the King of Prussia and innumerable dignitaries watched the procession from windows or the top of the ramparts. It pro-ceeded through the streets of Vienna, as the bells tolled, stop-ping in front of the Hofburg to be saluted by Francis II, then on to the suburb of Nussdorf. After a triple salute the military escort then retired, leaving the undertaker and a few intimates to climb as far as the cemetery on the Kahlenberg. Ligne is buried there, his wife (who died six years later) finally beside him.[31] The epitaph on his tomb connects him, in language and spirit, to the Roman Empire he had studied as a boy: *Carolo. Lamoralio. Princ. a. Ligne. Supr. exerc. duci. Praetor. Praef. Viro. Forti. Literatori. Consp. Nat. XXIII Maii MDCCXXXV. Ob. XIII. Dec. MDCC-CXIV* ('To Charles Lamoral Prince of Ligne, general in the army, Praetorian Prefect,* a brave man, a famous writer. Born on 23 May 1735, died 13 December 1814').[32]

The family found itself disoriented. Ligne had been so much the centre of its life that the least step, the slightest idea, seemed

* Commander of the Imperial Guard.

like a dagger wound: Princess Clary in particular was 'petrified with sorrow'.[33] Tributes flooded in from the Chancellery of the Golden Fleece, from the Empress Marie-Louise, and the Imperial family. 'You know how much I loved him whom you are mourning,' wrote Mme de Staël to Princess Clary. 'You know how much I admired his mind, which was as profound as it was graceful; he was unique.' Mme Eynard, like many others, was especially moved to learn that 'this good prince who said he was so poor, deprived himself of half his revenues to give them to the indigent'. So much for his alleged indifference to the poor (Ligne also desired that his memoirs' manuscript should be sold for the benefit of the soldiers of his companies of guards). A police report also referred to the Prince's kindness, and his fame throughout Europe: 'They say that the death of the Prince de Ligne will cause a profound sensation in all Europe. He was known, respected and loved everywhere, for he was fundamentally good. If at moments he was not good, it was out of mischief, out of *travers d'esprit*.'[34]

Forty years later, in another world, his goodness could still cause tears to flow. In 1853 a visitor to Windsor Castle reported that Ligne's last valet, Louis-François d'Albertanson, who had become a major-domo in the household of Queen Victoria, 'still likes to sing the praises of this gentleman and tells me many very good anecdotes on him, on his illness and death, which make him cry'.[35]

In the absence of an edition of his letters, particularly those to his wife, children and mistresses, it is difficult to make a final assessment of such a complex personality. When he was only seventeen, his friend the Duc de Croÿ had noticed that Ligne 'wanted to be a hero to such an extent that he might subsequently either become truly great or, if he followed his presumption or his imagination, turn out very badly'. To a certain extent, as Croÿ had feared, Ligne's 'presumption and imagination' had stopped him becoming 'truly great'. 'The desire to be everywhere' noted by his grandson Lolo Clary during the Congress of Vienna not only helped kill him, but stopped him realising many of his ambitions: his constant travels, his insistence on the supreme command, in 1792 and later, weakened his chances of becoming a great general. His presumption also led him to underrate opponents, among revolutionaries, ministers, generals, and lawyers; as a result, after 1790 he had to content himself with a spectator's role. His presumption even led him to falsify his son's and his own letters before publishing them, in order to present himself in a more flattering light.

In two ways, however, Ligne was indeed 'truly great': his open mind and open heart. The author who had seen and recorded both courts and lavatories, gardens and battlefields, the man who incarnated the originality and frankness of the eighteenth century, comparing the Hofburg to a synagogue and asking friends to make love on his grave, has few rivals as a witness to his age. His open heart not only led him into many love affairs; it also made him free of national and religious prejudices. Appreciating Christians, Jews and Muslims, he united different nationalities in his own life. So proud of being 'from Flanders, from Flanders, from Flanders', he also loved France, 'the country where I enjoy myself most'. Austria was *chez nous*; Germany, 'our Germany'; Poland, 'that fine country, which I idolise'; he had always been 'tenderly attached' to Hungary; yet felt no resentment for the Russian colossus. Knowing how to think, live and act as a European, the Prince de Ligne is a man for our time.

Appendix: Letters

Twenty-five letters by the Prince de Ligne. Letters 4, 7, 8, 11, 12 and 14 are published here for the first time. The others were published for the first time in the French edition of this biography. Original spellings and punctuation have been kept.

1. To Prince Kaunitz, State Chancellor, c.1772.[1]

Mon Prince

Il y a bien des gens dans le monde occupés de Vous. Il y en a qui disent que Vous aimez à faire du bien. D'autres que vous en faites faire. Les uns parlent de grands talens. Les autres de grandes virtus. Ce n'est pas là ma façon de faire votre éloge. Je dis que vous avez des bontés pour moi: parce que cela fait voir que vous remarquez que je suis celui de tous les hommes qui vous ont juré le plus d'attachement, celui qui en aura davantage toute sa vie. Et puis aussi, Mon Prince, cela prouve Votre indulgence et tout cela vaut mieux, à mon gré, que de faire enrager [?] des Russes, des Suédois, et des Français.[2]

Il y aura encore assez d'occasions de vous admirer. Je préfère celles de vous aimer. C'était chez ce pauvre grand Prince[3] que cela m'était permis. C'est encore une autre raison pour moi de regretter un des hommes les plus aimables qu'il y ait jamais eu. Je vous annonce, Mon Prince, que je vous poursuivrai partout où vous passeres vos Soirées. Je romps une lance avec le meilleur ami, le plus brave volontaire, et le cousin le plus chéri s'il est plus heureux que moi.

J'aurais été Vous faire ma cour cette année-cy; mais on prend part de loin comme de près aux grands évènemens. Et j'avais peur de mêler à la joye générale un air de sollicitation qui convient peu aux fêtes.

Comme je n'en serai jamais, Mon Prince, que ce ne soit pour vous: que je regarderoi les graces de la Cour, encore plus graces vous les devant, je vous supplie de faire ressouvenir Leurs Majestés[4] que La Toison[5] à toujours été dans ma maison sans interruption.

Il n'y a jamais eu de promotion ou nous n'ayons eu part, lorsqu'elle n'y était plus, par la mort de celui qui l'avait. Je compte beaucoup sur la première si vous vous en mêlez Mon Prince. C'est la seule chose que je suis dans le cas de demander, étant très sûr d'avance en fortune militaire, si la guerre revient, à force de zèle. J'attens le Régiment qu'on m'a fait espérer, avec toute la résignation possible. Je désire encore plus que tous les honneurs une façon de penser avantageuse de votre part. Je sais ce qu'il faut pour l'avoir: et je ferai toujours tout mon possible pour le mériter.

Mais pour La Toison je ne sais comme on s'y prend. Je suis un pauvre Jason. Ce qu'il y a de sûr, c'est que j'aime mieux aller à Vienne qu'en Cochide pour la chercher. Je pense à toutes les bontés qu'on y a eu pour moi, à tout ce que j'avois l'honneur de vous dire l'année passée qui me fait préférer ce pays-là à tant d'autres que j'ai vus. Je fais icy le bon flamand malgré moi. Je meurs d'envie d'avoir une occasion de remercier mes souverains plutôt que de les solliciter.

Comme Vous m'avez ordonné d'avoir confiance en vous, Mon Prince, que vous savez bien l'inspirer, je joindrai ce sentiment de plus au respectueux attachement, et j'ose dire bien tendre. Si vous me le permettez, à la parfaite vénération avec laquelle j'ai l'honneur d'être,

Mon Prince,
Votre très humble et très obéissant serviteur
le Prince de Ligne

Vous avez toujours la bonté, Mon Prince, de me donner cinq ou six ans de plus que je n'ai. Cela peut servir à ne pas étonner la Cour de ma demande. D'ailleurs je suis une vieille gueuse. Un autre vous demanderait pardon de vous écrire comme cela. Mais vous aimez à protéger sans avoir l'air de protecteur. Aussi je vous sauve la cérémonie du protegé. C'est toujours à vous, Mon Prince, que [end of phrase missing].

2.　To M. Vandenbroucke[6]

Je vous ai dit, mon cher Vandenbroucke, que lorsque je vous verrais en train de mettre nos affaires au net, je ne vous ferais plus de mistère, en voici la preuve.

Vous souvenez vous d'un contrat de 3500 florins pour lequel je ne sais quel notaire demande son salaire? Je ne voulus pas vs en rendre compte alors, mais à présent que ma confiance est au dernier point, je vous dirai qu'après avoir vécu avec Eugénie[7] pendant 7 ans, elle devint grosse il y a

3 ans, et qu'elle alla accoucher à Lyon. L'enfant est mort. Mais je ne voulus pas la rendre plus malheureuse qu'elle ne l'était, puisqu'elle savait bien qu'après les premiers 6 mois je ne l'aimais plus.

M. Desandroin à qui j'ai payé la Rente de 300 ducats voudrait avoir de l'argent comptant. Comme c'est l'intérêt à 4 pour cent, ce qu'il en a joui 3 ans, il consent à me rendre ce qu'il a reçu, pour avoir le capital. C'est à peu près 5000 florins. Moyennant quoi, donnes lui en 3000 le plutôt possible. J'en serai quitte. C'était sur la terre de Rumpré comme vous verres, par ces papiers, que j'avois établi cette Rente qui m'a fort gêné.

Après avoir employé ces 25,000 pour lesquels je signe, comme vous l'aves fort bien décidé, songes à ces 30,000 sur les premières parties que vous vendrez.

Ecrives aussi à Théaulon de s'informer chez le Prince de Nassau, des moyens de retirer des papiers de 30,000 livres, que j'ai pris autrefois avec lui à condition de les ravoir au même prix que nous les avions vendu, c'est à dire dix mille. Peut être qu'on les aura même à moins. Ou le Prince de Nassau ou son intendant en donnera les éclaircissements ou les facilités à théaulon, qui d'ailleurs sait ce que c'est que ces agiotages de papiers puisqu'avec moins d'argent comptant que cela, on en a pour beaucoup plus. Je ne dois pas un sou au jeu ny d'ailleurs; voilà ma confession générale. Je ne donne ny fête, ny course de traineau ny mascarade. Il me faut une lettre de change sur Paris ou Lyon de 2 ou 300 Louis pour mon carême. Du reste je paye tout plein de comptes de [?], de mes 200 ducats par mois dont je suis très avare.

Que lorsque Étienne et je ne sais qui encore, à mémoire, ou lettre de change, soyent payés avant le 1 de février que je serai à Paris.

Pressez M. de Champ à l'affaire de Salm. J'ai rompu avec de Rasse qui me demande d'être remboursé des frais. Je l'ai envoyé promener. Je suis tout à vous de tout mon coeur,

Mon cher Vandenbroucke, votre serviteur et ami

ce 12 ou 13 [June 1774]

Le P. de Ligne

3. Versailles ce vendredi [July or August 1776][8]

Tout va à merveille mon cher Vandenbroucke. Mais si je n'avais pas été icy, nous étions perdus. Je travaille comme un enragé. Mais je vous avertis que si je n'avais pas promis mille louis à quelqu'un, nous étions au diable. Quitte à en payer l'intérêt de ma poche tous les ans. Je les

emprunterais icy, si on achève le service qu'on me rend. Prépares
quelque honnête homme à les faire remettre icy, [?] à 6 pour cent. Il faut
du crédit pour soutenir le crédit.

Notre bavard fait des merveilles. Voilà sa lettre d'aujourd'hui. Je
n'employerai les bontés de la Reine qu'en cas que l'injustice de la justice
ne me traitera pas bien. En attendant M. le Comte d'Artois et son
Chancelier Mr. Bastard m'ont rendu de grands services. Cette chienne
de famille du Cardinal [de Luynes], à cause de son apoplexie, demandait
encore des délais. J'ai dit au Roy que cela serait affreux. Il me demande
tous les jours s'il a perdu sa terre. Il n'y a que M. de La Galaizière qui lui
a dit qu'il ne le perdrait pas. Il s'en souviendra s'il y contribue.

Adieu, mon cher Vandenbroucke, je vous embrasse.

4. To M. Vandenbroucke, February 1777[8]

Vous avez très bien vu, ou prévu, mon cher Vandenbroucke: et je suis
aussi sûr de battre les Français à la guerre que vous en affaires. Car les
plus sensés n'ont pas le sens commun. Suivez donc votre premier plan.
J'irai vraisemblablement à Paris dans 3 semaines: ce sera le tems de
Corbie. M le Clerc me parait le seul honnête homme du gouvernement:
ce sera le rapporteur de ma requête: J'espère infiniment [?] toujours le
jugement: si la mémoire que je vous conseille de faire imprimer, ne suffit
pas, mes parents [?] seront notre seconde ligne: d'ailleurs pour les avoir,
il faut bien que l'arrêt du conseil d'état soit cassé.

Employez le diable, de l'argent, d'Hennin[9] et M le comte d'Artois par
lui, la Reine par la princesse de Ligne et Mde de Brionne. Parlez aux
gens d'affaires de m de lauraguais, pour savoir ce qu'aura sa fille, ou ce
que [illegible] nous échapper, ce que je ne crois pourtant pas. Mais il
vaut mieux en avoir deux [illegible]. Je vous assure mon cher
Vandenbroucke de toute mon amitié.

5. Vienne, ce 4 [April 1778][8]

Comme Me. de Ligne a écrit à l'une de ses soeurs qu'elle se donnait tant
de peines qu'elle rangeait tout ce qui était dérangé et qu'elle a beaucoup
à courir, et à travailler, je vous prie mon cher Vandenbroucke, d'arrêter
ce grand zèle dont je ne me soucie pas du tout. Je vous recommande
d'abord de faire observer à la lettre, mes instructions, de lui dire de n'en
déranger aucun article, et celui de Baudour, surtout, où si elle vouloit
aller, je vous prie de lui dire que je ne le veux pas; non plus que de faire

travailler, ou réparer, à Beloeil et ailleurs. On dirait, en vérité, que ny vous ny moi n'avons soin de rien. Heureusement sa soeur qui la connait a ri de sa lettre, et moi aussi.

Je ne crois pas qu'il y ait guerre; et pour diminuer notre dépense, et n'en pas faire d'inutile, je ne puis pas me résoudre d'acheter ny des tentes, ny des Mulets. Je ne joue pas. Je suis dans la plus grande économie. Je ne couterai sûrement pas plus que nos 3000 florins par mois.

Adieu mon cher Vandenbroucke, à vous revoir peut-être plutôt que je ne pensais; je vous assure de mon amitié, de ma reconnaissance de vos soins, et de ma confiance.

6. To the Maréchal Duc de Croÿ, Antoing, 10 August 1783

Ne suis-je pas bien malheureux, Monsieur le Maréchal? J'étais tout près de vous, dans ma vieille chaumière Romaine d'Antoing, sur le Champ de Bataille où le brave Colonel de Royal Roussillon [Croy himself] s'est distingué, comme partout, et dont je n'ai pas oublié un mot sage qu'il m'a dit là-dessus, il y a 30 ans. Je me ressouviens de ce que vous avez entendu dire à Mr. de Lowendal, lorsque le Maréchal de Saxe lui parla pendant la bataille: Car heureusement pour moi je me souviens de tout ce qui vient de vous, ou qui vous concerne. C'est dans cette masure que j'occupe pendant tout le temps de l'exercice, que j'écris depuis 7 heures jusqu'à une heure qu'arrivent une zone d'officiers de Mon Régiment que je ramène à Tournay à l'exercice à 5 heures, sur mon joli petit vaisseau; après m'être égosillé pendant 2 heures, je m'en retourne icy de la même manière; et j'y travaille jusqu'à minuit, comme un diable, à achever mon catalogue raisonné de tous les livres militaires qui existent, que j'ai commencé il y a 10 ans. C'est une petite analyse, un petit jugement, quelques commentaires, à l'usage des paresseux qui aimeraient mieux me croire que d'y aller voir et dont je ferai mon premier hommage dès qu'il sera fait à mon cher maître en guerre et en Jardins. Je suis si [?] de ce que vous avez bien voulu être content de celui de Beloeil et de ma petite Ile que je ne puis assez me glorifier de l'approbation du créateur de l'Hermitage et de tant de choses ou sublimes ou jolies ou agréables ou utiles. J'y irai tout de suite; mais je suis obligé d'aller à l'ouverture du nouveau bassin d'Ostende qui ne servira plus qu'aux [?] du pays et que l'on n'a commencé que lorsqu'il devait être fini. Je m'en vais y recevoir l'archiduchesse[10] et puis l'amener diner le 16 icy dans ma baraque où vous devriez bien, mon cher duc, me faire l'honneur de diner avec elle et toute

votre famille que j'aime et respecte de toute mon âme. Au moins venez à
sa tête au mois de septembre à Ostende. Permettez-moi de vous présenter
mon vieux Baudour rajeuni. A propos de vieux, je ne suis pas inquiet du
vieux Maréchal.[11] M. de Voltaire a singé le vieux malade pendant 40 ans.
Le vieux Colonel de Royal Roussillon l'était par les connaissances, et le
travail, et mon vieux voisin fera notre bonheur, et notre admiration des
tours, des belvédères, des bosquets, des canaux et des galopades pendant
40 ans encore. Je me mets à ses pieds et ceux de la princesse belle fille et
belle femme; et je leur jure et rejure par mon gros juron le plus tendre et
le plus respectueux attachement qui ne finira qu'avec ma vie.

7. To M. Vandenbroucke, Vienna, 15 April 1786[12]

La Réforme dans la Maison, mon cher Vandenbroucke, n'est guère possible: et il ne faut pas que la princesse se prive de 2 chevaux et d'un pos-
tillon. Je ne le veux pas du tout ni qu'elle s'apperçoive en rien d'un
changement à faire excepté dans les soupers qui pourraient être moins
nombreux, et moins fréquens et moins illuminés, puisque nous ne
sommes pas chargés de faire les honneurs de la ville, qu'il y a d'autres
maisons, où elle est invitée, et qu'on pourrait s'arranger comme autrefois de n'avoir qu'un souper chez soi par semaine. Il y avait bien de la
différence pour l'économie. Et les comptes de baptiste en font foy. 2 ou 3
petits diminueroient la dépense de plus de deux tiers.

Comme la somme des ouvrages trop prononcés par les zélés [illegi-
ble] et [illegible] a effrayé M de Calonne[13] j'aime bien mieux avoir 50 ou
60 mille livre's de rentes viagères sur nos 3 têtes: et de mieux vendre les
biens roturiers et Jumon et Hastrod [illegible]. D'ailleurs le bruit que
fait dans l'Europe la donation de l'Impératrice en Tauride[14] l'engage à y
ajouter sûrement du profit à l'honneur. Je lui ai déjà proposé 1000 brig-
ands que l'angleterre promet de débarquer à Cherson: et j'espère qu'elle
m'en donnera une partie pour travailler, labourer et peupler: car c'est le
parti le plus riche du monde: il ne faut que des hommes: et les grecs en
étaient les plus habiles avant que l'ignorance et la cruauté des bachas,
soit venu devaster ces beaux pays.

J'y irai avec L'impératrice au mois de janvier prochain, Porter l'oeil
du Maître: et je suis bien sûr que cela nous vaudra quelquechose de bon.
Si la coupe extraordinaire paye les plus criards des créanciers, et la vente
les matières les plus arriérées, ce que nous tirerons de Koeurs et des
revenus, et des améliorations, nous mettra bientôt au courant: et d'icy là,
mon cher Vandenbroucke, de la patience pour nous et pour les autres.

Votre amitié, et les réponses qu'elle vous fournit, pourra nous tirer d'affaire. Je verrai tout cela avec vous, depuis les 1ers jours de juin, jusqu'aux derniers de Xbre.

Nous avons reçu et envoyé quelques documens à Pradel, et des procurations. Il y a grande apparence que la petite Charles[15] est grosse. Voilà 3 semaines que nous le croyons. Si cela est elle retournera aux pays bas, au mois de 7bre. Adieu mon cher Vandenbroucke, je vous embrasse de tout mon coeur.

8. Bruxelles, 17 April 1786[16]

Vous savez mon cher Vandenbroucke que j'ai dit, il y a longtemps que si j'étois Roy de France je vous ferois contrôleur général. Voicy ce qui nous arrive.

Le Roy de Pologne vient de faire écrire par le Prince de Nassau que l'imbecille Xavier est a la mort, condamné à ne vivre tout au plus que 3 mois, et entouré de fripons, à l'ordinaire qui veulent lui faire désheriter la petite Charles,[15] et lui faire faire un testament en faveur d'une palatine de Novgorod, je crois. Le Roy me demande pour cela et pour la Diette. Mes occupations militaires, et Fontainebleau,[17] où ma présence rende notre procès de Koeurs immanquable, m'empêchent d'y aller. J'ai écrit à Charles et à sa femme d'y aller, dût-elle même y accoucher: mais on ne peut pas compter sur une Tête comme celle là. Elle empêchera même son mari d'y aller.

J'ai pensé à une chose. Pour vous dédommager des sacrifices que vous me feriez, du couple de mois, je serais trop heureux qu'une pension de cent louis vous témoignât, mon cher Vandenbroucke, ma nouvelle reconnaissance, car je suis sûr, que faisant peut être un solécisme en Latin, mais jamais en affaires; que vous finiries avec L'Evêque, étant soustenus par le prince de Nassau, et le Roy, pour qui je vous donnerais une lettre, et que nous aurions l'héritage de Xavier. Sans cela je ne prévois pas que nous puissions y réussir. Madame de Marsan, à qui j'écrirais, ne la trouverait mauvais sûrement. Mandes moi ce que vous pensez la-dessus, et soyez persuadé, telle chose qui arrive, que je ne vous en serai pas moins tendrement attaché pour la vie.

9. To King Stanislas Augustus, 10 April 1787, a few days before the journey to the Crimea.[18]

Sire,

Je supplie Votre Majesté de me plaindre de ne pas arriver à la tête de la jeune Caravane: mais comme je n'aurai jamais rien de caché pour elle, j'aurai l'honneur de lui dire que c'est pour faire ma cour à Votre Majesté que je ne lui fais pas ma cour. *On* [Catherine II] trouverait icy, où *l'on* craint toujours et où *l'on* croit que nous nous ennuyons; que le plaisir conduit à Kamiew, outre le devoir de l'hommage: et je suis sûr qu'*on* me dirait: vous vous amuseres mieux qu'icy, où la société continue vous est peut-être à charge. J'aime mieux me sacrifier, dans ce moment cy, prolonger, au moins pour moi l'entrevue, ou la devancer, si je puis; et rester à Kiovie le plus fidèle et le plus zélé des Apôtres qui prêchent la bonne Religion; qui en serait martyre, s'il le fallait; mais qui aura le plaisir de voir rentrer tout le monde, dans la croyance. Il n'y aura dans tout cela d'autre Passion que celle que vous inspires, sire, aux belles et bonnes âmes. Je suis bien fâché de me séparer du passioné qui porte la Sienne sur son front calme et serein. Il m'a pourtant presque grondé, et Comte Edouard Dillon, de la démarche que j'ai osé faire de prier Votre Majesté de le comprendre dans quelque promotion de ses ordres. Je me suis justifié, en lui disant, que c'était par ce que je lui avais entendu dire: Voilà donc un roy à qui il serait doux, et glorieux, pour quelque marque d'estime d'appartenir en quelque chose. Je suis sûr que si Votre Majesté, sans me trahir, lui faisait la surprise, à son départ, de daigner lui conférer son ordre de St. Stanislas, le bonheur de recevoir ces signes de bonté de sa part, par un cordon de son nom, et son institution, lui flatterait plus que l'aigle blanc dont d'ailleurs votre Majesté pourrait l'honorer ensuite, comme officier général, ou ministre à quelque cour, ainsi qu'on a déjà voulu le faire. Je vous demande pardon, sire, de cet excès de confiance de ma part: mais j'aime autant les gens qui sont attachés a V. Majesté, et qui ne seront pas ingrats, que je déteste ceux qui le sont.

J'espère que la Flotte célébrant la Fête de S. Stanislas, au Port ou la Porte de Kamiew: il n'y a que cela qui puisse me consoler de ce qu'elle est encore à la voile. Je n'ennuyerai plus Votre Majesté de ma façon de penser. Je ne dirai seulement pas que sa Lettre pleine de grâce et de bonté m'a enchanté et pénétré. Et la seule chose inutile que je repétérai, mais nécessaire puisqu'il faut bien [?] d'être trop confiante, c'est que j'ai l'honneur d'être avec le plus respectueux attachement, plus que personne au monde,

Sire
>de Votre Majesté
>>Le Très humble et Fidèle Sujet
>>>Ligne
à Kiovie ce mardi
10 avril [1787]

10. To the Baron de Grimm from Moscow, 3 July 1787[19]

On vous aime beaucoup, monsieur le Baron, on parle souvent de vous, mais vous écrit-on? *Catherine le Grand* (car elle fera faire une faute de françois à la Postérité), n'en a peut-être pas le tems. Peut-être ces très petits détails que je viens de dicter vous donneront-ils une idée, quoique bien foible, de ce que nous avons vu; D'ailleurs c'est *indignatio fecit* relation [see end of letter], car je suis outré de la basse jalousie qu'en Europe l'on a conçue contre la Russie. Je voudrois apprendre à vivre à cette petite partie de l'Europe qui cherche à déshonorer la plus grande. Il est extraordinaire, par example, que les grâces aient sauté notre Saint Empire à pieds joints pour venir de Paris s'establir à Moscou et deux cens Werstes encore plus loin où nous avons trouvé des femmes charmantes, mises à merveille, dansantes, chantantes, et aimantes peut-être comme des anges.

L'Empereur a été extrêmement aimable les trois semaines qu'il a passées avec nous. Les conversations de deux personnes qui ont soixante millions d'habitans et huit cent mille soldats, ne pouvoient être qu'intéressantes en voiture où j'en profitois bien, les interrompant souvent par quelque bêtise qui me fesoit rire en attendant qu'elle fit rire les autres, car nous avons toujours joui de la liberté qui seule fait le charme de la société, et vous connoisses le genre simple de celle de l'Impératrice qu'un rien divertit, et qui ne monte à l'élévation du sublime que lorsqu'il est question de grands objets.

Il faut absolument, Monsieur le Baron, que nous revenions ici ensemble, ce sera la moyen que je sois encore mieux reçu. Ce n'est pas que vous ayes besoin de rappeler à l'Impératrice tout ce que vous avés d'aimable, car absent elle vous voit, mais elle sera fort aisé de dire présent, je le trouve.

Vous ferés de charmantes connaissances. M. de Mamonow,[20] par example, est un sujet de grande espérance, il est plein d'esprit, d'agrémens et de connaissances. Vous vous doutés bien de l'agrément que le Comte de Ségur[21] a répandu dans tout le voyage. Je suis désolé qu'il soit presque fini.

J'ai fait bâtir un Temple dédié à l'Impératrice par une inscription près d'un rocher où étoit celui d'Iphigénie et un autel à l'amitié pour le Prince Potemkine, au milieu des plus beaux et gros arbres à fruits que j'aie vus, et au bord de la mer où se réunissent tous les torrens des montagnes. Cette petite terre que m'a donnée l'Impératrice s'appelle *Partheniȥȥa* ou le *Cap Vierge*, et est habitée par cinquante six familles Tartares qui ne le sont pas autant que les déesses et les rois qui exigeoient de durs sacrificies, comme tout le monde sait. Je ne connais pas de site plus délicieux, je pourrais dire:

> Sur les bords fortunés de l'antique *Idalie*
> lieux où finit l'Europe et commence l'Asie

car on découvre les montagnes de la Natolie [Anatolia]. Ce qu'il y a d'assés singulier, c'est que c'est sur les bords de la mer noire que, tranquille et vivant au milieu des Infidèles, j'ai appris que les fidèles sujets de la maison d'Autriche se révoltaient sur les bords de l'Océan.[22] Je ne m'attendois pas qu'il y eut plus de sûreté pour moi dans mes terres du Pont Euxin que dans celles de la Flandre.

Auriés vous la bonté de faire remettre ce paquet à son adresse et de recevoir les assurances de la considération distinguée que je partage pour vous avec tous ceux qui vous connaissent ou ont entendu parler de vous, de même que je partage avec vos amis le tendre attachement que vous inspirés si vite et avec le quel j'ai l'honneur etc etc

[signed] le Prince de Ligne

From Moscow, 3 July 1787 (new style):

Il y a aujourd'hui deux mois que nous sommes partis de Kiovie et nous arrivons ici tous en bonne santé du voyage le plus intéressant, le plus triomphal et le plus magnifique qui se soit jamais fait, sans la moindre contrariété et sans le plus petit accident. Il ne m'est pas possible de m'empêcher de dire que les gazettes qui ont eu la bonté de s'occuper de nous, nous ont bien amusés.

Pour rassurer tant de gens bien intentionnés pour la Russie, je leur dirai qu'après une navigation charmante sur le Boristhène nous avons trouvé des ports, des armées et des flottes dans l'état le plus brillant; Que Cherson et Sébastopol surpassent tout ce qu'on peut en dire, et que chaque jour étoit marqué pour quelque grand événement; tantôt c'était la manoeuvre de soixante-dix escadrons de Troupes régleés et superbes qui chargeoient en ligne à merveille, tantôt un nuage de cosaques qui exerçoient au tour de nous à leur manière, tantôt les Tartares de la Crimée qui, infidèles jadis à leur Kan Sahin-Guerai[23] parce qu'il voulait les enrégimenter, avoient formé d'eux-mêmes des Corps pour venir au devant de l'Impératrice. Les espaces de désert qu'on avait à traverser pendant deux ou trois jours aux lieux d'où Sa Mté. l'Impératrice a chassé les Tartares Nogaïs et Zaporoviens qui, il y a deux ans encore, ravageoient ou menaçoient l'Empire, étaient ornés de tentes magnifiques aux dinées et aux couchées; et ces campemens de pompe asiatique, avec l'air de fête qui sur l'eau comme sur terre nous a suivi par tout, présentaient le spectacle le plus militaire. Que ces déserts même n'alarment pas trop les gens bien intentionnés, comme les Gazetiers du bas Rhin, de Leyde, Le Courier de l'Europe etc, ils seront bientôt couverts de grains, de bois et de villages; on y en bâtit déjà de militaires qui, étant l'habitation d'un Régiment, deviendront bientôt celle de paysans, qui s'y établiront à cause de la bonté du terrain. Si ces Messieurs apprennent que dans chaque ville de Gouvernement l'Impératrice a laissé des présens pour plus de cent mille écus, et que chaque jour de repos étoit marqué par des dons, par des bals, des feux d'artifice et des illuminations à deux ou trois lieues à la ronde, ils s'inquiéteront, sans doute, des finances de l'Empire. Malheureusement elles sont dans l'état le plus florissant, et la banque nationale sous la direction du Comte André Schuvalow, l'un des hommes qui a la plus d'esprit et de connoissances, source inépuisable pour la Souveraine et les sujets, doit les rassurer. Si, par humanité, ils sont inquiets du bonheur des sujets, qu'ils sachent qu'ils ne sont esclaves que pour ne pas se faire du mal ni à eux ni aux autres, mais libres de s'enrichir, ce qu'ils font souvent, et ce qu'on peut voir par la richesse des différens costumes des Provinces que nous avons traversées. Pour les affaires étrangères, que les bien intentionnés s'en rapportent à l'Impératrice elle-même; elle travailloit tous les jours en voyage le matin avec le Comte Bezborodko, Ministre du plus grand mérite, et qu'ils apprennent, outre cela, que le Prince Potemkin, homme du génie le plus rare, esprit vaste, ne voyant jamais qu'en grand, seconde parfaitement les vues de l'Impératrice ou les prévient, soit comme chef du département de la guerre et des armées ou chef de plusieurs Gouvernemens. L'Impératrice, qui ne craint pas qu'on l'accuse d'être gouverné par quelqu'un, lui donne, ainsi qu'à ceux qu'elle emploie, toute l'autorité et la confiance possibles; il n'y a que pour faire du mal qu'elle ne donne de pouvoir à personne. Elle se justifie de sa magnificence en disant que donner de l'argent lui en rapporte beaucoup, et que son devoir est de récompenser et d'encourager; d'avoir créé beaucoup d'emplois dans ses provinces, parce que cela fait circuler les espèces, élève des fortunes et oblige les Gentilshommes à y demeurer plutôt qu'à s'entasser à Petersbourg et à Moscou; d'avoir bâti en pierres 237 villes, parce qu'elle dit que tous les villages de bois, brûlés si souvent, lui coûtaient beaucoup; d'avoir une flotte superbe dans la mer noire, parce que Pierre 1er aimoit beaucoup la Marine. Voilà comme elle a toujours quelque excuse de modestie pour toutes les grandes choses qu'elle fait. Il n'y a pas d'idée à se faire du bonheur qu'on a eu de la suivre. On fesait quinze lieues le matin, on trouvait au premier relai à déjeuner dans un joli petit palais de bois, et ensuite à dîner dans un autre, et puis encore quinze lieues et un plus grand, plus beau et meublé à merveille pour coucher, à moins que ce ne fût dans les villes de Gouvernement où les Gouverneurs généraux ont par tout de superbes résidences en pierres, colonnades et toutes sortes de décorations. Il y a des marchands très riches dans toutes les villes et beaucoup de commerce depuis Krementschuk, Kaursk, Orel, Toula jusqu'ici, et une surprenante population dont l'Impératrice est adorée. Dans le dénombrement qu'on en rapporte quelquefois dans les papiers publics on ne parle que des mâles, et dans les autres pays on compte tout. Si les bien intentionnés, (car je n'écris que pour eux) craignent que la Tauride ne soit une mauvaise acquisition, qu'ils se consolent en apprenant qu'après avoir traversé quelques espaces abandonnés par des familles Tartares qui demandent aujourd'hui à y revenir, on trouve le pays le mieux cultivé; qu'il y a des forêts superbes dans les montagnes; que les côtes de la mer sont garnies de villages en amphithéatre, et tous les vallons plantés en vignes, Grenadiers, Palmiers, figuiers, abricotiers et toutes sortes de fruits et plantes précieuses de beaucoup de rapport. Je trouve enfin qu'il ne suffit pas que nous ayons été fort heureux de suivre l'Impératrice et que ses sujets le soient, mais qu'il faut encore que les Gazetiers et ceux qui les ont crus, le soient en apprenant la fausseté de leurs nouvelles, et qu'ils nous aient une éternelle obligation de les avoir rassuré au point qu'ils peuvent promettre de notre part une récompense de mille louis à celui qui prouvera la fausseté d'un seul des faits que nous avons rapportés ici par l'intéret le plus pur pour leur instruction, ce qui leur fera croire qu'en conservant nos mille louis, nous n'avons pas mis autant de soins à économiser notre tems.

11. Moscow, 7 July 1787[24]

Je ne demande pas mieux, mon cher Vandenbroucke, que de vendre le contrat de Ma Tante, à Paris s'il n'y a pas de perte. Mais prenez garde qu'on ne nous attrape: car c'est ce qui se fait le mieux dans ce pays là. Pour le nôtre je vois qu'on n'a jamais songé à m'y rendre service, et que Messieurs les richards aiment mieux sottement leur argent et méritent les banqueroutes et les malheurs que je leur souhaite.

Si l'on peut lever de l'argent sur le contrat de Paris, cela vaudra encore mieux. Enfin demandons encore du tems à ces créanciers qui étaient si patins du leur dans mon procès. Ce qu'il y a de sûr, c'est que las de faire du bien, sans qu'on m'en fasse, je me souviendrai d'eux s'ils s'avisent seulement de faire une saisie. Si je voulais abuser des facilités qu'on m'accorde dans ce pays cy, en revanche on me fournirait tout ce que je voudrais, car il y a des capitalistes fort obligeants: je compte tirer quelque parti de mes deux charmantes terres de Nickita et de Parthenizza situés sur le bord de la Mer Noire. Il y a 56 familles Tartares. Je fais bâtir quelques maisons pour des vignerons et planter des vignes. Il y a des figuiers, des palmiers des [illegible] partout. Je passerai par Varsovie où j'espère terminer nos affaires. Je n'ai confiance qu'en vous pour toutes les miennes. Ainsi mon cher Vandenbroucke, je me recommande sans cesse à votre amitié, et vous assure de la mienne à la vie et à la mort.

12. Copy of the report of the F. Z. M. Prince de Ligne to the Emperor, from the Russian headquarters, 12 May 1788[25]

C'est pour ce coup-ci que les expressions me manquent. Tout ce que je puis dire à V. M. Ile. c'est qu'elle dispose de toute notre existence, notre Sang, notre fortune, notre vie, est plus que jamais à elle. Heureux si je puis payer de la mienne quelque succès sous ses yeux, lorsque V. M. daignera me rappeler d'ici, où tout étant une fois en train va de soi même: ainsi que la Pologne qui s'échauffe un peu. Petersbourg qui ménace un peu et Berlin qui parait s'arrêter pour voir si l'on pense sérieusement à s'opposer à ses funestes projets.

Mon bonheur de ce que V. M. Ile daigne dire de faire pour Charles a été bien diminué par mes regrets de ne l'avoir pas rencontré sur ce parapet où le nom, l'activité et la présence de V. M. Ile a fait plus d'effet, et en fera plus que notre artillerie.[26] J'envie le sort du moindre des soldats qui a été de cette superbe expedition.

J'ai enfin tiré au clair ce qui avait l'air d'être l'effet de la mauvaise volonté et qui ne l'est que d'un mal entendu occasionné par ce prétendu plan d'opération que je trouve si vague et si peu prononcé que si je n'arretois pas quelquefois mon zèle, il y auroit de plus fortes scènes[27] que celles que je suis pourtant obligé de faire de tems en tems: car sans cela ce serait bien pis, et rien n'iroit du tout.

Dans le premier projet du Prince [Potemkin] envoyé par moi à V. M. Ile il y a 6 mois, il n'y avoit que battre l'ennemi s'il venoit nous chercher et point d'Oczackow qu'après. Au moins le voicy en train. L'Attaque du Liman est prête, et dez que celle de terre le sera, on prendra la forteresse vraisemblablement. Ou l'on en fera le siège qui ne peut pas durer plus de 8 jours. Adieu Mr. de Lafitte.[28]

Si le Prince [Potemkin] ne m'avoit pas acordé d'écrire cette lettre au Maréchal [Romanzov] ou sans pouvoir lui donner des ordres il l'invite encore plus particulièrement dans la lettre qui est partie hier par le courrier qu'il lui a envoyé exprès de passer le Niester sans délai; j'en envoyais une à S. M. l'Imperatrice.

Celle ci que lui portera M. de Herbert est accompagnée d'une bien caressante de ma part pour le piquer d'honneur. S'il ne fait rien j'ecrirai directement à S. M. l'Imperce pour me plaindre des procédés de ces deux maréchaux qui sont bien les maîtres de s'attraper tous les jours, pourvu que ce ne soit pas aux depens du meilleur des alliés. Peut être même que ce que j'ai laissé entrevoir ici de mon intention à cet égard a fait effet. Car on n'a jamais écrit si vite.

S. M. l'Impératrice a écrit hier pour la première fois avec force au sujet des lenteurs. Que ne l'at'elle fait plutôt! Et encore c'est d'après l'impatience de l'ambassadeur à qui je faisais part des miennes exprès par le courrier russe parce que je voulais être lu, puisqu'il m'est égal de me brouiller pour me raccomoder quand je le veux bien.

Il ne me convient pas de dire mon avis à V. M. Ile mais qu'Elle le pardonne à trop de zèle. Il y a tant de jalousie, de malice ou d'ignorance, si peu d'envie et tant de prétextes de ne pas faire grand chose dans le genre offensif, que pour n'avoir pas contre nos trouppes toutes celles de l'Empire ottoman, il n'y a qu'une bonne paix à faire lorsque V. M. Ile après avoir pris une partie de ce qui lui convient, se fera donner le reste par un traité. La Russie sent si bien la faiblesse de son Colosse, que contente qu'on ne lui demande plus la Crimé [*sic*], qu'on s'arrange pour le Caucase, d'avoir Oczakow et de pouvoir donner le nom d'Oczakowsky et le Grand Cordon de St. George au Pce Potemkin, elle ne demandera pas mieux. Elle ne songe ni à la Moldavie, ni à la Vallachie, et si elle obtient que Bender et Chotzim soit rasé pour avoir la navigation du Niester libre, elle aura tout ce qu'elle désire. Tous les beaux projets de chasser les Turcs de l'Europe et de mettre Constantinople en République sont évanouis.

V. M. Ile. après avoir resisté dans la guerre de 1778 au Cabinet de Vienne (ce qui était le plus difficile) de Berlin, de Versailles et de Petersbourg, arrêté, repoussé le génie du Roy de Prusse et eu toujours des avantages, a commencé alors sa carrière de gloire. Elle y met le comble à présent par ses actions d'éclat; la prise de Belgrad et une bataille qu'elle va gagner et tout ce qui se passe tous les jours sous ses yeux ou par ses ordres: comme la conquête de la Moldavie qui ne nous coûte que deux marches et ayant coûté aux Russes deux campagnes a si bien excité leur envie que c'est à cause de cela que nous avons trouve cette petite difficulté-ci que j'espère avoir vaincu.

Ce que j'ai gagné aussi, c'est que le Pce. Potemkin a fait décider l'Impératrice sur le corps de Troupes destiné contre le Roy de Prusse. Ce sera l'armée du Maréchal Romanzow après avoir laissé ici, à ce qu'il m'a promis hier, ce qu'il faudra pour soutenir le Prince de Cobourg et la Moldavie. Ainsi l'On pourra compter sûrement sur 20,000 hommes pour arrêter le Projet sur Dantzig, Thorn et la Samogitie.

Le Cabinet de Petersbourg est très content d'avoir pensé à imaginer que la Diète de Varsovie soit confederée, et on faira alors sa Déclaration. Il sera trop tard alors, et le parti prussien est enchanté qu'on attende jusqu'à là, et qu'on suspende moyennant cela ce qui était en train. Le Prince Potemkin a de l'argent et des armes prêtes pour les conféderations. En cas qu'il s'en forme avant ainsi que je l'espère, malgré les arrangements de Petersbourg.

On avait mandé ici de même la prétendue manière de sommation du Prince de Cobourg pour Chetzim. Avant de savoir qu'elle n'avoit pas été faite, comme on l'avoit écrit. J'ai juré que cela n'étoit pas vrai, et que si cela l'étoit, ce seroit contre l'intention De V. M. Ile.

Je n'ai point entendu dire que le Pce de Cobourg ait voulu faire ce marche avec le Commandant de Kaminicek dont je vois les rapports et les envoye dès que je les ai reçues au Pce. Potemkin.

Le Général de Wesmilinow, qui étoit sous ses ordres ainsi que ses quatre Bataillons ont été extrêmement content des soins et des bons arrangements du Pce de Cobourg, et l'ont quitté avec peine.

N'ayant pas pu m'empêcher de témoigner encore aujourd'hui au Pce Potemkin mes regrets d'être chez lui au lieu d'être au siège de Belgrad, où mon Père mes oncles mon grand Père avaient été, et où mon fils sera, et mon mécontentement de ne pas voir assez d'activité de sa part, ni de clarté dans ce qu'il va faire, voici ce qu'il vient de m'envoyer, qui vaut mieux que son premier plan de soidisants opérations dont je m'étais plaint. Je viens de l'en remercier: et il me promet d'être plus autrichien que jamais, et de faire voir qu'il reconnait les obligations qu'il a, ainsi que la Russie, à V. M. Ile.

Notre avantgarde passera le Bog après demain. Voici le plan que le Prince de Nassau m'a envoyé de son attaque qui parait infaillible. Je suis bien aisé que l'attaque de terre puisse me procurer une partie de dédommagement, quoique bien faible, de n'avoir pas donné la main à Charles sous le parapet où il m'aurait aidé à grimper.

Je mets aux pieds de Votre Majesté Impériale encore une fois ma reconnaissance et le Profond respect avec lequel je suis

Ligne F. Z. M.

P.S. le Pce Potemkin dans l'intention de réussir plus sûrement a engagé le [?Maréchal] à passer le Niester, lui a fait entendre qu'en cas de besoin il croyoit que le Pce de Cobourg pourroit alors lui être assigné. J'espère que le Maréchal cessera de commander son armée de 600 Werst. C'est je crois la première fois que c'est arrivé.

Je demande pardon à V. M. Ile de mon Griffonage. Mais à peine trouve-t'on ici des plumes et du papier.

13. Copy of the report of the F. Z. M. Prince de Ligne to the Emperor, Nimierow 7 June 1788[29]

Tout commence à s'eclaircir et Votre Mté Imple qui est accoutumée à mieux voir que tous ceux, qui ont l'honneur d'être employés à son auguste service, a bien eu raison de me faire la grâce de me mander qu'Elle n'ajoutoit plus foy aux bluettes et aux lueurs d'espérance.

Le Prince[30] m'a dit il y a près de trois semaines, avant que je le quittai, qu'il ne croyait pas que le Maréchal[31] passeroit le Niester. Le Maréchal m'a dit il y a 15 jours qu'il ne croyoit pas que le Prince fît le Siège d'Oczakow, et ils ont raison tous deux, car ni l'un ni l'autre n'ont envie de faire ce qu'ils ont promis: celuici m'a dit aujourd'hui qu'il ne vouloit pas avoir sa gauche en l'air, et qu'il ne se fioit pas à la droite du Prince, qui à peine passeroit le Bog, il n'y a rien de passé encore et il est à Elizabeth.

Je lui ai écrit hier que las de demander à Votre Majesté Imple des fausses suppositions et des mensonges, je la prierois, si cela continuoit, d'avoir la bonté de me rappeler, si je n'étois pas assez heureux pour lui être utile et savoir au juste, au moins, quand il passeroit la rivière et feroit son siège auquel personne ne croyoit: j'attends ici sa réponse: et serai bien étonné, s'il me mande quelque chose de positif. Votre Majesté Imple aura su par le Prince de Cobourg le contrordre donné à la Brigade

Russe que j'avois eu l'honneur de lui annoncer dans ma dernière lettre devoir joindre le Prince de Cobourg. Le Baron de Herbert estimé généralement de tout le monde et toujours rempli de zèle alla trouver tout de suite le Maréchal, et lui parla très fortement la dessus: celuici lui répondit que c'étoit pour faire marcher tout le corps de Soltikoff à la fois.

Pendant ce tems là, étant allé voir de très près Chotzim et le Prince de Cobourg, pour prévenir les malentendus qui peuvent survenir des Courriers qui se croisent, et des correspondances Russes, j'attendois cette Brigade, et m'étois déjà arrangé avec le Général Mellin qui la commandoit pour la partager près de Chotzim et la faire paroitre plus grande qu'elle n'étoit, en manoeuvrant surtout avec les Cosaques, sur les deux rives: et je crois que le garnison auroit pris le parti de sortir, pour s'échapper, d'autant plus que j'avois engagé le Général de Vitte à le conseiller à Osman Bacha, en lui annonçant l'arrivée d'un Corps considérable russe: et que ce Bacha lui avoit écrit la veille pour lui demander des nouvelles.

Je suis retourné chez Mr. de Soltikoff qui se mettoit en marche et compte passer le Niester dans 3 jours à Merlinozzi à 8 Werst audessous de Chotzim, avec dix mille hommes: je l'ai prié d'envoyer ses Cosaques au delà du Pruth pour allarmer le Prince de Walachie et rassurer les sujets bien intentionnés pour nous. Il m'a promis d'établir un poste à Stephanouze et je suis revenu ici pour prier le Maréchal de ne plus au moins cette foisci donner de contre ordre: il me l'a promis: et cependant je n'ose l'assurer, ayant été trompé si souvent par les deux Maréchaux.

Je n'ai que lieu de me louer de leur amitié, malgré les choses un peu dures que j'ai été obligé souvent de leur dire et de leur écrire; mais je suis fâché de voir que tout ceci est le second Tome de la guerre de 36[32] où malgré la bonne volonté de l'Impératrice Anne, le Maréchal Munich ne fit rien que nuire aux intérêts de l'Empereur Charles six: et le Général Bernclau représentoit, sollicitoit et écrivoit les mêmes choses que moi.

Je plains S. M. l'Impératrice des soupçons injustes que l'Europe a conçus de sa bonne foy, et de sa foiblesse à ne pas faire faire tout ce qu'elle désire. On verra aussi le manquement total d'argent et de moyens de son Empire.

La Pologne est pleine d'officiers et de soldats Prussiens. Un Lieutenant, qui étoit chez le Maréchal aujourd'hui, lorsque je suis entré chez lui, s'est sauvé tout de suite et lui a eu l'air un peu embarrassé. Le Comte Soltikoff me paroit le plus zélé pour nous, et me jure, au moins, un attachement sans bornes pour l'auguste Maison [of Austria].

Plusieurs Polonais et entre autres les Potocki m'assurent aussi que si Votre Majesté Imple. avoit besoin d'eux, ils donneroient leurs biens pour des confédérations, comme par example, s'il s'agissoit de s'opposer au Roi de Prusse. Je n'ose seulement que détruire ce que le parti prussien avoit debité sur les vues de Votre Majesté Impériale pour la Podolie.

Je ne conçois pas, pourquoi la cour de Petersbourg a fait publier des Manifestes de protection en Moldavie, sous pretexte d'appui pour la Religion greque, dans le tems qu'il n'est pas entré un Russe, et que tout est dû aux troupes de Votre Majesté Impériale qui s'y sont conduites avec tant de valeur.

Je désire que le Grand Vizir aille la chercher pour se faire battre et que Belgrad rendu en soit la suite. Mes espoirs et mes désespoirs pour ces deux armées cy ont souvent alterné: mais il me semble si présent qu'il est bien prouvé qu'on ne veut que défendre la Crimée, Cherson et Kinbourn, attendre les Evénemens chez Votre Majesté Imple et obtenir Oczakow et Ackerman pour la paix.

Puisse mon zèle aux dépens de ma vie et sous les yeux de Votre Majesté Imple, quand elle le daignera juger à propos, être plus heureux et mettre bien à découvert le véritable et vif attachement dont je suis pénétré, et qui est égal au profond respect avec lequel je suis. [no signature]

14. To Prince Joseph Poniatowski, nephew of King Stanislas Augustus, who was leaving the Austrian army to serve in the Polish, from Semlin [September or October 1789][33]

Je reçois la lettre de mon cher Prince, je la lis et dans mon premier Mouvement je lui réponds. Il n'y a dans ceci d'affligeant que pour l'armée Impériale qui vous adore et qui a prononcé sur votre compte il y a longtems. Ce que vous avez fait l'année passée, ce que vous avez essayé et ce que vous avez vengé si ardemment, prouve assez qu'elle avait raison. Comment vous seul qui ne vous connoissez pas assez, peut ignorer à quel point vous êtes aimé et estimé, pouvez vous croire que ce que l'on sait être l'effet du premier de vos devoirs, puisse vous faire du tort. La première cause de mes larmes, en vous lisant, c'est que j'ai pensé à la peine que vous avez dans ce moment cy et qu'avec le Talent que vous avez de n'en pas manquer une, vous vous en feriez mille et de mille manières. Je ne vous parle pas de moi. Si notre maudite position d'incertitude avait finie, je me destinais à vous avoir de grandes obligations. Ma Tête et mon coeur travaillaient pour vous: et Charles en me contrefesant, là dessus, pourraitpendant 2 heures. Quel plaisir j'eusse eu de contribuer à votre gloire. Et quel plaisir pour votre âme sensible et ardent d'être utile à votre meilleur ami, père de votre meilleur ami.

Me voilà perdu auprès de mes [illegible] de mon [illegible] et de tous mes postes avancés, qui vous attendaient avec tant d'impatience. J'avais déjà préparé un diner d'une 20eme de votre diner polonais, pour le jour de votre arrivée.

Apparemment, Cher Prince, que je vous aime plus que je ne pensais: car ce que j'éprouve est bien fort. Avec cela, je serais désolé que vous ne prissies pas le parti de vous en aller. Vous vous devez à votre belle et illustre nation que votre exemple peut relever. Votre sûreté, votre contenance, votre fidélité et votre suite déjoueront ceux qui chez vous, en manquent et les Têtes Légères et intriguantes et inconsequentes se reformeront peut être. Vous serez la seule consolation de Notre Roy, le soutien de sa gloire, et le bonheur de ses vieux jours.

Le Stanislas qui n'est pas auguste,[34] quoique avec beaucoup de mérite, n'est pas fort aimé. Vous l'êtes de tous les partis. Vous les [illegible] faisant Vos beaux yeux aux leurs, et vos gros yeux aux autres. Enfin, je vous prédis les plus belles destinées.

Ayez l'esprit de les goûter d'avance, et de ménager votre santé. J'ai demandé à vos gens si vous n'aviez pas besoin d'argent, et quoiqu'ils fûssent en pleurs aussi, de ma sensibilité, et de quitter un pays, où vous êtes adoré, ils ont ri quand j'ai dit, tristement, Je n'en ai pas, moi, mon dieu[?], j'en volerai s'il le faut.

Adieu, cher, bon et joli Prince. Le mot d'adieu m'a coûté, parce que c'est un adieu militaire: mais ne m'effrayez pas autrement, car nous nous aimons trop pour ne pas nous chercher et nous rencontrer sans cesse.

15. To M. de Calonne [March 1791][35]

Tout ce que j'ai éprouvé ne se conçoit pas: et lorsque je suis rentré chez moi, je me suis trouvé dans l'ivresse du plaisir, de l'espérance, de l'horreur, et du désespoir. Tout s'est peint à mon âme, excepté la crainte. Vous avez prêché un converti, charmant apôtre: et mon résultat est toujours (ou tout ce qu'on a répondu à tout ce que j'ai dit là dessus) qu'il faut appuyer ainsi que nous avons dit cette nuit-cy.

1o. Certitude du danger par l'inaction.

2o. Incertitude du danger par l'opération.

3o. Espérance de non danger par le manifeste pour lequel je prêche depuis 3 mois.

4o. Espèce d'obligation forcée par les corps de l'Empire exagérés même, si l'on veut dans une occasion semblable pour lequel on laisse agir les Princes attaqués dans leurs droits.

5o. Certitude du succès si la Reine échappe à tous les dangers, (ce que je crois) de la remettre sur le Trône.

6o. Eloignement de l'idée du bien particulier et ambitieux de la part d'un jeune prince[36] dont j'ai [vu] croître chaque jour, avec admiration, l'honneur avec la grâce, les agréments avec les vertus et l'esprit, et les talens se développer sans rien perdre de la candeur charmante avec laquelle il est venu au Monde.

Puisse-je en sortir glorieusement pour la gloire et le bien d'une nation que j'adorais. Il me verra [?], si on me le permet, lui porter des étendards d'Autriche ou de l'empire sur les rives du Rhin ou de l'Escaut, pour aller égorger des monstres *sur les bords charmans de la Seine*.

Puisse le plus illustre, le plus [?], le plus ferme des ministres, et le plus loyal et le plus aimable des hommes, mettre fin à son grand [?], parler comme de moi au jeune gentilhomme que j'aime, admire, et respecte, dans le même genre qu'un ancien bourgeois de Paris de son propre [aieul?] qui s'appelloit Henri 4; [four words illegible] l'un et l'autre de ma fidelité, ma discretion et ma tendresse.

Quoique je n'aime point à mentir, Je ne dirai pas ce soir, à l'empereur,[37] que je me suis engagé à lui dire tout cela. Je dirai que je n'ai rien promis et aurai l'air de lui laisser tomber toutes ces idées par une suite de l'attachement que j'ai véritablement pour lui, dont l'intérêt me semble, ainsi que je le lui ai déjà exprimé, se trouve lié, avec sa dignité, sa gloire, et son humanité.

Adieu, vous que j'aime, come on vous aime, c'est tout dire.

16. To Prince Kaunitz c.1793[38]

Mon Prince,

La Perte du bonheur de ma vie[39] m'empêcherait de penser à celle des Trônes, puissances, dominations, si dans la retraite où je me suis plus condamné que jamais, un zèle patriotique tres peu encouragé, ne venait pas quelquefois se réveiller à mon reveil. D'ailleurs on est fâché de voir crouler un bel édifice. Votre altesse en avait été l'architecte; et des maçons trop illuminés ou trop peu éclairés y ont malheureusement mis la main.

Sans me mêler d'affaires j'en ai beaucoup vu autour de moi: et Je me souviens que sous le beau Règne de l'Impératrice Reine que Votre altesse avait rendu si glorieux, si ferme, si rempli de l'élévation qui est dans votre âme, mon Prince, on demandait des plans de campagne aux Maréchaux et generaux d'infanterie et de Cavallerie qui avaient commandé des corps. On les examinait et on n'en faisait pas [illegible] aussi vague que celui de cette année cy.

Nous avons vu arriver Votre Altesse en fixer [illegible] avant la Bataille de Colin et je ne m'aviserois pas de parler à Celui qui sait tout depuis le cèdre jusqu'a l'hysope, si tant de gens qui n'en savent pas plus que moi, n'étaient pas souvent consultés. Je connais mieux les Pays-Bas qu'eux: et c'est ce qui me fait prendre la liberté de écrire à Votre Altesse, en la suppliant de ne la dire à personne: car grâce à Dieu, je n'ai jamais voulu jouer un Role. Je suis mort avec le Maréchal Loudon; et je ne dirai jamais la hardiesse que j'ai aujourd'hui depuis qu'on s'imagine que je veux ressusciter.

Nos Troupes ne s'étant jamais retournés depuis Mons, je ne sais pourquoi, pour attaquer en mare la canaille française, que l'embarras même de sa nombreuse et pesante artillerie aurait fait battre, sont poursuivis jusqu'au Rhin. Je voudrais quelles ne rentrassent plus aux Pays-bas abandonnés pendant quelque tems à leur malheureux sort: et qu'on fit une diversion qui en fit sortir, au moins, les deux tiers des Troupes francaises.

Pour y réussir on couperait en passant à Mannheim, ou asiégerait Mayence. Le reste de nos forces chercherait à prendre Strasbourg et Landau. Il n'y a jamais eu dans le système Vonckiste, protégé si fort, contre mon avis, par les Gouverneurs Généraux,[40] que Mons, Namur, Tournay, un tiers de Bruxelles. Les deux autres tiers, ath, gand, bruges, ostende, nieuporte, malines, anvers, louvain, Vandernoottistes, fanatiques, furieux de l'impiété française, redeviennent, tous les jours, plus Royalistes. En les flattant, et ménageant, on pourrait les engager à faire des vêpres Siciliennes des français qui, malgré la diversion, seraient restés aux Pays Bas. Les Troupes flamandes qu'ils lèvent pour eux serviraient pour nous: et nous y rentrerions sans dépenser hommes ny argent.

Je soumets tout cela à Votre Altesse: et je ne le croirai faisable qu'à moins qu'elle ne la trouve. Je n'y mets de prix que sur la discretion que je demande, et que je garderai bien sûrement. Pardon, mille fois pardon, Mon Prince. Ce qui me rassure sur ma démarche, c'est l'assurance de vos bontés paternelles.

C'est de cela dont je suis le plus fier. J'oublie que j'aurais sauvé les Pays Bas si, suivant la justice et le sermon de l'inauguration, on m'avait rendu le gouvernement militaire du Hainaut. La connaissance de tous les chemins de la province, où sont toutes mes Terres, confisquées à ce que je crois, m'aurait fait tourner et prendre à dos M. du Mourier⁴¹ fort aisement.

Je suis bien aisé aussi de me fournir une occasion de présenter à Votre Altesse le renouvellement des sentiments tendres et respectueux qui sont dans mon coeur depuis si longtemps, et la vénération, et admiration, avec laquelle j'ai l'honneur d'être

Mon Prince

de Votre Altesse

Le tres humble et tres obéissant serviteur

Ligne

Ce matin mardi

17. To M. Vandenbroucke, Vienna, 24 August 1795[42]

Quoique vous m'ayez rendu bien des services, mon cher Vandenbroucke, amélioré toutes mes terres, mis de l'ordre dans mes affaires etc. Le plus grand de tous est de m'avoir envoyé un homme qui est bien intelligent et que j'envoye à Basle et à Paris, aux ministres Prussiens et à la convention. J'ai écrit au roy de Prusse;[43] et quoique ma paix particulière ait l'air d'une plaisanterie, j'ai prévenu l'Empereur à ce sujet. J'ai ajouté le double de raisons bien fortes, bien plausibles, et un peu mieux historicisés au mémoire d'harmignies, qui n'était pas assez bien appuyé.

J'en envoye à M. Barthelemi,[44] et ailleurs encore. Je presse Legros de la faire partir bien vite de Vienne. Il est déjà parti hier d'icy. J'augure bien de tout cela et de la justice de la république. Vous lui rendrez service, mon cher Vandenbroucke, en même tems qu'à moi: car on voit que depuis qu'elle s'est débarrassée des Monstres qui auroient sûrement ruiné Beloeil, s'ils avoient vécu, le régime est doux et plein d'équité, et même d'obligeance, à ce qui parait. Recevez les assurances de ma reconnaissance et de mon amitié, sans compliment, mon cher Vandenbroucke, et à l'ordinaire. Ligne.

18. To the Marquis de Bonnay, 28 June 1802[45]

[Ligne refers to the death of his friend the Chevalier de Saxe, son of Prince Xavier of Saxony, uncle of Louis XVI, by his morganatic marriage to Comtesse Clara Spinuzzi. After fighting a duel with Count Nicolas Tcherbatoff, with whom he had a feud dating from 1795, the Chevalier had died from his wounds on 23 June 1802 at Teplitz.]

Avec assez peu de Talent pour bien Mentir, je m'en suis servi pour raccommoder l'affaire du malheureux chevalier, en disant qu'elle l'était. C'en était un moyen; et publiant le rendez-vous, aux frontières de Saxe, c'etait le rendre indispensable.

Quand vous m'avez rencontré dans la rue, la veille de mon départ, je lui portais une seconde lettre de Zouboff,[46] je prêchai encore le chevalier, à la porte de la maison de Mde. Lanckaronska, et j'articulai les vilains mots des vilaines choses que les gazettes renouvelleraient en remontant à l'origine.

Si je l'avais déterminé à y renoncer, Scherbatoff ne serait point arrivé: et nous n'aurions à pleurer celui qui, par je ne sais quel sentiment, quel rapport invisible et inexplicable, fait plus mon malheur, dans ce moment cy, que jamais j'aurais pu le croire.

La sotte acceptation du défi de Gelgut, les mensonges que me fit Zouboff sur tout cela, ont rendu l'affaire du Chevalier indispensable. Il n'a eu malheureusement aucun tort: et Scherbatoff par son air de repentir de l'origine de cette malheureuse histoire, sa bonne contenance et ses regrets en disant que c'est à present qu'il est le plus malheureux des hommes et se jettant par terre, n'a que trop bien réparé les torts de ses quinze ans. Mais celui qui a songé à le faire arriver à bien à se reprocher. Quoique deux Gouvernemens ayent été informé des deux duels, je n'aime pas à nommer le second du Chevalier, contre qui la police sera [?], instruite de ce qui se passait à Vienne.

Mais je défie de s'être conduit dans tout ce qu'il a dit, fait et réglé avec plus de justice, de justesse, de trait, de raison, d'honneur, s'opposant à ce qu'on batte à 4 pas, disant que cela pouvait convenir à celui qui avait autrefois refusé de se battre, mais non au chevalier dont la réputation était faite.

Chacun d'eux, n'ayant qu'un pistole, puisqu'ensuite ils devaient se battre au sabre, et tirant à volonté, il est inouï qu'un coup parti à 17 ou 18 pas, fasse le malheur de nos jours.

D'autres détails me sont encore trop sensibles pour avoir la force de vous les mander. Hélas! Le Chevalier, en y allant, me serra la main, d'une manière a me faire trembler, moi superstitieux. Christine fondit en larmes. Le Chevalier n'était pas caressant, comme vous savez: ny caressable, car je n'ai jamais eu le plaisir de lui dire combien je l'aimais. Il fut si parlant, si gay toute la journée, qu'on aurait dit qu'il ne voulait pas se laisser aller à un pressentiment.

Le second, avec une force incroyable qu'il paya, sur le terrain, en se trouvant mal, après ... et depuis, par du crachement de sang, et un État de Malaise et de tristesse, cache toutes les craintes auxquelles il n'est pas porté. En voilà assez. Pour cette fois-cy que fera Gelgut? Où est allé Scherbatoff? S'est il arrêté à Vienne? Quand part Zouboff de Prague? pour où? Le chevalier, sur un mot, un regard de son second, ne l'ayant pas tué, et m'obéissant en lui donnant le coup de sabre précisément où je le lui ai dit, s'est couvert de gloire, finissant ensuite, sans souffrir, une existence dont il ne faisait pas grand cas, car sa famille la laissait trop équivoque,[47] pour qu'elle lui fut chère.

Je crois que vous partages notre situation. C'est pour cela que malgré moi je vous en parlai: et j'ai peut-être un espoir de consolation, en vous disant que je vous embrasse de tout mon coeur.

Teplitz ce 28 [June 1802]

19. To Hugh Eliot, British minister to the court of Saxony, undated[48]

S'il vous manque un Valet de Chambre, mon cher ami, et si vous voulez de moi, je vais tout de suite à votre Service. Mais si vous pensez comme l'ami du [illegible] que je ne sers pas bien; prenez je vous prie celui que je vous envoye. Il vous servira mieux que Pitt et Cobourg, et nos quatre [defeated Austrian Marshals] de l'Italie. Il ne vous fera pas de mic-mac. Si vous n'en avez pas besoin, vous me ferai le plus grand plaisir de le placer dans quelque bonne maison anglaise, car je m'y intéresse infiniment. C'est le frère de mon valet de chambre Angelo Molinari. Si vous le prenez, je serai, je crois, son envieux, moi qui ne le suis de personne: mais je sens si bien le bonheur de vous voir, sans cesse, qu'il est permis d'en être jaloux.

Ne soyez pas si aimable, ou si rare, Venez nous voir encore. Ce n'est que par hasard que je vous fais une déclaration. Mais jamais homme ne m'a autant inspiré l'envie de passer ma vie avec lui. Jamais on n'a réuni autant de choses distinguées, piquantes, neuves, bonnes, attrayantes et essentielles que l'aimable ministre que l'Angleterre a la bêtise de laisser à Dresde.

Nous allons avoir une nuée de doubles émigrés, assez *simples* pour croire que leurs projets toujours à demi conçus et leur indiscrétion ne les ferait point chasser. Je craignais bien qu'on n'en fit une S. Barthelemi et de Barthelemi[49] lui même. Voilà pour la vigilance et la modération insidieuse des démons français l'Europe à tous les diables: et le Rhin qui va se républicaniser comme le Po. Heureusement pour moi qui ne m'embarrasse pas plus des quatre parties du Monde qu'elles ne s'embarrassent de moi, je ne m'occupe que de mon plaisir, ramasse de tems en tems les débris de mon coeur et de mon tempérament, et ne parle qu'au très petit nombre de gens que j'aime, à la tête desquels vous êtes, mon cher mauvais voisin.

20. To Hugh Eliot [undated][50]

Vous n'avez jamais refusé aux femmes de leur faire plaisir. Celle que j'ai, et celles que je voudrais avoir veulent que vous veniez avec nous, en bateau, à Meissen. Nous avons besoin d'un Ministre d'une puissance maritime pour une pareille navigation. Bonjours, cher ancien ami, l'homme le plus aimable des 3 royaumes,[51] et tel que je n'en ai peu vu dans 3 empires et une demi douzaine de Républiques.

21. To Francis II[52]

Sire,

Je demande pardon à Votre Majesté Impériale de ce que mon zèle m'inspire pour le soumettre aux Lumières qu'elle a reçues de la Nature, ayant Toujours un sens si juste et si droit dans toutes ses affaires. J'ai tant de confiance en Votre Majesté que ce n'est pas à mon auguste souverain que j'adresse ce petit Mémoire; c'est au premier officier de son armée et au plus loyal Gentilhomme de son Empire. Ce sont ces deux Titres que je réclame pour que Votre Majesté ne dise à personne que j'ai pris cette Liberté, ne voulant pas avoir la réputation d'un homme à projet, qui cherche à se faire valoir, et qui pense plutôt à son bien qu'a celui de sa Patrie.

D'ailleurs, grâce aux bontés de Votre Majesté Impériale, je ne puis rien demander: mais mon Tendre attachement (si je puis me servir de ce terme) pour son auguste et Loyale personne m'a engagé à ces observations. Encore, ce n'est qu'en partant de Presbourg que j'ose les lui envoyer: car je serais embarrassé de les présenter moi-même à Votre Majesté.

Je voudrais qu'elle pût en oublier l'auteur: mais malheureusement, sire, Vous avez une mémoire que je n'ai vue à personne. Je réitère mes excuses, mes prières pour le secret et les assurances de ma reconnaissance, et de l'éternel et respectueux dévouement avec lequel je suis

De Votre Majesté Impériale

Le plus humble et le plus

obeisst. et le plus fidèle des sujets

Ligne

Presbourg Ce 4 Obre 1808

22. To Metternich[53]

Je Vous ordonne comme doyen, de ne pas me répondre. Je ne suis pas fâché d'avoir une bonne recrue dans mon corps,[54] où j'avais besoin de gens de mérite: et je vous embrasserai cher comte, ex officier, de tout mon coeur. De plus en plus je vous trouve votre beau grand père,[55] occupant bien sa place. Je voudrais que vous occupassiez son sallon de la même manière: c'est à dire que sans vous ennuyer et ruiner par de grands soupers, on peut s'y promener depuis le spectacle jusqu'à 11 heures qu'on s'en irait souper chez soi, ou qu'on vous verrait souper en Famille, pour sortir de chez Vous pour aller souper ailleurs.

Vous expédieries vos Ministres Étrangers, en vous promenant sans être accablé d'audiences longues et fatigantes le Matin. Point de thé ny de Tables de Jeu. Point l'air roide d'une assemblée. Vous n'auriez que la bonne compagnie qui irait Vous chercher et se chercher elle même. Et avec quelques grands diners tous les 15 jours, Vous expédieriez tous les ennuyeux.

Pas plus que 3 ou 4 personnes que ne se feroient pas annoncer viendraient diner avec vous s'ils y trouvaient place, sans un plat de plus, pour cela. Malgré la dépense et la bonne chère du bon, honnête et intéressant Stadion,[56] qu'on aimait avec raison, on s'ennuyait chez lui; et il faisait des mécontens. Père et Fils Kaunitz, Colloredo, et Starhemberg ont eu la toison ensemble: mais il n'y a que père et Fils Metternich qui auront les deux ordres.

Vous méritez tout, Vieux Prince Kaunitz, puisque grâce à vous je ne passerai plus la Scythe. Sans y être obligé,[57] je vous embrasse de tout mon coeur.

Ce dimanche matin. [1810]

23. To the Duke of Weimar[58]

Le papier bleu, Monseigneur, qui cet été se promène aussi à Vienne m'a fait le plus grand plaisir. Les bains de Teplitz entretiennent ma santé, parceque Votre Altesse Sérénissime vient l'y chercher, et que j'ai toujours besoin de la voir. Comme vous êtes, Monseigneur, le Meilleur garçon Libraire qu'il y ait, je prends la liberté de Vous envoyer ces 5 volumes pour en faire imprimer un de ce que j'ai marqué. Les substituts de Votre Altesse Sérénissime, mon ancien Brigadier Muffling, et Mr. de Rull, l'aideroit. Comme ce sont des Fragments, il faudrait les mettre à linéa comme par exemple au 1er tôme.

Le 18 juin 1757 nous passâmes, etc, et puis, ce qui va jusqu'aux derniers mots *pas accoutumés* et puis *le 16 août nos Grands gardes* ainsi du reste: pour faire voir que ce sont des fragments qui n'ont aucune liaison.

Ces Messieurs à qui je me recommande verront bien d'abord pour le sens, et puis pour une lettre de l'Alphabet où l'article commence et finit, par exemple d'un A, à un autre A ainsi du reste comme [illegible word] Ligne qui est a côté. Ce qui m'engage Monseigneur à vous prier de vous charger de cela, c'est Votre goût pour les crimes de Faux, en Mensonges, signatures etc…

J'espère que les Cornes ne feront pas peur à V. A. S. et que ce ne sera pas de mauvais augure pour la noce. J'aurois voulu que c'en eût été une autrichienne, car il n'y a quelles. Vous savez tous les genres de mérite de la Princesse. Je ne crains pour la Vertu que l'usurpateur catholique chef de votre maison[59] dont les moeurs devenant corrompues à Paris et à Varsovie lui font faire des entreprises à ce qu'on dit sur toutes ses parentes.

Il faudra alors, Monseigneur, que vous vous en vengiez sur son épouse si elle d'a [*sic*] son pannier.

Nous avons légitimé Titine qui au lieu du nom de sa mère qui en avoit 2 ou 3 s'appelle Mademoiselle de Ligne, mais toujours Titine pour ceux qui ont de l'amité pour elle.

Si votre imprimeur gagne trop d'argent avec mes mensonges, Monseigneur, je prie encore que ce petit profit de son édition soit pour les veuves et les Enfans des Héros Weymariens d'Espagne,[60] quoique leurs Prières Luthériennes m'eloigneront du Paradis plutôt que de m'y faire entrer. Il n'y a pas là de Confédération pour les hérétiques. S. A. Royale de Constance, Erfurt, Mayence, et Francfort[61] n'a pas fait de concordat avec S. Pierre. Il vaut mieux être battu et se sauver.

Étudiez bien Monseigneur, avec mes deux autres Protecteurs, Mers de Muffling et de Rull, Votre Leçon du Commencement de ma Lettre. Épousés, Faites Épouser, et puis venez recevoir à l'Englische Gruss, les Tendresses Respectueuses de Celui qui de Vos pieds se jettera dans Vos Bras si V. A. S. le permet à l'homme qui l'aime le plus. Teplitz ce 12 juin 1810. La petite avocate arrive et veut voir vos pieds, [two words illegible] pour Vous juger. Nous avons déjà bien parlé de V. A. S.

24. To the Duc d'Arenberg, Vienna, 23 January 1813

[Arrived in Paris on 11 February[62]]
Copy

Je suis si penetré de reconnoissance, mon cher, et bien cher Duc![63] de ce que vous avez bien voulu me faire dire par le Prince Auguste[64] qu'il m'est impossible de ne pas vous le témoigner. Si la paix se fait cet hiver j'irai sûrement au printems que mon service de Capitaine des Gardes finit, voir mon bon Louis.[65]

J'en sens un besoin extrême, car son état me fait une peine que je ne puis exprimer. Je ne pourrai pas profiter de votre aimable obligeance. Tous mes souvenirs de Bruxelles, l'hôtel d'Arenberg, où nous avons été tous si heureux, celui que j'ai perdu,[66] Vos jolis petits entresols offerts avec tant de grâces, me feroient trop de peine. J'en aurai bien à vaincre mes souvenirs de Beloeil; mais il le faut absolument pour soulager mon coeur. C'est moi, cher Duc, qui vous prie à genoux d'y venir, pendant le mois que je voudrai y passer dès que les circonstances le permettront.

Quel plaisir de vous serrer contre mon coeur tout de suite après mon cher Louis! Ce ne sera pas sans une arosée de larmes, en me rappellant sa jolie et brillante carrière, et les pertes déchirantes que vous et moi nous avons faites. Pourquoi cette sotte petite flamande, à t-elle été lui faire de la peine, à ce brave Louis ? Ne pourrait-il donc pas essayer encore quelques bains? On en connait en Suisse d'extrèmement salutaires, dit-on; je suis bien heureux d'avoir ici le Prince Auguste; mais j'ai été bien inquiet du sort des Princes Prosper et Pierre. Mettez moi aux pieds de Mme la Duchesse. Si elle ne pourroit pas venir à Beloeil, j'irai pour quelques heures à Bruxelles, seulement pour jouir du bonheur de l'admirer. Vos deux santés m'intéressent bien, et sont heureusement bien rassurantes, j'en demande toujours des nouvelles. Voilà nos deux maisons qui tiennent à bien peu de chose. Donnez vous des petits fils, cher Duc: et redevenez heureux en famille, quel bonheur ne meritez vous pas par votre belle âme!

Mes occupations dans mon lit, jusqu'à 3 heures, mes 4 filles, compris la Comtesse Maurice Odonel me font passer une Vie bien douce. Quelquefois de superbes chasses, quelques spectacles de societé, où je suis toujours grondé, des ballets lorsque Duport y danse, y ajoutent des agrémens. Un fier appetit, une bouteille de Vin de Champagne entière, lorsque, par hazard, je dine ailleurs; Tout cela me fait plaisir aussi. Mais le plus grand sera de vous revoir, cher Duc! et mon Louis, et de vous dire que mon tendre attachement est et sera toujours le même jusqu'à la fin de mes jours.

25. To Metternich[67]

Qu'est ce que les affaires de l'Europe en Comparaison de celles de mon Coeur. Comme je ne compte plus être aimé de cette partie du Monde, et comme l'Asie vient de remplacer l'Amérique que j'ai perdue; en grâce, cher comte, glisses ce petit Mémoire dans la poche de quelque Prince ou Duc pour celui dont j'aime le Consulat dans la personne de la Grecque sa toute belle Épouse.[68]

Votre chancellerie d'État croit sûrement que Cecy est d'importance, et elle aura raison. Pour achever notre Conversation interrompue l'autre jour par la Maitresse de la Maison, non, de son humeur, je vous dirai que je suis Sûr de la Continuation de la bonne Attitude que nous avons, et qu'après avoir conservé l'existence de notre Monarchie, vous trouverez moyen de l'améliorer.

Vous savez, mon Excellent Excellence, combien j'aime vos succès, et Votre Très aimable Personne
ce Jeudi [October or November 1814]

Notes

CHAPTER I *Beloeil*

1. See Pierre Mouriau de Meulenacker, 'Les princes de Ligne marquis de Mouy', *Nouvelles Annales Prince de Ligne* (hereafter referred to as *NAPL*), XIII, 2001, 7–132.

2. Félicien Leuridant, *Une éducation de Prince au XVIIIe siècle*, 1923, 14n; cf. *Annales Prince de Ligne* (henceforward referred to as *APL*), V, 1924, Frederick William III of Prussia to Ligne, 29 August 1810, beginning *Cher cousin*; ibid., XIII, 1932, p. 82, Charles-Theodore Elector of Bavaria to *Monsieur mon Cousin!*, 11 August 1783.

3. Prince de Ligne, *Fragments de l'histoire de ma vie*, 2 vols., ed. Jeroom Vercruysse, 2000–2001 (hereafter referred to as *Fragments*), I, 116.

4. Jeroom Vercruysse, 'L' éducation du Prince de Ligne', *NAPL*, 2001, XIII, 136.

5. *Fragments*, II, 349. In addition the Lignes had claims to the Kingdom of Naples and the Duchy of Lorraine.

6. *Fragments*, I, 50–1, 56.

7. University of Ghent, Archives, Vandenbroucke papers (hereafter referred to as Ghent), 1777 (2), *Plan de direction que présente l'Intendant Vandenbroucke à S.A. Monseigneur le Prince de Ligne relativement aux affaires de sa Maison.*

8. Ligne, *Mémoires*, 1914, pp. 3–4; *Fragments*, I, 90; Leuridant, *Une Education de Prince au XVIIIe siècle*, pp. 10–11.

9. *Fragments*, I, 156 and n.

10. *Fragments*, I, 88; P. J. Goyens, 'L'oncle mystérieux', *APL*, VII, 1926, pp. 75–84.

11. Prince de Ligne, *Nouveau Recueil de Lettres*, 1926 edn, p. 144.

12. Basil Guy, 'Le Prince et le Maréchal: Ligne et les Rêveries du Maréchal de Saxe', *NAPL*, I, 1986, 20.

13. *Fragments*, I, 54, 59.

14. *Fragments*, I, 91; Paul W. Schroeder, *The Transformation of European Politics 1763–1848*, Oxford, 1994, viii, 28.

15. Leuridant, *Education*, pp. 37, 47; *Fragments*, I, 116n.; Prince de Ligne, *Mélanges Militaires, Littéraires et Sentimentaires*, 34 vols., Dresden, 1795–1811 (hereafter referred to as *Melanges*), X, 3.

16. *Fragments*, I, 91.

17. *Fragments*, I, 213.

18. René Pomeau, *L'Europe des Lumières. Cosmopolitisme et unité européenne au siècle des Lumières*, 1991 edn, pp. 60, 81; and Rivarol, *Discours de l'Universalité de la langue française*, 1991 edn, passim.

19. Quoted in Prince de Ligne, *Lettres à Eugénie sur les Spectacles*, ed. Gustave Charlier, 1922, p. vi.

20. Leuridant, *Education*, passim and p. 17; Jeroom Vercruysse, 'Le petit Charles Joseph de Ligne et son précepteur indélicat l'abbé du Verdier', *NAPL*, XIII, 1999, pp. 141, 151.

21. *Fragments*, I, 52–4; Leuridant, *Education*, pp. 29, 48–9.

22. *Fragments*, I, 55; *NAPL*, VIII, 35.

23. Leuridant, *Education*, pp. 52, 60; *Fragments*, I, 101; talk by Marc Fumaroli, Ecole Normale Supérieure, Paris, 3 July 2001.

24. Leuridant, *Education*, pp. 40–2.

25. *Fragments*, I, 48–9; Leuridant, *La Bibliothèque du Prince de Ligne*, Brussels, n.d., p. 18.

26. See catalogue on *Charles-Alexandre de Lorraine*, 2 vols., Brussels, 1987.

27. Bibliothèque de l'Institut Mss 1651, Journal du Duc de Croÿ, November 1753, 20 September, 15 November 1754.

28. Freidrich Heer, *The Holy Roman Empire*, 1968, p. 116.

29. Frederick II, *Mémoires pour servir à l'Histoire de la Maison de Brandenbourg*, 3 vols., Berlin, 1758, II, 20.

30. *Mélanges*, XXVII, 71.

31. *Fragments*, I, 81.

CHAPTER 2 *Austria*

1. Ligne, *En marge des rêveries du maréchal de Saxe*, 1919, pp. 5, 65; *Mélanges*, X, 230.

2. Victor-L. Tapié, *L'Europe de Marie-Thérèse*, 1973, p. 105; cf. Ligne, *Mémoires et Mélanges*, 5 vols. 1829, V, 136.

3. Tapié, *L'Europe de Marie-Thérèse*, p. 21.

4. Derek Beales, *Joseph II*, I, 'In the Shadow of Maria Theresa', 2 vols., 1987.

5. A. J. P. Taylor, *The Habsburg Monarchy*, 1970 edn, p. 12.

6. M. Gachard, *Etudes et Notices historiques concernant les Pays-Bas*, 3 vols., Brussels, 1890, III, 348–9; Leuridant, *Education*, p. 16.

7. Leuridant, *Education*, 7; *Fragments*, I, 49n. His other names were François – probably after the Emperor's son-in-law Francis Duke of Lorraine; the Ligne family name of Lamoral; and, probably after his mother Elizabeth Alexandrina, Alexis.

8. Sir Robert Murray Keith, *Memoirs*, 2 vols., 1849, II, 165, 180: Duke of Montagu to Sir Robert Murray Keith, 6 September 1783, Keith to Sir Andrew Drummond, 27 September 1780.

9. *Mélanges*, X, 230, 'Mémoire sur Vienne'.

10. Vera Oravetz, *Les impressions françaises de Vienne (1567–1850)*, Szeged, 1930, 11, 21.

11. M. de Guibert, *Journal de Mon Voyage en Allemagne*, 2 vols., 1803, I, 290.

12. *Fragments*, I, 60.

13. *Maria-Theresa*, exhibition catalogue, Schönbrunn, 1980, 97.

14. Vienna Haus-, Hof- and Staatsarchiv (henceforward referred to as HHSA), Diary of Count von Zinzendorf (henceforward referred to as Zinzendorf), 5 July 1763.

15. W. H. Bruford, *Germany in the Eighteenth Century: the Social background of the Literary Revival*, Cambridge, 1965, p. 80; *Mélanges*, XIII, 398.

16. Lady Mary Coke, *Letters and Journals*, 4 vols., 1970, III, 329–30, 30 November 1770; Zinzendorf, 9 April 1773, 29 November 1770.

17. *Fragments*, I, 134.

18. J. F. Marmontel, *Mémoires*, 4 vols., 1804, II, 10.

19. Michael Levey, *The Life and Death of Mozart*, 1988 edn, pp. 37, 90, 164–5.

20. Nathaniel Williem Wraxall, *Memoirs of the Courts of Berlin, Dresden, Warsaw and Vienna in the Years 1777, 1778 and 1779*, 2 vols., 1799, II, 331.

21. *Fragments*, I, 70, 87, 90.

22. *Fragments*, I, 53.

23. *Fragments*, I, 87.

24. *Fragments*, I, 70.

25. Institut Mss., 1650, Croÿ, Journal, 16 November 1755.

26. Coke, IV, 25, 8 February 1772.

27. *Mélanges*, V, vi.

28. *Mélanges*, XXVIII, passim.

29. Coke, III, 322, 17 November 1770.

30. Michael Kelly, *Reminiscences*, 2nd edn, 2 vols., 1826, I, 218; Guibert, II, 8, 19 July 1773.

31. Nathaniel William Wraxall, *Memoirs of the Courts of Berlin, Dresden, Warsaw and Vienna in the Years 1777, 1778 and 1779*, 3rd edn, 1806, II, 139, 257.

32. Ligne, *Préjugés Militaires*, 2 vols., 1780, I, 150.

33. Earl of Chesterfield, *Letters to His Son*, 4 vols., III, 6 June 1751.

34. *Mélanges*, XIII, 22, 45; XX, 92.

35. *Mémoires et Mélanges*, V, 205.

36. *Mélanges*, XII, 347.

37. *Mélanges*, XIX, 28.

38. *Mélanges*, II, 42–3.

39. Ligne, *Mémoires et Mélanges*, V, 136; Tapié, *L'Europe de Marie-Thérèse*, pp. 47, 58, 75–6.

40. *Fragments*, I, 119.

41. Christopher Duffy, *The Army of Maria Theresa*, 1977, 43–4; cf. A. von Arneth ed., *Maria Theresia und Joseph II. Ihre correspondenz*, 3 vols., 1867, II, 104, Joseph to Leopold, 1 January 1776.

42. M. S. Anderson, *War and Society in Europe of the Old Regime 1618–1789*, 1988, p. 160.

43. Vicomte Charles Terlinden, 'Le Prince de Ligne et les grandes guerres de son temps', *APL*, XVI, 1935, 183.

44. *Fragments*, I, 91.

45. *Fragments*, II, 21.

46. Château d'Antoing, manuscripts (henceforward referred to as Antoing), *Mes Livres rouges*, IX (4), 'Je regrette bien une journée où je n'ai ni lu ni écrit'.

47. *Mélanges*, IV, 215–16; Pierre Mouriau de Meulenaker, 'Le prince de Ligne et les mémoires du Comte de Bussy-Rabutin', *NAPL*, IX, 86, 98.

48. Duffy, p. 13.

49. *Mélanges*, XIV, 59.

50. *Mélanges*, XIV, 23, 47, 'Mon Journal de la Guerre de Sept Ans, Campagne de 1757 et 1758'.

51. *Mélanges*, XIV, 45–6.

52. *Mémoires*, 42–3.

53. Tapié, p. 161.

54. *Fragments Militaires*, II, 182.

55. Terlinden, p. 184.

56. Lt-Gen. Baron Guillaume, *Histoire des Régiments nationaux des Pays Bas au Service d'Autriche*, Brussels, 1877, pp. 49, 74–6; *Fragments*, I, 71.

57. *Fragments*, I, 73.

58. Tony Sharp, *Pleasure and Ambition. The Life, Loves and Wars of Augustus the Strong*, 2001, p. 219.

59. *Fragments*, I, 86.

60. R. Waddington, *La Guerre de Sept Ans*, 5 vols., 1899, III, 233, 238; IV, 102; *Mélanges*, XV, 98.

61. *Mélanges*, XXVII, 79; XIX, 117; *Fragments*, I, 82, 147–8.

62. *Mélanges*, XVI, 50; IV, 102; Budapest, Hungarian National Archive, 1808 Autobiography.

63. *Mélanges*, XVI, 46–7; XIV, 33; XV, 170.

64. *Mélanges*, XXVIII, 59.

65. *Fragments*, I, 144.

66. Zinzendorf, 17 June 1763.

67. *Fragments*, I, 110; HHSA; Zinzendorf, 14 October 1766, 17 June 1763.

68. There were so many foreign princes in the Austrian army that at the manoeuvres of 1770, when Ligne presented one after the other to Frederick II, the King exclaimed: 'Comment! Encore?': *Mémoire sur le roi de Prusse Frederic le Grand*, by Mgr. le P. de L****. Berlin, 1789, 22.

69. M. Hochedlinger, 'The Militarisation of the Habsburg Monarchy 1740–1790', talk given at the Institute of Historical Research, London, 27 May 2002.

70. HHSA, Nachlass Lacy, Lacy to Ligne, 24 November 1769, 25 June 1770.

71. HHSA, Nachlass Lacy, Lacy to Ligne, 27 December 1768, 18 September 1769.

72. *Préjugés Militaires*, I, 1, 57.

73. Johannes Willms, 'Mes mémoires de guerre de 1757 à 1762', *NAPL*, VI, 1991, 59.

74. HHSA, Nachlass Lacy, Lacy to Ligne, 13 July 1763.

CHAPTER 3 *The Republic of Letters*

1. Elizabeth L. Eisenstein, *Grub Street Abroad. Aspects of the French Cosmopolitan Press from the Age of Louis XIV to the French Revolution*, Oxford, 1992, pp. 1, 17; Dena Goodman, *The Republic of Letters. A Cultural History of the French Enlightenment*, Ithaca, 1994, passim.

2. *Fragments*, I, 66; Ligne, *Amabile suivi de quelques portraits*, ed. Jeroom Vercruysse, 1996, p. 58.

3. *Amabile*, p. 18.

4. Raymond Trousson, 'Ligne, Voltaire et Rousseau', in *Bulletin de l'Académie royale de langue et de littérature françaises*, Bruxelles, 1985, 194, 203; Frederick A. Pottle, *Boswell on the Grand Tour*, 1953, 273–96, 24–29 December 1764; *Mélanges*, X, 257–68, 'Mes conversations avec M. de Voltaire'.

5. Theodore C. Besterman, ed., *Correspondance de Voltaire*, 51 vols., 1968–1977, XXVII, 69, 230, Ligne to Voltaire, 29 November 1763, 18 February 1764; XXX, 250, Ligne to Voltaire, 1 June 1766; XXXII, 180, id. to id., 30 June 1767.

6. Besterman, XXXIV, 146, Ligne to Voltaire, 20 November 1768.

7. Basil Guy, *Oeuvres choisies du Prince de Ligne*, Saratoga, 1978, p. 230.

8. Roger Chartier, *Les origines culturelles de la Révolution française*, 2000 edn, pp. 85–6.

9. *Mélanges*, X, 268–77, 'Mes Conversations avec Jean-Jacques'.

10. *Mélanges*, XXVII, 70; Rousseau, *Correspondance Complète*, XXXVIII, 48.

11. For the date of these notebooks, which are in the Château d'Antoing, see *Mes livres rouges*, vol. X, 274, which refers to September 1768; for his habit of writing *en courant la poste*, see X, 254; for his hopes of success, X, 130. He wrote his accounts of campaigns in *Mes livres jaunes* and his meditations on war in *Mes livres verts*, since lost; Johannes Willms, 'Mes mémoires de guerre de 1757 à 1762,' *NAPL*, VI, 1991, 51.

12. Roland Mortier, 'La littérature de la langue française', in *La Belgique Autrichienne*, Brussels, 1987, p. 286.

13. *Mes livres rouges*, X, 119, 206; IX, 347.

14. *Mélanges*, XII, 67; cf. *Oeuvres Légères*, 2 vols., n.d., II, 33.

15. *Mes livres rouges*, IX, 64.

16. Cf. Michael Hunter and David Wootton, eds., *Atheism from the Reformation to the Enlightenment*, Oxford, 1992 edn, pp. 183–4.

17. Besterman, XXXII, 213, Voltaire to Ligne, 17 July 1767.

18. *Mes livres rouges*, X, 50, 78, 82, 244; IX, 100, 348.

19. *Mes livres rouges*, IX, 34, 104, 134.

20. Leuridant, *Education*, p. 11.

21. Ghent, 1777 (2), *Plan de direction que présente l'Intendant Vandenbroucke à S. A. Monseigneur le Prince de Ligne relativement aux affaires de sa Maison*.

22. Archives du château de Beloeil, *Payements faits aux officiers et livrée de la Maison*, 1771–3.

23. *Mes livres rouges*, IX 20, 21, 130. In a later paragraph he claims that hair-dressers 'y sont extrèmement portés', and that, outside England, 'les petits garçons attaquent prèsque partout ailleurs la pudeur': XI, 108.

24. Cf. *Mes livres rouges*, IX (25): 'Frottement par frottement la main qui fait venir vers les organes de la géneration la liqueur seminale n'est pas plus nuisible que ce qui est destiné à la recevoir.'

25. *Fragments*, I, 58.

26. The volumes of *vers de société* and the texts of *supplément à Apprius* and *Les Deux Amis* are among the manuscripts at the Château d'Antoing. The only contemporary equivalent was the recently discovered *Histoire des deux amis* by William Beckford, first published 2003 in *Vathek et ses épisodes*, ed. Didier Girard.

27. Besterman, XXXII, 180, Ligne to Voltaire, 30 June 1767.

28. *Préjugés Militaires*, I, 153, *Mélanges*, XI, 4, 21.

29. André Delcourt, *Le Duc de Croÿ*, 1983, p. 235; Zinzendorf, 3 January 1770.

30. Prince de Ligne, *Lettres à Eugénie sur les spectacles*, 1922 edn, p. xxxvii.

31. Zinzendorf, 3, 31 March 1773; Marthe Oulié, *Le Prince de Ligne*, 1926, p. 61.

32. *Mélanges*, XI, 4.

33. Leuridant, *Lettres et Billets inédits du prince de Ligne et ses familiers*, Brussels, 1956, p. 94; Bruno Colson, 'Les lectures militaires de Charles-Joseph de Ligne d'après le catalogue raisonné de sa bibliothèque', *NAPL*, XIV, 31.

34. Pierre Mouriau de Meulenaker, 'Le Prince de Ligne et les mémoires du Comte de Bussy-Rabutin', *NAPL*, IX, 79–147.

35. Jeroom Vercruysse, 'L'histoire de Préjugés et Fantaisies Militaires. Le Prince écrivain, l'illustrateur, et les imprimeurs', *NAPL*, I, 1986, 72, 86, 91, 96.

36. *Préjugés Militaires*, I, 149; II, 6.

37. *Préjugés Militaires*, II, 51.

38. For general discussions of Ligne and gardens, see Monique Mosser's essay on 'Paradox in the Garden', in *The History of Garden Design: The Western Tradition from the Renaissance to the Present Day*, (1991), ed. Monique Mosser and Georges Teyssot, pp. 263–81; and Basil Guy, ed., *Coup d'oeil at Beloeil and a Great Number of European Gardens*, Berkeley, 1991, pp. 1–70.

39. W. S. Lewis, ed., *Horace Walpole's Correspondence*, III, 333n.

40. Besterman, XXXII, 374–6, Ligne to Voltaire, October 1767; *Mélanges*, XIII, 359.

41. Guy, pp. 158, 162–4.

42. Zinzendorf, 10 November 1770; Frederic Hayez, Jeroom Vercruysse, 'L'imprimerie privée des princes de Ligne au XVIIIe siècle', *NAPL*, II, 1987, pp. 9, 25, 44, 47; Charles intended to print a copy of *Coup d'oeil sur Beloeil* for Catherine II with his own hands: Lucien Perey, *Figures du Temps Passé*, 1900, p. 114, Ligne to Catherine II, 15 February 1781.

43. Guy, pp. 153, 193, 217.

44. Guy, p. 267.

45. Guy, pp. 265–6.

46. Guy, p. 202.

47. *Coup d'Oeil*, ed. Ganay, p. 204.

48. Guy, p. 218.

49. Guy, pp. 128–9, 252–3, 259–61.

50. Guy, pp. 73–5.

CHAPTER 4 *Paris*

1. *Fragments*, II, 93.

2. *APL*, 1923, p. 178, Lacy to Ligne, 22 January 1766; cf. Lacy to Ligne, 8 March 1768, 13 February 1773; he finally obtained it through Marshal Lacy in 1772. Also: Maria Theresa, *Briefe an Ihre Kinder*, IV, 385, Maria Theresa to Marshal Lacy, 30 November 1771. The first Ligne to obtain the Golden Fleece was Jean IV, in 1481.

3. Prince de Ligne, *Amabile suivi de quelques portraits*, ed. Jeroom Vercruysse, 1996, p. 18; HHSA, Ligne to Mercy, 1 September ?1770; *Fragments*, I, 295.

4. *Fragments*, I, 204, 244; Mouriau de Meulenaker, p. 59.

5. Arneth and Geffroy, III, 10, Mercy to Maria Theresa, 17 January 1777; HHSA, NL, Lacy to Ligne, 27 December 1768, 28 April 1771, 14 June 1773; *APL*, V, 1924, p. 30, Lacy to Ligne, 23 December 1778.

6. Lord Byron, *Letters and Journals*, IX, 78, letter of 12 December 1821.

7. *Fragments*, I, 204; Daniel Acke, *Les cosmopolitismes du prince de Ligne*, *NAPL*, VIII, 65.

8. Archives du château de Beloeil, *Payements faits aux officiers et livrée de la Maison*, 1771–3.

9. *Fragments*, I, 126.

10. Stanislas Auguste Poniatowski, *Mémoires*, 2 vols., St Petersburg, I, 97.

11. Pomeau, pp. 225–6.

12. Earl of Bessborough, *Lady Bessborough and her Family Circle*, pp. 18–19, journal of Lady Harriet Spencer, 3 August 1772; Guy, p. 181.

13. *NAPL*, XII, 12.

14. Ligne, *Mémoires et Mélanges*, V, 412; Zinzendorf, 14 October 1766, 17 June 1763.

15. *Préjugés Militaires*, I, 5.

16. Comte d'Escars, *Mémoires*, 2 vols., 1890, II, 150; Baronne d'Oberkirch, *Mémoires*, 1970 edn, p. 239.

17. *Fragments*, II, 374, 425; Marquis de Bombelles, *Journal*, I, Geneva 1977, 180, 14 December 1782.

18. *Mémoire sur le Roi de Prusse Frédéric le Grand par Msgr. le P. de L.*****, Berlin, 1789, p. 6.

19. *Mémoires*, p. 47; Zinzendorf, 10 November 1770, 11 January 1770.

20. HHSA, NL.

21. M. Risbeck, *Lettres sur l'allemagne*, Vienna, 1787, p. 262; *Fragments*, I, 295; Zinzendorf, 27 April 1770.

22. *Mélanges*, XXVII, 66.

23. M. de Stassart, *La Collection d'Autographes*, Brussels, 1879, p. 109; O. Uzanne, *Contes du Chevalier de Boufflers*, 1878, p. ixn.

24. Antoing, *Histoire trop véritable*, f. 4.

25. *Fragments*, I, 112–13.

26. Zinzendorf, 29 December 1766, 13 July 1769; Ghent, 1778, Cattoir to Vandenbroucke, 10 July 1778.

27. Comte Fédor Golovkine, *La Cour et le règne de Paul Ier*, 1905, p. 218.

28. Brno, Czech Republic, Statni Oblastni Archiv, Kaunitz Papers, Ligne to Prince Kaunitz, 9 October 1767; cf. Zinzendorf, 16 February 1794, for a reference to the Princess's relationship with Flemming.

29. Zinzendorf, 4 January 1767; Ghent, 1774, Abbé Villette to Vandenbroucke, February 1774; *Fragments*, I, 261.

30. *Fragments*, I, 195.

31. Prince de Ligne, *Oeuvres Romanesques*, ed. Roland Mortier and Manuel Couvreur, I, 2000, pp. 33, 87n., 91n., 98n.

32. Risbeck, p. 261; Erica-Marie Benabou, *La Prostitution et la Police des Moeurs au XVIIIe Siècle*, 1987, p. 265.

33. *Oeuvres Légères*, I, 101; *Fragments*, I, 147.

34. Manuel Couvreur, ed., *Le Grand Théâtre au XVIIIIe Siècle*, Brussels, 1997, p. 222.

35. *Fragments*, II, 421–2; Bachaumont, X, 275, 9 November 1777; *Mélanges*, XXVII, 31.

36. André Britsch, *La jeunesse de Philippe Egalité (1747–1785)*, 1926, p. 17; *Mélanges*, XXVII, 95; Mme de Genlis, *Mémoires inédits*, 8 vols., 1825, III, 3.

37. Pomeau, pp. 220–24.

38. Leuridant, 1919, p. 33n.; *Fragments*, I, 227n.–9.

39. *Fragments*, II, 23; *Mélanges*, VII, 7n.

40. *Mes livres rouges*, X, 24.

41. *Fragments*, II, 290.

42. *Fragments*, I, 147; *Mélanges*, XXVII, 47–9.

43. G. Capon et R. Yve-Plessis, *Vie Priveé du Prince de Conty*, 1907, pp. 263, 287–9.

44. *Mélanges*, XXVII, 49.

45. Paul Morand, *Le Prince de Ligne*, 1964, p. 181; *Fragments*, I, 138.

46. *Mélanges*, XXVII, 22; cf. Zinzendorf, 15 April 1767, 'Diné chez Madame Geoffrin avec le Prince de Ligne'.

47. W. S. Lewis, ed., *Horace Walpole's Correspondence*, III, 333, Du Deffand to Walpole, 3 August 1767; cf. IV, 434, id. to id., 15 July 1770.

48. Benedetta Craveri, *Madame du Deffand et son monde*, 1987, p. 349; *Mélanges*, XXVII, 73.

49. *Mélanges*, XXVII, 7, 65, 253; *Fragments*, II, 364.

50. Ghent, 1774, Théaulon to Vandenbroucke, 3 May 1774; Guy, p. 86; Jean Stern, *A l'Ombre de Sophie Arnould*, 2 vols., 1930, I, 32–4; *Mémoires*, p. 84.

51. *Mélanges*, VIII, 22–31; Guy, pp. 81–4, 90–3.

52. *APL*, X, 1929, Journal, p. 30, letter of 9 November 1775; Ghent, 1775, Tiroux to Vandenbroucke, 9 November 1775.

53. Stern, I, 32–3.

54. Ghent, 1775, Ligne to Vandenbroucke, July 1775; Albert of Saxe-Teschen, *Journal*, September 1781, kindly communicated by Professor Derek Beales.

55. Leuridant, pp. 5, 31; cf. Ghent, 1778, Ligne to Vandenbroucke, 4 April 1778.

56. *APL*, X, 1929, 115–16.

57. *APL*, II, 1921, 227–9, 'Les deux châteaux'; Bibliothèque Royale de Belgique Mss, Sauveur Legros, Mes Babioles, f. 47, and f. 211 for Ligne's verses in praise of Legros written at Beloeil on 22 August 1791; N. Loumayeur, *Sauveur Legros*, Brussels, 1856, passim.

58. *APL*, X, 1929, pp. 104, 168, 177.

59. Gallerie Beloeilloise, Brussels, 1932, pp. 42–4; *APL*, XII, 1931, p. 119.

60. Jean-Philippe van Aelbrouck, 'Quelques notes sur Angélique d'Hannetaire, muse du prince de Ligne', *NAPL*, XIV, 145–58.

61. *APL*, X, 1929, 62, 64, 170; Guy, *Oeuvres Choisies*, pp. 102–9.

62. Couvreur, pp. 224–5.

63. *APL*, 1929, pp. 26, 79; Ghent, 1778, Leygeb to Vandenbroucke, 14 April 1778, Ligne to Vandenbroucke, 30 May 1778.

64. *Fragments*, I, 125.

65. *Fragments*, II, 261.

66. *Mémoires*, p. 81; *Fragments*, I, 81.

67. Ghent, 1779, Leygeb to Vandenbroucke, 30 December 1779, for Ligne's supper parties; and Charles de Lorraine, *Journal secret*, Brussels, 2000, pp. 89, 136, 296, 310, 1 January 1768, 30 March 1769, 8 January, 9 June 1774; *Fragments*, I, 107; for other stories of Ligne's constant lateness, see e.g. Zinzendorf, 17 May 1770, 7 December 1772.

68. Couvreur, p. 200; *APL*, V, 1924, p. 32, Lacy to Ligne, 31 August 1779.

69. *Mélanges*, XXVI, 303; XXVIII, 42; *APL*, VII, 1926, p. 7.

70. *Fragments*, II, 164.

71. Ghent, 1769–71, Cattoir to Vandenbroucke, 10, 13 July 1771.

72. *Fragments*, II, 163.

73. *Fragments*, II, 222; Prince de Ligne, *Lettres Inédites*, Brussels, 1878, p. 24.

CHAPTER 5 *Versailles*

1. Ghent, 1772, Théaulon to Vandenbroucke, 11 April, 1 May 1772.

2. Archives du château de Beloeil, *Premier Chapitre de Recette*, 1771.

3. Leuridant, 1919, pp. 40–42, Ligne to Vandenbroucke, March 1772.

4. Stern, I, 22–5; AN (Archives Nationales, Paris), T 582, 1, Papers of M. Théaulon, banker, letters of 12 June, 6 August 1773 from Belanger to Vandenbroucke.

5. *APL*, 1929, 170; Guy, pp. 102–9.

6. AN, T 582, 2, 1774–7.

7. Leuridant, 1919, p. 37; AN, T 582, 2, letter of 15 October 1773 to Mercy-Argenteau, and T 582, 3, *Affaire de m. le Prince de Ligne*; Hampshire Public Record Office, Malmesbury Papers, Ligne to Lord Malmesbury, 28 October 1780.

8. Ligne called Du Barry *le plus honnête et le meilleur des hommes*, and himself *quelqu'un qui vois est attaché de tout son coeur depuis longtemps*: Ghent, 1774 (2), f. 81, Ligne to du Barry, ?October 1774.

9. Hubert Cole, *First Gentleman of the Bedchamber*, New York, 1965, pp. 243–5.

10. Claude Saint-André, *Madame du Barry*, 1909, p. 121.

11. Ghent, 1769–1771, Théaulon to Vandenbroucke, 19 February 1772.

12. *Mélanges*, XXIX, 269.

13. Institut Mss, Croÿ, III, 92–3, May 1774.

14. *Fragments*, I, 109.

15. Ghent, 1774, Villette to Vandenbroucke, 9 May 1774, announcing Ligne's departure the day before; Besterman, XLI, 36, Ligne to Voltaire, June/July 1774.

16. Ligne, *Nouveau Recueil de Lettres*, ed. Henri Lebasteur, 1928 (henceforward referred to as *NRL*), p. 336.

17. Ligne, *Lettres à la Marquise de Coigny* (henceforward referred to as *Coigny*), 1914, p. 49.

18. *Fragments*, II, 170.

19. *APL*, 1929, X, 106.

20. *Fragments*, I, 151; *Coigny*, p. 50.

21. Ghent, 1776, Théaulon to Vandenbroucke, 20 August 1776; A. von Arneth and M. Geffroy, eds., *Correspondance entre Marie-Thérèse et le Comte de Mercy-Argenteau*, 3 vols., 2nd edn, 1874–5, II, 493, 529–30, Mercy-Argenteau to Maria Theresa, 17 September, 15 November 1776; A. von Arneth, ed., *Maria Theresa und Marie Antoinette. Ihr Briefwechsel*, 1865, p. 176, letter of 14 September 1776.

22. *Fragments*, I, 177; *Mélanges*, XXVII, 32.

23. *Mémoires*, p. 240; *Joseph II und Leopold*, 2 vols., 1872, II, 130, Joseph II to Leopold, 29 April 1777.

24. *Fragments*, I, 193.

25. *Mémoires*, p. 55; *Fragments*, II, 69; *Mélanges*, XXVII, 37.

26. Arneth and Geffroy, II, 493, Mercy to Maria Theresa, 17 September 1776; *Fragments*, I, 84.

27. *Fragments*, I, 235, Ligne to Charles de Ligne, 10 December 1780; *APL*, V, 1924, 'Le Chevalier de Lisle', pp. 54, 61, 67, Delisle to Ligne, 15 January 1779, 15 March 1781, 28 March 1782.

28. Prince de Ligne, *Coup d'oeil sur Beloeil*, Beloeil, 1781, pp. 229–30; *Englebert*, 1982, p. 48; Dazincourt, M., *Mémoires*, 1810 edn., p. 151.

29. *Fragments*, I, 236, Ligne to Charles, 10 December 1780.

30. Chevalier Delisle, *Lettres au Prince de Ligne*, Brussels, n.d., p. 82, letter of 24 November 1782; *Mémoires*, pp. 59, 61, 69.

31. M. de Pimodan, *Le Comte F. C. de Mercy-Argenteau*, 1911, p. 141n., Madame du Barry to Mercy-Argenteau, 8 April ?1775; *Fragments*, I, 110; Ligne, *Oeuvres Romanesques*, I, 115–16.

32. *Fragments*, II, 98.

33. Arneth et Geffroy, II, 457, Marie Antoinette to Maria Theresa, 26 July 1776.

34. *Fragments*, I, 129; G. Dansaert, *Le Prince Louis de Ligne*, 1933, pp. 21, 30, Kaunitz to Maria Theresa, 31 August 1776.

35. Leuridant, 1919, pp. 127–8; Ghent, Vandenbroucke to Ligne, 26 August 1787; Adam Zamoyski, *The Last King of Poland*, 1992, pp. 229, 245; Princess Hélène de Ligne, *Mémoires*, 2 vols., 1887, II, 20.

36. Mouriau de Meulenacker, p. 129.

37. *Fragments*, II, 164; Jean Jadot, *Une Lettre Inédite du Prince de Ligne*, Brussels, 1956, letter of 3 August 1779.

38. Leuridant, 1919, pp. 36–7; Ghent, 1774, Ligne to Vandenbroucke, 12 or 13 June 1774; 1777, Ligne to Théaulon, 8 September 1777; 1778, Ligne to Vandenbroucke, 4 April 1778.

39. AN, T 582 1, letter of 2 April 1774, and of Delatour, *conseilller au Châtelet*, to Ligne, 12 June 1776; Ghent, 1778, Ligne to Vandenbroucke, 4 April 1778. Ligne had also nearly been arrested for debt in 1772: see Ghent, 1772, Théaulon to Vandenbroucke, 7 May 1772.

40. Hélène de Ligne, II, 3.

41. Ghent, 1776, Dechent to Vandenbroucke, 14, 17, 21 October 1776; Théaulon to Vandenbroucke, n.d.

42. Ghent, 1776, Dechent to Vandenbroucke, 24 October 1776; Ligne to Vandenbroucke, 26 October 1776; Dechent to Vandenbroucke, 28 December 1776.

43. *Mémoires*, p. 57; *Mémoires et Mélanges*, IV, 151; *Mélanges*, XXV, 41; XXVII, 38, 73; XXIX, 273.

44. *Mélanges*, XXIX, 271–2. Ligne frequently attended the *soupers dans les cabinets*: *Fragments*, I, 193.

45. Comtesse de Laage, *Souvenirs*, Evreux, 1869, LXX–LXXII, diary for 13/14 May 1789; Marquis de Bombelles, *Journal*, II, 213, 235, 247, entries for 18 July, 15 September, 10 October 1788.

46. *Fragments*, I, 235, Ligne to Charles de Ligne, 10 December 1780.

47. Clary Archives, State Archives, Decin, Czech Republic (henceforward referred to as Decin), D102, letter of 1787, from Kiev.

48. Delisle, p. 79, letter of 9 October 1782.

49. Jeanne Arnaud-Bouteloup, *Le Rôle politique de Marie-Antoinette*, 1924, p. 102; [Ligne], *Mélanges de Littérature*, 2 vols., [Brussels], 1783, II, 126–46, 'Mémoire sur Paris'.

50. *Fragments*, I, 205.

51. François Fejtö, *Joseph II*, p. 108; Beales, I, 166, 185; *Fragments*, I, 173, 190.

52. Beales, I, 330–5; *Fragments*, II, 412.

53. *Fragments*, II, 412.

54. *Fragments*, I, 190.

55. Beales, I, 185, 208; *Fragments*, I, 114; Henry Swinburne, *Memoirs of the Courts of Europe*, 2 vols., 1895, I, 351, diary for 12 September 1780. Ligne's friendship with Kaunitz is confirmed in Marquis d'Aragon, *Un Paladin au 18e Siècle*, 1893, p. 72.

56. Arneth, von, *Maria Theresa und Joseph II*, I, 366, Joseph to Leopold, 26 March 1772.

57. *Vergennes*, exhibition catalogue, Galérie de la Séita, Paris, 1987, number 100, Breteuil to Vergennes, 21 December 1780.

58. Beales, I, 120, 129.

59. Karl A. Roider, *Austria's Eastern Question 1700–1790*, Princeton, 1982, pp. 143, 149; Duffy, pp. 209–10; Lord Herbert, *Pembroke Papers*, 1950, p. 89, Major J. Floyd to Lord Herbert, 13 February 1781.

60. Arneth and Geffroy, III, 36, 138, Mercy to Maria Theresa, 18 March, 19 November 1777; Harold Acton, *The Bourbons of Naples*, 1974 edn, pp. 172, 178.

61. Arneth and Geffroy, III, 10, Mercy to Maria Theresa, 17 January 1777.

62. Bombelles, IV, 240, diary for 12 September 1794. Many of Ligne's Paris friends – Delisle, Belanger, Boufflers, Mme de Brionne – came from Lorraine, homeland of the Emperor Francis I and the Duc de Choiseul, whose ruling house and nobles had a tradition of hostility to the Bourbons.

63. *Mémoires*, pp. 58, 65; *Fragments*, I, 99; cf. *Mélanges*, XXIX, 270, 'Toujours dans l'ivresse de l'ambition et des plaisirs on n'avait ni le temps d'aimer, ni d'estimer, ni de juger.'

64. *Mélanges*, XII, 345.

65. Institut Mss, Croÿ, 1677, f. 13, January 1781; *Marie-Antoinette, Joseph II und Leopold II*, 1866, p. 39, Marie Antoinette to Joseph II, 22 September 1784.

66. Pimodan, pp. 208, 229, Mercy to Kaunitz, 30 September 1783, Kaunitz to Mercy, 18 March 1787.

67. *Fragments*, I, 179.

68. John Hardman and Munro Price, eds., *Louis XVI and the comte de Vergennes: correspondance 1774–1787*, Oxford, 1998, p. 190, Louis

XVI to Vergennes, 11 April 1775; Orville T. Murphy, *Charles Gravier Comte de Vergennes. French Diplomacy in the Age of Revolution: 1719–1787*, Albany, 1982, p. 430, Vergennes to Louis XVI, 29 March 1784. Cf. Hardman and Price, pp. 247–50, 256, Vergennes to Louis XVI, 12 April 1777, Louis XVI to Vergennes, February 1778 for further evidence of French hostility to Austria.

69. Ghent, 1777, Ligne to Vandenbroucke, January 1777; *Mélanges*, XXVIII, 268.

70. Such plans, showing Austria's desire for geographical unity and the possibility of an independent Belgian nation, had been proposed since the early eighteenth century: Klaus Malettke, 'Les pays-bas autrichiens au XVIII siècle', *NAPL*, VIII, 21.

71. Beales, I, 397; Ghent, 1778, J. B. Grisset to Vandenbroucke, 28 June 1778; *Fragments*, I, 232, letter of 26 June 1778. Cf. Arneth, von, *Maria Theresa und Joseph II*, III, 42, to Maria Theresa, 12 August 1778.

72. *Fragments*, I, 233, Ligne to Charles de Ligne, 26 June 1778; *Amabile*, p. 104.

73. *Fragments*, I, 130; Mélanges, XVII, 57–8; Leuridant, 1919, pp. 98, 113, letter of 25 October 1778.

74. Ghent, 1778, J. B. Grisset to Vandenbroucke, 3 September 1778.

75. *Mélanges*, XVII, 68; Beales, I, 417, 422.

76. M. Gachard, *Etudes et Notices historiques concernant les Pays-Bas*, 3 vols., Brussels, 1890, III, 366n; Arneth, von, *Maria Theresa und Joseph II*, II, 253, letter of 18 May 1778; cf. for Maria Theresa's distrust of Ligne's boastfulness and frivolity, her letter of 2 September 1776 to Marie Antoinette, in Arneth and Geffroy, II, 485.

CHAPTER 6 *Russia*

1. Ghent, Ligne to Vandenbroucke, 13 October 1779; *Fragments*, II 164.

2. British Library Mss, 6852, f. 79, Ligne to Sir Andrew Mitchell, 10 January 1762, expressing desire to visit *le héros du siècle*, whom he was then fighting; *Préjugés Militaires*, I, 153.

3. *Boswell on the Grand Tour*, p. 23, 13 July 1764; David Fraser, *Frederick the Great*, 2000 edn, p. 126.

4. *Mélanges*, XXVIII, 163.

5. Cracow, Czartoryski Library, Mss 2775, f. 112, *Notice à l'occasion de cette lettre*.

6. *Mémoire sur le Roi de Prusse*, p. 28; Antoing, 3, Frederick to Ligne, 11 July 1780.

7. *Mémoire*, pp. 1, 7, 30–2.

8. *Mémoire*, pp. 11, 47.

9. *Mémoire*, pp. 26, 35, 44, 52.

10. *Mémoire*, p. 38.

11. Antoing, *Vers de société*, III, f. 83, 'Fragment d'une Epitre à un Roi qui ne lui a jamais été Envoyée':

> Vos gardes sont pleins de Césars,
> Qui vous traitent en Nicomède.
> Servant Priape ainsi que Mars,
> Epris du feu qui les possède,
> Ils vous prouvent ainsi qu'à nous,
> Que vis à vis d'aussi beaux hommes
> Il faut bien avoir le dessous.
> En France pour de grosses sommes
> Louis est entre deux genou …
> A Berlin on économise,
> En mettant à tout les soldats.

12. *Mémoire*, pp. 28, 50.

13. Guy, p. 243; *Mémoire*, pp. 11, 52, 54; *Oeuvres Légères*, II, 83.

14. *Mélanges*, XXII, 131–4; cf. XX, 103.

15. Frederick II, *Politische Correspondenz*, 46 vols., Berlin, 1879–1939, XXXXIV, 354, Frederick to Princess of Orange, 13 July 1780; K. M. S. Roedenbeck, *Tagebuch oder Geschichtskalendar an Friedrich des Grossens Regentensleben*, 3 vols., Berlin, 1840, III, 234.

16. *Fragments*, I, 163.

17. Warsaw, Central Archives, Zbior Popielow 165, Papers of King Stanislas Augustus, Correspondence with Ligne (henceforward referred to as Warsaw), Ligne to King Stanislas, September 1787.

18. Pomeau, p. 243; *Sbornik* (proceedings of the Russian Imperial History Society), XXIII, 185, 646, Catherine to Grimm, 7 September 1780, 11 September 1795.

19. Public Record Office (PRO), SP 91/106, Sir James Harris to Lord Stormont, 15/26 September 1780; *Josef II und Graf Ludwig Cobenzl. Ihr Briefwechsel*, 2 vols., 1901 (henceforward referred to as *Cobenzl*), I, 53–7, Cobenzl despatch of 17 September, diary of September 1780; Lucien Perey, *Figures du Temps Passé*, 1900, p. 129, Ligne to Catherine, 15 February 1786; *Fragments*, I, 94.

20. Guy, pp. 170–1.

21. Simon Sebag Montefiore, *Prince of Princes: the Life of Potemkin*, 2000, pp. 135–6, 139, 161.

22. *APL*, V, 98, Lacy to Joseph, 3 February 1781; *Cobenẓl*, I, 53, 114, Cobenzl to Joseph II, 17 September 1780, 4 February 1781; cf. Chevalier de Corberon, *Journal intime*, 2 vols., 1901, II, 376, diary for 27 September 1780.

23. PRO, SP 91/106, despatches to Viscount Stormont, 15/26 September, 25 September/6 October 1780.

24. Chevalier de Corberon, *Journal Intime*, 2 vols., 1904, II, 391–2, 6 October 1780. Seven years later Ligne was still on terms of such intimacy with the empress that Cobenzl judged her intentions 'd'après ce que l'Impératrice a dit au Prince de Ligne': *Cobenẓl*, II, 199, Cobenzl to Joseph II, 12 September 1787.

25. *Fragments*, I, 94–5; *Mélanges*, XX, 237–56, *Portrait de feu Sa Majesté l'Impératrice de toutes les Russies*.

26. *Joseph II und Katharina von Russland. Ihr Briefwechsel* (henceforward referred to as *Joseph II*), 1869, p. 12, letter of October 1780; Corberon, II, 390, 5 October 1780.

27. Budapest 1808 autobiography by Ligne (henceforward referred to as *Budapest 1808*), f. 9.

28. Perey, *Figures*, pp. 109, 113, 137, Ligne to Catherine, 1780, 15 February 1781, 15 November 1786.

29. *Mélanges*, IX, 330, 'Mémoire sur la Pologne'.

30. Eugène Mottaz, *Stanislas Poniatowski et Maurice Glayre*, 1897, p. 172, Glayre to Comte de Moret, 22 November 1780; *Fragments*, I, 79; for references to Ligne's Polish uniform, see Antoing, King Stanislas to Ligne, 5 October 1791; Ghent, 1781, Abbé de Wiazewicz to Ligne, 24 February 1781.

31. Hampshire Record Office, Malmesbury Papers, letters to Lord Malmesbury, Ligne to Malmesbury, 28 October 1780.

32. *Fragments*, I, 234, Ligne to Charles de Ligne, 10 December 1780; cf. Lucien Perey, *La Princesse Hélène de Ligne*, p. 270, 10 September 1779, to Prince Charles de Ligne; Ghent, 1786, Abbé de Wiazewicz to Ligne, 24 February 1781.

33. Warsaw, Ligne to King Stanislas, September 1787; Ghent, 1786, Ligne to Vandenbroucke, 10 January 1786.

34. *NRL*, p. 112; *Fragments*, I, 244; II, 25, 164.

35. Ghent, Prince de Ligne et Evêque de Vilna, Prince de Ligne to Vandenbroucke, 28 October 1780, 11 December 1780.

36. Alex Carmes, 'L'entrée du Prince de Ligne à Luxembourg en 1781',

NAPL, VIII, pp. 262–325; E. Hubert, *Le voyage de Joseph II dans les Pays-Bas*, Brussels, 1900, pp. 42, 328, 365.

37. *Fragments*, II, 25.

38. *Fragments*, II, 26; *APL*, V, 1924, p. 103, Lacy to Ligne, 12 June 1782.

39. *Fragments*, II, 165.

40. Institut Mss, 1680, ff. 5–6, Croÿ diary for 16 August 1783, f. 39vo, Ligne to Croÿ, 8 August 1783; *APL*, VII, 1926, p. 177, Margrave of Baden to Ligne, 22 February 1785.

41. Georges Englebert, 'Le Marquis de Bombelles et le Prince de Ligne', *NAPL*, III, 1988, 95.

42. Comte Valentin Esterhazy, *Lettres à sa Femme 1784–1792*, 1907, p. 47, letter of 29 September 1784.

43. Ghent, 1780, Leygeb to Vandenbroucke, 4, 15 February 1780.

44. Zinzendorf, 19 April 1789.

45. Whitby, Mulgrave archives, Mrs to Mr Dillon Lee, 26 July 1781.

46. See e.g. Ghent, 1784, Charles de Ligne to Vandenbroucke, 14 June 1784; yet despite his fear of bankruptcy, he bought a house in Paris: ibid., Claus to Vandenbroucke, 23 August 1784.

47. Guy, p. 139; *Fragments*, I, 191; II, 368.

48. *Cobenzl*, II, 6, Joseph to Cobenzl, 22 January 1785.

49. Gachard, III, 355–6; *Mélanges*, XVII, 103.

50. Englebert, 'Bombelles', p. 97, diary for 5 June 1785.

51. Hardman and Price, p. 378, Vergennes to Louis XVI, 13 September 1785.

52. *Mélanges*, XVII, 112, 113n., 'Espèces de Campagnes de 1784 et 1785'.

53. Esterhazy, p. 125, letter of 25 September 1785; *Fragments*, I, 133, 266; *Budapest 1808*, f. 11.

54. Ghent, 18, Ligne to Vandenbroucke, 22 January 1786, Théaulon to Vandenbroucke, 2 March 1784, Princesse de Ligne to Vandenbroucke, 8 April 1786.

55. Renate Zedinger, 'Le prince Charles-Joseph de Ligne et Vienne', *NAPL*, XV, 2002, p. 33; Adam Bartsch, *Catalogue raisonné des dessins originaux des plus grands maîtres anciens et modernes qui faisaient partie du Cabinet de feu le Prince Charles de Ligne*, Vienna, 1794, passim.

56. Ghent, 1782, Princesse de Ligne to Vandenbroucke, 12, 27 April 1782.

57. Ghent, 18, Ligne to Vandenbroucke, 17 April 1786; *Correspondance inédite de la Comtesse de Sabran et du Chevalier de Boufflers*, 1875, p. 128, letter of 6 June 1786; *Fragments*, I, 197; II, 420; cf. Ghent, 19,

Bricard to Vandenbroucke, 1 September 1787 for Vergennes' role in Ligne's loss of the lawsuit.

58. Félicien Leuridant, 'Histoire d'une principauté d'Empire', *APL*, VII, 1926, pp. 133–44.

59. Roider, p. 162; Catherine II, *Lettres…au Prince de Ligne*, ed. Princesse Charles de Ligne, 1924, pp. 34, 53, letters of 1 October 1780, 12 September 1785. These letters have been checked against the originals in the Château d'Antoing.

60. Zinzendorf, 9 February, 8, 21 March, 2 May 1786; Perey, *Figures du Temps Passé*, p. 128, Ligne to Catherine, 15 February 1786; *Joseph II*, p. 286, Catherine II to Joseph II, 12 March 1787.

61. Sebag Montefiore, p. 357.

62. *Sbornik*, XXIII, 400, Catherine II to Grimm, 4 April 1787; Comte de Ségur, *Mémoires, Souvenirs et Anecdotes*, 2 vols., 1890, I, 422–3.

63. Ghent, 19, Leygeb to Vandenbroucke, 15 June 1787.

64. Ségur, II, 15; *Sbornik*, XXIII, 407, Catherine II to Grimm, 6 April 1787.

65. *Cobenzl*, II, 134, 137.

66. *Fragments*, II, 65, 200, 382.

67. Gaston Maugras, *Le duc de Lauzun*, p. 185; *Coigny*, pp. xxvi, 7–9.

68. PRO, FO 65/15, f. 171vo, Fitzherbert to Carmarthen, 3 May 1787; Ségur, II, 29, 44.

69. *Coigny*, pp. 21, 24; Ségur, II, 40–3, cf. Marquis d'Aragon, *Un Paladin au 18e Siècle*, 1893, pp. 145–6, Prince to Princess of Nassau-Siegen, 21/2 May 1787; PRO, FO 65/15, f. 191, despatch from Fitzherbert, 27 May 1787.

70. Warsaw, Ligne to Monseigneur, no date, to Stanislas, 23 March, 10 April 1787.

71. *Coigny*, p. 22; Ségur, II, 38; Warsaw, Ligne to Stanislas, 13 May 1787.

72. *Joseph II*, pp. 353, 357, Joseph to Lacy, 19 May 1787; *Mélanges*, XXIV, 4; *Fragments*, II, 66.

73. *Fragments*, I, 168.

74. *Coigny*, p. 36.

75. *Coigny*, pp. 26, 35, 39; cf., for confirmation of discussions of the partition of the Ottoman Empire, *Cobenzl*, II, 153, Cobenzl to Kaunitz, 3 June 1787.

76. *Coigny*, pp. 30–1, 76; A. W. Fisher, *The Russian Annexation of the Crimea*, 1970, p. 146; the palace had been reconstructed after a fire in 1740: see *Encyclopedia of Islam*, new edition, articles Baghce Seray, Kirim.

77. Ségur, II, 73; Aragon, pp. 160–1, Nassau-Siegen to Princess of Nassau-Siegen, 1 June 1787; *Mélanges*, XXIV, 7.

78. Ghent, Ligne to Vandenbroucke, 7 July 1787.

79. *Coigny*, pp. 47–8, 57–9; Aragon, 167–70, letter of June 1787; cf. Institut Mss, 1651, Journal du Duc de Croÿ, November 1753, 20 September, 15 November 1754.

80. *Joseph II*, 357, Joseph II to Lacy, 19 May 1787.

81. *Cobenzl*, II, 176, Cobenzl to Kaunitz, 22 June 1787; *Coigny*, p. 87.

82. *Mélanges*, XXVII, 14; *Coigny*, pp. 82–7.

83. This view is confirmed by the admiring letters of the hyper-critical Joseph II to Marshal Lacy: *Joseph II*, pp. 358–76.

84. *Cobenzl*, II, 192, Cobenzl to Joseph, 9 August 1787; *Mélanges*, XXIV, 5, 11, 14; *Théâtre de l'Hermitage de Cathérine II*, 2 vols., 1799, I, 417–36.

85. *Mélanges*, XXIV, 183, Ligne to Kaunitz, 15 December 1788; XXVII, 13–15; *Cobenzl*, II, 84, 192, Cobenzl to Joseph II, 1 November 1786, 9 August 1787.

86. *Coigny*, pp. 83, 85; *Mélanges*, XXVII, 15.

87. Paris Archives du Ministère des Affaires Etrangères (AAE), Correspondance Politique Turquie, 176ff., 72vo, 87vo, 98, 100, 195vo, Choiseul-Gouffier to Montmorin 3, 9, 10, 25 August 1787.

88. W. Bruce Lincoln, *The Romanovs*, New York, 1981, p. 344; *Mélanges*, XXIV, 11.

89. Ghent, 19, Princesse de Ligne to Vandenbroucke, 20 December 1787.

90. *Coigny*, pp. 55–68; Aragon, p. 162, Nassau-Siegen to Princess of Nassau-Siegen, June 1787.

CHAPTER 7 *Turkey*

1. *Fragments*, I, 108.

2. Sebag Montefiore, p. 391.

3. *APL*, XIII, 1932, 93, *Résumé des différent entretiens du prince de Ligne avec le comte Cobenzl*, 31 October 1787; Antoing, Joseph II to Ligne, 14 October, 25 November 1787.

4. Catherine II, *Lettres ... au Prince de Ligne*, 1924, p. 89, Catherine II to Potemkin, 18 October 1787; *Cobenzl*, II, 201, Cobenzl to Joseph II, 12 September 1787.

5. *Mélanges*, XXIV, 15.

6. *Mélanges*, XXIV, 76, 93, 150, 155, Ligne to Joseph II, 13 May, 12 July, 22 October, 19 November 1788; Hélène de Ligne, II, 148–9, Ligne to Charles de Ligne, 30 July 1788.

7. *Mélanges*, XXIV, 13.

8. *Mélanges*, VII, *Lettres sur la Dernière Guerre des Turcs*, 151, 155, Ligne to Ségur, 1 December 1787, 15 February 1788.

9. Ghent, 1787, Princesse de Ligne to Vandenbroucke, 29 November 1787; *Fragments*, II, 322.

10. Comte Roger de Damas, *Mémoires*, 2 vols., 1912, I, 19, 26; *Mélanges*, VII, 176, Ligne to Ségur, 1 August 1788.

11. Léonce Pingaud, *Choiseul-Gouffier*, 1887, pp. 96, 184; Ghent, 1788, Ligne to Vandenbroucke, 12 April 1788; Warsaw, Ligne to King Stanislas Augustus, autumn 1787.

12. Karl A. Roider, *Baron Thugut and the Austrian Reaction to the French Revolution*, Princeton, 1987, p. 179; *Mélanges*, XXIV, 127, 180; German State Archives Merseburg Geheime Staatsarchiv, Rep. 9 Polen Nr. 27–233, Buchholtz to Frederick William II, 17 October 1788, enclosing a letter from Ligne to Czetwertynski; cf. Jean Fabre, *Stanislas Auguste et l'Europe des Lumières*, 1952, p. 480.

13. *Mémoires et Mélanges*, II, 50–82.

14. Antoing, Joseph II to Ligne, 13 October 1787.

15. Antoing, Joseph II to Ligne, 28 May, 6 June 1788; HHSA Staatskanzlei Vorträge 145 (supplement), Ligne to Joseph II, 12 May 1788, enclosed in Joseph to Kaunitz, 27 May 1788.

16. Antoing, Joseph II to Ligne, 25 April, 14 October 1788; Warsaw, Charles de Ligne to Ligne, 4 May 1788 (copy); *Fragments*, I, 236, Ligne to Charles de Ligne, 12 May 1788.

17. *Mélanges*, XXIV, 21; VII, 171–4, Ligne to Ségur, 1 August 1788.

18. *Mélanges*, XXIV, 45, 182, Ligne to Joseph II, February 1788, to Kaunitz, 15 December 1788.

19. *Fragments*, I, 238, Ligne to Charles de Ligne, 8 June 1788; Antoing, Romanzov to Ligne, 30 September 1788, Joseph to Ligne, 25 October 1788.

20. *Fragments*, I, 238, Ligne to Charles de Ligne, 8 June 1788; *Mélanges*, VII, 164, 2 July 1788, to Ségur; Damas, I, 51.

21. *Mélanges*, VII, 169, 195, Ligne to Ségur, 1 August, 1 October 1788; cf. Philip Longworth, *The Art of Victory*, 1965, p. 147, for confirmation of the astonishment caused by Potemkin's failure to attack Ochakov; *Mélanges*, XXIV, 120, Ligne to Joseph II, 3 August 1788.

22. Antoing, Potemkin to Ligne, 28 July, 15 September 1788; *Mélanges*, XXIV, 32.

23. Catherine II, p. 97; *Mélanges*, XXIV, 150–1, Ligne to Joseph II, 22 October 1788; John T. Alexander, *Catherine the Great*, 1989 edn, pp. 264–5.

24. Ghent, Ligne to Vandenbroucke, 25 November 1788, 15 April 1788; Antoing, Coburg to Ligne, 13 November 1788.

25. *Coup d'Oeil*, p. 294; *Mélanges*, VII, 200–5, 209, Ligne to Ségur, 1 December 1788.

26. *Cobenzl*, II, 315, Philip to Ludwig Cobenzl, 5 January 1789; M. S. Anderson, *War and Society in Europe of the Old Regime 1618–1789*, 1988, p. 196.

27. *Mélanges*, XXIV, 191–2; Decin, 102, Ligne to Christine, 1789.

28. *Mélanges*, VII, 182, 186, 192, 221–6, Ligne to Ségur, 1 September 1788.

29. *Mélanges*, XXIV, 221, 227, 248.

30. *Mélanges*, XXIV, 249; VII, 218–19, Ligne to Ségur, 18 October 1789; Antoing, Laudon to Ligne, 8 October 1789.

31. Philip Mansel, *The Court of France 1789–1830*, Cambridge, 1991 edn, p. 18.

CHAPTER 8 *Belgium*

1. The full meaning of this celebrated question, provoked by the uprising of the great Tyrolean patriot Andreas Hofer in 1809, is not apparent unless Tyroleans' ancient exemption from Austrian war taxes, and from obligatory military service outside the Tyrol, are remembered.

2. *APL*, I, 1920, p. 166, 'Mémoire sur les Pays-Bas Autrichiens que je donnai à Joseph II qui devait y venir'.

3. *Joseph II und Leopold II*, II, 17, Joseph to Leopold, 14 May 1786; *La Belgique Autrichienne*, Brussels, 1989, p. 231.

4. Jeroom Vercruysse, 'Le Prince de Ligne et la révolution belgique 1787–1790', *NAPL*, V, 1990, 29.

5. *Mélanges*, XXII, 46, *Discours à la Nation Belgique*.

6. Sir Robert Murray Keith, *Memoirs and Correspondence*, 2 vols., 1849, II, 211, Keith to Carmarthen, 3 August 1787.

7. Ghent, Ligne to Vandenbroucke, 10 February 1789.

8. *Oeuvres Légères*, I, 80; *Mémoires et Mélanges*, V, 102–3n. A poem in praise of Flanders, in which the last line of every verse reads *aux pays bas*, is at Antoing.

9. *Mélanges*, XXVIII, 50.

10. *Fragments*, I, 222; *Mémoires*, pp. 81–3; *APL*, 1920, I, p. 170, 'Mémoire sur les Pays-Bas autrichiens'; *Mélanges*, XXII, 49, 'Discours à La Nation Belgique'. On the other hand there were limits to Ligne's love of his fellow-countrymen. As early as 1782 his

wife had written to Vandenbroucke: 'the prince is discontented with the way of thinking of the Beloeil people. He talks about it every day': Ghent, 1782, letter of 16 May 1782.

11. Ghent, XXIV, Princesse de Ligne to Vandenbroucke, 10 September 1795.

12. Dansaert, p. 46; Ghent, Princesse de Ligne to Vandenbroucke, 9 February 1790; cf. Jeroom Vercruysse, 'Le Prince de Ligne et la révolution belgique 1787–1790', *NAPL*, V, 1990, p. 85. Although this author differs with M. Vercruysse over the attitude of the Prince to the Belgian revolution, there is agreement about that of the Princess.

13. *Fragments*, I, 417; Ghent, 1789–90, Ligne to Leygeb, 10 February 1789.

14. *APL*, III, 1922, 'Espèce de Campagne de 1790', pp. 50–1; *Mélanges*, XXIV, 185, Ligne to Kaunitz, 10 November 1789, 269; cf. Jeroom Vercruysse, 'Le Prince de Ligne et la révolution belgique 1787–1790', *NAPL*, V, 1990, p. 39.

15. Dansaert, pp. 47, 55.

16. HHSA, Familienarchiv Sammelbände, 72, Lacy to Joseph II, 13 December 1789; *Mélanges*, XXIV, 269; Dansaert, pp. 58–9; cf. *APL*, I, 1920, p. 139, Ligne to Legros, 3 January 1790, for further expressions of admiration for the patriots.

17. *APL*, II, 1922, p. 52; Ghent, 1789–90, Princesse de Ligne to Vandenbroucke, 9 February, 16 May 1790.

18. Cracow Academy of Sciences, Archives Poniatowski, rkps III, 4582, letter of 4 or 5 January 1790.

19. Zinzendorf, 13 January 1790.

20. Ghent, Ligne to Vandenbroucke, 7 April 1790.

21. *APL*, VI, 1925, p. 87, Ligne to Mercy-Argenteau, 14 February 1790.

22. *APL*, III, 1922, 'Espèce de Campagne de 1790', pp. 50, 54; Ghent, Ligne to Vandenbroucke, 7 April 1790.

23. *APL*, III, 1922, 'Espèce de Campagne de 1790', p. 54; *Fragments*, I, 118.

24. *APL*, III, 1922, 'Espèce de Campagne de 1790', p. 59.

25. M. de Bray, *Quelques considérations sur la Révolution des Provinces Belgiques*, Brussels, 1908, pp. 98, 106–8, letter of October; Zinzendorf, 14, 16 January 1791, says the real reason for Ligne's anger was that he was going to be made a marshal with two others, rather than by himself; *Fragments*, I, 104, Leopold II to Ligne, 15 December 1790.

26. Klarwill, *Mémoires et Lettres*, p. 29.

27. Duc de Broglie, *Souvenirs*, 4 vols., 1886, I, 85; Axel von Fessen, *Daybook*, 4 vols., Stockholm 1925–36, II, 478; Bibliothèque Royale de Belgique, Mss G2135, contract of 28 June 1790 (copy). The year that Ligne first rented his two properties is not known, but in 1790 he was already well installed; see Zinzendorf, 31 May 1790.

28. Zinzendorf, 20 May 1792; Guy, p. 131; Thomas Baring, *A Tour through Italy and Austria in 1814*, second edn 1817, p. 79.

29. Mme Vigée-Lebrun, *Souvenirs*, 2 vols., 1867, I, 282, 293; Guy, p. 132.

30. Zinzendorf, 5, 10 January, 7, 9 February, 24 September, 3 October 1790; Ghent, Princesse de Ligne to Vandenbroucke, 20 June 1791.

31. *Mélanges*, XXIV, 186, Ligne to Kaunitz, 10 November 1789; *Coup d'Oeil*, ed. Ernest de Ganay, p. 297.

32. *APL*, VI, 1925, p. 91, Ligne to Mercy-Argenteau, 14 November 1790.

33. Antoing, *Mes livres rouges*, XI, 7; X, 62; Ghent, 1782, Théaulon to Vandenbroucke, 7 March 1782. In 1780 Ligne had a scheme to buy salt wholesale and distribute it free to his peasants, and thereby pay for their weddings. Ghent, Prince de Ligne et Evêque de Vilna, Ligne to Vandenbroucke: 'Vienne ce 25 vous saurez le mois mais je ne le sais pas.'

34. Ghent, 1789–90, Ligne to M. de Busscher, 6 May 1789; *NRL*, p. 350.

35. *Mélanges*, XXV, 39.

36. *Mélanges*, XXVII, 131; XXV, 43–4.

37. *Mélanges*, XIII, 44; F. Barrière, *Tableaux de Genre et d'Histoire*, 2 vols., 1828, I, xvi; *Mémoires et Mélanges*, IV, 135, 'Sur l'Armée Française avant la Révolution'; *Mélanges*, II, 171.

38. *Ma napoléonide*, 1921, p. 38.

39. Claude Arnaud, *Chamfort*, 1988, p. 276.

40. Guillaume, p. 122n.

41. *Amabile*, p. 85.

42. *Fragments*, I, 112.

43. *Mélanges*, XXII, 126–9, Ligne to Ségur, 6 October 1790.

44. Gaston Maugras, *Les Dernières Années du Duc de Lauzun*, n.d., p. 406, letter of 1 September 1791, to M. de Biron.

45. Ghent, 1787, Bricard to Vandenbroucke, 1 September 1787, complaining about Calonne's lack of help; PRO, PC1/129/572, letters of Ligne and Calonne, January 1791; cf. Duc des Cars, *Mémoires*, 2 vols., 1890, II, 187–9.

46. Marquis de Bombelles, *Journal*, III, Genève, 1993, 173, 3 February 1791; 204, letter of 28 March 1791.

47. Hans Schlitter, ed., *Briefe der Erzherzogin Marie Christine...an Leopold II*, 1896, p. 307, Leopold to Mercy, 14 May 1791; Antoing, Leopold to Ligne, 10 February 1790.

48. Catherine II, p. 139, Catherine to Charles de Ligne, n.d.; cf. Perey, *Figures*, p. 181, Ligne to Catherine, n.d.

49. Ghent, Princesse de Ligne to Vandenbroucke, 21 October 1790, 27 April 1782.

50. Klarwill, p. 284, Ligne to Princess Hélène de Ligne, 15 January 1791.

51. Dansaert, p. 71; Ghent, 1791, Princesse de Ligne to Vandenbroucke, 22 August 1791.

52. *Mélanges*, XXII, 122–4, letter of 8 April 1792.

53. Archiver duchateau de Beloeil, 'Note de l'Entrée Solonelle de S. A. Mgr le Prince de Ligne à Mons...du 8 Août 1791'; P-P-J Harmignie and N-J-H Descamps, *Mémoires sur l'Histoire de la Ville de Mons*, Mons, 1882, p. 42, diary for 8 August 1791; Albert-Joseph Paridaens, *Journal historique*, 2 vols., Mons, 1902, II, 81–6, diary for 8–13 August 1791; Ghent, 1791, Princesse de Ligne to Vandenbroucke, 14 August 1791.

54. Gachard, III, 372n.

55. Heinrich von Zeissberg, *Zwei Jahre Belgischer Geschichte*, 2 vols., Vienna, 1891, I, 120, Charles to Francis, 9 October 1791; Perey, *La Princesse Hélène de Ligne*, pp. 418–19; Gachard, III, 376, letter of Ligne, 11 October 1791.

56. Guy, *Oeuvres choisies*, p. 88.

57. Perey, *Figures*, p. 189, Ligne to Catherine (misdated 15 February 1792); Archives du Ministère des Affaires Etrangères, Paris, CP Autriche 362, f. 251, Noailles to Delessart, 30 November 1791; *Leopold II und Marie-Christine. Ihr Briefwechsel*, 1867, p. 281, Leopold to Marie-Christine, 28 November 1791.

58. *APL*, VI, 1926, pp. 112–16, *Mémoire sur l'etat présent des Pays-Bas autrichiens*; Zinzendorf, 8 January 1791; Ghent, 1791, Princesse de Ligne to Vandenbroucke, 16 December 1791.

59. Léonce Pingaud, ed., *Correspondance Intime du Comte de Vaudreuil et du Comte d'Artois*, 2 vols., 1889, II, 83, Vaudreuil to Artois, 19 April 1792.

60. Zinzendorf, 5 January 1792, 2, 18 March 1792.

61. Gachard, III, 380, 386–9, Estates to Ligne, December 1791, Ligne to Estates, 8, 13 March 1792.

62. Hungarian National Archives (henceforward referred to as HNA), 1808 autobiography of Ligne, ff. 12, 17; Ghent, 1792, Princesse de Ligne to Vandenbroucke, 2 December 1792.

63. Ghent, 1792, Ligne to Vandenbroucke, 1 February 1792, Ligne to Claus, 5 May 1792, Princesse de Ligne to Vandenbroucke, 20 November 1791, 10 August 1792.

64. Cracow, Academy of Sciences, Archives Poniatowski, rkps 111, Charles de Ligne to Joseph Poniatowski, n.d. [1792].

65. Georges Englebert, 'La mort du prince Charles Antoine de Ligne', *NAPL*, IX, 200.

66. *Fragments*, I, 94.

67. Perey, *La Princesse Hélène de Ligne*, pp. 438–46, will of Prince Charles de Ligne.

68. *NAPL*, XI, 1996, 218, Princess Clary to Prince Clary, 8, 12 November 1792.

69. Ibid., Princess Clary to Prince Clary, 21 October 1792.

70. *Catherine II*, pp. 171–2, letter of 1 November 1792; Harmignie et Descamps, p. 50, 7 November 1792.

71. Ghent, 1792, Princess de Ligne to Vandenbroucke, 11 October, 11 November 1792; Zinzendorf, 20 October 1792.

72. Ghent, Maison de Ligne 1793–5, Princesse de Ligne to Vandenbroucke, 4 April 1793, Ligne to Vandenbroucke, 17 April 1793: *Fragments*, ed. Leuridant, II, 378.

73. *APL*, IV, 1923, pp. 85–8, 'Un Salon'; BRB Mss, Sauveur Legros, 'Mes Babioles', f. 138. At this time Ligne lent the great counter-revolutionary writer Rivarol a book-lined pavilion in the park. See M. de Lescure, *Rivarol et la Société Française*, 1883, p. 400, letter of Rivarol, 21 February 1794.

74. Cf. Baron R. M. de Klinckowstrom, *Le Comte de Fersen et la Cour de France*, 2 vols., 1877, II, 105, diary of Count Fersen, 16 December 1793: *J'ai remarqué le prince de Ligne chez le baron de Breteuil; il est très mécontent de ne pas être employé et blâme par conséquent tout ce qui se fait.*

75. *Fragments*, II, 356; *Mélanges*, II, 163; XXV, 41.

76. Ligne, 'Contre-réflexions aux Réflexions' [de Dumouriez], *APL*, II, 1921, pp. 292–308.

77. Antoing, Archduke Charles to Ligne, 20 November 1793, Coburg to Ligne, 25 November 1793; Harmignie and Descamps, p. 67, 19 August 1793; see *APL*, I, 1920, p. 178, Ligne to Metternich, November 1793; HHSA, DD Abt B Fasz, 121, 122, Ligne to Metternich, 31 January 1794.

78. HHSA, DD Abt Fasz, 121, 122, Ligne to Metternich 'ce 19' [?] February 1794.

CHAPTER 9 *Vienna*

1. J. B. S. Morritt, *A Grand Tour*, 1985 edn, pp. 26, 40, 308, letters of 22 May, 24 June 1794, 15 June 1796.
2. Des Cars, II, 161; Zinzendorf, 11 December 1789.
3. Frances Trollope, *Vienna and the Austrians*, 2 vols., 1838, I, 317.
4. Borje Knos, *L'Histoire de la Littérature Néo-Grecque*, Uppsala, 1962, pp. 514, 534, 550–1, 585, 690.
5. Kelly, Michael, *Reminiscences*, 1975, I, 199, 204.
6. Thayer's *Life of Beethoven*, Princeton, 1964, 2 vols., I, 170, Beethoven to Simrock, 2 August 1794.
7. Madame Vigée-Lebrun, *Souvenirs*, 2 vols., 1896, I, 282.
8. *Fragments*, II, 216; Decin, 102, *Fragments de lettres du Prince de Ligne à la Princesse Clary*, Pest, 1809.
9. Madame du Montet, *Souvenirs*, 3e edn, 1914, p. 107; Rosalie Rzewuska, *Mémoires*, 4 vols., Rome, 1939–50, I, 219.
10. Ghent, Princesse de Ligne to Vandenbroucke, 21 August 1795; Rzewuska, I, 222, 219.
11. Rzewuska, Rosalie, *Memoires*, 4 vols., Rome, 1939–50, I, 219; Du Montet, p. 107.
12. *Fragments*, II, 216, 137; Cracow, Charles de Ligne to Prince Joseph Poniatowski, n.d. ?1791.
13. Du Montet, p. 108; Rzewuska, I, 222–3.
14. Countess Potocka, *Memoires*, New York, 1900, pp. 178–80, 214.
15. Countess Lulu Thurheim, *Mein Leben. Erinnerungen aus Österreichs Grosser Welt*, 4 vols., München, 1913–14, I, 81; Prince A. Clary, *A European Past*, 1978, pp. 13–15.
16. Thurheim, II, 143–5; there was so little 'real warmth' that in the 1820s Sidonie de Ligne unsuccessfully sued her cousin Prince Eugène de Ligne for possession of Beloeil; Decin, 104a, Flore to Ligne, 6 May 1803; Countess Potocka, pp. 111–12; Rzewuska, I, 218.
17. Perey, *Figures*, p. 208, Ligne to Catherine II, 13 April 1795; Ligne, *Mon Réfuge; ou Satyre sur les Abus des Jardins Modernes*, London, 1801, p. 26.
18. Lund University Library, Dept. Mss., diary of Count de La Gardie (henceforward referred to as La Gardie), 11 October 1800.
19. NRL, p. 353, letter of 1810 to Legros; *Fragments*, II, 285.
20. *Fragments*, II, 106; Ghent 1800–1808, Ligne to Vandenbroucke, 15 December 1799.

21. Ghent, Maison de Ligne 1795–1801, G. Lambinet to Vandenbroucke, 30 August 1797.

22. Couvreur, pp. 228–9.

23. La Gardie, 20 July 1800; *Charles-Joseph Fürst de Ligne*, Albertina, Vienna, 1982, pp. 137–8; *Mélanges*, V, 1, preface of 1 January 1795; *Fragments*, II, 97–8; Dansaert, pp. 101, 111.

24. Decin, 104a, note by Harmignies, 29 December 1793; Dansaert, pp. 129, 143; Ghent, XXVII, Ligne to Vandenbroucke, 1 June 1806.

25. BRB Mss., Sauveur Legros, 'Mes Babioles', f. 24, cf. ibid., f. 102, 7 January 1795; many of his poems and letters are in the Château d'Antoing Mss., box 2; *NRL*, p. 341.

26. *Mélanges*, XIII, 22; *APL*, VI, 1925, pp. 240–5.

27. Georges Englebert, 'Emile Legros Adjutant du prince de Ligne', in *Revue Belge d'histoire militaire*, XVIII, September 1970, pp. 491–5; other adjutants were a Walloon called Augustin Docteur and Lieutenant Dettinger, whose journey to Brussels in 1789 had aroused the suspicion of Joseph II, and who later brought a lawsuit against Ligne.

28. Roider, p. 341, to Thugut, 3 July 1800.

29. Lady Jackson, ed., *The Bath Archives*, 2 vols., 1873, II, 353, letter from Sir George Jackson, 17 November 1813; Dorothy Gies McGuigan, *Metternich and the Duchess*, New York, 1975, p. 330.

30. Kelly, I, 207.

31. Maria Ullrichova, ed., *Clemens Metternich–Wilhelmine von Sagan. Ein Briefwechsel 1813–15*, Graz-Köln, 1966, p. 249, Metternich to Wilhelmine von Sagan, 21 April 1814; Earl of Minto, *Life and Letters*, 3 vols., 1874, III, 71, letter of Lord Minto, 1799; Walter C. Langsam, *Francis the Good*, New York, 1949, p. 155; Alan Sked, *The Decline and Fall of the Habsburg Empire*, Harlow, 1989, p. 81.

32. Finnish National Archives, Helsinki, Armfelt Mss., Armfelt to Auguste von Armfelt, 18 May 1803; *Fragments*, I, 133; II, 241; Freiherr von Aretin, quoted in James J. Sheehan, *German History 1770–1866*, Oxford, 1990, p. 278.

33. Gunther Rothenburg, *Napoleon's Great Adversaries*, 1982, p. 14.

34. Zinzendorf, 23 November 1796, for Ligne speaking in favour of peace; Ligne, *Mémoires*, pp. 134–7.

35. Klarwill, p. 32.

36. Perey, *Figures*, p. 201, letter dated April 1793 (in reality 1794).

37. Ghent, XXIV, Ligne to Vandenbroucke, 24 August 1795; *Fragments*, I, 131; II, 92; cf., for confirmation of Thugut's suspicions of Ligne, Klarwill, pp. 32–3.

38. Ligne, *Mémoires*, pp. 126–9; Roider, *Thugut*, p. 228.

39. Roider, *Thugut*, p. 246; *Mémoires*, p. 131; Zinzendorf, 1 March 1798.

40. Historical Manuscripts Commission, *Dropmore Papers*, V, 227, Lord Mulgrave to Lord Grenville, 2 August 1799.

41. Catherine II, p. 180n.; *Figures*, p. 199, Ligne to Catherine II, April 1793 [1794].

42. *Mémoires*, p. 153; Antoing, Paul I to Ligne, 2 July 1798; *Fragments*, I, 165, 433, Ligne to Paul I, 1 January 1800, II, 133, 279.

43. Antoing, Colloredo to Ligne, March 1800.

44. See e.g. Antoing, Archduke Charles to Ligne, 23 July 1797.

45. *Fragments*, II, 104.

46. *Mon Réfuge; ou Satyre sur les Abus des Jardins Modernes*, London, 1801, p. 26.

47. Rzewuska, I, 39; Decin, 103, Ligne to Bonnay, *ce 25*.

48. *Fragments*, I, 171; *Mélanges*, XXXI, 96; *NRL*, p. 277.

49. Comte S. Ouvaroff, *Esquisses Politiques et Littéraires*, 1848, p. 132; Alexandre Wassiltchikov, *Les Razoumovski*, 5 vols., 1893, II, 80; Guy, *Oeuvres Choisies*, p. 241.

50. *Fragments*, I, 310; *NRL*, p. 355; Zinzendorf, 17 October 1811, 10 January 1812, describes conversation at the Liechtensteins' salon when Ligne was there.

51. Basil Guy, 'Quelques documents méconnus sur la mort du prince de Ligne', *NAPL*, XIII, 184, Custine to Mme de Custine, 10 November 1814.

52. *Fragments*, II, 106, 356.

53. *Mélanges*, XXVI, 284–5; Zinzendorf, 28 March 1794, 9 March 1803, 11 February 1810, notes Ligne's brief appearances before dinner.

54. Zinzendorf, 30 April 1790, 29 January, 24 April 1791.

55. Zinzendorf, 30 April, 31 May 1790, 29 January, 24 April 1791, 18 May 1794, contains references to the Prince's smell and dirt.

56. Axel von Fersen, *Dagbok*, 4 vols., Stockholm 1925–36, II, 478–9, 27 February 1796, cf., II, 514, 1 May 1796.

57. Ilsa Barea, *Vienna: Legend and Reality*, 1966, p. 35; Zinzendorf, 16 October 1806; *Fragments*, I, 169; for a similar view of life in Vienna see Mme de Staël, *De l'Allemagne*, 2 vols., London, 1814, I, 53, 56–7.

58. Trollope, II, 3, 213.

59. Joseph Freiherr von Hammer-Purgstall, *Erinnerungen aus Meinen Leben*, 1940, pp. 27, 180, 417; *NRL*, pp. 373n, 379; Friedrich Heer, *The Holy Roman Empire*, 1968, p. 237; *Mélanges*, XXVI, 278.

60. Paul R. Sweet, *Friedrich von Gentz*, Madison, 1941, p. 68; National

Library of Scotland, Edinburgh (henceforward referred to as NLS), Mss. 12998, Eliot to Ligne, n.d. (draft).

61. Gentz, *Briefe von und an Friedrich von Gentz*, 3 vols., Munich and Berlin, 1913, II, 364, 372, Gentz to Adam Muller, 16 July 1802, 25 September 1802; III, 131, Gentz to Brinckmann, 4 June 1803; Decin, 103, Ligne to Bonnay, 1 August 1802.

62. *Mélanges*, XXII, 120–1.

63. Du Montet, p. 35.

64. Bombelles, IV, 269, Ligne to Bombelles, 10 December 1794.

65. [Comte de Salaberry], *Voyage à Constantinople, en Italie, et aux Iles de l'Archipel*, 1799, p. 38; Des Cars, II, 151.

66. The plan is in Englebert, *Le prince de Ligne et son temps*, Beloeil, 982, p. 92; Du Montet, p. 33. Another *émigré* friend of Ligne was *ce pauvre d'Auteuil tout à moi*, who died in 1808. His last letter was to Ligne.

67. *Mélanges*, XX, 213–14, for Ligne's views on, and scepticism about, friendship.

68. Cracow, Czartoryski Library, autograph collection of Isabella Czartoriska, Mss. 2777, f. 409, Louis of Wurttemberg to Ligne, 26 August 1762.

69. Hampshire Record Office, Malmesbury papers, letters of 28 October 1780, 4 November [1784], and *ce 20*.

70. Aragon, p. 255.

71. Rzewuska, I, 204; Decin, 103, Ligne to Bonnay, 25 August 1803; Pierre Escoubé, *Sénac de Meilhan*, 1984, pp. 271, 294–5.

72. Decin, 103, Ligne to Bonnay, 25 August 1803.

73. *Amabile*, p. 99.

74. *Souvenirs du chevalier de Cussy*, I, 1909, 67, 70; Decin, 103, Bonnay to Ligne, 14 July 1812.

75. Rzewuska, I, 97.

76. Decin, 103, letter of 22 June 1803.

77. Ibid., Bonnay to Ligne, 7 September 1803.

78. Ibid., Bonnay to Ligne, 27 August, 26 November 1803.

79. Ibid., Bonnay to Ligne, 17 August 1803. For poems exchanged between Ligne and Bonnay see *Mélanges*, XXI, 192–4; XXII, 264, 288; *APL*, 1934, XV, 106–9.

80. J. M. P. McEarlean, 'L'Indicible Secret de Napoléon Bonaparte et de Charles-André Pozzo di Borgo', in *Annales Historiques de la Révolution Française*, Oct.–Dec. 1974, 218, pp. 674–84; Rzewuska, I, 47.

81. *Fragments*, I, 214; *NRL*, pp. 197–200, Ligne to Pozzo di Borgo, 6 October 1804; this conversation is referred to in a letter of Christopher Hughes to the Duke of Wellington, 3 April 1835 (Southampton University, Wellington Papers WP2/31/90).

82. Wassiltchikov, *Les Razoumovski*, II, part 4, p. 70, Ligne to Razumovski, 6 November 1795; *Fragments*, I, 353; Finnish National Archives, Helsinki, Armfelt to Auguste von Armfelt, 25 December 1802.

83. *Fragments*, I, 310; *Mélanges*, XVIII, 102.

84. Antoing, note on the English; Earl of Minto, *Life and Letters*, 3 vols., 1874, III, 120, Lady Minto to Lady Malmesbury.

85. Rzewuska, I, 29; Decin, 103, Bonnay to Ligne, 20 July 1803; Hungarian National Archives, Budapest, Mss. 84496–7, letters from Ligne to Batthyani, n.d.

86. Antoing, Survorov to Ligne, 20 December 1794, 4 February 1795. On account of his pro-Russian sympathies, Charles de Ligne's father-in-law the Bishop of Vilna had been hanged by Polish Jacobins, which may explain Ligne's enthusiasm for the Russian occupation.

87. Rudolf Maixner, 'Un Ragusain Ami du Prince de Ligne', in *Revue de Littérature Comparée*, 1957, pp. 576–7.

88. Robert S. Wistrich, *The Jews of Vienna in the age of Franz Joseph*, Oxford, 1990, pp. 10–11, 16, 20; Hilde Spiel, *Fanny von Arnstein. Daughter of the Enlightenment 1758–1818*, Oxford, 1991, p. 72.

89. Ghent, 1780, Leygeb to Vandenbroucke, 15 February 1780; Gentz, *Briefe*, II, 227, Gentz to Brinckmann, 19 September 1804; *Fragments*, I, 369.

90. *APL*, XI, 1930, pp. 94–104, 'Lettres à la Baronne de Grotthus'; Decin, 103, Ligne to Madame Regina, n.d.

91. *Mémoires et Mélanges*, II, 28–49, cf. Baruch Hagani, *Le Sionisme Politique. Le Prince de Ligne*, 1920; *Fragments*, ed. Leuridant, I, 249–50.

92. *Fragments*, I, 171.

93. J. F. Reichardt, *Vertraute Briefe auf einer Reise nach Wien*, 2 vols., München, 1915, I, 167, letter of 10 December 1808.

94. *Bermerkungen eines Jungen Bauers*, München, 1808, pp. 85–7.

95. Spiel, pp. 149, 151, 182, 188, 204; Gentz, II, 218, Gentz to Brinckmann, 22 August 1804.

96. Comte S. Ouvaroff, p. 132.

97. Rzewuska, I, 134, 203; Zinzendorf, 29 December 1810.

98. Thurheim, II, 146; Gentz, II, 131, to Brinckmann, 4 June 1803. Only an English visitor called Mrs Trench failed to be amused by the Hôtel de Ligne: 'In general conversation at Vienna seems to me but meagre; little events are magnified as in a small town; politics never, and literature very seldom mentioned.' Mrs Trench, *Remains*, 1862, p. 69, diary for 13 April 1799.

99. *Fragments*, I, 213; II, 169.

100. Bibliothèque Nationale, Charavay Mss. 48933, Louis XVIII to Gentz, 30 May 1804.

101. *Mélanges*, XXII, 244.

102. *Mélanges*, XXV, 72, Ligne to Vaudreuil, 1802, 42; Ouvaroff, pp. 138–9.

103. Georges Englebert, 'Sauveur Legros Secrétaire Intime du Prince de Ligne, homme d'esprit, littérateur et artiste', *NAPL*, VIII, 1994, p. 103; cf. Baron Hue, *Souvenirs*, 1904, p. 258n.; Du Montet, p. 135.

104. NRL, p. 72, to Tilly, 1797; Decin, 103, Ligne to Bonnay, 16 August 1803.

105. Decin, 103, Bonnay to Ligne, 12 October 1803, Ligne to Bonnay, 28 August 1805.

CHAPTER 10 *Bohemia*

1. Edith J. Morley, ed., *Crabb Robinson in Germany*, Oxford, 1929, p. 87, October 1801.

2. Elof Tegner, *Gustaf Mauritz Armfelt*, 3 vols., Stockholm, 1893, III, 17–18, 398, Ligne wrote of the Courland family, when he heard that one of their ladies-in-waiting complained to M. Gualtieri that he was compromising her princess:

Le sang auguste de Courlande
Ne souffre point d'amour la contrebande.
J'observe Demidoff et j'ai chassé Palffy.
J'ai pris Taxis sur moi. Cesse Gualtieri
Dans notre cour d'étaler une offrande
Qui peut me compromettre et surtout me fâcher.
Oui, je me sacrifie, épargnons une Princesse.
D'une Dame d'honneur fais plutôt ta maîtresse
Tache donc de la rechercher
Elle me permet de l'afficher.

3. *Mélanges*, XXV, 106.

4. *NRL*, p. 152; Decin, 102, Bonnay to Ligne, 1 August ?1802.

5. Princess Louise of Prussia, *Forty-five Years of my Life*, 1912, p. 185; cf. for their friendship, *Mélanges*, XXVI, 356–9.

6. Prince de Ligne, *Fragment sur Casanova suivi de Lettres à Casanova*, 1998, passim and p. 52, Ligne to Casanova, 22 November 1794; Octave Uzanne, 'Les Relations de Ligne et de Casanova', *APL*, I, 1920, p. 237.

7. *APL*, IV 1923, 'Quelques Remarques de Casanova', p. 8; *APL*, I, 1920, p. 154.

8. *Lolo. Le journal du Prince Charles-Joseph Clary-Aldringen*, 1, 1795–1798, Utrecht 1996, p. 67, 7 September 1795.

9. Prince de Ligne, *Fragment sur Casanova suivi de lettres à Casanova*, p. 68; *APL*, I, 1920, p. 335, letter of September 1794.

10. *Fragment sur Casanova*, p. 55, letter of 17 December 1794.

11. *APL*, I, 1920, p. 338.

12. *Fragment sur Casanova*, p. 71.

13. *APL*, I, 1920, p. 239, Ligne to Casanova, 16 December 1795.

14. *APL*, I, 1920, p. 321, 17 December 1794, to Casanova, p. 237.

15. *Fragment sur Casanova*, p. 70.

16. *APL*, I, 1920, p. 237, Ligne to Casanova, 17 December 1794; *APL*, II, 1921, pp. 117–18, Ligne to Casanova.

17. *Fragment sur Casanova*, pp. 69–70, letter of 22 September 1794.

18. *Fragments*, II, 270, cf. I, 224–5, 'voici la liste de mes petits malheurs'.

19. *Mélanges*, XXVI, 283, 285.

20. Simon Askenazi, *Le Prince Joseph Poniatowski Maréchal de France*, n.d. pp. 17–19; Cracow, Polska Akademia Nauk, Archives Poniatowski, rkps 111, letters of Prince Charles de Ligne and his father to Prince Joseph, 1789–90.

21. Ligne, *Fragment*, pp. 9, 10, 45.

22. *Mélanges*, IV, 1–42, 'Fragments sur Casanova', 291–4, portrait of 'Aventuros'.

23. Comte Alexandre de Tilly, *Mémoires*, 3 vols., 1965, pp. 34, 39; *APL*, VII 1926, p. 47; *Mélanges*, XXII, 162; de Tilly, III, 1828, 295.

24. Richard Friedenthal, *Goethe: His Life and Times*, 1989 edn, pp. 165–7, 196, 199.

25. Friedenthal, pp. 173, 185, 216.

26. Karl August, Duke of Saxe-Wiemar, *Briefwechsel*, 3 vols., Bern, 1971, I, 227, 267, Duke to Goethe, 17 June 1797, 26 November 1798.

27. *Lolo. Le journal du Prince Charles-Joseph Clary-Aldringen*, 1, p. 184, 30 May 1797.

28. Staatsarchiv Weimar, HAA, XIX, 78.

29. J. W. Goethe, *Annals*, New York, 1901, p. 151; A. Sauer, *Goethe und Oesterreich*, 1902, pp. 117–21, 125–6; Johannes Urzidil, *Goethe in Böhmen*, Zurich, 1965, pp. 73–5.

30. *Mémoires et Mélanges*, II, 205.

31. *Fragments*, I, 254–6; Perey, *La Comtesse Hélène Potocka*, pp. 253–4.

32. Perey, *Hélène Potocka*, pp. 309, 314, 315, 317, letters of December 1806, 25 March, 1 May 1807, to Vincent and Hélène Potocka.

33. Perey, *Hélène Potocka*, p.386; *Fragments*, I, 302.

34. Ghent, XXIV, Princesse de Ligne to Vandenbroucke, 10 September 1795, when she was at Teplitz.

35. *Fragments*, II, 444.

36. Zinzendorf, 28 November 1795.

37. Decin, 102, *Fragments de lettres du prince de Ligne à la Princesse Clary*.

38. Guy, *Oeuvres choisies*, p. 9; Zinzendorf, 28 November 1796.

39. *Oeuvres romanesques*, I, 146n.

40. *Fragments*, I, 120.

41. *Fragments*, I, 260.

42. Decin, 103, Bonnay to Ligne, 24 August 1803; Decin, 104a, unsigned letter of 23 June 1799.

43. *APL*, IV, 1923, pp. 165, 168, 169, 172, letters of 7, 30 July, 16 August 1805.

44. *Fragments*, I, 271–2; *Mélanges*, XXX, 297–300; *APL*, IV, 1923, pp. 162–74.

45. *Fragments*, I, 303, 370; Balayé, p. 262, Ligne to Mme de Staël, 7 June 1808.

46. *Fragments*, II, 444.

47. Metternich, *Memoirs*, 2 vols., New York, 1880, I, 41.

48. Central State Archives, Prague, Metternich papers, Ligne to Metternich, n.d.

49. Metternich, I, 39; *Fragments*, I, 370.

50. Basil Guy, 'The Prince de Ligne and the Exemplification of Heroic Virtue in the Eighteenth Century', *Studies in Eighteenth Century French Literature presented to Robert Niklaus*, ed. J. H. Fox *et al.*, Exeter, 1975, p. 86; Archduke Charles wrote to thank him for the military catalogue on 16 October 1793.

51. Albert Ward, *Book Production, Fiction and the German Reading Public*, Oxford, 1974, p. 88.

52. *Fragment sur Casanova*, p. 49, to Casanova, n.d.; *NRL*, pp. 330, 332, 351.

53. *Mélanges*, XXI, 117.

54. Decin, 103, Bonnay to Ligne, 22 June 1803.

55. Decin, 103, Ligne to Bonnay, 6 July 1803.

56. Guy, 1962, p. 267.

57. *Mélanges*, XXXI, 164, 203; XXVI, 269; XXV, 63.

58. Decin, 103.

59. *Mélanges*, XXI, 96; XIX, 98.

60. Louis Wittmer, *Le Prince de Ligne, Jean de Müller, Frédéric de Gentz et l'Autriche*, 1925, p. 63, letter of 18 July 1802.

61. *Mélanges*, XXXV, 52.

62. *Mélanges*, II, 163; XX, 273.

63. *Mélanges*, XXVI, 11, 53, 143n., 278; *Mémoires et Mélanges*, V, 242–3, 395.

64. Lady Morgan, *France in 1829*, 2 vols., 1830, II, 389–90.

65. Decin, 103.

66. *Mélanges*, XX, 121, 193.

67. *Mémoires et Mélanges*, II, 253–4.

68. *Mes écarts*, p. 36.

69. *Fragments*, I, 15; *Mémoires et Mélanges*, II, 275; *APL*, IV, 1923, p. 130.

70. *Mélanges*, XII, 81, 90–1.

71. *Mélanges*, XXII, 233.

72. *Fragments*, I, 244; *Fragments* (ed. Leuridant), I, XXXIV, to Walther, 21 April 1809.

73. *Fragments*, I, 48.

74. *Fragments*, I, 80 and n.

75. Institut Mss, Croÿ, III, 92, 4 May 1774.

76. *Fragments*, I, 17, 21, 35, 435.

77. *Fragments*, II, 102, 241.

78. *Fragments*, ed. Leuridant, I, XXV.

79. *Fragments*, I, 79–81.

80. *Fragments*, I, 15; II, 338; Mortier, 287–8.

81. *Fragments*, II, 441–4.

82. *Mélanges*, XXXII, 218; *APL*, VI, 1925, pp. 274–5, Ligne to Walther, 21 February 1811.

83. *Fragments*, I, 342–3, 360.

84. *Fragments*, I, 383.

85. *Fragments*, I, 201.

86. *Fragments*, I, 73.

87. *Fragments*, I, 392.

88. *Fragments*, I, 9.
89. Ghent, letter of 22 August 1791.
90. Henri Lebasteur, 'Le Prince de Ligne et la Religion'; *APL*, XI, 1930, p. 60.
91. *Mémoires et Mélanges*, 1827, II, 243.
92. Lebasteur, p. 60; Guy, p. 227.
93. Lebasteur, p. 65.
94. Francis Ley, *Madame de Krüdener et son temps*, 1962, p. 291.
95. *Suppléments aux Ecarts*.
96. *Philosophie du Catholicisme*, Berlin, 1816 edn, Ph. Marheinecke, pp. 6, 18; cf. *APL*, II, 1921, p. 74, Mme de Krüdener to Mme de Stourdza, 15 December 1814.
97 *APL*, IV, 1923, pp. 199, 200, *Ma Profession de Foi*, *c*.1810; *Fragments*, I, 310, 383, 407.
98. *Fragments*, I, 271.

CHAPTER 11 *Napoleon*

1. Dansaert, p. 140.
2. AAE, Austria, 372, f. 508, Czartoryski to Ligne, 8/16 August, 8/16 September 1802 (copies): Alexander I was probably influenced by his Foreign Secretary Prince Adam Czartoryski, who had met Ligne during an enjoyable stay in Vienna in 1798.
3. Decin, 103, letter of 1 June 1803.
4. *NRL*, p. 27, Ligne to Christine Clary, 12 May 1803 (misdated).
5. Decin, 104a, *Journal du voyage du Prince de Ligne à Edelstetten*; *NRL*, pp. 30–1, Ligne to Christine Clary, 29 May 1803 (misdated).
6. Decin, 103, Ligne to Bonnay, 2, 6–8 June 1803.
7. Decin, 103, Ligne to Bonnay, 11 June 1803; *Fragments*, I, 157, 161; cf. *NRL*, p. 235.
8. Decin, 104a, *Journal de Voyage du Prince de Ligne à Edelstetten*, act of 19 June 1804; Félicien Leuridant, 'Histoire d'une principauté d'empire', *APL*, VII, 1926, p. 165; *Fragments*, I, 160, 198.
9. *Mélanges*, XXII, 207.
10. *Fragments*, II, 132.
11. *Ma napoléonide*, pp. 11, 36–7.
12. *Fragments*, I, 313; *Ma napoléonide*, 'Sur Bonaparte', pp. 10–11, 37.
13. *Ma napoléonide*, p. 10.
14. *Ma napoléonide*, pp. 70–1, Ligne to Francis II, n.d.
15. Wittmer, p. 135; Wassiltchikov, V, 122–3, Ligne to Razumovski, October 1804.

16. Prague, Central State Archives, Metternich Papers, Ligne to Metternich, 28 August 1804.

17. *Fragments*, II, 137.

18. Sheehan, p. 373; *Mes écarts*, p. 43.

19. *APL*, XIII, 1932, p. 60, Ligne to Gentz, n.d.; Klarwill, pp. 34, 301; *Fragments*, I, 175. Building on this visit, in February 1805 Ligne sent a long memoir called 'Attitude respective de l'Autriche et de la Prusse depuis cent ans' to Jean de Muller, a friend from the Imperial Library who had moved to Berlin to become Historiographer to the King. Again he demanded military commands for himself and Prince Louis Ferdinand, in order to 'de-Charlemagnise' Napoleon, who 'takes possession of the Empire of the West and ... gives the portrait of Charlemagne whose name he uses on every occasion to accustom Europe to see him take his place': Wittmer, pp. 172, 180, 182, Ligne to Jean de Müller, 14 February 1805.

20. *Fragments*, II, 314; Rothenburg, p. 77; Stella Musulin, *Vienna in the Age of Metternich*, 1975, p. 42.

21. Wittmer, p. 243, 10 September 1805 to Müller, cf. p. 220, 27 August 1805 to Müller; HHSA, Sammelbände 41, Ligne to Francis II, 27 August 1805; Decin, 103, Ligne to Gentz, 11 October 1804.

22. Musulin, p. 43; *Fragments*, I, 293.

23. *Fragments*, II, 314–19.

24. *Fragments*, II, 378–9; Rothenburg, p. 80.

25. *Fragments*, I, 288; II, 299–302; *Ma napoléonide*, pp. 89–94.

26. Emile Dard, *Napoléon et Talleyrand*, 1935, p. 114, Talleyrand to Napoleon, 5 December 1805.

27. Jeroom Vercruysse, 'Cinq Lettres du Prince de Ligne à Talleyrand', *NAPL*, IX, 1995, 154, 156.

28. *NAPL*, IX, 1995, 154, Ligne to Talleyrand, 5 December 1805; *Fragments*, II, 304–5, 378.

29. *Fragments*, II, 304.

30. Dard, *Napoléon et Talleyrand*, p. 135, Talleyrand to Ligne, 31 December 1805; *Fragments*, I, 229.

31. *Ma napoléonide*, pp. 40–1, Ligne to Gentz, 20 February 1806; Zinzendorf, 26 December 1805; cf. Rothenburg, pp. 104, 106, for equally forthright denunciations of the Emperor by the Archduke Charles; Ley, p. 287, diary of Juliette de Krüdener, 24 August 1807.

32. Zinzendorf, 8 August 1806.

33. *Ma napoléonide*, pp. 1, 7, 12; *Fragments*, I, 250.

34. Weimar Staatsarchiv, Ligne to Weimar, 11 September 1806; Decin, 103, Ligne to Roger de Damas, 1806.

35. *Fragments*, I, 300–1.

36. *Fragments*, I, 302; *Ma napoléonide*, pp. 15–18, 15 August 1807.

37. *Fragments*, II, 301; Musée Royal de l'Armée, Brussels, Cercle d'Histoire Militaire, Mss. 593, Francis II to Count Von Schaffgotsch, 13 June 1807.

38. Georges Englebert, 'Le Prince Charles-Joseph de Ligne Capitaine des Trabans Impériaux et Royaux', in *Carnet de la Fourragère*, December 1954, pp. 265–71; *Fragments*, I, 400.

39. *Fragments*, I, 307–11; Damas, II, 29, 35, notes of 6 January 1808; Zinzendorf, 17 January 1808.

40. *Fragments*, I, 321.

41. *Fragments*, I, 324.

42. *Fragments*, I, 323; cf. *NRL*, pp. 331–4, Ligne to Flore de Ligne, 10 September 1808; Emile Brouwet, *Collection d'autographes*, 3 vols., London, 1936, II, 117, Ligne to an unnamed relation, 25 October 1808.

43. Ghent, Ligne to Vandenbroucke, 19 April 1791.

44. *Fragments*, I, 116, 325.

45. *Fragments*, I, 309.

46. Rzewuska, I, 97, 105; Henri Deherain, *La Vie de Pierre Ruffin*, 2 vols., 1930, II, 179, Rzewuski to Pierre Ruffin, 15 January 1809.

47. Perey, *Hélène Potocka*, p. 392.

48. *NRL*, p. 70; Rzewuska, I, 105.

49. Rzewuska, I, 218, 237–8; Decin, 103, Ligne to Christine Clary, 1809.

50. Rzewuska, I, 188; III, 17; Du Montet, p. 187.

51. Jean Mistler, *Madame de Staël et Maurice O'Donnell*, 1926, p. 33; Simone Balayé, 'Lettres inédites du Prince de Ligne à Madame de Staël', in *Bulletin de l'Académie royale de Langue et de Littérature françaises*, XLIV, 3–4, 1966, p. 241, Mme de Staël to Benjamin Constant, May 1808.

52. Guy, *Oeuvres Choisies*, p. 149; General Dirk van Hogendorp, *Mémoires*, La Haye, 1887, pp. 235–6; Balayé, Ligne to Mme de Staël, 28 December 1807; Mistler, pp. 82–3, 93.

53. Rzewuska, I, 94; Balayé, pp. 248, 250; *APL*, XVI, 1935, p. 115, Ligne to Mme de Staël, 1808; Daniel Acke, 'Le prince de Ligne et l'Allemagne', *NAPL*, XII, 1999, 129.

54. Jeroom Vercruysse, 'Le portefeuille de Marie Caroline Murray', *NAPL*, XI, 1998, 55–139.

55. Leuridant, *Le Prince de Ligne, Madame de Staël et Caroline Murray*, 1920, pp. 11, 13, 14.

56. Balayé, pp. 6n, 18n.

57. Maria Ullrichova, *Lettres Inédites de Madame de Staël conservées en Bohème*, Prague, 1959, p. 61; Balayé, p. 270, Ligne to Mme de Staël, 25 September 1808.

58. *Lettres et Pensées*, I, iv, vii.

59. François Métra, *Correspondance secrète politique et littéraire*, 18 vols., London, 1787–90, XV, 65–8; Miklos Bardo, 'Le comte Janos Fekete de Galantha 1741–1803, un disciple hongrois du prince de Ligne', *NAPL*, XIII, 1999, 190.

60. Basil Guy, in *NAPL*, V, 1990, pp. 199–200; Balayé, pp. 268, 270; idem, 'Les premiers succès littéraires du prince de Ligne dans la presse parisienne en 1809', *NAPL*, IX, 1995, passim and pp. 61, 66.

61. Madame de Rémusat, *Lettres*, 2 vols., 1881, II, 349, Madame to Monsieur de Rémusat, 21 July 1810; Balayé, pp. 268, 270.

62. John C. Isbell, 'Les premiers succès littéraires du Prince de Ligne dans la presse britannique en 1809', *NAPL*, XI, 1997, pp. 143, 145, 170, 175.

63. Balayé, p. 283, Ligne to Mme de Staël, 8 July 1811.

Chapter XII, War and Peace

1. Zinzendorf, 4, 9 February 1809.

2. Musulin, p. 66; W. C. Langsam, *The Napoleonic Wars and German Nationalism in Austria*, New York, 1930, 31n., Dodun to Champagny, 18 March 1809.

3. *Fragments*, I, 311–12; Balayé, 266, Ligne to Mme de Staël, 20 September 1808.

4. 'Ma profession de foi sur les Anglais', *APL*, IV, 1923, 36–41; *Fragments*, I, 304.

5. *Fragments*, II, 175.

6. Decin, 103, 'Réflexions' of 20 and 21 April 1809.

7. Richard Kralik, *Histoire de Vienne*, 1932, p. 312; *Fragments*, II; *NRL*, 83–4; Zinzendorf, 13 May 1809.

8. *NRL*, 86, Ligne to Mlle C., 20 May 1809; Rothenburg, p. 155; *Fragments*, II, 328–30, 336; cf. *Ma napoléonide*, p. 114, 16 May 1809.

9. *Fragments*, I, 341–2.

10. Gentz, *Tagebücher*, 4 vols., Leipzig, 1861, I, 140, 191, 201. Ligne had also heard guests of Princess Françoise Leichtenstein say that the Emperor was going to be replaced by his brother Ferdinand; Zinzendorf, 9 May 1809.

11. Paul Sweet, *Friedrich von Gentz*, Madison, 1941, p. 157; Guillaume de Bertier de Sauvigny, *Metternich*, 1986, 112–14; *Fragments*, I, 339–40.

12. *Fragments*, ed. Leuridant, II, 215n.; *Ma napoléonide*, 'Sur cette dernière campagne', 95–100; *APL*, XVI, 1935, 193–209, Grünne to Ligne, 23–30 September 1809; Zinzendorf, 5 November 1809.

13. Klarwill, 42; *Fragments*, II, 347–9 and n.; HHSA, Sammelbände, 41, Ligne to Francis II; Zinzendorf, 14 January 1810. Ligne did not stop. In 1810 he published in Paris the *Mémoires du prince Eugène de Savoie*, in reality a fresh attack against the campaign of 1809. He wrote to Christine: 'It seems to me that I made Prince Eugène say what we should have done for the defence of Vienna', *NRL*, 7n.

14. *Ma napoléonide*, p. 23.

15. *Fragments*, II, 344; Balayé, p. 229, Mme de Staël to Mme Récamier, adding, 'c'est dommage qu'il soit vieux'. Younger and more nationalist than Ligne, Gentz was shocked to meet Napoleonic officers at the Prince's table: Gentz, *Tagebücher*, I, 243, 4 March 1810.

16. *Lolo. Le Journal du Comte Charles de Clary-Aldringen*, II, Utrecht, 2000, 175, 8 March 1810; *Ma napoléonide*, p. 103; Bonnay's letters to Ligne stop in 1812; there is no mention of Ligne in the second volume of Roger de Damas's memoirs, describing life in Vienna from 1806 to 1814; cf. Potocka, p. 180.

17. Broglie, I, 85–6; Rzewuska, p. 217.

18. *Fragments*, I, 354–94; Zinzendorf, 23 February 1810.

19. *Fragments*, I, 358–9; Cecilia Sternberg, *The Journey*, 1977, 60; Prague, Central State Archives, Metternich Papers, Ligne to Metternich, 1810. In his autobiography, Ligne does not mention his efforts to secure this job.

20. Du Montet, p. 106; Thurheim, II, 145; Rzewuska, I, 220.

21. Prince Charles de Clary-et-Aldringen, *Trois mois à Paris lors du mariage de l'Empereur Napoléon Ier*, 1914, pp. 73, 79–80, letters of 3 April 1810.

22. Ibid., p. 83, 2 April.

23. Ibid., pp. 8, 131, 21 March, 12 April 1810.

24. Ibid., pp. 37, 62, 86, 362, 27 March 1810, 1, 3 April 1810, 5 April 1810, 21 June 1810.

25. Ibid., p. 249, 14 May 1810.

26. *Fragments*, I, 361; *APL*, XI, 1930, 109, Ligne to Rahel Levin, 16 November 1810; Decin, 103, Bonnay to Ligne, 8 July 1810; Zinzendorf, 20 December 1810; McGuignan, p. 218, Countess to Count Metternich, 5 May 1814.

27. *Fragments*, I, 256; *NRL*, p. 4, cf. Balayé, p. 280n.

28. Guy, *Oeuvres Choisies*, p. 95.

29. New York Public Library, Mss. and Archives, Miscellaneous Papers – Ligne, Ligne to Weimar, 12 June 1810; Dr Richard Maria Werner, *Goethe und Gräfin O'Donell*, Berlin, 1884, 39; Balayé, pp. 281 and 285.

30. *Ma napoléonide*, pp. 26–7.

31. Balayé, p. 285, letter of 8 July 1811.

32. *Mélanges*, VII, or VIII, 15; a copy of Charles's letter dated 4 May 1788 is in the archives of King Stanislas Augustus in Warsaw.

33. Thurheim, II, 144.

34. Mistler, p. 280; Prague, Central State Archives, Metternich Papers, Ligne to Metternich, 6 June 1812.

35. Metternich, I, 41; Prague, Central State Archives, Metternich Papers, Ligne to Metternich, 1812; *APL*, II, 1921, 219–31, Ligne to Louis Starhemberg, 2 March 1812; *Ma napoléonide*, pp. 75–6.

36. *Fragments*, I, 401.

37. *NAPL*, XI, 1997, 230, Charles Clary to Louise, 3 July 1812.

38. *Fragments*, I, 407, 412.

39. Maréchal de Castellane, *Journal*, 5 vols., 1896–7, I, 206, 8 December 1812; *Fragments*, I, 404; Rzewuska, I, 217–18.

40. General Bertrand, *Cahiers de Sainte-Hélène*, 3 vols., 1949–1959, II, 16 April 1818; Klarwill, pp. 45–6.

41. Prague, Central State Archives, Metternich Papers, Ligne to Metternich, 15, 21 July 1813.

42. Arenberg Archives, Enghien, 41/16, Ligne to the Duke of Arenberg, 23 January 1813; *Fragments*, I, 429.

43. Prague, Central State Archives, Metternich Papers, Ligne to Metternich, 5 July 1813. Since Metternich wished to keep Napoleon as a counterbalance to Russian power, Ligne hoped that Napoleon or his son would keep the throne of France. He affirmed that the Bourbons had no partisans and that the Emperor of Austria would not depose his grandson. Perhaps because of Rosalie Rzewuska, he hoped that Poland would become a hereditary monarchy; Du Montet, p. 85; Rzewuska, I, 216–17.

44. G. de Bertier de Sauvigny, *Metternich*, 1986, pp. 166–8; *APL*, I, 1920, 364, Ligne to Frederick William III (misnamed Francis I), 15 September 1813.

45. Klarwill, pp. 46–7, note dated 30 September 1813; cf. *Ma napoléonide*, 59–65, for criticism concerning the conduct of the campaign.

46. Trebon, Czech Republic, Statni Oblastni Archiv Ligne to Schwarzenberg, February 1814.

47. Théodore Bramsen, *Promenades d'un voyageur prussien*, 2 vols., 1818, I, 72; *Fragments*, I, 428; John Cam Hobhouse (Lord Broughton), *Recollections of a Long Life*, 2 vols., 1909, I, 63–4; Ligne's friendship with Hobhouse explains why Charles de Ligne's heroism at the siege of Ismail is celebrated in Canto VII in Byron's *Don Juan*.

48. Decin, 103.

49. *Fragments*, I, 432–3; the letters that Ligne wrote to Rosalie Rzewuska in 1814 are on religion, cf. *APL*, XIV, 1933, 19–23; Rzewuska, I, 223, 236.

CHAPTER 13 *Europe*

[The *Souvenirs du Congrès de Vienne*, by the Comte de Lagarde-Chambonas, a friend and distant cousin of Ligne, have not been used in this chapter. Among other errors it describes the triumphs of Rosalie Rzewuska in Vienna, when she was on her estates in Poland.]

1. Du Montet, p. 112; Enghien, archive 9/25, anonymous to Prince Auguste d'Arenberg (formerly Comte de la Marck), 21 July, 16 October 1814.

2. Klarwill, p. 48.

3. Enghien, archive 9/25, anonymous to Prince Auguste d'Arenberg.

4. Jean-Gabriel Eynard, *Journal*, 1914, 119, 13 November 1814.

5. *APL*, II, 1921, 69, Ligne to Talleyrand, n.d.

6. Bibliothèque municiplaale de Génève, mss., 1959, Journal of Mme Eynard (hereafter called Eynard), p. 4, 5 October 1814.

7. Enghien, 9/25, anonymous to Prince Auguste d'Arenberg, 16 October 1814.

8. *APL*, 1920, I, 72, Clary to Golovkine, 23 December 1814.

9. Enghien, 9/25, anonymous to Prince Auguste d'Arenberg, 16 October 1814.

10. Charles-Otto Zieseniss, *Le Congrès de Vienne et l'Europe des princes*, 1984, p. 98; Eynard, 10 October 1814.

11. Eynard, pp. 15, 44–6, 10, 19 October 1814.

12. Leopold I, *Lettres*, 1943, p. 61, letter dated 8 November 1814.

13. Klarwill, p. 48; Cdt m-H. Weil, *Les Dessous du Congrès de Vienne*, 2 vols., 1917, I, 29, 127, 498, 569, notes to Baron von Hager, 18 July, 27 September, 9 and 21 November 1814.

14. Weil, I, 483–4, report dated 8 November 1814.

15. Pauline Adelaide Alexandra Panam, *Mémoires d'une jeune Grecque*, London, 1823, pp. 248 and 250; cf. a letter by Leopold of Saxe-Coburg to his sister: 'Old Ligne is taken by her and all his clan protects her in a very astonishing manner': Leopold I, *Lettres*, Liège, 1973, p. 115.

16. Enghien, 9/25, anonymous to Prince Auguste d'Arenberg, 16 September 1814; Weil, I, 191, 352, 577, and 647, police reports dated 2 and 12 October, 22 November, and 6 December 1814.

17. Eynard, 27 November 1814, 13 December, 1 and 3 November 1814, letter dated 4 February 1815 to Mme Delessert.

18. Eynard, 161–2, 28 November 1814; Weil, I, 145, Gagern to Prince of Orange, 28 September 1814; Enghien, 9/25, anonymous to Prince Auguste d'Arenberg, 28 November 1814.

19. Weil, I, 182, 452, report of 30 September, 2 November 1814.

20. Weil, I, 161, 170, notes to Hager, 29, 30 September; *Ma napoléonide*, pp. 123–8, Ligne to Talleyrand, November 1814.

21. Zieseniss, p. 89; A. Fournier, *Die Geheimpolizei auf der Wiener Congress*, 1913, 205, report dated 26 October 1814.

22. Bertier de Sauvigny, pp. 174–5, Metternich to Wilhelmina of Sagan, 2, 6 November 1813; Ullrichova, p. 100, Metternich to Wilhelmina of Sagan, 16 November 1813.

23. Prince Eugène de Ligne, *Souvenirs et Portraits*, 1930, p. 46.

24. Bertier de Sauvigny, p. 251; *Ma napoléonide*, p. 127.

25. Weil, I, 541, 601, and 609, reports to Hager, 16, 26, 27 November.

26. Paul Schroeder, *The Transformation of European Politics 1763–1848*, Oxford, 1994, pp. 517–83.

27. *Ma napoléonide*, pp. 126–7, Ligne to Talleyrand; Eynard, p. 97; Edouard Gachot, *Marie-Louise intime*, 2 vols., 1911, II, 55, 151, Marie-Louise to the Duchess of Montebello, 22 June, 14 December 1814; Jean de Bourgoing, *Le Fils de Napoléon*, 1932, 56.

28. Decin, 103, *Derniers vers du Prince de Ligne la dernière nuit avant sa maladie, à un journaliste obligeant le 31 11bre 1814.*

29. *APL*, I, 1920, 69–73, Clary to Golovkine, 23 December 1814; *APL*, XV, 1934, 110–14, *Relation des derniers moments du Prince de Ligne*, by surgeon Puttemans.

30. Basil Guy, 'Quelques documents méconnus sur la mort du prince de Ligne', *NAPL*, XIII, 2000, 184–5; *APL*, XV, 1934, 110–14, *Relation des derniers moments du Prince de Ligne*, by surgeon Putterman.

31. C. Bertuch, *Tagebuch*, Berlin, 1916, p. 71, 15 December 1814; Franz Patzer, *Wiener Kongresstagebuch*, 1981, 77–8, 15 December 1814;

Jeroom Vercruysse, 'La tombe du prince de Ligne', *NAPL*, XV, 2002, p. 143.

32. Vercruysse, 'Tombe', pp. 144–5.
33. *APL*, I, 1920, 69, Clary to Golovkine, 23 December 1814.
34. Eynard, 13 December 1814; Klarwill, pp. 50, 328; Balayé, p. 289.
35. Extracts from the journal of Carl Haag, Windsor Castle, 13 October 1853, and information kindly provided by F. W. P. Broadley, a descendant of Louis-François d'Albertanson.

Appendix: Letters

1. Brno, Czech Republic, Moravsky Zemsky Archiv, Kaunitz Papers.
2. Allusion to the role of Prince Kaunitz in Austrian foreign policy.
3. Possibly the Prince's uncle by marriage, Prince Joseph Wenzel Liechtenstein, who had died in 1772.
4. Maria Theresa and her co-Regent, her son Joseph II.
5. The Order of the Golden Fleece, the first of Austria's chivalric orders, founded by the Duke of Burgundy in 1430.
6. Ghent University Library, Manuscripts, Vandenbroucke Papers.
7. His mistress Eugénie d'Hannetaire.
8. Ghent University Library.
9. The Prince d'Hénin, a friend of Ligne and *Capitaine des gardes du corps* of the Comte d'Artois.
10. The Archduchess Marie-Christine, Governor-General of the Austrian Netherlands, with her husband Duke Albert of Saxe-Teschen.
11. Croÿ himself.
12. Ghent University Library.
13. Contrôleur Général des Finances in France, and friend of the Prince.
14. Of land to the Prince de Ligne.
15. The wife of his eldest son, Charles de Ligne.
16. Ghent University Library.
17. The French court's annual autumn journey to Fontainebleau.
18. Warsaw, Central Archives, Zbior Popielow 165, Papers of King Stanislas Augustus, correspondence with Ligne.
19. Gustavus III Papers, Uppsala University Library, Sweden.
20. The Empress's current lover.
21. French ambassador to Catherine II.
22. The start of the revolution in the Austrian Netherlands.
23. The Khan of the Crimea.
24. Ghent University Library, Vandenbroucke Papers.

25. Vienna, HHSA, Staatskanzlei Vorträge 145, Supplement.
26. A reference to the Austrian victory at Sabacz in 1788.
27. With the Russian commander Prince Potemkin.
28. The French engineer who, in accordance with the French policy of strengthening the Ottoman Empire, had recently helped strengthen the defences of Oczakow.
29. Vienna, HHSA, Staatskanzlei Vortrage 145, Supplement.
30. Potemkin.
31. Romanzow.
32. The war of 1736–9 between Austria and Russia as allies, and the Ottoman Empire.
33. Cracow, Polska Akademia Nauk, Poniatowski archives, rkps 111.
34. The King of Poland, whom, to his face, Ligne called the best and handsomest of kings.
35. London Public Record Office, PC1/129/572.
36. The Comte d'Artois, leader of the emigration.
37. Leopold II.
38. Brno, Czech Republic, Moravsky Zemsky Archiv, Kaunitz Papers.
39. The Prince's beloved elder son Prince Charles de Ligne.
40. Marie-Christine and Albert.
41. Dumouriez, the French Commander-in-Chief.
42. Ghent University Library.
43. His old friend Frederick William II, who was making peace with the French Republic at Basle.
44. French ambassador in Switzerland.
45. Decin, Czech Republic, State Archives, Clary Papers, 103.
46. Catherine the Great's last lover, and one of the murderers of Paul I – an allusion to which by the Chevalier de Saxe had helped lead to the duel.
47. Owing to the fact that he was the son of a morganatic marriage.
48. Edinburgh National Library of Scotland, Mss. 12998, Eliot Papers.
49. A French diplomat.
50. Edinburgh National Library of Scotland, Mss. 12998, Eliot Papers.
51. England, Scotland and Ireland.
52. Vienna, HHSA Sammelbände, 41.
53. Prague, Central State Archives, Metternich Papers, Acta Clementina 8–10.
54. Either the Trabant or the Hofburg Guard.
55. Prince Kaunitz, grandfather of Metternich's wife.
56. The principal Austrian minister, 1806–9.

57. Cf. supra, p. 96, 'What, monsieur, without being obliged to!'
58. Weimar, Staatsarchiv HAAXIX, 78.
59. Frederick Augustus, King of Saxony, Grand Duke of Warsaw by the grace of his ally Napoleon.
60. The Grand Duke had been obliged to send troops to help his French allies in Spain.
61. Charles Theodore de Dalberg, last Archbishop Elector of Mainz, later, thanks to Napoleon, sovereign of Erfurt and Grand Duke of Frankfurt.
62. Arenberg Archives, Enghien, Belgium, Mss. 41/16.
63. The Duc d'Arenberg, a cousin of the Prince.
64. The Duke's younger brother, former protector of Mirabeau, who lived in Vienna.
65. Prince Louis de Ligne, the Prince's surviving son, who lived in Beloeil.
66. The Prince's adored elder son Prince Charles de Ligne.
67. Prague, Central State Archives, Metternich family papers, Acta Clementina.
68. Pauline Panam.

Bibliography

AUTHOR'S NOTE

The story of Ligne's archives is as complicated as that of his life. After 1794 some papers, mainly estate documents and juvenilia, stayed in the château of Beloeil, where, closely guarded, they remain today. Other documents accompanied the Prince to Vienna. Some of the Prince's manuscripts were dispersed after his death but, in some cases, repurchased by his grandson Prince Eugène de Ligne, and returned to Beloeil. Further papers – particularly, but not exclusively, letters received and manuscripts written while at Teplitz – remained among the papers of his daughter Princess Clary and are now, with the Clary papers, in the State Archives in Decin in the Czech Republic. Some of Ligne's most personal papers, including the *livres rouges* and the letters addressed to him by sovereigns and generals, were inherited by a junior branch of the family and are in the Château d'Antoing.

Manuscripts

1. Château d'Antoing, Belgium [cited as Antoing]:
   Lettres Autographes adressées a S. A. la Maréchal Prince de Ligne
   Souverains, Hommes d'État, Hommes de Guerre, Auteurs
   Vers de Société, 14 vols., 1759–1815
   Mes Livres Rouges, 3 vols.
   Notebooks of Sauveur Legros
2. Brno, Czech Republic, Moravsky Zemsky Archiv:
   Kaunitz Papers, letters of Ligne to Prince W. A. Kaunitz
3. Brussels, Bibliothèque Royale de Belgique:
   II 2065, Sauveur Legros, 'Mes Babioles ou Recueil de differéns à propos de Société'
4. Budapest, Hungarian National Archives:
   Autobiography of Ligne, written in 1808
   Letters from Ligne to Count Szechenyi and Prince Louis Batthyany
5. Cracow, Academy of Sciences:

Archives Poniatowski, rkps 111, letters of Prince Charles de Ligne
and his father to Prince Joseph Poniatowski, 1787–1792
Czartoryski Library Mss 2775, 7, autograph collection of Princess
Isabella Czartoriska

6. Decin, Czech Republic Statni Oblastni Archiv:
   Clary papers [cited as Decin] 102–104, letters and manuscripts of the
   Prince de Ligne

7. Edinburgh, National Library of Scotland:
   Mss. 12998 Eliot papers, letters of Ligne to Hugh Eliot

8. Enghien, Belgium:
   Archives d'Arenberg 41/16, letters of Ligne to Duc d'Arenberg
   9/25 anon. letters to Prince Auguste d'Arenberg from Vienna in
   1814

9. Geneva, Bibliothèque Municipale:
   Archives Tronchin 188
   Archives Saussure 6, letters of Prince de Ligne
   Mss. Suppl. 1959, Journal de Madame Eynard, 1814–15

10. Ghent, University Library:
    Vandenbroucke Papers. Affaires de la Maison de Ligne, 24 volumes,
    1769–1806 [cited as Ghent]

11. Helsinki, National Archives of Finland:
    Armfelt mss, letters of Count Armfelt to his daughter Auguste from
    Vienna in 1800–1804

12. London, Public Record Office:
    PC1/129/572, letters of Ligne to Calonne, 1791
    SP 91/106, despatches of James Harris to Lord Stormont, 1780
    FO 65/15, despatches of Mr Fitzherbert to Marquess of Carmarthen,
    1787

13. Lund, University Library:
    Diary of Count de La Gardie, Vienna, 1799–1800

14. Mulgrave Castle, Whitby:
    Mulgrave archives, L 416, Ligne to Henry Phipps, 1776

15. Paris Archives du Ministère des Affaires Etrangères (AAE):
    Correspondance Politique Turquie 176, Choiseul-Gouffier to
    Montmorin, 1787
    Autriche 372, f. 508, Czartoryski to Ligne, 8/16 August, 8/16
    September 1802 (copies)

16. Paris, Archives nationales (AN):
    T 582 1, 2, 3, papers of Prince Charles de Ligne and the banker
    Théaulon

17. Paris, Bibliothèque de l'Institut:
    Mss. 1650–2, 1670–80, Journal du Duc de Croÿ
18. Prague, Central State Archives:
    Metternich papers, Acta Clementina 8–10, letters of Ligne to Metternich [cited as Metternich]
19. Trebon, Czech Republic, Statni Oblastni Archiv:
    Letters of Ligne to Prince Charles Schwarzenberg
20. Vienna, Haus-, Hof- and Staatsarchiv [HHSA]:
    Mercy-Argenteau papers, letters of Ligne to Mercy-Argenteau
    DD Abt B Fasz 121, 122, letters of Ligne to Count Metternich
    Sammelbände, 41, letters of Ligne to Emperor Francis II
    Nachlass Lacy III, 3–6, letters of Lacy to Ligne, 1761–1773
    Staatskanzlei Vorträge 145, Supplement, Ligne to Joseph II, 1788
    Count von Zinzendorf, Tagebuch 1761–1813 [cited as Zinzendorf]
21. Vienna, Österreichisches Nationalbibliothek:
    Letters of Ligne to Comte de Mercy-Argenteau
22. Warsaw, Central State Archives:
    Zbior Popielow 165, Papers of King Stanislas Augustus
    Correspondence with Ligne [cited as Warsaw]
23. Warsaw, Archivum Glowne akt Dawnych:
    Archivum Radzillow Nieborowa, letters to and portrait of Princess Angélique Radziwill by Ligne
24. Weimar, Staatsarchiv:
    HAAXIX 78, letters of Ligne to Duke Karl August
25. Winchester, Hampshire Public Record Office:
    Malmesbury Papers, letters of Ligne to Lord Malmesbury, 1780–84

Published works

Unless otherwise stated, books in French are published in Paris, books in English in London, books in German in Vienna.

WORKS BY THE PRINCE DE LIGNE:

Amabile suivi de quelques portraits, 1996, ed. Jeroom Vercruysse.
Coup d'oeil sur Beloeil, Beloeil, 1781.
En Marge des Rêveries du Maréchal de Saxe, Brussels, 1919.
Fragment sur Casanova, suivi de lettres à Casanova, 1988.
Fragments de l'histoire de ma vie, 2 vols., 1928.
   Idem, ed. Jeroom Vercruysse, 2 vols., 2000–2001.
Lettres Inédites, Brussels, 1878.
Lettres à la marquise de Coigny, 1914.

Lettres et Pensées du maréchal prince de Ligne, 2 vols., 1909, ed. *Mme de Staël*.

Ma napoléonide, 1921.

Mémoires, 1914.

Mélanges de Littérature, 2 vols., a Philosophopolis [Brussels], 1783.

Mélanges Militaires, Littéraires et Sentimentaires, 34 vols., Dresden, 1795–1811.

Mémoire sur le Roi de Prusse Frédéric le Grand, Berlin, 1789.

Mémoires et Lettres, 1923, ed. Victor Klarwill.

Mémoires et Lettres du maréchal prince de Ligne, 2 vols., 1809.

Mémoires et Mélanges Historiques et Littéraires, 5 vols., 1827–9.

Mes écarts, Brussels, 1990.

Mon refuge ou Satyre sur les abus des jardins modernes, London, 1801.

Nouveau recueil de lettres, ed. Henri Lebasteur, 1928.

Oeuvres Légères, n.d.

Oeuvres choisies du Prince de Ligne, ed. Basil Guy, Saratoga, 1978.

Oeuvres Romanesques, ed. Roland Mortier and Manuel Couvreur, I, 2000.

Préjugés militaires, 2 vols., 1780.

GENERAL WORKS:

Alexander, John T., *Catherine the Great*, 1989.

Anderson, M. S., *War and Society in Europe of the Old Regime 1618–1789*, 1988.

Annales Prince de Ligne, 19 vols., Brussels, 1920–38.

Anon, *Bemerkungen einers Jungen Bauers*, Munich, 1808.

Antoine, Michel, *Louis XV*, 1989.

Aragon, Marquis d', *Un Paladin au 18e Siècle*, 1893.

Arendt, Hannah, *Rahel: the Life of a Jewess*, New York, 1956.

Arnaud, Claude, *Chamfort*, 1988.

Arnaud-Bouteloup, Jeanne, *Le Rôle Politique de Marie-Antoinette*, 1924.

Arneth, A. von and M. Geoffroy eds, *Correspondence entre Marie-Thérèse et le Comte de Mercy – Argenteau*, 3 vols., 2nd edn 1874–5.

Balayé, Simone, 'Lettres inédites du prince de Ligne à Madame de Staël', in *Bulletin de l'Académie Royale de langue et de littérature françaises*, Brussels, 1966.

Barea, Ilsa, *Vienna: Legend and Reality*, 1966.

Baring, Thomas, *A Tour through Italy and Austria in 1814*, 2nd edn, 1817.

Beales, Derek, *Joseph II*, 2 vols., 1987.

——, *La Belgique autrichienne*, Brussels, 1989.

Bertier de Sauvigny, Guillaume, *Metternich*, 1988.

Besterman, Theodore C., *Correspondance de Voltaire*, 51 vols., 1968–77.

Bled, Jean-Paul, *Histoire de Vienne*, 1998.

Bombelles, Marquis de, *Journal*, Geneva, 1978–.

Bourgoing, Jean de, *Le Fils de Napoléon*, 1932.

Bramsen, Théodore, *Promenades d'un voyageur prussien*, 2 vols., 1818.

Britsch, André, *La Jeunesse de Philippe Égalité*, 1926.

Broglie, Duc de, *Souvenirs*, 4 vols., 1886.

Bronne, Carlo, *Beloeil et la Maison de Ligne*, Beloeil, 1979.

Brouwet, Émile, *Collection d'autographes*, 3 vols., London, 1936.

Capon, G., *Vie Privée du prince de Conti*, 1907.

Caussy, Fernand, 'Le Prince de Ligne à Paris', in *Revue Bleue*, September 1906, pp. 284–8.

Catherine II, *Lettres ... au Prince de Ligne*, 1924, ed. Princesse Charles de Ligne.

Chapuisat, Édouard, *Le Prince chéri et ses amis suisses*, Lausanne, 1944.

Charlier, Gustave, *Les Derniers vers du prince de Ligne*, Brussels, 1946.

Clary et Aldringen, Prince Charles de, *Trois Mois à Paris*, 1914.

Cobenzl, *Josef II und Graf Ludwig Cobenzl*, 2 vols., 1901.

Coke, Lady Mary, *Letters and Journals*, 4 vols., 1970.

Couvreur, Manuel, *Le Grand Théâtre au XVIIIe Siècle*, Brussels, 1997.

Craveri, Benedetta, *Madame du Deffand et son monde*, 1987.

Damas, Comte Roger de, *Mémoires*, 2 vols., 1912.

Dansaert, Adrien, *Le Prince Louis de Ligne*, 1933.

Dard, Émile, *Napoléon et Talleyrand*, 1935.

Davis, Walter, *Joseph II: an Imperial Reformer for the Austrian Netherlands*, The Hague, 1974.

Dazincourt, M., *Mémoires*, 2nd edn, 1810.

Delcourt, André, *Le duc de Croÿ*, 1983.

Duffy, Christopher, *The Army of Maria Theresa*, 1977.

——, *Russia's Military Way to the West*, 1981.

Du Montet, Madame, *Souvenirs*, 3rd edn, 1914.

Englebert, Georges, 'Le prince Charles-Joseph de Ligne, Capitaine des Trabans Impériaux et royaux', in *Carnet de la Fourragère*, December 1954, pp. 265–71.

——, 'Emile Legros, Adjutant du Prince de Ligne', in *Revue Belge d'Histoire Militaire*, XVIII, Septembre 1970, pp. 491–5.

——, *Wallonen in Kaiserlichen Diensten*, Heeresgeschichtliches Museum, Vienna, 1978.

Englebert, Georges, and Martine Englebert, *Charles Joseph Fürst de Ligne*, Albertina, Vienna, 1982.

——, *Le Prince de Ligne et son temps*, Beloeil, 1982.

Escars, Duc d', *Mémoires*, 2 vols., 1890.

Esterhazy, Comte Valentin, *Lettres à sa Femme 1784–1792*, 1907.

Evans, R. J. W., *The Making of the Habsburg Monarchy 1550–1700*, Oxford, 1979.

Eynard, J-G., *Journal*, 1914.

Faber, F., *Histoire du théâtre français en Belgique*, 5 vols., 1878.

Fabre, Jean, *Stanislas-Auguste et l'Europe des Lumières*, 1952.

Fersen, Axel von, *Dagbok*, 4 vols., Stockholm, 1925–36.

Fisher, A. W., *The Russian Annexation of the Crimea*, 1970.

Friedenthal, Richard, *Goethe, his Life and Times*, 1989.

Fumaroli, Marc, *Quand l'Europe parlait français*, 2001.

Gachard, M. A., *Études et Notices historiques concernant l'histoire des Pays-Bas*, 3 vols., 1890.

Gachot, Édouard, *Marie-Louise Intime*, 2 vols., 1911.

Gagliardo, John G., *Reich and Nation*, Bloomington, 1980.

Gentz, Friedrich von, *Briefe von und an*, 3 vols., Munich–Berlin, 1913.

——, *Tagebücher*, 4 vols., Leipzig, 1861–4.

Gérard, Jo, *Marie-Thérèse impératrice des Belges*, Brussels, n.d.

Goethe, Wolfgang von, *Truth and Fantasy from my Life*, 1949.

Guibert, M. de, *Journal de mon voyage en Allemagne*, 2 vols., 1803.

Guillaume, Lt-Gen. Baron, *Histoire des Régiments nationaux des Pays-Bas au service d'Autriche*, Brussels, 1877.

Guy, Basil, ed. and tr., *Coup d'oeil at Beloeil and a Great Number of European Gardens*, Berkeley, 1991.

Hagani, Baruch, *Le Sionisme politique*, 1920.

Hammer-Purgstall, Joseph Freiherr von, *Erinnerungen aus Meinem Leben*, Vienna/Leipzig, 1940.

Hardman, John and Munro Price, eds., *Louis XVI and the Comte de Vergennes: correspondence 1774–1787*, Oxford, 1998.

Harmignies, P. P. J. and N–J–H Descamps, *Mémoires sur l'histoire de la ville de Mons*, Mons, 1882.

Hedwig Elizabeth Charlotte, Duchess of Sudermania, *Dagbok*, 19 vols., Stockholm, 1902–42.

Heer, Friedrich, *The Holy Roman Empire*, 1968.

Hobhouse, John Cam (Lord Broughton), *Recollection of a Long Life*, 2 vols., 1909.

Hubert, E., *Le Voyage de Joseph II dans les Pays-Bas*, Brussels, 1900.

Hunter, Michael and David Wootton, eds., *Atheism from the Reformation to the Enlightenment*, Oxford, 1992.

Hunter, William, *Travels through France, Turkey and Hungary to Vienna in 1792*, 2 vols., 3rd edn, 1803.

Jadot, Jean, *Une lettre inédite du prince de Ligne*, Brussels, 1956.

Karl August, Duke of Saxe-Weimar, *Briefwechsel*, 3 vols., Bern, 1971.

Keith, Sir Robert Murray, *Memoirs*, 2 vols., 1849.

Kelly, Michael, *Reminiscences*, 1975.

Kerner, Robert J., *Bohemia in the Eighteenth Century*, New York, 1932.

Langsam, Walter C., *Francis the Good*, New York, 1949.

———, *The Napoleonic Wars and German Nationalism in Austria*, New York, 1930.

Landon, H. C. Robbins, *Mozart and Vienna*, 1991.

Lapouge, Gilles, *The Battle of Wagram*, 1989.

Leeflang, Marc, *Lolo. Le journal du Prince Charles-Joseph Clary-Aldringen*, 2 vols., Utrecht, 1996–2000.

Leuridant, Félicien, *Une éducation de Prince au XVIIIe siècle*, Brussels, 1923.

———, *La Bibliothèque du prince de Ligne*, Brussels, n.d.

———, *Galerie beloeilloise*, Brussels, 1932.

———, *Lettres et Billets inédits du prince de Ligne et de ses familiers*, Brussels, 1919.

———, *L'Abbé Pagès et ses chansons*, 1932.

———, *Le Prince de Ligne, Mme de Staël et Caroline Murray*, Brussels, 1920.

Levey, Michael, *The Life and Death of Mozart*, 1988.

Ley, Francis, *Mme de Krüdener et son temps*, 1961.

Ligne, Prince Albert de, *Histoire généalogique de la Maison de Ligne*, Brussels, 1950.

Ligne, Princess Hélène de, *Memoirs*, 2 vols., 1887.

Longworth, Philip, *The Art of Victory. The Life and Achievements of Generalissimo Suvorov*, 1965.

Lorraine, Charles de, *Journal secret*, Brussels, 2000.

Loumayeur, N., *Sauveur Legros*, Brussels, 1856.

Magris, Claudio, *Danube*, Paris, 1988.

Maixner, Rudolf, 'Un Ragusain ami du prince de Ligne', in *Revue de Littérature Comparée*, 1957.

Maria Theresa, *Briefe an Ihre Kinder und Freunde*, 4 vols., 1881.

Maria Theresia and Marie Antoinette, *Ihr Briefwechsel*, 1865.

Marheinecke, Philipp, *Philosophie du catholicisme*, Berlin, 1816.

McErlan, J. M. P., 'L'Indicible Secret de Napoléon Bonaparte et de Charles-André Pozzo di Borgo', in *Annales Historiques de la Révolution française*, Oct.–Dec. 1974, 218, pp. 674–84.

McGuigan, Dorothy Gies, *Metternich and the Duchess*, New York, 1975.

Metternich, Prince von, *Memoirs*, 2 vols., New York, 1880.

Mistler, Jean, *Madame de Staël et Maurice O'Donnell*, 1926.

Morand, Paul, *Le Prince de Ligne*, 1964.

Morgan, Lady, *France in 1829*, 2 vols., 1830.

Morley, Edith J., ed., *Crabb Robinson in Germany*, Oxford, 1929.

Morritt, J. B. S., *A Grand Tour*, 1985.

Mottaz, Eugène, *Stanislas Poniatowski et Maurice Glayre*, 1897.

Musulin, Stella, *Vienna in the Age of Metternich*, 1975.

Nouvelles Annales Prince de Ligne, Brussels, 1986–present.

Oberkirch, Baronne d', *Mémoires*, 1970.

Oravetz, Vera, *Les impressions françaises de Vienne (1567–1850)*, Szeged, 1930.

Oulié, Marthe, *Le Prince de Ligne*, 1926.

Ouvaroff, Comte, *Esquisses politiques et littéraires*, 1848.

Panam, Mme Pauline Adélaïde Alexandre, *Mémoires d'une jeune Grecque*, 1823.

Paridaens, Albert-Joseph, *Journal historique*, 2 vols., Mons, 1902.

Pasteur, Claude, *Le Prince de Ligne*, 1980.

Patzer, Franz, *Wiener Kongresstagebuch*, 1981.

Perey, Lucien, *Charles de Lorraine et la cour de Bruxelles sous le règne de Marie-Thérèse*, n.d.

——, *Histoire d'une grande dame au XVIIIe siècle: la princesse Hélène de Ligne*, 1888.

——, *La Comtesse Hélène Potocka*, n.d.

——, *Figures du temps passé*, 1900.

Pick, Robert, *Empress Maria Theresa*, 1966.

Pimodan, M. de, *Le Comte F.-C. de Mercy-Argenteau*, 1911.

Pomeau, René, *L'Europe des Lumières. Cosmopolitisme et unité européenne au XVIIIe siècle*, 1991.

Potocka, Countess Anna, *Memoirs*, New York, 1910.

Pottle, Frederick, A., ed., *Boswell on the Grand Tour*, 1953.

Prussia, Princess Louise of, *Forty-Five Years of My Life*, 1912.

Razumovsky, Maria, *Les Razoumovsky 1730–1815. La saga d'une famille dans la Russie des Tsars*, 1999.

Reichardt, J. F., *Vertraute Briefe auf einer Reise nach Wien*, 2 vols., Munich, 1915.

Risbeck, M., *Lettres sur l'Allemagne*, Vienna, 1787.

Roider, Karl A., *Austria's Eastern Question*, Princeton, 1982.

——, *Baron Thugut and the Austrian Reaction to the French Revolution*, Princeton, 1987.

Rothenberg, Gunther, *Napoleon's Great Adversaries: the Archduke Charles and the Austrian Army 1792–1814*, 1982.

Rzewuska, Rosalie, *Mémoires*, 4 vols., Rome, 1939–50.

Schroeder, Paul W., *The Transformation of European Politics, 1763–1848*, Oxford, 1994.

Sebag Montefiore, Simon, *Potemkin*, London, 2000.

Ségur, Comte de, *Mémoires, Souvenirs et Anecdotes*, 2 vols., 1890.

Schoutedens-Wery, J., *Charles de Lorraine et son temps*, Brussels, 1943.

Sheehan, James J., *German History 1770–1866*, Oxford, 1990.

Sked, Alan, *The Decline and Fall of the Habsburg Empire*, Harlow, 1989.

Spiel, Hilde, *Fanny von Arnstein*, Oxford, 1991.

Stäel, Mme de, *De l'Allemagne*, 2 vols., London, 1814.

Stern, Jean, *A l'Ombre de Sophie Arnould*, 2 vols., 1930.

Swinburne, Henry, *Memoirs of the Courts of Europe*, 2 vols., 1895.

Tapié, Victor, *L'Europe de Marie-Thérèse: Du Baroque aux Lumière*, 1973.

Tegner, Elof, *Gustaf Maurit̄ Armfelt*, 3 vols., Stockholm, 1893.

Thurheim, Grafin Lulu, *Mein Leben. Erinnerungen aus Österreichs Grosser Welt*, 4 vols., Munich, 1913–14.

Tilly, Comte Alexandre de, *Mémoires*, 1965.

Trollope, Frances, *Vienna and the Austrians*, 2 vols., 1838.

Ullichova, Maria, ed., *Clemens Metternich-Wilhelmine von Sagan. Ein Briefwechsel*, Graz–Cologne, 1966.

——, *Lettres inédites de Madame de Staël conservées en Bohême*, Prague, 1959.

Urzidil, Johannes, *Goethe in Böhmen*, Zurich, 1965.

Uzanne, O., *Contes du chevalier de Boufflers*, 1878.

Vaudreuil, Comte de, *Correspondance intime du ... et du Comte d'Artois*, 2 vols., 1889.

Vercruysse, Jeroom, 'Le portefeuille de Marie-Caroline Murray', *Nouvelles Annales Prince de Ligne*, XI, 55–139.

Vigée-Lebrun, Mme, *Souvenirs*, 2 vols., 1896.

Voltaire et l'Europe, 1992.

Waddington, R., *La Guerre de Sept Ans*, 5 vols., 1899.

Wandruszka, Adam, *The House of Habsburg*, 1964.

Wassiltchikov, Alexandre, *Les Rāoumovski*, 5 vols., 1893.

Weil, Cdt. M-H., *Les Dessous du Congrès de Vienne*, 2 vols., 1917.

Werner, Richard Maria, *Goethe und Gräfin O'Donnell*, Berlin, 1884.

Wittmer, Louis, *Le Prince de Ligne, Jean de Müller, Friedrich de Gentz et l'Autriche*, 1925.

Wraxall, Nathaniel William, *Memoirs of the Courts of Berlin, Dresden, Warsaw and Vienna in the Years 1777, 1778 and 1779*, 3rd edn, 2 vols., 1806.

Zamoyski, Adam, *The Last King of Poland*, 1992.

Zeissberg, Heinrich von, *Zwei Jahre Belgischer Geschichte*, 1891.

Index